D0753477

WITHDRAWN
UTSA LIBRARIES

IMPROVISED
CITIES

HELEN
GYGER

ARCHITECTURE
URBANIZATION
& INNOVATION
IN PERU

IMPROVISED

CITIES

University of Pittsburgh Press

Graham Foundation

Furthermore:
a program of the J.M. Kaplan Fund

This publication has been supported by grants from the
Graham Foundation for Advanced Studies in the Fine Arts
and Furthermore: a program of the J. M. Kaplan Fund.

Published by the University of Pittsburgh Press, Pittsburgh, Pa., 15260
Copyright © 2019, University of Pittsburgh Press
All rights reserved
Manufactured in the United States of America
Printed on acid-free paper
10 9 8 7 6 5 4 3 2 1

Cataloging-in-Publication data is available from the Library of Congress

ISBN 13: 978-0-8229-4536-9
ISBN 10: 0-8229-4536-3

Cover art: El Ermitaño, Lima, 1965. Ongoing consolidation of dwellings,
proceeding at varying rates: three years after the invasion, some dwellings are still of *esteras*. John F. C. Turner Archive.

Cover design: Alex Wolfe

Library
University of Texas
at San Antonio

CONTENTS

PREFACE

I did not set out, exactly, to write this history. I imagined a more straightforward narrative, along the lines of a critically informed postoccupancy study, built upon a detailed analysis of three or four projects from design and implementation to use and transformation.

It soon became clear that my object of study—aided self-help housing in postwar Peru—was more elusive than I had anticipated, its nature more complex, variable, diffuse. As it was defined and redefined by architects and policymakers of diverse ideological formations, it acquired subtly different qualities and promised benefits. The projects were heterogeneous, both in the completion and refinement of the dwellings produced and in the contributions required of architects and participants. Moreover, the projects shifted between different registers of architectural production, ranging from the close on-site collaboration of architects and self-builders on a community-development model to the mass construction of sites-and-services schemes directed by unnamed professionals to the auteurist proposals of a 1960s avant-garde. As a further complication, proposals were often only partially realized, or their outlines were transformed during execution, which could span years and overlap with the contingencies of occupation and use.

Given this fundamental incommensurability, a straightforward comparative study of built projects would be not only unfeasible but completely insufficient to convey the breadth of practices involved. Beyond the projects themselves, I would need to write a history of the framing of aided self-help housing as it had evolved in this context and as it was understood by a range of actors engaged in its production. To capture these refractions, I have deployed a shifting perspective that encompasses the contributions of politicians and policymakers, anthropologists and development experts, architects and self-builders themselves. Each viewpoint generated its own documentary evidence—from planning legislation and policy papers to architectural plans—and demanded its own mode of analysis. Each entailed a particular approach to history writing, whether political or geopolitical, intellectual or cultural. Yet for all these polyphonic elements, this is fundamentally a history of the built environment—of architecture and of urban form. To this end, it draws upon traditional tools of architectural history, from a biographical approach to explore the professional trajectories of key practitioners to the formal analysis of proposals and built works.

In other ways, this history does not conform to the established contours of the discipline. Rather than guiding readers into unfamiliar terrain by charting the trajectory of a recognizable actor from the North Atlantic world—the figure of the "global expert 'off radar'" richly explored in a recent journal issue—it invites them to negotiate the territory from within.[1] As architectural theories and practices are echoed from one context to another, they shift in translation, resonating in a particular key in each setting. Accordingly, this case study is forged from the specificities of the Peruvian experience, yet it is precisely the fine grain of a situated history that allows it to transcend its national context and come into dialogue with research grounded elsewhere.

Rather than following criteria of aesthetic excellence or originality to quarantine the designs of the pragmatic problem solver away from those of the auteur, it places them in the same field of analysis. Avant-gardist proposals are measured against solutions devised by architects working closer to the ground, whose everyday expertise in infrastructure provision, techniques of participation, or financing mechanisms could generate equally innovative strategies to refine aided self-help housing.

Rather than positioning the architect as either the innocent, socially engaged advocate for a vulnerable constituency or the compromised agent of state power governing that constituency via the instrument of housing provision, it recognizes the fundamental ambivalence of this mode of practice. The architect's approach could veer between paternalistic and genuinely collaborative—and not just from one practitioner to another, or from project to project across a career, but moment by moment within the same project.

Rather than viewing the architect as the principal author of these projects, it acknowledges the distributed agency of their production. The context of architectural practice within the Peruvian housing bureaucracy parallels that described by Kenny Cupers in *The Social Project: Housing Postwar France*, where designs were "shared and shaped by government officials, construction companies, residents' associations, developers, and social scientists alike." Cupers also notes that residents exercised their agency "as active subjects of the urban environments provided for them" by initiating modifications to their planned neighborhoods to rectify deficient amenities; while in France such instances were exceptional, in Peru they were pervasive enough to be the rule.[2] Moreover, aided self-help housing schemes were highly dependent on the actions or inactions of self-builders: their resistance during the planning process and on the building site could sharply alter the shape of designs conceived in the architectural office. This blurred or hybrid agency at the core of aided self-help housing presents a particular challenge to architectural history, but accounting for the interactions of architect and self-builder, in a relationship that is as contentious as it is collaborative, is crucial to this narrative.

While aided self-help housing—along with the unaided self-building of urban informality—is only now coming into the consciousness of architectural history, the postwar surge in squatter settlements around the globe is now decades old, and is being considered from a historical perspective within other disciplines. In the case of Latin America, this includes social scientists drawing upon a career of fieldwork to bring a longitudinal perspective to their analyses, whether refining earlier conclusions (Janice Perlman) or proposing policies for the future evolution of these settlements (Peter M. Ward). Equally pertinent is the work of historians broadly focused on the right to the city, for many of whom a key point of reference is James Holston's work on urban citizenship, defined as conferring "rights to inhabit the city, appropriate its space, not to be excluded from it, participate in its production." Holston observes that in rapidly urbanizing low-income nations, many of the most marginalized residents have created large swathes of the city, building their own homes and developing their neighborhoods via collective demands for the installation of urban services. This improvised, grassroots work of urban development fosters "insurgent" claims for urban citizenship propelled by an emerging political awareness: "Contributing to city-making gives people the conviction that they deserve a right to it." While powerful countervailing forces—notably neoliberalism—challenge this dynamic, in ideal conditions of broad-based political mobilization, this insurgent urban citizenship allows for "an alternative public sphere of the city" in contrast to that of national citizenship, where the urban poor frequently face entrenched discrimination.[3]

Recent histories examining the formation of urban citizenship through struggles over housing include Edward Murphy's research on squatters' claims to "proper" minimum housing in postwar Chile and Brodwyn Fischer's study of how Brazilian law (from planning and property codes to criminal and social welfare statutes) has demarcated the rights of poor urban residents. Particularly instructive for architectural history is Alejandro Velasco's *Barrio Rising: Urban Popular Politics and the Making of Modern Venezuela*, whose focus is the 23 de Enero, a showcase mass housing project designed by Carlos Raúl Villanueva and expressing the modernizing vision of General Marcos Pérez Jiménez. In the two days following the fall of the Pérez Jiménez regime in 1958, over three thousand of the project's as-yet unfinished apartments were occupied via a spontaneous squatter action, quickly followed by the construction of improvised dwellings in the interstices of its blocks. While this may suggest the familiar tale of a failed modernism, for Velasco it marks a popular rewriting of the project. Its status as a privileged architectural object was not incidental to this process. Rather, the prestige it was afforded by Pérez Jiménez as an embodiment of the new Venezuela gave its residents a sense of their role as members of a social vanguard; having become the modern citizens that the developmentalist dictatorship aimed to produce, they surpassed its intentions with their own unruly assertion of urban citizenship.[4]

In Velasco's account, the rewriting of the 23 de Enero sets the scene for a site-specific history of the emergence of popular democracy, grounded in the materiality of modernist housing and the dynamics of urban space. Within architectural history, similar user-generated transformations of modernist buildings have been viewed from a very different perspective, largely limited to questions of creative agency. In an early example of the genre, Philippe Boudon argues that resident-built modifications to Le Corbusier's Pessac project reveal not the design's failure but its success, because "it not only allowed the occupants sufficient latitude to satisfy their needs, by doing so it also helped them to realize what those needs were." Similarly, in a recent study of a 1950s housing project in Sidi Othman, Casablanca, one of the architects asserts that their goal had been "to find a structure which was destruction-proof in an aesthetic sense" while simultaneously claiming credit for facilitating residents' alterations: "It was this structure that made [their] creativity possible in the first place!" By suggesting that such modifications are essentially fulfilling the original design, inventiveness and agency remain positioned on the side of the architect. By contrast, editors of a recent journal issue on "appropriate(d) modernisms" insist that resident transformations express a creative drive "to construct an alternative spatial practice to that foreseen by an imposed structure." By "appropriating" buildings for new purposes, these interventions potentially subvert the architecture's original meaning and intent, suggesting "the starting point of a new grammar of 'city-making' [*faire-ville*]."[5]

Here, Holston's concept of insurgent urban citizenship reemerges as the constructive agency of the self-builder—with the caveat that without the benefit of in-depth resident interviews (as Velasco conducted) the intention remains opaque, as physical reworkings and formal disruptions of the built fabric cannot be assumed to express an oppositional stance. Nonetheless, simply recognizing these practices as part of a language of city-making grants them a new legibility that is also instructive for a discussion of aided self-help housing; it allows for consideration of an extended and layered timeline of architectural production that may incorporate a range of self-built insertions into approved plans, enacted from construction site to postoccupancy transformation.

Working at the intersection of architectural design, housing provision, and urban informality, the range of scholarship I have referenced, along with the research of earlier scholars of housing in Peru, outline possible approaches to my topic. My aim is to broaden access to architectural practices that have been on the borderlines of architectural knowledge, and that are more complex and multifaceted than a cursory reading of their modest forms and materialities may suggest. With this research, I hope to reinforce some tentatively drawn routes into this unfamiliar territory, and to contribute toward opening up new ones.

ACKNOWLEDGMENTS

This project would not have been possible without the assistance of numerous people. My sincerest gratitude to all those who contributed to its realization.

Firstly, my thanks to John F. C. Turner for his immense generosity, both personal and intellectual, in granting extensive access to his papers and sharing his thoughts in a series of interviews, conversations, and emails. Many thanks also to the architects, engineers, and other experts, in Peru and elsewhere, who shared their knowledge with me: Santiago Agurto Calvo, Michel Azcueta, Adolfo Córdova, Frederick Cooper Llosa, Miguel Cruchaga, Carlos Escalante Estrada, Lidia Gálvez, Kathrin Golda-Pongratz, Juan Gunther Doering, Sandy Hirshen, Sara Ishikawa, Helan Jaworski, Doscenko Josic, Sharif S. Kahatt, Peter Land, Francisco Leo, Wiley Ludeña Urquizo, Raquel Machicao, Fumihiko Maki, Federico Mevius Andersen, Heinz Müller, Gustavo Riofrío, Diego Robles, Juan Tokeshi, E. Howard Wenzel, and in particular Marcia Koth de Paredes, Ernesto Paredes, and Rodolfo Salinas, for their invaluable assistance in Lima.

My thanks to the staff of the key archives I drew upon, particularly: Maria Seminario Sanchez and Ramón Cuevas Pillman at the Centro de Documentación e Información, Ministerio de Vivienda, Construcción y Saneamiento, Lima; Elaine Penn at the University of Westminster, London; and Mary Nelson at the Wichita State University Libraries, Wichita, Kansas. Thanks also to Germán Samper and the Archivo de Bogotá, the Centre Canadien d'Architecture/Canadian Centre for Architecture, Igor Bodhan Hansen, and Tess van Eyck Wickham for facilitating access to the archives in their care, and to Fredy Quispe Aguilar for his professionalism and persistence in carrying out followup research in Lima.

My thanks to the faculty at Columbia University who helped to shape and refine the framework of this research: to Reinhold Martin, for provocative exchanges on the architectural, historiographical, theoretical, and political issues at stake, and for not trying to dissuade me from pursuing this topic; to Kenneth Frampton, for illuminating conversations about the architects involved in PREVI, and more generally for rich insights into reading architecture; to Robert A. Beauregard, for sharp questions at the edges of disciplinary boundaries; to David Smiley, for many stimulating discussions about the trees as well as the woods; to Felicity D. Scott, for her intellectual curiosity and assiduous critical reading; to Claudio Lomnitz, for guidance in navigating the rich field of urban anthropology in postwar Latin America; to Mary McLeod, for her early suggestion to expand my research to include John F. C. Turner.

My thanks to conveners or respondents of panels and other forums where I presented various iterations of this research: Carol McMichael Reese and Thomas Reese, David Smiley, Pilar Rau, Dianne Harris, Timothy Hyde, Alessandro Angelini, David Rifkind, Leandro Benmergui and Mark Healey, Frederique van Andel, Deanna Sheward and Luis Castañeda; in addition, my particular gratitude to Luis for his boundless generosity in sharing his insights into Peru. My thanks also to Jesús Escobar and Meredith TenHoor for support at critical moments and for intellectual community within the discipline.

My thanks to the many PhD colleagues at Columbia University who offered feedback, and provided me with a home in architectural history, especially: Patricio del Real, Irene Cheng, María González Pendas, Marta Caldeira, Leslie Klein, Ginger Nolan, Ayala Levin, Daniel Barber, Peter Minosh, Daniel Talesnik, Andrea J. Merrett, Alexandra Quantrill, James D. Graham, Diana Martinez, Hollyamber Kennedy, Norihiko Tsuneishi, and Chris Cowell.

My thanks and sincere appreciation to those organizations that supported the initial research for this project: the Graham Foundation for Advanced Studies in the Fine Arts through the Carter Manny Award, the Society of Architectural Historians, the Paul Mellon Centre for Studies in British Art, and the Buell Center for the Study of American Architecture, Columbia University. Many thanks also to Eugenie L. Birch and David Brownlee of the H+U+D (Humanities, Urbanism, Design) Initiative at the University of Pennsylvania, for facilitating my participation in the Mellon Junior Fellow program, which was invaluable in completing followup research. Finally, my thanks to the Graham Foundation for Advanced Studies in the Fine Arts and Furthermore: a program of the J. M. Kaplan Fund for their support of the production of this book, as well as the team at the University of Pittsburgh Press, above all Dianne Harris and Abby Collier, for their enthusiasm in backing this project and their guidance in steering it toward completion.

LIST OF ABBREVIATIONS

Archives

CDI-MVCS	Centro de Documentación e Información, Ministerio de Vivienda, Construcción y Saneamiento, Lima
JFCT-UW	John Francis Charlewood Turner Collection, University of Westminster, London
MMA	Maryknoll Mission Archives, Maryknoll, NY
RG 56; NACP	General Records of the Department of the Treasury, 1775–2005, Record Group 56; National Archives at College Park, College Park, MD
RG 286; NACP	Records of the Agency for International Development, 1948–2003, Record Group 286; National Archives at College Park, College Park, MD
RG 469; NACP	Records of US Foreign Assistance Agencies, 1942–1963, Record Group 469; National Archives at College Park, College Park, MD
UN-ARMS	United Nations Archives and Records Management Section, New York, NY
WHC-WSUL	Jean and Willard Garvey World Homes Collection, Wichita State University Libraries, Special Collections and University Archives, Wichita, KS

Agencies, etc.

APRA	Alianza Popular Revolucionaria Americana (American Popular Revolutionary Alliance)
CIAM	Congrès Internationaux d'Architecture Moderne (International Congresses of Modern Architecture)

CINVA	Centro Interamericano de Vivienda (Inter-American Housing Center)
CNV	Corporación Nacional de la Vivienda (National Housing Corporation)
CRAV	Comisión para la Reforma Agraria y la Vivienda (Commission for Agrarian Reform and Housing)
CUAVES	Comunidad Urbana Autogestionaria de Villa El Salvador (Self-Managing Urban Community of Villa El Salvador)
ENACE	Empresa Nacional de Edificaciones (National Building Enterprise)
FNSBS	Fondo Nacional de Salud y Bienestar Social (National Fund for Health and Social Welfare)
IDB	Inter-American Development Bank
INADUR	Instituto Nacional de Desarrollo Urbano (National Institute for Urban Development)
ININVI	Instituto Nacional de Investigación y Normalización de la Vivienda (National Institute for Housing Research and Standardization)
INVI	Instituto de la Vivienda (Housing Institute)
IU	Izquierda Unida (United Left)
JNV	Junta Nacional de la Vivienda (National Housing Board)
MLM	Municipalidad de Lima Metropolitana (Municipality of Metropolitan Lima)
MSP	Movimiento Social Progresista (Progressive Social Movement)
MV	Ministerio de Vivienda (Ministry of Housing)
OATA	Oficina de Asistencia Técnica de Arequipa (Arequipa Technical Assistance Office)
ONDEPJOV	Oficina Nacional de Desarrollo de Pueblos Jóvenes (National Office for the Development of Young Towns)
ONPU	Oficina Nacional de Planeamiento y Urbanismo (National Office for Planning and Urbanism)
PLANDEMET	Plan de Desarrollo Metropolitano Lima-Callao (Metropolitan Development Plan for Lima-Callao)

PREVI	Proyecto Experimental de Vivienda (Experimental Housing Project)
SINAMOS	Sistema Nacional de Apoyo a la Movilización Social (National System of Support for Social Mobilization)
UCV	Unidad Comunal de Vivienda (Communal Dwelling Unit)
UPIS	Urbanización Popular de Interés Social (Popular Urban Settlement of Social Housing)

IMPROVISED
CITIES

INTRODUCTION

This narrative turns on the limits—and limitations—of architecture as a means to provide housing under conditions of crisis: it examines the challenges to the universalist claims of architectural modernism in the postwar period when it was faced with an unsettling world of rapid demographic growth, very low-income populations, intensifying economic modernization, and increasing rural-urban migration, which resulted in extensive unplanned urban development. The prototypes first devised in Europe in the 1920s to provide affordable reform housing, which by this period had already gained a canonical status for architects, needed to be radically rethought. More than adjustments to create culturally appropriate residential forms, or regionally inflected aesthetics, or technical adaptations to different climates, building materials, and technologies, this would require a profound conceptual recalibration to accommodate unfamiliar economic and social conditions. In Peru, as elsewhere, the sheer scale of the housing deficit and of the incursions of improvised construction on illegally occupied land, combined with the scarcity of resources, tested the limits of conventional modernist mass housing. Aided self-help housing presented itself as a response to the constraints and apparent opportunities of this situation: its essential premise was to bring together the benefits of "formal" architecture (an expertise in design and construction) with those of "informal" building (substantial cost savings, because residents themselves furnished the labor). Yet this formal/informal interface hardly represented a seamless alliance. Even at its most collaborative, the relationship between architect and self-builder remained to a degree conflictual, reflecting the inevitable friction as architecture sought to reorder the patterns of informal, or unplanned, urbanism—to remake or redeem the improvised city through design.

This examination of aided self-help housing, or technical assistance to self-builders, presents a case study of Peru, the site of significant (albeit sporadic) trial projects in the technique. The discussion centers on three interrelated contexts: the circumstances that made Peru a fertile site for innovation in low-cost housing under a succession of very different political regimes; the influences on, and movements within, architectural culture that prompted architects to consider self-help housing as an alternative mode of practice; and the environment in which international development agencies came to embrace these projects as part of their larger goals. The narrative unfolds over eight chapters focused on key episodes in this history, alternating its viewpoint between these contexts.

Over the three decades covered by this research (1954–1986), aided self-help housing projects were initiated in many countries. Since much of this history remains to be written, it is all but impossible to determine whether projects in Peru were more successful than trials elsewhere—whether more effective in their planning and implementation or more substantial in their social, economic, or urbanistic impacts. However, the Peruvian case is unequivocally significant in other respects—firstly, for the ongoing, deeply engaged debates about low-cost housing in general, and aided self-help techniques in particular, which involved key public figures and politicians, theorists and practitioners, over several decades. Some of these actors were prominent within Peru but little known outside the country, such as economist and newspaper owner Pedro G. Beltrán, or architect and politician Fernando Belaúnde Terry; others did their formative work within Peru but developed an international audience for their writing, such as English architect and self-help housing theorist John F. C. Turner and Peruvian neoliberal economic thinker Hernando de Soto. Taken together, their contributions generated a remarkable level of discourse around aided self-help, providing a rich background to a discussion of the projects themselves. Secondly, Peru was pioneering in enacting a policy of land tenure regularization in squatter settlements, passing legislation to enable these efforts in 1961 as part of an initiative to reassert control over urban development. The legislation envisaged that once the status of illegally occupied urban land was resolved, planning professionals would guide the construction of high-quality aided self-help housing to replace the squatters' own improvised dwellings. As Julio Calderón Cockburn has observed, it was a decade before other countries in Latin America followed Peru's lead in regularizing tenure, with Mexico passing similar legislation in 1971, and Chile, Brazil, and Argentina following suit after Habitat, the first United Nations (UN) Conference on Human Settlements, held in Vancouver in 1976.[1] Finally, from the perspective of architectural history, Peru is notable for organizing PREVI (Proyecto Experimental de Vivienda, or Experimental Housing Project), which included an international design competition held in the late 1960s that invited prominent avant-garde architects to devise low-cost housing that would incorporate elements of aided self-help. While most aided self-help housing schemes tend to be modest in their formal ambitions, PREVI challenged participants to explore the design potential of an architecture devised at the intersection of formal and informal construction processes.

Efforts to make aided self-help housing work—technically, administratively, financially—took a variety of forms in Peru over these decades. Primarily, "aided" or "directed" self-help housing projects were intended to be carried out with active, on-site technical assistance from architects, harnessing the energy of do-it-yourself building and directing it toward more accomplished outcomes. The architect could offer improvements to the planning of urban layouts, to the design of building components and methods, to construction standards and structural engineering, or to the internal disposition of the house (separating functional zones, maximizing available light and air, or minimizing wasted space). More broadly, professional expertise could be deployed to produce efficiencies in the management of resources (usage of time, labor, materials, money) and to shape the social dimensions of the project (skills training, organization of work groups, promoting community development). Finally, the housing agencies sponsoring such projects could facilitate the participants' access to subsidized loans, in an effort to speed up the often protracted process of self-help construction.

While a small number of projects discussed here were aimed at coordinating the remediation of existing unauthorized settlements, construction ex nihilo was regarded as far preferable, because a well-planned urban framework ensured that any subsequent installation of services would be more straightforward and therefore more affordable than working around improvised structures. These planned settlements took a variety of forms. Most commonly, following the sites-and-services model, they offered an urban layout, graded roadways, residential lots with a one- or two-bedroom *núcleo básico* (basic core unit), and essential services—water, sewerage, electricity—but only on a shared basis at the outset, with standpipes and latrines but no domestic plumbing connections, with street lighting but no domestic electricity. With the additional advantage of secure tenure (and the future possibility of gaining legal title), the expectation was that these fragmentary settlements would eventually cohere into more or less conventional urban areas, with more or less adequate dwellings. At times, however, the sites-and-services model stretched the *Existenzminimum* to its extreme: in their most reduced form, known in Peru as *lotes tizados* (surveyed lots outlined with chalk), they offered residents only rudimentary shared services and guaranteed tenure on the outline of a lot.

Other architect-designed projects went beyond the sites-and-services minimum, including a more substantial core house, which could be expanded and completed over time by the residents, following the architect's plans. Experiments with housing on this model of progressive development (also called the "growing house") go back to at least the 1920s, in Europe and elsewhere. In Peru this approach appealed not just to low-income households but also to lower-middle-income families, since it could provide an alternative path to achieving a standard modern dwelling, built incrementally as the family's needs demanded and its budget allowed. In another variant of the "growing house" model, known as supervised credit, financing would be disbursed in stages, with a technician inspecting and approving each phase of construction before the next installment was paid out. This offered technical assistance at a remove, in the form of quality control, and was a more cost-effective use of the expert's time—intervening at key junctures to ensure that work was proceeding in the right direction, rather than managing the entire process.

Significantly, the term *aided self-help housing* evokes ideologies of self-improvement, signaling the fact that it aimed not just to provide housing but also to transform participants into better citizens, better workers, better community members. However, the Spanish terms used to designate the technique vary considerably over this period. A key early study, published in 1953 by the Centro Interamericano de Vivienda (CINVA, or Inter-American Housing Center) in Bogotá, based on trial projects in Puerto Rico, used a pairing of terms—*ayuda propia* (self-help) and *ayuda mutua* (mutual help or mutual aid)—which it defined in tandem as "the deliberate effort of a group of families that joins together to study its problems, formulates plans to resolve them through its own efforts, and organizes itself for direct action, counting on minimum aid from the government." The roots of the technique lay in "universally recognized sociological concepts": specifically, the widespread phenomenon that "the individual has felt the need to participate in social institutions larger than the family."[2] Although some later theorists would insist on drawing a clear distinction between the singular and plural modes of the "self" that is the subject of aided self-help, the CINVA experts maintained that individual effort was inseparable from collaborative work in the successful realization of these projects.

In Peru, architect Eduardo Neira wrote a report in 1954 on measures to address unauthorized settlements in the city of Arequipa, in which he proposed "ayuda mutua" for housing construction, emphasizing the cooperative dimension. Significantly, Neira would later argue that forms of cooperative work were indigenous to traditional Peruvian society reaching back to the pre-Columbian era[3]— an idea that was frequently repeated elsewhere, often evoking the Quechua terms *ayni*, meaning reciprocity or mutualism, or *minga* (or *mink'a*), meaning collective labor to benefit the community, sometimes characterized as an Inca mutual self-help. This framing naturalized these practices and effectively set the stage for the adoption of mutual-aid self-help schemes as a key element of housing policy within Peru. A situation of crisis, with citizens forced into the arduous process of constructing their own dwellings, was given the reassuring patina of tradition, ensuring that the focus remained on their undoubted resourcefulness and creativity rather than the structural inequality that had necessitated it in the first place.

In his somewhat later study evaluating a realized project in Arequipa, Turner employed the term *ayuda mutua dirigida* (managed mutual aid), underscoring the contribution of professional guidance. The designation *autoconstrucción* (self-building) appeared in a Peruvian housing agency document from 1961, referring to two linked modes of self-help: ayuda mutua and esfuerzo propio (one's own effort).[4] In more recent documents, autoconstrucción is used alone, absent association with any outside "assistance"—it is object-centered rather than process-centered in its connotations, and entirely detached from the abstract values of personal and community development. Of course, all these terms serve to mask the difficulties of participating in the capitalist labor market while simultaneously employing one's labor to build one's own house, obscuring the extent to which "self-help" housing requires drafting the efforts of the entire household, including children, or is outsourced to local builders when that is judged to be a more efficient use of time and money.

Similarly, the phenomenon of informal or unauthorized urban settlement has been described by a number of different terms within Peru. By using the terminology of the original documents throughout the text, the aim is to foreground this shifting conceptual and ideological construction. While in English the recently revived and problematic term *slum* is frequently used to designate informal settlements,[5] in Peru, both in popular usage and professional discourse, these are two distinct urban forms: *tugurio* (slum) refers to degraded housing of various kinds, generally occupied on a rental basis and situated in inner-urban areas, but not to neighborhoods self-built by residents. Early references to unauthorized urban development are firmly within the tradition of regarding it as a form of "cancer" or other malady, with one government document from 1956 using the phrase "'barrios hongos' (insalubres)"—insalubrious, mushrooming—or fungal—neighorhoods.[6] In general, the terminology employed throughout the 1950s is less colorful, with more neutral descriptive modifiers, albeit with pejorative undertones: *barrio clandestino* (clandestine neighborhood), *barrio espontáneo* (spontaneous neighborhood), *barrio marginal* (marginal neighborhood), or, more colloquially and most commonly, *barriada* (shantytown). A more sympathetic denomination, and the one usually preferred by the residents themselves, was *urbanización popular* ("popular" or low-income urban settlement).

Writing documents for the Peruvian housing agencies that employed him, Turner tended to use "urbanización popular"; writing in English for a wider audience, he used "barriada" as well as "squatter settlement"—a term that underscored the illegal occupation of the underlying land, forcibly claimed by residents unable to find a footing elsewhere in the urban housing market. After 1968, the leftist Gobierno Revolucionario de la Fuerza Armada (Revolutionary Government of the Armed Forces) sought to eliminate the use of barriada, with all its pejorative connotations, by actively promoting the substitute term *pueblo joven* (young town, or young community), emphasizing the emerging economic and social potential, and anticipated future consolidation, of these neighborhoods. After the military regime ended in 1980, the official term was changed again, rejecting the ideological associations that had developed around pueblo joven in favor of *asentamiento humano* (human settlement), a more technocratic denomination popularized by Habitat in 1976. The usage *asentamiento informal* (informal settlement) seems to have been introduced by de Soto in his 1986 book *El otro sendero: La revolución informal* (first published in English in 1989 under the title *The Other Path: The Invisible Revolution in the Third World*). In this context, de Soto's employment of "informal" underscores his broader argument that the "formal" channels of law and bureaucratic procedure only serve to stifle the dynamism and economic potential of self-built neighborhoods; for de Soto, informal settlements succeed precisely by opposing themselves to the constraints of formal urban development.

Currently, "informal" is the prevailing term in Anglophone architectural discourse, where its somewhat blurry usage often fails to take account of the term's connections to neoliberal economic thought, and furthermore merges together related but distinct phenomena, which in practice do not always overlap.[7] On the one hand, "informal" or unauthorized settlements: these are extralegal in two senses, since they are established on land that has been occupied illegally by the residents, and they do not conform to prevailing legal standards for the development of urban subdivisions, lacking basic services such as water and sewerage lines, electricity, and graded roadways. On the other hand, "informal" or improvised construction: housing that is self-built rather than guided by architects, engineers, or building permits. Complicating matters, in Peru as elsewhere, "informal" or improvised construction is not confined to "informal" or unauthorized settlements—dwellings in legally established neighborhoods will often begin with conventional construction but will subsequently be modified or extended on an ad hoc basis via self-building.

Ironically, the influence of de Soto's ideas within Peru means that on a quite literal level, the term "informal" may be facing imminent redundancy: de Soto's call to recognize the economic potential of informal settlements has led to the widespread implementation of "formalization" programs aimed at clarifying and securing legal property title for residents (albeit without requiring improvements in their everyday conditions of life by bringing urban services up to code). Alternative terms such as *barrio popular* ("popular" or low-income neighborhood), and *ciudad emergente* (emerging city) have begun to appear—the latter term recalling pueblo joven in its evocation of an urbanism in the process of becoming, whose present deficiencies wait to be resolved. Perhaps these legally titled, "formalized" neighborhoods—which remain "informal" in the sense that they fail to meet established planning standards—could be best described as "nonconforming" settlements.

Before turning to the narrative structure of the book, it is worthwhile to explore the wider context surrounding practices of aided self-help housing: first, debates within the social sciences concerning how to understand the patterns of urbanization shaping postwar Latin America; second, the positioning of self-help housing within architectural history, focusing on aided self-help housing per se, and the relationship of aided self-help and the "growing house" model.

Urbanization—Unbalanced, Marginal, Dependent, Informal

From the early 1950s, the discourse on Latin American urbanization—understood as encompassing demographic change, the sociocultural changes experienced by rural-urban migrants, and the physical changes affecting the shape of cities—was intricately enmeshed with theories of modernization and development. The narrative of modernization, since complicated and compromised, was almost universally accepted in this period. As James Ferguson has suggested, its straightforward and self-evident appeal could be summarized in the upward trajectory of a diagonal line on a graph defined by a horizontal axis of "time" (aiming toward the "universal telos" of modernity) and a vertical axis of "status" (promising elevation within the global economic system, as "the passage of developmental time . . . raise[d] the poor countries up to the level of the rich ones").[8] Promoting development in countries that were determined to be lagging in relation to markers of economic and social progress became a widely shared goal of international agencies such as the UN and national governments alike, with elites in many "developing" nations setting agendas to transform their own societies, and the already "developed" nations selectively supporting these initiatives via foreign aid.

In Latin America, political elites had long sought to foster modernization, which was often seen as virtually synonymous with industrialization. In this view, modernization meant economic growth and diversification, entailing a shift from agricultural to industrial production, the transformation from a predominantly rural to an urban society, and with it the emergence of a particular kind of city (and citizen), unmistakably modern in character. Rather than entrusting the path of development to market forces, Latin American nations emulated the kind of state-run modernization programs undertaken in nineteenth-century Germany and Japan.[9] Accordingly, as the sense grew that somehow the anticipated patterns of development and its associated urbanization were not being followed in postwar Latin America, large-scale planning emerged as a preferred solution.

Typical of this thinking was the assessment of urban planner Francis Violich, who, writing in a 1953 UN publication, identified as an issue of concern the region's characteristically "unbalanced" economies, with their ad hoc industrial programs and unevenly distributed employment opportunities, which had resulted in a "high concentration of urban population in a few major cities." For Violich, the answer was regional planning: "With greater guidance of resource development and a basic policy for industrial locations, the urban pattern would be more balanced and a more stable type of development would result." Meanwhile, in the main cities, the population surge combined with "the utter lack of systematic zoning" had created an "anarchic pattern of land use."[10] While effectively enforced urban planning could alleviate this problem, Violich concluded that such measures would only fully succeed within a comprehensive program for national development, synchronizing networks of major cities, secondary centers, and sites of industrial or agricultural production. Coordinated initiatives to redirect the flow of migrants would relieve the pressure on overloaded poles of attraction and stimulate emerging urban areas, ultimately benefiting both the national economy and the cities themselves.

One element of the "anarchic" urban growth that Violich observed was the illegal construction of "conspicuous shacktowns" on vacant sites. Violich did not speculate on their socioeconomic origins or role in the urban ecosystem; he simply applauded instances of "direct slum clearance" where shacktowns were "demolished for urgent sanitary reasons or for purposes of pure aesthetics" and the residents rehoused, arguing that any attempts to ameliorate conditions in these settlements "only add to the permanency of the miserable dwellings."[11] For Violich, the shacktowns were an epiphenomenon, a temporary side effect of the region's unbalanced urbanization that would disappear as these developing economies regained their equilibrium.

Half a decade later, sociologist and demographer Harley Browning reiterated the concern with Latin America's uneven urban growth, or, as he termed it, its "high primacy pattern" of urbanization, whereby the "first city is many times larger than the second city" and tends to monopolize economic opportunities and social resources, such as access to improved education and healthcare. Although there were doubtless some advantages to this concentration, the disadvantages were very clear. Second- or third-tier cities risked being left behind, while the favored cities faced their own challenge—becoming "overurbanized"—because "city growth is running ahead of economic development" as urban centers attracted far more migrants than the nascent industrial sector could absorb. In this way, Latin American cities appeared to be sidestepping established models of modernization: rather than urban development arising out of economic growth, cities were increasing in population and complexity and sheer physical size without the requisite economic development. The issue was not just an imbalance among cities, then, but a fundamental disjunction between urban and economic development. Nonetheless, Browning viewed "overurbanization" as preferable to minimal urbanization, which signified social and economic stagnation. Furthermore, the shift toward a more urbanized population was a positive in itself: migrants were "shedding some of their rural-based conceptions" and adapting themselves to the city, beginning a process of acculturation that would culminate in their full integration into the life of the modern nation.[12] Browning only obliquely addressed the issue of unplanned settlements. While acknowledging the substandard living conditions endured by many migrants, he noted that the situation was far worse in rural areas; despite the challenges they faced, new urban arrivals had already improved their lot simply by "urbanizing" themselves, and thereby offered encouragement for others to migrate.

The culmination of this strand of thinking was the Seminar on Urbanization Problems in Latin America held in 1959 in Santiago, Chile, cosponsored by three UN agencies—the Bureau of Social Affairs, the Economic Commission for Latin America (ECLA), and United Nations Educational, Scientific and Cultural Organisation (UNESCO)—along with the International Labour Organization (ILO) and the Organization of American States (OAS). Bringing together a range of experts from across the region, the multidisciplinary nature of the investigation is exemplified by the three contributors from Peru: anthropologist José Matos Mar, social psychologist Humberto Rotondo, and urban planner Luis Dorich. In its summary of the seminar's findings, the Rapporteurs' Report once again noted the disjunction between Latin America's urban and economic development. Yet rather than interpreting this as pathological, the authors argued that urbanization in Western Europe and the United States had been similarly "haphazard, regulated only by spontaneous market forces." These earlier models of urbanization seemed coherent only in hindsight; in fact, disorder and disequilibrium were constitutive of urbanism under capitalist economic development, and thus the experience of Latin America was not an aberration. However, in contrast to those earlier waves of modernization, experts now had the benefit of a scientific understanding of urbanization processes, such that planned development offered a viable tool to remediate its ill effects. Echoing Violich and Browning, the seminar concluded that development initiatives "should be used to achieve a better balance of urban-rural growth" in an effort to "moderate the excessive flow of migrants."[13] With such measures, a realignment of urban and economic development would eventually be achieved.

In Peru, concrete policies along these lines were proposed by the 1956 Comisión para la Reforma Agraria y la Vivienda (CRAV, Commission for Agrarian Reform and Housing), which explicitly connected substandard barriada housing in Lima to migration driven by insufficient access to arable land in rural areas. Its recommendations to slow migration included enacting agrarian reform to draw potential migrants back toward working the land and promoting regional development projects to counterbalance the gravitational pull of the capital. Realized initiatives included limited schemes for the resettlement of barriada residents via internal colonization, as part of the government's strategic "marcha a la selva" (march to the forest) to clear, cultivate, and secure the territory of the Peruvian Amazon. Foreshadowing later, more systematic colonization efforts, in July 1960 fifty families from the San Martín de Porres barriada in Lima established the *colonización* "La Morada" (The Residence) in the Huallaga Central area of Peru's Amazon basin, with each household granted title to 30 hectares of land. The "settlers" received technical assistance from a number of government bodies, including the Ministries of Agriculture, Health, Defense, and Transport, and the Fondo Nacional de Salud y Bienestar Social (FNSBS, National Fund for Health and Social Welfare), the primary body concerned with the well-being of barriada residents. Four years later, in May 1964, eighty heads of household from Lima barriadas embarked for another Amazonian colony, "La Buena Esperanza" (Good Hope) in Oxapampa, joining two hundred other settler families from around the country. Depending on the size of the household, they would receive 30 to 50 hectares of land, suitable for growing crops such as cacao, coffee, and rubber.[14]

Beyond its recommendations concerning planned development, the UN seminar acknowledged that urgent measures were needed to address the increasing prevalence of "shanty-towns" in rapidly growing cities. Yet it cautioned that the fundamental problem was the low level of household income, which would be resolved only with economic growth. In the meantime, the focus should be on realistic, achievable goals, such as "the provision of basic urban services to the mass population in cities" and perhaps very basic housing programs meeting "minimum standards of sanitation and comfort." In addition to these pragmatic physical planning solutions, the seminar addressed the "social welfare aspects" of urbanization, proposing measures such as "the creation of reception centres for newcomers . . . to ensure their integration into the city community." Channeling Georg Simmel, the Rapporteurs' Report framed such issues as falling within the "psycho-social aspect of urban culture": this demanded a "new type of personality" characterized by a "receptive attitude to foreigners, . . . emotional detachment, and the capacity for abstract thought." The urbanization of the individual required shedding rural personality traits (xenophobia, strong emotional connections) in favor of a more rational subjectivity, suitable for cultivating the "impersonal relationships" proper to urban life.[15] This psychological transformation also entailed replacing the traditional, inherited value system that had broken apart with the migrant's transplantation with a new set of values based on innovation, creation, and change—qualities that were closely connected to (and needed for effective participation in) economic development.

José Matos Mar's contribution to the seminar report, an anthropological study of barriadas in Lima, provided a vivid illustration of the challenges involved. According to his analysis, the sharp contrast of rural (traditional) and urban (modern) cultures led "to serious conflicts which are reflected in mental, social, and economic maladjustment that militates against satisfactory integration."[16] Evidence for this lack of "integration" was abundant: under- or unemployment, inadequate living conditions, ill health and poor nutrition, matrimonial and domestic instability, and consequent vagrancy and vice. In sum, these migrants exhibited the economic, social, and psychological pathologies fitting the contemporary definition of a "marginal" existence—hovering on the periphery of mainstream society, seeking in vain a new rootedness in urbanity.

The pervasiveness and persistence of the discourse of marginality in discussions of Latin American urbanization in this period was comprehensively unraveled by Janice Perlman in *The Myth of Marginality* (1976). Noting the fluidity of the concept—which had been "popularized as a coherent theory even though . . . it is based on a set of loosely related, rather ambiguous hypotheses"—Perlman enumerated several distinct modes of marginality.[17] Its intellectual origins lay in the "psychosociological" mode introduced by Robert E. Park's "Human Migration and the Marginal Man" (1928), which described the migrant's hybrid existence, stranded on the edges of two cultures, one he had not fully left behind and the other he had not fully embraced. Although this marginality was experienced on an individual, psychological level, it was rooted in larger sociological processes. The concept gained a widespread legitimacy in the 1950s throughout Latin America, offering a framework to understand the new sociocultural landscape emerging as a consequence of accelerating urbanization. The "ethnographic" mode of marginality articulated in this context explicated the cultural dislocation experienced by rural-urban migrants. Matos Mar's analysis of Lima's barriadas fit firmly within this tradition. Other variants identified by Perlman were closely related offshoots. The "modernization" mode addressed the sociopsychological challenges of urban integration for the individual, as well as the political-economic challenges for the modern nation-state overseeing this integration, in order to produce the kind of citizenry required for political stability and economic growth. The "radicalism" mode took this preoccupation to its logical conclusion, suggesting that the inadequate integration of the neither-here-nor-there "marginal man" could lead to discontent, political instability, and even revolution, threatening the foundations of society as a whole.

Another important aspect of the marginality concept was that its descriptive power applied not only to social groups but also to the physical space of cities. Perlman denominated this the "architectural-ecological" mode of marginality, as it focused on identifying problematic neighborhoods by their physical characteristics: their marginal location on vacant sites, wasteland, or literally on the urban periphery, as well as their functionally marginal infrastructure and marginal construction. In this circular environmental determinist reading, "marginal settlements" were both a symptom of underlying social problems and the disease itself: socioeconomically marginal citizens built marginal neighborhoods; inhabiting a marginal neighborhood exacerbated and confirmed the residents' socioeconomic marginality.

With the rise of these debates, the discourse on Latin American urbanization shifted its conceptual framework. While for observers like Violich, focused on unbalanced urbanization, the "shacktown" was an epiphenomenon that would disappear when national development found its point of equilibrium, "marginal settlements" were now seen as a core problem, both in urbanistic terms (as unauthorized settlements subverting efforts at rational urban planning) and in social terms (as the home of an unintegrated mass of marginals).

In this new discursive context, aided self-help housing came to have a particular resonance. As a case in point, despite describing the barriadas as unstable and unhealthy, Matos Mar's study for the UN seminar also provided a clear-sighted view of the role of self-help—albeit unaided and improvised—in these settlements. His detailed observations of the process of barriada formation noted that self-organized residents carefully managed the occupation and settlement of their sites, overseeing tasks such as allocating lots among the group, and collectively executing public works from roads to sewer trenches. These residents, he concluded, "have been compelled to help themselves by organizing on an ad hoc basis." Furthermore, while he regarded the residents as "underdeveloped people of peasant mentality" yet to be integrated into urban life, he nonetheless endorsed the practices of cooperative work that he argued they had brought with them from their rural communities, interpreting this as an important continuation of traditional Peruvian communitarian values. In developing their barriadas, "the help which they give to projects for the common good is steady and effective and is perhaps their most valuable contribution."[18]

The UN seminar's Rapporteurs' Report also underscored the significance of such practices: "Evidence was presented for a number of cities indicating that the shanty-town dwellers had considerable initiative and, with proper leadership and guidance, could be mobilized for effective self-help types of community development activity that would notably improve their housing and environment."[19] Unaided self-help was already operative; by introducing technical assistance (that is, "proper leadership and guidance") its impacts could be amplified and refined. In this way, aided self-help could be engineered to provide a dual-use solution: delivering concrete improvements to improvised settlements (upgrading their "marginal" conditions) while building social integration (assimilating their "marginal" residents via community development). This deployment of aided self-help housing as part of programs to counteract the challenges of marginality would continue to find echoes in the language of "popular participation" and "social mobilization" of the Peruvian Revolution in the early 1970s, and once again in discussions around democratization and political engagement in the early 1980s.

Although marginality discourse continued to reverberate into the 1970s, by the late 1960s anthropologist William Mangin, among others, started to question some of its underlying assumptions. Mangin conducted fieldwork in Lima barriadas beginning in the late 1950s and collaborated with Turner on research documenting processes of barriada formation (discussed below). Mangin's article "Latin American Squatter Settlements: A Problem and a Solution" (1967) drew on a range of recent scholarship, including his own research on Lima, to debunk pervasive myths about squatter settlements, much of them shaped by marginality discourse. In Mangin's view, there was little evidence of the social pathologies described by Matos Mar. While families faced challenges due to low levels of income, the rates of violence, crime, and social breakdown were no higher in squatter settlements than in other neighborhoods with similar socioeconomic profiles. While these settlements were often unsightly to the casual observer and their living conditions difficult for residents, the general trend was slow but steady improvement. There was ample evidence of productive economic activity, seen in each family's small-scale investment in improving their housing, and numerous home-based businesses. Participation in the formal labor market was uneven, but a majority of residents did have stable employment of some form—as skilled or unskilled laborers, domestic workers, small-scale entrepreneurs, midlevel public service employees (teachers, white-collar workers)—demonstrating that there was more economic diversity in the barriada than was often imagined.

To Matos Mar's charge that barriada residents were struggling to adapt to urbanity, Mangin responded that they negotiated institutions of urban life from a pragmatic standpoint, having been "compelled to acculturate strategically in order . . . to defend themselves." He noted that many demonstrated a keen awareness of laws, bureaucratic procedures, and political debates that could potentially benefit or harm their interests. They had learned to lobby powerful outsiders for support, cultivating clientelistic relationships with politicians who could legitimate their settlements by guaranteeing secure tenure or the installation of urban services. In this way, they astutely leveraged the promise of their electoral support into gradual but tangible improvements in their neighborhoods. Far from being motivated by radical politics, any collective mobilization was guided by concrete goals and unapologetic economic self-interest. Mangin observed that residents had retained some elements of their rural culture—although he doubted whether cooperative work was one of them, suggesting that most "had never heard of *mingas* before they read about them in newspapers"—but this did not interfere with their ability to function in the urban sphere. They negotiated a new hybrid identity easily, without the trauma suggested by Matos Mar. In sum, for Mangin the squatter settlement was not the "problem" anxiously examined by earlier observers: he did not see it (as per modernization theory) as an unfortunate side effect of dysfunctional urbanization, nor (as per marginality theory) as evidence of social breakdown. Rather, it was a grassroots "solution" to an otherwise intractable housing shortage: the self-organized self-help of the barriada represented "a process of social reconstruction through popular initiative"—and it was now an integral part of Latin American urbanization.[20]

Mangin's work contributed to a wave of scholarship that fundamentally changed how unauthorized settlements were understood. This shift was due in part to new evidence and interpretative approaches, and in part to the emergence of a very different theoretical paradigm—dependency theory—which emphasized a structural rather than a cultural interpretation of poverty. Peruvian sociologist Aníbal Quijano wrote an influential essay on the urban implications of dependency while he was the principal researcher on urbanization and marginality at ECLA in the late 1960s. Quijano argued that Latin American societies—with the exception of post-revolutionary Cuba—occupied "a position of dependency" within a globalized "system of relationships of interdependency formed by capitalist countries." This was not a new phenomenon: from the outset of its colonial occupation, Latin America had been "constitutively dependent"—although the precise contours of its dependency had evolved with the transformations of capitalist markets and modes of production, as successive metropolitan powers in Europe (and later the United States) claimed dominance in the global economy.[21] Importantly, these relations of dependency were not simply imposed by metropolitan powers; rather, they resulted from transnational alliances of external capital and internal elites whose own interests would be furthered by faciliating the local economy's position as a dependent, subordinate actor in the international system.

Latin American urbanization was likewise dependent, the configuration of its urban networks subject to the evolving demands of capital, whether a colonial framework of mining centers and administrative nodes to streamline metal exports or a postcolonial—read: imperial—model of ports along the Atlantic coast to serve British-dominated commercial shipping. Viewing the contemporary situation, Quijano observed that relations of dependency were only intensifying, as international capital shifted into manufacturing and services, resulting in another reshaping of both urban networks and urban society. The new urban networks were dominated by ever more influential industrial centers that were drawing workers away from the rural economy, creating the unbalanced urbanization identified by earlier observers. In Quijano's view, this increasingly asymmetrical dynamic between the urban and rural spheres, and between primary and secondary cities, was symptomatic of internal relationships of dependency. In parallel, the emerging urban society was defined by recent rural-urban migrants whose lives were now circumscribed by the limited opportunities for stable employment that "dependent industrialization" entailed: "Its very logic contains the inevitability of the *marginalization* of growing sectors of the urban population."[22] In this reading, recognized phenomena associated with unbalanced or marginal urbanization were reconceived within a new theoretical framework that viewed the global economic system as the driving force of urban change.

The challenge for those such as Quijano who decried the destructive effects of dependent urbanization was how to move beyond its apparent structural determinism. That is, if dependent urbanization was an expression of global structural inequality—and of internal structural inequality within Latin American societies—it would persist as long as current geopolitical and economic relations held firm. In his conclusions, Quijano pointed to one possible alternative future: the disruptions caused by intensifying urbanization might well lead to a reckoning with the social problems that it had inflamed, because "cities in Latin America fulfill an ambivalent function, serving . . . as vehicles for the penetration and expansion of dependency" while also stimulating "the most broad and rapid diffusion of clear forms of social consciousness in dominated groups."[23]

In an essay a few years later, Manuel Castells underscored that in its dependent state, Latin American urbanization was directed not by the coherent, self-determined plans of developmentalist states but by the needs of capital in its imperial mode: "The transformation of Latin American space is not, then, a 'march toward modernization' but the specific expression of the social contradictions produced by the forms and rhythms of imperialist domination." In essence, the region's dependent urbanization had resulted in a series of unwanted effects, the most striking in spatial terms being *the development of intraurban segregation and the constitution of vast ecological zones called marginal in a process of 'wild urbanization' [urbanización salvaje].*" Viewing this landscape through a Marxist lens, Castells concluded that the key issue now was to determine whether there was a meaningful relationship between the ecological and social stresses created by dependent urbanization, and whether the breakdowns this unveiled opened the possibility of new political movements and alliances, as Quijano had suggested.[24]

A decade on, Castells returned to this theme in *The City and the Grassroots* (1983), a study focused on the dynamics of urban social movements. Castells explicitly identified Latin American squatter communities—the architects of "wild urbanization" and the archetype of social marginality—as potentially "a bank for an alternative political scheme, mak[ing] them at once dangerous and necessary" for existing and nascent political systems alike. In particular, Castells explored the tensions in the relationship between squatters and the state, examining "the dialectics between social integration and social change, since urban populism always walks on the thin edge between clientelism and the triggering of urban social movements."[25] On one side was assimilation to the dominant political system via clientelism; on the other, disrupting it via the construction of a new politics.

In this discussion, Castells refined and to an extent redefined the concepts of marginality and dependency, introducing a new term: the dependent city. Drawing an analogy with the asymmetrical relationships of dependency in the international system, the "dependent city" is characterized by the dependencies that govern its most disempowered residents: squatters. Rather than viewing marginality as a side effect of dependent urbanization, Castells now saw it as a tool to forge dependency: marginality is "socially constructed by the state, in a process of social integration and political mobilization in exchange for goods and services which only it can provide." These goods range from guaranteeing secure tenure to granting title to infrastructure provision (and, by extension, overseeing aided self-help housing schemes). The squatters' extreme need and precarious status—their constructed marginality—binds them to the rules of clientelism, within which their demands may only be met on the state's terms. As squatters, even their physical presence within the city is "an exception to the formal functioning of the economy and of the legal institutions"—and as such is sustainable only under the protection of a patron-client relationship. Ultimately, since squatters are constituted by patronage rather than legal rights, they lack the citizenship required to hold the state accountable. Thus, Castells concludes, "The dependent city is a city without citizens."[26] Nonetheless, even though urban popular politics has a strong tendency toward cooptation by clientelism, it is still only a "thin edge" away from the eruption of urban social movements, potentially triggered by squatters empowered to reject their stable but impoverished situation of dependency, and to demand instead—echoing James Holston's terminology—the recognition of their urban citizenship, their right to the city.

Following a very different theoretical pathway, in the early 1970s some critics of dependency theory, who nonetheless accepted a structural interpretation of poverty, sought to develop a less deterministic viewpoint about its causes and the possibilities of social change. One of the most influential of these was the "dualist" economic theory developed by Keith Hart and others, focused on the complex interrelationships between the "formal" and "informal" economic sectors, generating much debate about how to define their particular characteristics. While earlier theories had viewed informal production and labor markets as a drag on efforts to modernize the economy and spur national development, according to the dualist theory the informal sector had its own logic and dynamism, which was indispensible to the productivity of the formal sector.

The informal sector came to the forefront of debates about urban settlements in the 1980s, largely due to the influence of de Soto's *El otro sendero*. However, while Hart and his contemporaries perceived complex and productive interconnections between the formal and informal sectors, de Soto framed the relationship as inherently antagonistic: the "formal" signified the bureaucratic operations of the state, and the "informal" signified economic vitality, seen to be under constant threat from a state trying to contain entrepreneurial spirit via needless rules and regulations. In his discussion of three areas of economic activity—housing, trade, and transport—there is no mention of the formal economy, as if economic activity per se can be generated only by the informal sector.

On the surface, this would seem to be a deliberate misreading of dualist theories; however, Ray Bromley convincingly argues that de Soto simply has little interest in engaging in such debates. Rather, his intellectual roots lie elsewhere, in a range of conservative and libertarian influences, including economic ideas derived from Adam Smith and Friedrich Hayek, Thomas Paine's political theory, and conservative critiques of dependency theory that attribute Latin America's underdevelopment to its political elites and institutions. Accordingly, de Soto looks at the informal from a "sociolegal" viewpoint, focused on the intersection of law and economics, considering the social impacts of regulations that shape the borderline between the formal and informal sectors. He defines the informal as hovering somewhere between formal and criminal activity, with each of the three sectors characterized by a particular means/end profile. While formal activities seek legal ends via legal means, and criminal activities seek illegal ends via illegal means, "informal activities have legal ends, but are conducted illegally because it is difficult for the participants to comply with official regulations."[27]

In contrast to the black markets of criminal activity, the informal sector functions in a grey zone—rendering a legitimate, necessary service via widespread under-the-table practices (such as operating without a permit or avoiding tax) that are, strictly speaking, illegal, but generally socially sanctioned. The problem with this arrangement, according to de Soto, is that there are considerable costs to the household or business owner operating in this grey zone, adversely affecting the dynamism and productivity of the informal sector. Long-term solutions include streamlining bureaucratic processes and reducing regulations, while in the short term the answer is to "formalize" informal housing and businesses, thereby removing the shadow of illegality.

In the case of informal housing, de Soto argues that through developing their informal settlements, squatters have "created considerable wealth . . . by causing land values to rise and investing in the building of their own homes, thereby dispelling a myth . . . that Peruvians of humble origins are incapable of satisfying their own material needs and must be provided for, guided, and controlled by the state."[28] For de Soto, the state's only legitimate role is to eliminate these settlements' extralegal status: gaining formal title would free the homeowner to borrow money, using the home as collateral to access capital to start a small business or invest in some other enterprise. The economic implications of formalization are seen to be overwhelmingly positive, both in the immediate materialization of home equity for the individual householder and the promised boon to the national economy, as the entrepreneurial spirit of countless residents of self-built settlements is set free. By contrast, the urbanistic implications of formalization are of no concern to de Soto: he does not consider the potential negative impact for overall urban development of granting legal status to any and all self-built housing, no matter how poor the physical condition of the structure, or how ill-planned the neighborhood. Urban planning regulations are only ever seen as compromising the self-determination of the individual householder; de Soto does not acknowledge that the state may have a legitimate right, and even a responsibility, to use planning law to shape the evolution of the city as a whole, for the maximum collective benefit of the urban community.

The conceptual framings of urbanization discussed here—unbalanced, marginal, dependent, and informal—sometimes overlap or blend into one another; paradigm shifts are rarely marked by hard and fast boundaries, even less so when they are translated into policy positions and on-the-ground projects. Nonetheless, it is clear that each of these framings identified particular urban problems, and proposed particular solutions, which could be summarized as follows. In the "unbalanced" paradigm, the problems of overurbanization and associated urban ills (such as shantytowns) can be resolved by recalibrating development to correct urban imbalances. In the "marginal" paradigm, the problems of marginal citizens and settlements can be resolved by programs to integrate the marginal into the mainstream. In the "dependent" paradigm, unbalanced urbanization, marginality, and "wild urbanization" all result from dependency, and can only be remedied through radical structural reform; urban popular politics offered a possible route to creating a less dysfunctional and inequitable city, but—in Castells's reading—was torn between cooptation (social integration) and empowerment (social change). In the "informal" paradigm, improvised settlements are not the problem they appear to be; the solution is to accept this as its own form of urban development, and aim to facilitate, rather than overregulate or restrict, its dynamism.

Likewise, each of these framings of urbanization could be said to present a particular position on the role of aided self-help housing. For the "unbalanced" paradigm, aided self-help is moot, because the shantytown is a transitory epiphenomenon; once its root causes are addressed, it will disappear of its own accord—or be cleared away. For the "marginal" paradigm, aided self-help is a powerful tool, and its impacts are twofold: improving physical living conditions while fostering social integration. For the "dependent" paradigm— again following Castells's reading—"goods and services" such as aided self-help programs seem to occupy an ambivalent position— most likely functioning as a tool of the clientelism that permeates state-squatter exchanges, but possibly a venue for the alternative politics of urban social movements. For the "informal" paradigm, aided self-help is unnecessary, because independent self-helpers are already developing their settlements and their wealth, unaided, and any state assistance is simply another constraint undermining their self-sufficiency.

While there is a particular resonance between aided self-help and the conceptual framework of marginal urbanization, its implementation was not only due to the influence of that position. Rather, aided self-help was a recurrent theme of housing policy in Peru, though pursued with varying degrees of enthusiasm and efficacy, while the arguments supporting it were modulated in response to theoretical, political, and ideological shifts. Nevertheless, in practice, the unaided self-help of the barriada, shantytown, marginal neighborhood, or informal settlement was responsible for the bulk of urban housing production over these decades, remaining a constant throughout these conceptual reframings of the city.

Architectural Encounters with Self-Help Housing

Self-help housing, whether aided or unaided, has been peripheral to architectural history. Yet there are significant points of intersection between these practices and established historical narratives. The focus here will be on two such instances: the history of aided self-help housing per se, and the relationship of aided self-help and the "growing house" concept.

As Richard Harris has shown, the history of aided self-help housing extends far beyond the postwar programs in the developing world often associated with the term. Promoted in Sweden as early as 1904, it first emerged as a widespread solution during the housing crisis following World War I, with programs implemented in several Western European countries and the Soviet Union. Notably, Ernst May worked extensively with self-help projects during his tenure directing the provincial housing authority in Silesia (1918–1925). In addition to supervising a self-help housing program at Neustadt, he experimented with different building methods and materials to improve their efficiency, produced pamphlets demonstrating simple construction techniques, and devised a manually operated brick press for self-builders.[29]

Beyond Europe, Patrick Geddes's *Town Planning towards City Development: A Report to the Durbar of Indore* (1918) includes an important, if brief, theoretical discussion of aided self-help housing. While Geddes addressed the topic in only a few pages of his lengthy and wide-ranging two-volume report, which revolves around plans for a new industrial town, the passages are worth examining in detail, as they foreshadow many of the arguments that were made in favor of aided self-help housing in the postwar period. Addressing the issue of providing mass housing for industrial workers, Geddes argued: "For the needed thousands of houses, we cannot often hope to start with capital more than to admit of an initial single room and veranda, especially in *pukka* [first-class, complete construction]. We must even be content in a good many cases with *kucha* [makeshift, unfinished construction]; and this has the advantage of more cheaply and easily ensuring the adequate floor-space and air-space which are prime essentials of health. Moreover in *kucha* construction, labour can often, at least partly, be given by the worker himself." Geddes continued by suggesting that the state should foster these efforts by providing security for deposits invested in promoting housing construction—this being, in effect, an investment with a guaranteed return in future economic growth, since both state and city governments would be "enriched and strengthened by every increase of material property within their limits, and by every tax-payer whose prosperity and permanence they can assist." In addition, better housing would make for a more stable workforce: "Nothing fixes people like a good house." (Realizing this house with the personal investment of the owner-resident's labor would seem to give additional weight to its anchor.) Returning to the subject in a subsequent chapter, Geddes claimed that many manual laborers had time to spare, and were "sturdy fellows, handy, willing, and often intelligent: and what better outlet can a man find for these virtues, or for increasing them, even acquiring them, than in the construction of his own home?" This proposal was complicated, Geddes lamented, by the fact that the processes of modernization in India had transformed housing construction from "one of the most widely diffused aptitudes" into a specialized occupation; therefore the authorities needed to find "some capable overseers . . . men who could keep up the standards of planning and execution, yet utilize and train the more or less unskilled labor of its employees into satisfactory house-building."[30]

Here are many themes familiar from postwar debates: the reduction of construction costs through self-help; the deployment of state-backed financial resources to expand homeownership, and thereby elevate the household income of self-helpers and stimulate overall economic growth; the increased work-discipline of the industrial labor force; the moral improvement of the self-helper/homeowner; and the importance of sound technical assistance to direct the work.

The key point of connection between Geddes and postwar practice is Jacob L. Crane, director of the International Office of the United States Housing and Home Finance Agency (HHFA, 1945–1954). As documented by Harris, Crane, "who coined the term 'aided self-help housing' in about 1945"—thereby foregrounding the role of experts in guiding such projects—was influenced in his approach at least in part by Geddes, whom he had met in 1921 shortly after Geddes left India. Crane's firsthand experience of the practice came from his time working as director of project planning for the United States Housing Administration, beginning in 1938. This involved overseeing the provision of low-cost housing in Puerto Rico, including an early sites-and-services project in the city of Ponce, whereby the housing authority drew up lots, paved the streets, and at the intersection of every four-lot grouping installed a utility unit with individual toilet, shower, and laundry facilities for each family. The housing itself was provided either "in the traditional way" by unaided self-building or by moving the family's existing house to the newly appointed site. For Crane, the next logical step was to improve the outcomes of these "traditional ways" by providing technical assistance in the design and construction of the housing unit, and by streamlining building via cooperative work—hence "aided mutual self-help." Harris has argued that Crane became a key promoter of the practice and the professionalization of its techniques by using his office at the HHFA to gather and disseminate information via a network of "well-placed individuals throughout the developing world."[31] His closest contact in Peru seems to have been David Vega Christie, a prominent housing official from the late 1940s onward.

Within the international sphere, the UN's advocacy of aided self-help dates to the late 1940s. Initially, the UN's interest in housing was limited to postwar reconstruction in Europe, through the auspices of the UN Housing and Town and Country Planning Program, situated within the Bureau of Social Affairs (in 1964 the unit was granted greater autonomy as the UN Centre for Housing, Building and Planning, and in 1978 it was expanded into the UN Centre for Human Settlements, or UN-Habitat, now the UN Human Settlements Programme). In 1947 the UN Social Commission officially widened its housing focus to encompass areas beyond Europe, and in mid-1949 the secretary-general proposed a study to address the lack of adequate housing in much of the world's "tropical and semi-tropical regions." Given the low incomes of these households, the recommendation was "to spread among the population concerned the knowledge required to enable them to build their own houses in a manner which will give them a greater degree of health and comfort"—in other words, via techniques of aided self-help.[32]

This call for action was quickly followed by two reports on low-cost housing that reiterated the support for aided self-help. In both cases, the influence of Crane is evident: the first was essentially a literature review that drew heavily on the HHFA's collection of materials; the second reported on a multination research mission to Asia led by Crane. While acknowledging that implementing aided self-help programs on a large scale presented logistical challenges, this report argued that it could "do more to reduce money cost and to achieve higher standards than any other combination of finance and technology."[33]

Shortly afterward, the January 1952 issue of *Housing and Town and Country Planning*, the bureau's information bulletin, focusing on the theme of housing in the tropics, again emphasized aided self-help. The issue included information on successful trial projects across several continents and the draft of a manual for organizing aided self-help programs, drawn up by the HHFA. According to the editorial statement, not only was this an effective solution in technical terms (allowing for "the rational application of local materials and skills") but it also offered individual self-improvement, drawing out the participants' existing capabilities (their "initiative and resourcefulness"), and enhanced community development through the shared task of building a neighborhood of houses. Furthermore, "there is every right to expect that by relating housing to a country's economic and social development, aided self-help can become a lever for continuous betterment of living conditions in general." This was followed by a number of UN consultants' reports that recommended the technique for the Gold Coast (now Ghana, 1956), Pakistan (1957), and the Philippines (1959).[34] These documents were not widely circulated at the time, but do indicate the extent to which the technique was embraced by UN-affiliated experts. M. Ijlal Muzaffar's research examining the deployment of aided self-help housing as an instrument of development in the postwar Third World provides a close reading of the discourse of expertise as it was framed in such documents.[35]

During the 1950s the ILO and the OAS added their support, and in 1953 the OAS-funded CINVA published a Spanish-language manual on aided mutual self-help housing based on trial projects in Puerto Rico. CINVA also operated as a training center on techniques of aided self-help, reaching housing officials from across Latin America. Also in 1953, mass-scale urban informality was introduced into the discourse of modern architecture, via representations of the "bidonvilles" (shantytowns) in France's North African colonies, at the ninth meeting of the Congrès Internationaux d'Architecture Moderne (CIAM). The displays by CIAM-affiliated groups in Morocco included ATBAT-Afrique's celebrated Sémiramis and Nid d'Abeille apartment buildings (1952), which were erected as part of a program to rehouse residents of the Carrières Centrales bidonville in Casablanca. In 1954 a managed, cooperative aided self-help housing project was launched as part of the same program. The site was laid out following the standard 8-by-8-meter housing grid designed by Michel Écochard and used throughout Carrières Centrales, accommodating a basic two-room patio house. The project was a trial of the "mouvement Castor" (Beaver movement) method: this cooperative model of aided self-help housing originated in working-class communities in postwar France, with roots in Catholic and labor union activism, and was responsible for the construction of some eight thousand dwellings throughout France in the early 1950s.[36] While North Africa is often framed as a colonial laboratory for projects devised by metropolitan architects, in this case the aided self-help model was trialed in the metropolis, then exported, pointing to the circulating nature of aided self-help between industrialized and industrializing nations.

When the aided self-help approach was first considered within Peru in the mid-1950s, the Puerto Rican projects were the best-known example of the technique. The US government actively promoted these projects to a wide audience, with the particular assistance of Pedro G. Beltrán, a conservative economist and publisher of the newspaper *La Prensa*, who was well-connected to housing officials in Washington. In August 1954 *La Prensa* published an article on the Puerto Rican projects, citing as its source a press conference held at the US embassy in Lima by Teodoro Moscoso, head of the Economic Development Association of Puerto Rico (and later head of John F. Kennedy's Alliance for Progress).[37]

A second point of intersection between architecture and aided self-help appears in the "growing house" concept—also known as incremental or progressive development. This model is often promoted by its advocates as replicating the traditional mode of construction in unaided self-built housing, where the dwelling is treated as an adaptable object, with no fixed or final form: typically, a basic livable shelter is completed quickly, then gradually improved as needed. The architect-designed "growing house" aims to be equally responsive to the constraints of budget and the rhythms of changing household composition, while providing a strict blueprint for all stages of the house's development. Early trials of progressive construction to reduce the cost of housing include Margarete Schütte-Lihotzky's explorations of the "core-house" in 1920s Vienna and Martin Wagner's advocacy of the "wachsende Haus" (growing house) in early 1930s Germany.

During the political and economic turmoil of World War I, it became apparent that the Viennese government could not guarantee adequate food or shelter for the city's two million residents. In response, squatters of the so-called wild settlement movement occupied public land, planting subsistence gardens and constructing their own dwellings. By 1918 over one hundred thousand people were living in self-built settlements and surviving on produce they had grown themselves. After the war, the municipal government's housing proposals included support for the construction of self-help settlements—no longer "wild" but organized within municipal guidelines. To this end, in 1921 the municipality established a design office (with Adolf Loos as chief architect) to produce master plans for new settlements. The municipality also undertook to provide the necessary materials via GEBISA (the settlers' cooperatively run building materials supplier) along with machinery and tools. Under the municipal model, prospective settlers were required to contribute two thousand to three thousand hours of work to build a new neighborhood; once construction was completed, each family would be allocated one of the collectively self-built houses.

In 1923 the municipality supported an exhibition to showcase the achievements of the settlement movement, including three model houses designed by Schütte-Lihotzky. These "core-houses" all employed a modular construction system, with prefabricated elements that allowed the structure to grow progressively, according to a set plan. The first stage (or "core") was a compact, two-story dwelling with a live-in kitchen on the ground floor and a small bedroom above, and featured traditional stylistic references such as a pitched roof. The designs received enthusiastic coverage in the press, and GEBISA announced that it could prefabricate the core-houses. However, this failed to convince the intended customers, who were accustomed to contributing their sweat equity as payment for the house. While using prefabricated elements would doubtless save them time, it would also require a much larger cash outlay upfront. Ultimately, a prefabricated core-house was simply less suitable for self-builders' budgets than a dwelling realized with labor-intensive (but low-cost) conventional materials and methods. As a result, fewer than two hundred were purchased.[38]

In the early 1930s, amid Germany's ongoing postwar housing shortage and concurrent economic crisis, Martin Wagner, the head of Berlin's municipal housing program, conceived the *wachsende Haus* explicitly in opposition to the *Existenzminimum* so enthusiastically promoted by Ernst May, his counterpart in Frankfurt. Wagner argued that the use of minimum standards—which were continually being revised downward due to the deteriorating economic situation—would permanently tie residents to barely livable conditions imposed in the throes of a national crisis. Instead, he proposed a simple *Kernhaus* (nucleus-house or core-house), built around a *Wohnungskern* (dwelling-core), which would evolve into a complete dwelling over time, thereby surpassing the constraints of the "minimum" as the family's finances improved. Wagner publicized the concept through a conference and a design competition, culminating in a presentation of full-scale prototype dwellings as part of the 1932 Deutsche Bauausstellung Berlin. From over one thousand submissions, twenty-four designs for single-family dwellings were selected, including projects by a number of prominent modernist architects, among them Walter Gropius, Ludwig Hilberseimer, Erich Mendelsohn, and Bruno Taut.

Wagner's conception of the "growing house" showed the influence of the *Laubenkolonien* (summerhouse colonies) that had arisen on the outskirts of many German cities. These were allotment gardens with very basic, part-time summerhouses—often little more than a toolshed—which in cases of extreme need were converted into full-time residences. Wagner responded to this prevailing form of emergency self-help housing by adopting its model of the compact single-family house on a generous lot with room for a subsistence garden. In this way, Laubenkolonien-inspired dwellings would be reconceived within a modernist architectural language, and provided with enough design integrity to function as adequate permanent housing.

Importantly, as in Vienna, Wagner's "growing house" assumed a technological solution—a prefabricated, modular design—but it was to be carried out by trained construction workers, not self-help builders. In fact, Wagner's description of the project offered a vigorous critique of self-help housing: citing one of his earlier writings, he characterized it as "construction industry dilettantism, which would make each settler into his own entrepreneur and his own fabricator of raw materials." Wagner's critique, from a socialist perspective, was that self-help was destructive to the building economy as a whole: do-it-yourself builders made it more difficult for trained construction workers to find employment, they produced poor-quality work that lowered the standard of the dwelling, they wasted materials and damaged machinery (all the while requiring extensive supervision), and they relied on outmoded, inefficient building methods because the sophistication of modern construction systems was incompatible with self-help labor. Finally, Wagner argued that although it promised to lower construction costs, self-help did not in fact produce any savings: "It is a dangerous self-deception, which makes plans to persuade the public that with this method something can be 'saved.' If capitalism had been able to save in the building sector through 'self-help' then it would have done so with the greatest consequences for the last century."[39] While Wagner is correct that self-help often fails to reduce overall costs—that is, the houses may not be cheaper than those built using the most efficient technologies—it does produce savings for the sponsoring housing agency: the sponsor "saves" because the self-builder expends labor in kind.

Wagner was forced to leave office shortly after the presentation of the "growing house" exhibition, as the political climate within Germany turned sharply to the right. As a consequence, his proposal was not implemented. However, in a postscript, Ernst May revisited Wagner's concept in a project for a "growing house" designed for a neighborhood in Mombasa, Kenya (1952–1953). Intended for low-income rural-urban migrants, the design was projected to incorporate family growth, including the possibility of accommodating extended family, in line with traditional living patterns. The intention was apparently to replace the kind of provisional housing that migrants tended to construct for themselves, resisting a permanent structure, knowing that their needs would change. Once again the proposal was unrealized. According to a recent assessment, the design was of a type that "could neither be afforded by the majority nor conveniently built by the government"[40]—since, as with any implementation of the "growing house" model, the housing authority would have faced considerable challenges in overseeing extensions to ensure that they were carried out in accordance with the established plan.

The "casa que crece" (growing house) model first appeared in Peru in 1954, in a design for low-cost housing by modernist architect Santiago Agurto. It does not appear that Agurto was aware of any European precedents; rather, his inspiration was the incremental construction of barriadas. By the early 1960s the casa que crece had been widely adopted in designs both for government housing projects and for private sector developments aimed at the lower-middle-income market. This was a conventional dwelling in the sense that it conformed to basic building codes and standards of services and was sited on legally acquired land, but it borrowed the barriada model of stage-by-stage construction to create an affordable dwelling.

As documented by Turner and Mangin in 1968, construction in barriadas tended to follow a regular pattern.[41] Once lots were allocated to each household, a provisional one-room dwelling of *esteras* (woven bamboo mats) was erected; this was quickly followed by a *cerco* (perimeter wall), also of esteras, delimiting and protecting the lot (fig. I.1). (According to one architect, the reason for this act of enclosure transcended the resident's need to secure the lot or create privacy: "Why? To hide his poverty, so that at six in the evening, the neighboring family cannot see whether or not he has now lit the fire to cook.")[42] In the next stage, the cerco was rebuilt in concrete block; over time, the provisional materials of the dwelling were replaced with permanent ones, and rooms were gradually added to fill out the lot, and finally extend upward with additional stories. In Lima and other cities in Peru's coastal desert, a mild climate combined with extremely low levels of rainfall facilitates the long-term use of such provisional materials, even for the roofing. However, it should also be noted that esteras and open flames used for light and heat in the absence of electricity make for a volatile combination, leaving these houses vulnerable to fire.

The most sophisticated explorations of the "growing house" model within Peru appear in proposals produced for the PREVI design competition held in the late 1960s, involving a number of leading avant-garde architects. Each architect was to present a twofold design: a core housing unit to be constructed by professional contractors and taking advantage of the economies of mass production, and a blueprint for gradual horizontal and/or vertical extension of the house over time to be carried out by self-help. As in Schütte-Lihotzky's core-houses, many of these designs proposed that the extensions be carried out using prefabricated components, which in this case were to be manufactured in an on-site factory. For the earlier generation of modernist architects, the "growing house" was viewed primarily through the lens of the innovative possibilities offered by prefabrication and modular construction;

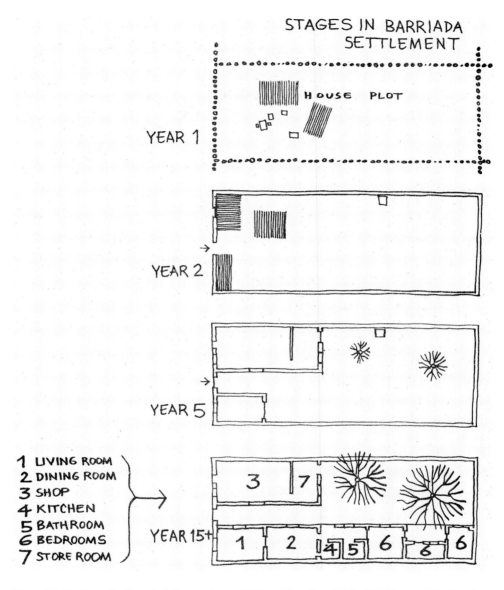

Figure I.1. The "growing" barriada house. *Source*: William Mangin and John F. C. Turner, "The Barriada Movement," *Progressive Architecture* 49 (May 1968), John F. C. Turner Archive.

for many of the architects involved with PREVI, the "growing house" model again suggested new constructional possibilities, but also strongly resonated with ideas about design for transformation, evolutionary potential, and open form. However, this did not necessarily translate into more meaningful participation for the self-help builder, who was to provide the labor to execute extensions that were carefully incorporated into the initial plans. Improvisations were discouraged, since any deviation could compromise the integrity of the design and its engineering. This points to an inherent tension in the architect-designed "growing house": although the concept was inspired by informal self-help practices, it redesigned—and formalized—the model it was emulating, placing the self-help builder's desire to shape the house according to evolving needs below the architect's desire to complete the growing house according to a static, preconceived design.

As a postscript to this review, it is worth noting that beginning in the late 1960s a number of architectural historians in Latin America began to address issues of urban informality, and along with it self-help housing. Notably, Francisco Bullrich framed his survey *New Directions in Latin American Architecture* (1969) as an overview of the region's architectural production considered "in relation to the problems which are now being confronted." To this end, the chapter on "Urban Utopia and Reality" pointedly concluded an extended analysis of Brasília by discussing the "spontaneous wild west, shanty-town life" of a self-built neighborhood on its outskirts that housed the low-wage workforce needed for the city's functioning but not provided for in its plan. Bullrich expressed skepticism that conventional mass housing schemes would ever entirely replace such shantytowns, and—referencing a 1963 issue of *Architectural Design* on the region's housing guest-edited by Turner—pointed to recent aided self-help initiatives in Peru as a more realistic solution. In Bullrich's view, these trials in "assisted" barriada construction challenged architects to rethink their practice, incorporating greater flexibility (since "the barriada is the paradigm of work in progress") and cultivating "a mutual respect of designer and owner-builder" (since effective collaboration was essential to such projects). More broadly, Bullrich interpreted this approach as exemplifying the imperative that Latin American architects devise local solutions to local problems, guided by a "crude realism" that was inspired by the profession's social engagement: "The new generation has varying attitudes towards the barriada experience, but in general it is entirely committed to the sense of public participation and design for change that are implicit in the experience."[43]

In contrast to Bullrich's embrace of the barriada model, other architects and historians aligned themselves with writers such as

Castells, viewing the shantytown as a highly compromised housing and urban solution, symptomatic of the region's dependency. Prominent among them, Cuban architect Fernando Salinas wrote a widely read critique of architecture in "underdeveloped" countries, identifying characteristics such as an intensifying housing deficit due to land speculation and a profit-focused real-estate market, with minimal government efforts to address the issue. This had left most with no other option than to house themselves via self-building, "in a spontaneous manner, with scattered dwellings in the countryside and huts and *barrios insalubres* [unsanitary neighborhoods] on the outskirts of the cities."[44]

América Latina en su arquitectura (1975), edited by Roberto Segre and featuring chapters by architects, planners, and social scientists from across the region, was broadly in line with this interpretation. Many of its chapters explored the challenges presented by unplanned urban development, but with widely differing assessments of the viability of self-help housing as a solution. Architect Germán Samper, who had worked on aided self-help housing projects in Colombia, foresaw "the *tugurio* and the incomplete dwelling" as the default low-cost housing options for the immediate future, and argued that architects could play a role in transforming these communities via the provision of "complementary institutions that make up for [their] deficiencies"—whether collective laundries, meeting halls, or childcare facilities. By contrast, Diego Robles, a colleague of Turner's on early aided self-help projects in Peru and subsequently the most senior architect in an agency focused on pueblos jóvenes under the Revolutionary Government, characterized "officialized *ayuda mutua*" as a "type of domination" that effectively undermined the unaided self-help efforts of the improvised city. Such programs were complicit in replacing self-builders' "mode of producing urban space socially" with a capitalist mode of city-making that reduced them to passive consumers, thereby reinforcing the existing socioeconomic order.[45]

Finally, Segre, the key historian of architecture in postrevolutionary Cuba, argued that the self-built housing of rural-urban migrants represented a degradation of both aesthetic and social values: rural creative traditions withered "in the context of marginality" in the urban shantytown, while self-builders' efforts to differentiate their dwellings from those of their neighbors demonstrated the "clear expression of the loss of the rural collectivist consciousness, supplanted by urban individualism."[46] Segre contrasted this to the experience of "microbrigadas" in Cuba, small voluntary work brigades that collaborated to build the multifamily housing that would become their homes, in some cases participating in the design process. This approach echoed aided self-help projects by relying heavily on the contributions of builder-residents, but surpassed them by utilizing modern building technologies, by allowing for the builders' creative input, and by producing collective housing blocks rather than single-family dwellings.

These contrasting positions toward self-help housing both aided and unaided—from optimism to pragmatism, to critique, to conviction that its underlying principles could find better form—demonstrate the range of theoretical and practical responses that these techniques could provoke among architects.

Practices of Self-Help Housing in Peru

This history unfolds via an episodic narrative that features a number of recurring figures, including Beltrán, Belaúnde, Neira, Robles, and Turner. Turner is particularly prominent, partly due to his position as a widely published and influential writer on self-help housing, partly due to the fact that I was able to interview him in some detail, and partly due to the survival of archival materials. The breadth and richness of Turner's personal archives allows for a close analysis of an early trial project in aided self-help housing that he managed, for example, and provides insights into the evolution of his thinking over many decades. Similarly, a self-help housing project that Turner worked on for the US-based company Hogares Peruanos (Peruvian Homes) is amply documented in the archives of the parent company, World Homes. By contrast, the records of Peruvian housing agencies have suffered from uneven custodianship, and as a result are fragmentary. There are no publicly available papers tracking internal debates about policy development, and the documentation of projects—whether proposed or realized—is scarce and often unreliable in the details. Furthermore, these projects tend to be presented in the standardized format of official reports, which does not allow for the voices of the individual architects who worked on them; to a certain extent, these viewpoints do come through in conference presentations and newspaper or magazine articles written by architects independently of their work at government agencies. Some of the policy debates can be traced through newspaper reports, particularly those in *La Prensa*, published by Beltrán, who was greatly concerned with the issue of affordable housing; however, since *La Prensa's* reportage faithfully reiterated Beltrán's political and policy positions, this is by no means a neutral account.

On the other side of the formal/informal divide, it is even more difficult to account for the voices of barriada residents and of participants in self-help housing programs. Their presence in the archives is almost always mediated: their behaviors and attitudes are filtered through the descriptions and analyses of anthropologists, architects, and officials; the words attributed to them in newspaper articles are set within a narrative framework established by the writer or editor. Whenever possible, I have included those rare documents where residents and self-builders present themselves and their viewpoints, such as petitions arguing their case in the public sphere. Nonetheless, as a result of archival gaps, this account is unavoidably incomplete. In the end, the construction of a historical narrative around these projects is a work of bricolage, assembled from the materials at hand.

The period covered here (1954–1986) encompassed great political and social change within Peru, starting with the tail end of the military regime of dictator Manuel Odría (1948–1956), followed by efforts to consolidate liberal democracy under Manuel Prado (1956–1962) and Fernando Belaúnde Terry (1963–1968), interrupted by a brief interlude of military rule (July 1962–July 1963). This was succeeded by a leftist military regime (1968–1980), and then a fragile return to democracy in the 1980s under Belaúnde (1980–1985) and Alan García (1985–1990), accompanied by the emergence of neoliberalism, as well as the guerrilla campaigns of leftist revolutionaries, most prominently Sendero Luminoso (Shining Path). In one way or another, each of these political shifts is reflected in the discourse around aided self-help housing.

The narrative begins in the mid-1950s, when debates on housing provision gathered new urgency. Chapter 1, "The Challenge of the Affordable House," examines contrasting positions on how to address the housing crisis—New Deal–inspired developmentalism to stimulate growth, market liberalization to promote homeownership, and structural reform to raise living standards—seen through the contributions of three figures: respectively, architect-politician Belaúnde, economist-publisher Beltrán, and architect Adolfo Córdova.

Chapter 2, "The Barriada under the Microscope," begins with the establishment of the Ciudad de Dios squatter settlement in Lima on Christmas Eve 1954, an event that prompted the government to introduce unprecedented legislative measures in an effort to solve the housing crisis. In addition, it considers the importance of anthropological research into the barriada as a tool for policymakers, politicians, and architects to understand, and thereby manage, the dense cultural context into which aided self-help housing projects would be inserted.

Chapter 3, "A Profession in Development," explores the intersection of aided self-help housing and modernist architectural culture through an individual career. It follows Turner's intellectual formation in England, his development of an architectural practice in Peru, working on early trials of aided self-help, and his subsequent shift from on-the-ground projects to theoretical work, which would culminate in a series of influential articles and books.

Chapter 4, "Mediating Informality," returns to the policy sphere, discussing innovations in Peruvian planning law that were designed to manage unauthorized settlements and reestablish control over the development of urban land. In particular, it analyzes Law 13517, which was conceived as a comprehensive effort to meet the challenge of the barriadas, and reviews a number of trial projects where these new approaches were implemented.

Chapter 5, "World Investments, Productive Homes," shifts to the international sphere, investigating the political appeal of aided self-help housing during the Cold War, deployed as a tool of both development programs and capitalist market expansion. The chapter begins with the establishment of new mechanisms for housing finance in Peru, and then assesses two very different projects, both funded by US government aid agencies under the umbrella of the Alliance for Progress: the Villa Los Angeles housing development in Lima, and the Perú-BID Plan Bienal 1962–1963, a nationwide program of aided self-help housing.

Chapter 6, "Building a Better Barriada," closely examines the UN-sponsored PREVI PP1 competition held in 1969, which challenged prominent avant-garde architects to develop proposals for affordable housing in Peru. This project transferred the growing house model into the realm of high architecture—an experiment that ultimately brought the conflicts between affordable housing and capital-A "Architecture" into high relief. The discussion also covers an associated project, PREVI PP3, planned as an entirely self-build program. In both cases, challenges in the implementation reveal the difficulties of devising a workable, affordable form for aided self-help housing.

Chapter 7, "Revolutions in Self-Help," explores how practices of aided self-help housing were reevaluated and reshaped during a period of leftist, revolutionary experimentation within Peru (1968–1980). The malleability of self-help in theoretical and ideological terms is demonstrated by the contrasting values and significance attributed to it by state agencies working with residents of pueblos jóvenes, by Turner's anarchist-inflected writings of this period, and by Habitat: UN Conference on Human Settlements, held in 1976.

Chapter 8, "Other Paths," reflects on how the self-help housing model was reframed from contrasting political positions, as the return to democracy in the 1980s brought about new alliances of leftist activists who saw in barriada communities the potential for an invigorated grassroots democracy, as well as the emergence of neoliberalism and its embrace of "informal" self-building as a route to economic development. The key link between debates within Peru and in the international sphere was de Soto's neoliberal manifesto *El otro sendero*, which contributed to a fundamental shift in the housing policies of development agencies such as the UN and the World Bank, whose consequences continue to unfold.

Aided self-help housing offered an innovative strategy to approach a problem that could not be resolved via conventional architectural techniques, promising a productive partnership of architect and self-builder that in practice proved to be more ambivalent. It quickly faced the specter of failure at many levels: at the political level, shifting and unreliable support, resulting in inadequate budgets; at the implementation level, the challenges of translating policies and regulations into design practice; at the organizational level, the complex social dynamics of self-help communities and building sites; and perhaps most crucially, at the funding level, the demand that programs be self-sufficient—the costs entirely reimbursed by their participants—belied the underlying economic reality, placing the sustainability of self-help housing programs into doubt. With the realization that those most in need of assistance were also the most difficult to incorporate into successful programs, funding tended to drift upward to the higher end of the low-income spectrum—that is, to more manageable target populations that posed less of a financial risk, such as low-level government employees with regular incomes. Moreover, despite the Peruvian state's pledges of technical assistance to self-builders, in practice it often failed to provide the needed resources and trained staff, revealing the emptiness of its rhetoric of "helping those who help themselves": as Jean-Claude Driant has argued, its glorification of self-help building "has long served as a pretext for the inaction of the state."[47]

As modest trial projects were overwhelmed by the rate of improvised urban development, the withdrawal of the state—and the architects it employs—from the provision of low-cost housing has seemed inevitable. Yet the undeniable shortcomings of these various initiatives in aided self-help housing need to be measured against the failures of the laissez-faire approach to housing and urban development that has taken its place, considering the impacts that a large-scale regime of unaided self-help construction has had, not just for individual households but for the neighborhoods and cities that have emerged. Returning to examine the limitations— but also the possibilities—of these trials presents the opportunity to reassess their potential and to reframe their strategies for contemporary practice.

1

THE CHALLENGE OF
THE AFFORDABLE HOUSE,
1954–1958

In 1949 Lima's modernist apotheosis appeared imminent: the Plan Piloto, the city's first master plan, had applied the techniques of scientific planning to analyze the city at its various scales—from the historic core to the agricultural areas supplying it with food—and to prescribe a logical course for "channeling urban development." But by the end of 1954 a followup study warned that "the overflowing vitality of the metropolis in its blind force of expansion" was setting in motion problems that would only intensify over time, necessitating decisive action: "The traffic congestion endlessly increases; the number of accidents multiplies; delinquency grows; the city is choking itself in a dreadful ring of clandestine dwellings; the food situation is causing a crisis; a drop in the standard of living threatens." All this was the result of an unprecedented rate of growth due to rural-urban migration, with the population almost doubling between 1940 and 1953, from an estimated 530,000 to around one million. Established planning processes were being overtaken by the rapid emergence of *barriadas*, as authorized housing could not be built quickly and cheaply enough to meet demand. Reluctantly, the study confessed: "An economical system of urbanization and construction that would allow us to avoid the overcrowded and unsanitary conditions that appear in the 'clandestine settlements' [*urbanizaciones clandestinas*] has not yet been devised."[1]

Two of the most influential figures in the development of housing policy in Peru differed sharply in their responses to the challenge of the barriadas. For Fernando Belaúnde Terry—architect, publisher of *El Arquitecto Peruano*, and politician, twice elected president of the republic (1963–1968, 1980–1985)—the barriada was an anathema that should be eliminated and replaced by planned, regulated urban development. For Pedro G. Beltrán—economist, ultraconservative owner/publisher of the national newspaper *La Prensa*, and (briefly) prime minister (1959–1961)—the primary goal was to promote homeownership, and the form of the dwelling was a secondary issue: low-cost conventional housing within planned neighborhoods would be the ideal solution, but the individual initiative of barriada settlers, made concrete in their self-built housing, should not be dismissed out of hand. For Belaúnde, an "economical system" to solve the crisis must necessarily be provided by modernist architecture, in the form of large-scale, state-backed housing projects in the service of a developmentalist agenda; for Beltrán, an ideal solution would emerge more indirectly, through reforms to mortgage finance that would encourage the flow of private capital into housing. From one perspective, the crisis called for a public sector powerful enough to drive the country's economic and social modernization, implementing a coordinated developmentalist program in the spirit of the New Deal; from the other, it underscored the need to strengthen the operations of the free market—a debate that would be echoed in discussions provoked by neoliberalism decades later.

A third position, advocating comprehensive structural reform, was articulated by architects associated with the Movimiento Social Progresista (MSP, Progressive Social Movement), such as Adolfo Córdova. Córdova is a pivotal figure here: he was a student of Belaúnde's, but also carried out research for a national commission on housing organized by Beltrán in 1956. For Córdova—and the MSP in general—the reduced economic capacity of most Peruvians was the major cause of the housing crisis. In this view, increasingly unregulated capital flows would, rather than providing a solution, only exacerbate existing inequalities. Instead, the MSP argued for *planificación* (large-scale physical planning) and wide-ranging structural reform—envisaging a powerful state with a redistributive role that was quite different from Belaúnde's conception.

These three positions outlined the politics of the affordable, modern house in this period, establishing the conceptual parameters for devising theoretical solutions and concrete policies toward housing provision. Negotiating the challenges of keeping costs low while maintaining acceptable standards would generate a range of contrasting proposals, which were at different moments in the ascendancy.

A School to Form Citizens

Fernando Belaúnde Terry spent much of his youth outside of Peru, first in Europe and then the United States, after his well-connected, patrician family was forced into exile in 1924. Belaúnde received his architecture degree from the University of Texas in 1935, and returned to Lima shortly thereafter, quickly becoming an influential figure in the area of housing policy, due less to his work as an architect than as an educator, a writer, a publisher, and a politician. He taught classes on housing at the Escuela Nacional de Ingenieros (now the Universidad Nacional de Ingeniería), the country's premier architecture school, and publicized the dire state of Lima's *tugurios* through denunciations in his magazine *El Arquitecto Peruano*. He was elected to the Peruvian congress in 1945, under President José Bustamante (1945–1948), and the following year was responsible for introducing the founding legislation for the Corporación Nacional de la Vivienda (CNV, National Housing Corporation), and subsequently vigorously promoted its work through *El Arquitecto Peruano*. Soon after, Belaúnde was instrumental in establishing the Oficina Nacional de Planeamiento y Urbanismo (ONPU, National Office for Planning and Urbanism) and the Oficina del Plan Regulador de Lima, the agency responsible for developing Lima's Plan Piloto. Belaúnde's parliamentary career ended in 1948, when a coup by General Manuel Odría suspended the democratic process, but he returned to politics in 1956, running as a reform-minded presidential candidate. Although this campaign was unsuccessful, it led him to form a new political party, Acción Popular, which established him as a major opposition figure and eventually brought him the presidency in 1963.

By and large, the CNV did not operate as a public housing authority per se, leasing and managing projects, but used the resources of the state to construct subsidized housing for those with sufficient resources to purchase it through a system of *alquiler-venta* (rental-sale). The dwellings were kept affordable by building on state land and selling bonds to finance construction. However, the need to provide a full return to private bondholders limited the kind of residents that the CNV could serve, resulting in a focus on the more profitable, upper end of the low-income population.[2] The CNV promised multifamily housing that conformed to the universal standards established by modernist reformers: reducing overcrowding, improving light and ventilation, and maximizing functional separation within the dwelling. In addition, it conceived of housing as one element of coordinated urban development, framing its projects within master plans that balanced residential, industrial, and agricultural zones in an effort to produce ordered and holistic growth.

The primary model for the CNV's initial projects was the *unidad vecinal* (neighborhood unit): a self-contained city in miniature, circumscribed by green space and shielded from through traffic, close to but separated from centers of work, and furnished with sufficient communal facilities (such as schools and markets) to satisfy immediate needs. The concept was introduced into Peru by Belaúnde, with influences leading back to Clarence Perry, and projects such as Radburn and the New Deal Greenbelt towns. In the latter case, Belaúnde—a student in the United States at the height of the Depression—was particularly impressed by the New Deal's demonstration of the state's ability to implement large-scale projects, and to deploy such projects to stimulate economic and social development. As Wiley Ludeña observed, the unidad vecinal's immediate point of influence was a project for Wayland, outside Boston, developed by students of Walter Gropius and Martin Wagner at Harvard, and discussed in detail by Belaúnde in an article published in *El Arquitecto Peruano* in 1944.[3] In contrast to the dysfunctional imbalance of the contemporary city, with overcrowding in the center and ever more diffused fringes pushed outward by population growth, the unidad vecinal presented a model for rationally planned, decentralized urban development, kept affordable by making use of inexpensive sites on the urban periphery.

The initial unidad vecinal program in Lima was conceived precisely along these lines, with projects located on seven greenfield sites; in parallel, five zones were slated for urban renewal, to be carried out in a second phase of construction (fig. 1.1). The CNV anticipated that the seven proposed unidades vecinales would de-

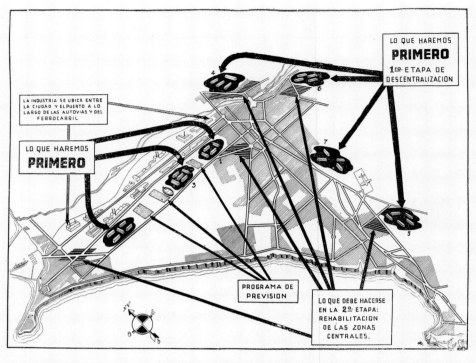

ESQUEMA GENERAL DE UBICACION

Expansión descentralizadora, primero; Rehabilitación de los tugurios centrales, después.

Figure 1.1. Lima as a rationally designed urban machine: "General Location Plan: Decentralized expansion first; Rehabilitation of central *tugurios* next." *Source*: *El Arquitecto Peruano* 9, no. 98 (Sept. 1945).

velop into self-sufficient nodes of economic activity, in the process
drawing population away from the historic center, relieving it from
congestion in preparation for rehabilitation. This decentralization
strategy was in keeping with the 1949 Plan Piloto, but like much of
the master plan, it remained incomplete, as only four of these unidad vecinal projects were actually realized. Belaúnde acted as consultant designer on the first of these, Unidad Vecinal No. 3 (1945–
1949), whose 1,112 units included a characteristic mix of walk-up
blocks and single-family houses, high-rise construction being too
expensive to consider as a solution in Peru at this time (fig. 1.2).[4]

At Belaúnde's urging, the VI Congreso Panamericano de Arquitectos, held in Peru in 1947, endorsed the unidad vecinal as a
quasi-canonical urban model, passing a resolution that "all the

Figure 1.2. Two of the first *unidad vecinal* projects in Lima: in the foreground, CNV (architects: Fernando Belaúnde Terry, Luis Dorich, et al.), Unidad Vecinal No. 3, 1945–1949; background right, CNV (architect: Santiago Agurto), Stage one of Unidad Vecinal Mirones, 1952–1953. *Source*: Servicio Aerofotográfico Nacional, Perú, 1954.

countries of the Americas should formulate master plans for their cities that establish unidades vecinales as basic elements for their structuring"; it could even be applied retroactively to achieve "the transformation of parts of the city already built" via urban renewal projects. The resolution argued that its model of spatial organization had social implications that resonated far beyond the technics of functional zoning. With humanism under threat in modern industrial society, a weakened sense of individuality had led to an impoverished culture of citizenship, creating a society of "mass spectators" rather than active participants. The antidote for this alienation was to foster civic engagement and "cooperation based in individual responsibility"—qualities that would promote "a high level of Democracy and social well-being." In this context, the special promise of the unidad vecinal was its potential to rebuild community life: being deliberately self-contained—its scale determined by the distance that could be comfortably walked in carrying out daily tasks—the unidad vecinal shaped everyday opportunities for the citizenry to interact. In this sense, it was antiurban in order to be procommunity. In later writings, Belaúnde shifted focus somewhat, placing particular emphasis on the "Peruvian" character of the unidad vecinal, drawing parallels with Inca territorial planning and the urban theories of Ebenezer Howard. Belaúnde viewed Inca practices of collective land ownership and *mink'a* as analogous to the cooperative ethos of Howard's garden city, which in fact, he claimed, "seems to have been inspired by ancient Peru"; he was careful to clarify that, like Howard, "the ancient Peruvians were not communists but cooperativists."[5] In this reading, the unidad vecinal emulated these precedents by reviving the timeless principle of building community through cooperation.

Belaúnde's vision of the unidad vecinal suggests Lewis Mumford as a major point of inspiration, reflecting a deeply held belief in the potential of architecture to reconstitute a modern communal life. Belaúnde's references to Mumford are rare but telling. Notably, in a 1953 article on barriadas (which Belaúnde labeled "a plague" and "an obstacle to urban expansion"), Mumford's research on "the culture of cities" was evoked to condemn the current situation in Lima, where rural migrants unable to find affordable housing were occupying vacant sites to create their own improvised neighborhoods. For Belaúnde, this demonstrated that "the advances derived from urbanism are now threatened by what we could call *LA INCULTURA de las ciudades*"—the lack of culture, or the unculturedness of cities. This "incultura" was revealed both in the actions of those building these chaotic and illegal settlements and in the inaction of "those who tolerate such agglomerations, . . . the entire community that sees this public danger with indifference." For his part, Belaúnde proposed the demolition of these substandard neighborhoods, synchronized with a resettlement program involving "the construction, on a vast scale, of Unidades de Emergencia [emergency urban units]" with very basic dwellings.[6] Here (despite pronouncements about "cooperation based in individual responsibility"), Belaúnde revealed himself to be a somewhat authoritarian New Deal technocrat, whose sincere commitment to the shared social responsibility of providing decent housing for all found expression in unilateral interventions from above.

In a similarly paternalistic vein, Belaúnde's 1944 article introducing the unidad vecinal argued that although the model had been developed in the United States, its strategy of economical, decentralized development was particularly applicable in "countries that have to measure out their resources and which find themselves, like Peru, with the unavoidable duty of educating their popular masses and raising their degrading level of present-day life." Accordingly, the rhetoric of the unidad vecinal as a training ground for democracy appeared more than once. In 1945, the announcement of the CNV's first building program characterized the unidad vecinal as a "cradle for the new generations that must build a better Peru." In 1949 Belaúnde announced that Unidad Vecinal No. 3 "is and will be a school to form citizens." Further, a CNV report from 1958 noted that in each of its unidad vecinal projects it had established a *superintendencia* (office of supervision) to perform this training. At Unidad Vecinal No. 3, which had the most complete services, the superintendencia functioned as arbiter and enforcer of civility: "Watches over the good use of the dwellings, and the observance of the Internal Regulations . . . ; Promotes and encourages cultural, social, educational, and sporting activities, and those of mutual aid [*de auxilios mutuos*] within the community, and of social assistance and social hygiene in coordination with the Sanitary Post."[7]

Here the universal modernist article of faith that an improved living environment would transform residents' lives met the particular conditions of postwar Peru: on one side, an urban elite having the "unavoidable duty of educating their popular masses" and on the other, waves of rural migrants bringing a radical shift in the class and ethnic identity of coastal cities, a transformation—and a threat—felt most acutely in the capital. In this era of mushrooming barriadas, the unidad vecinal's civilizing mission was clear: "educating" those recently arrived in the behaviors appropriate to urban life, and in the civic responsibilities of modern citizenship or in the terms of the archetypal dichotomy of Peruvian national identity, remaking the *paisano* (peasant, primarily of indigenous descent) as *criollo* (urbanite, primarily of European descent). This dichotomy contained an implicit hierarchy that privileged creole urbanity; further, as Cecilia Mendez has shown, the core *criollo-paisano* opposition seamlessly folded together race, class, and cultural prejudices that were echoed in corresponding dominant-subordinate pairings: "whites and Indians, the superior and the inferior, but also the civilized and the barbarian; that is, the oldest way of expressing . . . modern and traditional." (Paradoxically, as exemplified by Belaúnde's writings, the creole appropriation of pre-Columbian heritage to fashion a Peruvian identity frequently allowed "a rhetoric glorifying the Inca past [to exist] side by side with a contemptuous appraisal of the Indian.")[8] Mendez demonstrates that the social hierarchy built into this dichotomy had a long history: its seeds predated the foundation of the Peruvian republic and extended well into the twentieth century, maintained by an entrenched oligarchical system that reinforced the pervasive social inequality expressed in the tugurio and the barriada, and that kept the architects of the unidad vecinal at a comfortable distance from its residents, thereby granting Belaúnde the authority to speak as dutiful educator of the popular masses.

It would be difficult to overstate the influence of Belaúnde's unidad vecinal on planning professionals within Peru, largely due to his prominence as an educator and a writer on housing and urban issues. Indeed, the unidad vecinal concept recurs throughout urban planning discourse at least until the mid-1960s, even in contexts where its application would initially seem unlikely, such as barriada rehabilitation projects. From a position on the margins of modern architecture's customary map, Belaúnde's unidad vecinal asserted Peru's adherence to a shared vision of modern urbanism. As with Lima's Plan Piloto, this aspiration would remain unrealized.

A House that Grows

Pedro G. Beltrán studied at the Universidad Nacional Mayor de San Marcos in Lima, before transferring to the London School of Economics, where he earned his degree in 1918. Through his connections there he cultivated personal and professional relationships with a number of prominent free-market economists, most notably Ludwig von Mises, Friedrich Hayek, Milton Friedman, Wilhelm Röpke, and Ludwig Erhard. Beltrán popularized their thought through his newspaper *La Prensa*, and in some cases facilitated their visits to Peru.[9] Beltrán acquired *La Prensa* in 1934, and over the four decades of his ownership, he frequently used it as a vehicle to promote his conservative political views: defending the interests of agricultural landholders, attacking leftist political movements from communism to the Alianza Popular Revolucionaria Americana (APRA, American Popular Revolutionary Alliance), and critiquing the economic management of various governments. Beltrán's public service was fitful but significant. During the first presidency of Manuel Prado (1939–1945), he was appointed ambassador to the United States (1944–1945), and during his time in Washington he also served as Peru's representative at the UN's Bretton Woods Conference (1944). Upon returning to Peru, he waged a campaign via *La Prensa* to outlaw APRA, whose formidable organizing skills among the popular classes made it a significant threat to the elites. For this reason, he was initially supportive of Odría's 1948 coup and subsequent efforts to suppress APRA, and even served under Odría as president of Peru's Banco Central de Reserva (1948–1950). After Odría's policies took a populist turn and began challenging elite interests, Beltrán became an increasingly vocal opponent, culminating in his month-long imprisonment in 1956 for campaigning for an end to Odría's repressive rule. After the return to democratic government with Manuel Prado's second presidency (1956–1962), Beltrán briefly served as prime minister and minister of finance (1959–1961). In 1962 he launched his own run for the presidency, but ended his campaign after attracting little support.

Throughout Beltrán's career, the issue of housing was a central concern. In June 1954 he launched a major campaign via *La Prensa* to address the intensifying housing crisis.[10] Following his promarket views, the newspaper argued that the government could not solve the problem singlehandedly through the direct construction of low-cost housing. While the private rental market could make a valuable contribution (if given sufficient incentives to invest in the low-income sector), an alternative solution warranted greater support: the promotion of individual homeownership, since "the desire to have a *vivienda propia* [a dwelling of one's own, or a proper dwelling] is very natural, human, . . . understandable, and socially beneficial."[11]

Accordingly, *La Prensa* proposed a series of reforms to the mortgage financing system. The Banco Central Hipotecario (Central Mortgage Bank) had a monopoly on mortgage financing, but was unable to meet the demand because it had insufficient funds to lend, and its policy of financing no more than 50 percent of the property's value placed its terms beyond the capacity of most low-income households. Meanwhile, the Fondo Nacional de Salud y Bienestar Social (FNSBS), a key government agency charged with the provision of low-cost housing, could make better use of its funds by diverting them away from construction and into "the mobilization of private capital toward mortgage loans." Specifically, if the Banco Central Hipotecario lowered its minimum down payment to 10 percent, the loans would be subject to a considerably higher interest rate, making them more attractive to private investors; with additional capital at its disposal, the bank could increase its lending to low-income households—however, the higher interest rate need not be passed on to the prospective homebuyer, because FNSBS funds could be used to subsidize the mortgage repayments. Under this new policy—"favorable to investors as well as to those ... interested in having their own house"—a "decent but not lavish dwelling" that cost S/.20,000 could be had for a S/.2,000 down payment and S/.150 per month from the homeowner, with the balance of the monthly payment (roughly 35 percent) being paid by the FNSBS. In short, public funds would facilitate the purchase of housing built by private contractors and subsidize loan repayments to the ultimate benefit of the bank's private bondholders. *La Prensa* argued that this proposal would facilitate the construction of thousands of additional low-cost dwellings per year, and "with a monthly payment equivalent to rent, anyone could become the owner of an economical, healthy, and well-built house."[12]

La Prensa's extensive coverage of the housing crisis also included commentary that was hostile to the barriadas—notably, the opinions of the Asociación Nacional de Propietarios (ANP, National Association of Property Owners), which variously condemned them as presenting "deplorable conditions"; providing "the preferred hideout and residence of thugs pursued by the law"; constituting "a center of infection" and "a danger to society"; and in no way "manag[ing] to solve the housing shortage."[13] Touching on every anxiety the barriadas could possibly evoke—filth, lawlessness, disease, chaos—these articles reinforced the belief that squatters were besieging the city on all sides. Elsewhere *La Prensa* offered a far more sympathetic viewpoint. In a July 1954 article on Cerro San Cosme, one of Lima's oldest barriadas, the language of invasion was redeployed to evoke a pioneering spirit as "the invaders, the conquistadors of the hill" staged an assault—"armed with sticks, iron, bits of *esteras*, cartons, spades, and courage"—on the unforgiving terrain where they fought "to repair and improve their dwellings ... in an indescribable battle against the hill and against adversity." Regrettably, these dogged efforts were undermined by "their limited economic means and technical ability."[14] This account concluded with a degree of optimism, noting that *La Prensa* had already identified a solution to the nation's housing problem, which had been endorsed on all sides and only awaited implementation. In this way Beltrán appealed directly to low-income families by articulating moral support for self-help builders, framed as noble pioneers who struggled to improve their housing situation rather than the vandals of urbanity depicted by Belaúnde along with the ANP.

In relentless coverage promoting its plan, *La Prensa* published numerous articles over the succeeding weeks, presenting the testimony of various experts vouching for its economic viability and social necessity in curtailing the spread of the barriadas. Photographs of simple, low-cost dwellings were also published, allowing readers to envisage in concrete terms what could be achieved. These included a group of experimental patio houses designed by Carlos Morales Macchiavello and Eugenio Montagne and built by the CNV, using "a revolutionary construction system" that promised to cut costs by 20 percent. An article on recent projects in Puerto Rico presented a contrasting approach, describing the construction of more than one thousand "rural and working-class" houses by means of a "cooperative system"—that is, mutual aided self-help—with the state providing the resources of loans, machinery, and technical assistance.[15]

Belaúnde also contributed an article to the newspaper's campaign, in a rare moment of collaboration between the two men, rivals in the political sphere as well as the public sphere of the press. Belaúnde endorsed Beltrán's call for public-private partnership in solving the housing problem, and confirmed that *La Prensa*'s projected budgets were realistic for building low-cost housing. However, Belaúnde's article focused on the unidad vecinal program, rerouting Beltrán's campaign onto his own terrain. Emphasizing the achievements of the CNV—the state agency closest to his heart—he nonetheless accepted the need to increase its output, and agreed that FNSBS resources could be usefully employed in subsidizing mortgages. A map accompanying his article illustrated the many sites within a 15-kilometer radius of Lima's Plaza de Armas where housing development could be carried out economically because the land was of lower value, being distant from the city center, unsuitable for farming, or crossed with significant ravines. The large-scale development of planned settlements would make the installation of infrastructure on these peripheral sites affordable, and their relative isolation would facilitate their evolution into "self-sufficient satellite nuclei" in line with the decentralization policy established in the 1949 Plan Piloto. These urban "nuclei"—in the form of "unidades and sub-unidades vecinales"—would, he argued in an echo of his earlier writings, offer "a splendid opportunity for an urban structuring with a view to reestablishing communal life, which our era tends to destroy."[16] Despite his careful determination of the most rational solution, the technocratic logic of Belaúnde's decentralizing policy was completely at odds with the practical logic of barriada settlers, who preferred to establish their neighborhoods closer to the city center, accessible to jobs and urban facilities, without the challenges, time, and money required to arrange daily transit back and forth to "satellite nuclei" in the urban hinterland.

Concluding his article, Belaúnde proposed a design competition for "la casa elemental" (the basic house), both to encourage industry to develop cheaper building materials and to provide architects with the opportunity to devise a range of different housing prototypes, which could be deployed in combination to reduce the monotony of mass housing projects. Two weeks later, as the grand finale to its housing campaign, *La Prensa* adopted Belaúnde's proposal and announced that it would sponsor a competition for "la casa barata" (the low-cost house). Although Beltrán's and Belaúnde's interests coincided here, their motivations did not: while Beltrán saw a further opportunity to publicize his drive to expand the market for private homeownership, Belaúnde aimed to demonstrate that architects could meet the challenge of creating an "economical system" of minimum standard modern housing, even (or especially) within the constraints of a developing economy.

The competition brief called for an ensemble of four houses comprising two examples of two different models—a two-bedroom house (costing S/.15,000) and a three-bedroom house (costing S/.20,000). The ANP—already allied with Beltrán's call for reform—offered to finance the construction of the winning project. In order to demonstrate the viability of the design, construction was to begin immediately after the selection of the winner, to be completed within sixty days and within the specified budget. On August 12, Mario Bernuy Ledesma was announced as the winner out of a field of twenty-one entries (fig. 1.3 and fig. 1.4), with Santiago Agurto as runner-up. Twelve days later the newspaper reported that construction had begun on Bernuy's project, making use of a site on the campus of the Escuela Nacional de Ingenieros. The "casas gemelas"

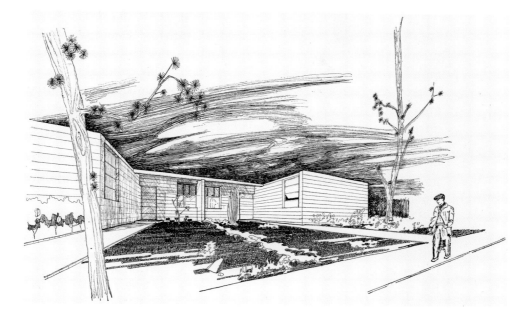

Figure 1.3. A pair of low-cost semidetached dwellings built in mirror image: the dividing line between the two lots is indicated by the party wall that projects forward to create a sheltered space for each entryway, and the center strip that separates the front yards. Mario Bernuy Ledesma, "Casas gemelas" (twin houses), 1954. *Source: El Arquitecto Peruano* 18, no. 204–5 (July-August 1954).

Figure 1.4. Two-bedroom (A) and three-bedroom (B) pairs of low-cost semidetached dwellings. Mario Bernuy Ledesma, "Casas gemelas" (twin houses), 1954. *Source: El Arquitecto Peruano* 18, no. 204-205 (July-August 1954).

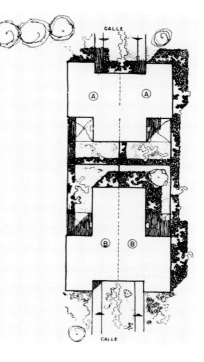

(twin houses) were designed to be built as semidetached, two-family dwellings, sharing a long party wall and the roofing structure as a cost-saving measure. Although they were small, maximum use was made of built space by eliminating corridors in favor of providing access to all rooms from the central living-dining area. In the future, part of the rear garden could be appropriated for an additional bedroom as needed. Seeing virtue in its simplicity of expression, the jury praised the design for its "frankness" and lack of "false ostentation" in the use of unfinished cement block, and for its attention to construction details, which promised to streamline and lower the cost of production.[17]

Once construction was under way, the newspaper closely covered its progress, featuring front-page photographs of the growing walls and the raising of the roof, and reporting on the interest it sparked among *La Prensa*'s readers—those struggling to find housing amid the ongoing policy debates (fig. 1.5). In the end, the houses were finished in thirty days, half the estimated time, and on October 17 they were handed over to the director of the Escuela Nacional de Ingenieros. It is not clear what happened to the houses afterward.

One week later, *La Prensa* announced the details of a new undertaking emerging from the competition: the construction of a second set of low-cost houses using the design by runner-up Santiago Agurto. This time, the five houses would be given away to readers in a lottery. Agurto studied civil engineering and architecture in Lima, and completed his postgraduate studies in architecture at Cornell University with a thesis project proposing a housing development for Lima. When he returned to Peru in 1947, he immediately assumed a key role with the CNV, since none of the fifty or so architects then in practice had been trained in social housing.[18] He was the lead architect on many CNV projects, beginning with Agrupamiento Angamos and Agrupamiento Miraflores (both 1948–1950), and Unidad Vecinal Matute (1952), Unidad Vecinal Rímac (1952-1953), and Unidad Vecinal Mirones (1952–1954).[19] He was also a partner in the architectural firm Agurto-Cayo-Neira with Javier Cayo Campos (who likewise enjoyed a long career within the CNV) and Eduardo Neira (a close colleague of John F. C. Turner's). Agurto was active in progressive politics for many years, serving as secretary-general of the MSP, and was discussed as a possible presidential candidate for the Frente de Unidad de Izquierda (United Leftist Front) in the 1962 elections.

Sus Viejos Sueños Ya Tienen Forma de Casa

Decenas de familias modestas **vieron ayer**, "con sus propios ojos", la realidad irrebatible de concreto y ladrillos de las "Casas Baratas" que obtuvieron el Primer Premio en el Concurso de Arquitectura organizado por LA PRENSA.

Figure 1.5. The construction site as stage for the performance of housing policy: "Their old dreams now take the form of a house." *Source: La Prensa*, Sept. 6, 1954.

Agurto's design, titled "La casa que crece" (The growing house) was conceived as a "célula habitacional flexible" (flexible dwelling unit) that could be developed over time as the family's needs and available resources changed (fig. 1.6). Stage one consisted of a compact dwelling with a small kitchen and bathroom, a bedroom for a couple with a young child, and a living-dining room that could be transformed into an extra bedroom at night—a pragmatic move that contravened the strict functional separation essential to modernist reform housing but reflected actual practice in low-income

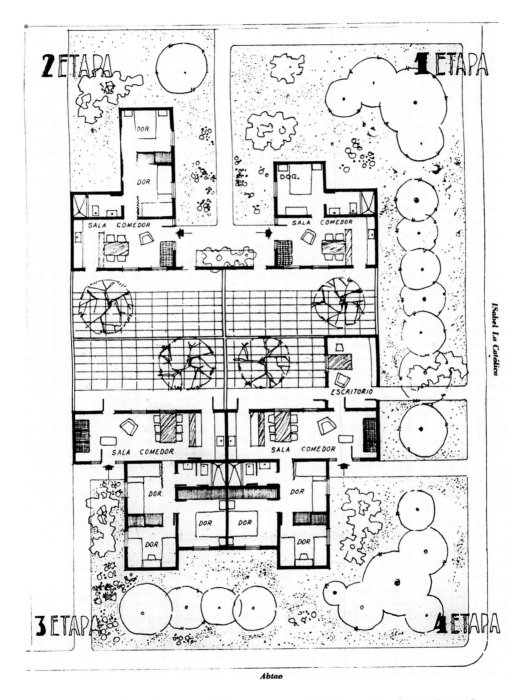

Figure 1.6. Santiago Agurto, Four stages of "La casa que crece" (the growing house), 1954. *Source: La Prensa*, Oct. 24, 1954.

Lima households. The 130-square-meter lot provided space to store a vehicle, and ample room to extend the house over three successive stages, adding one or two bedrooms, followed by a second, separate living space, a second bathroom, an expanded kitchen, and finally an all-purpose room at the front that could be used as bedroom, study, workshop, or even a shop, depending on the location of the lot. Agurto's design maintained a sense of spaciousness throughout its evolution: with the L-shaped core of the dwelling placed in the center of the lot, additional rooms were aggregated around three sides while preserving space for a rear patio and a small garden framing the front door. In this way, Agurto argued, the house followed the principle of "organic growth": rather than allowing the service and living areas to be overburdened as the household increased, each new bedroom would be complemented with enhancements to the supporting spaces, thereby maintaining the dwelling's optimum balance of functions. Agurto believed that this combination of adaptability and carefully staged growth was especially important for low-income families, since they did not have the resources to sell and relocate when the household grew, leaving them constrained by a dwelling that no longer met their needs.

Agurto claimed the Cerro San Cosme barriada as his inspiration: "There one appreciates, as in no other place, the obstinate constructive instinct of Peruvians. There they have built painstakingly, without having any technical knowledge, erecting houses on the rugged and steep foothills, making extraordinary works of engineering. And there's no Peruvian worker—driver, sweeper, laborer, or baker—who doesn't know how to handle a trowel, to place bricks one on top of another, to raise the walls of a house. And it's exactly this that must be made use of in the solution to the housing problem." Agurto's description references familiar tropes that serve to naturalize the prevalence of self-built neighborhoods: the barriada resident as conquistador, whose innate constructional abilities are framed as an essentially Peruvian trait that ultimately (like mutual aid) evokes the nation's Inca heritage. As a key element of his proposal, "La casa que crece" was designed "to be extended and improved by its own occupants"—a measure that would further contribute to the house's affordability. If this principle of actively engaging self-help labor were applied to the problem of housing provision at the national level, Agurto argued, the average 30 percent of construction budgets that covered labor costs could be eliminated; further, the 10 percent dedicated to "technical direction"

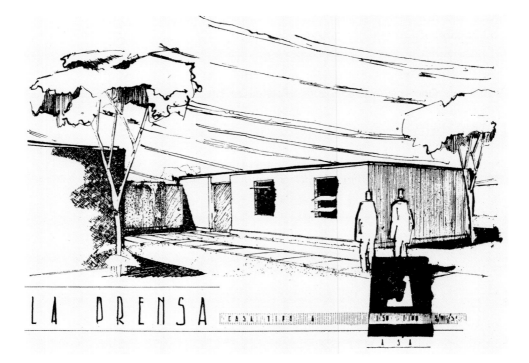

LA PRENSA

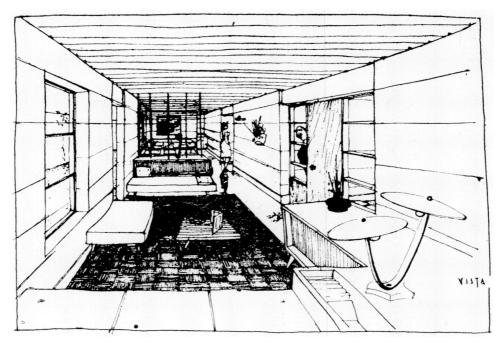

Figures 1.7 (*top*) and 1.8 (*bottom*). Santiago Agurto, "La casa que crece" (the growing house), 1954. *Source: El Arquitecto Peruano* 18, no. 204–5 (July–Aug. 1954).

could also be saved, provided that the self-builders were "under the supervision of a competent organization."[20]

Although unrealistic about the potential cost savings, and clearly minimizing the difficulties facing Peruvians building their own dwellings, Agurto's project was nonetheless a genuine effort to understand the economic necessities driving the protracted construction in barriadas, and to devise a model house that responded to this reality. At the same time, Agurto's design eschewed the usual pattern of barriada housing, which began with the construction of a *cerco*; rather, he proposed a freestanding house on an open lot. Moreover, the sketches present a strange disjunction between the unabashed austerity of the house's exterior and the interior's studied minimalism (figs. 1.7–1.8)—sparsely appointed in tasteful fashion, it evokes urbane modern living rather than the busy, well-populated spaces of a low-income household, as if Agurto had not quite succeeded in imagining the lives of its future inhabitants.

Ironically—but almost inevitably, in an eloquent demonstration of the increasing difficulty of acquiring land for low-cost housing in Lima—the day after *La Prensa* announced that the construction of "La casa que crece" had begun, efforts to start work on the selected site were obstructed by the arrival of a crowd of women and children armed with sticks and stones, claiming that the land was theirs. The nine hundred or so families had been there for over twenty-five years, and for the last ten they had been fighting to prove their legal claims. Court proceedings to determine the ownership of the site were still in process, but as far as the residents were concerned, the legitimacy of their claim was clear: "We have been property holders [*poseedores*] of this land for a long time, before anyone bought it."[21] In this conflict of de facto and de jure ownership, the residents claimed a moral right to the land not just by precedence but by virtue of having made something out of nothing, by "urbanizing" a site that had been little more than farmland. No doubt wary of engaging in a prolonged legal dispute with a group of people who represented the core constituency of its housing campaign, *La Prensa* swiftly moved to purchase an alternative site (while complaining in print about the expense).

Once construction was under way at the new site, progress was again closely followed in *La Prensa*, along with the drama leading up to the drawing of each of the five lottery winners. Although it took only twenty-two days to build the houses, the lottery to give them away was staged over nine months—excellent publicity for

Beltrán's plan to solve the housing crisis, and good business for *La Prensa*, since entry into the lottery required cut-out coupons from the newspaper. The winners included a twenty-five-year-old bachelor from Lima ("a poor and dignified person. . . . a young worker, studious and without vices"); a provincial police officer and father of three, ready to move to the capital to further his career; and a woman who had spent the last ten years of her "exemplary life" in the El Agustino barriada, gamely brightening up her surroundings with a flower garden, her assiduous domesticity now rewarded with a fully furnished residence for herself and her family.[22]

With the success of the lottery in material terms (for the winners) and in propaganda terms (for the newspaper), Beltrán's campaign had proved its point, but for the time being the experiment remained an isolated achievement. His focus now turned to the policy sphere.

Affording a House, or Not

In the 1956 presidential elections that marked the end of Odría's dictatorship, Belaúnde ran as a strong reformist candidate, but ultimately lost to Manuel Prado, a centrist and political ally of Beltrán. Within weeks of being inaugurated as president, Prado responded to intensifying concern over the barriadas by establishing the Comisión para la Reforma Agraria y la Vivienda (CRAV), appointing Beltrán as its head. In addition, CRAV charged Adolfo Córdova with preparing a comprehensive study on the nationwide housing deficit, while anthropologist José Matos Mar contributed a brief summary of his ongoing research on the barriadas—an early indication of the influence of his work on policy development.[23] The commission also counted on the advice of US experts, provided through the International Cooperation Administration (ICA, a precursor agency to USAID), who helped to produce draft legislation for a savings and loans system in Peru. Beltrán personally lobbied for the involvement of US consultants, beginning with a series of meetings with ICA officials in Washington in September 1956. Stanley Baruch, Latin American branch chief of the ICA's housing division, was eager to assist, since Beltrán had signaled that the commission would not consider "any of the myriad forms of public housing which so often are present in underdeveloped countries"; from the US perspective, CRAV offered a "unique opportunity and challenge . . . to participate in the creation of an all encompassing housing program which places principal emphasis on the role of private lending institutions and on 'home-ownership' in the purest sense of the term."[24] Indeed, Baruch was so impressed by the quality of the resulting report that he arranged for the ICA to translate it into English and distribute copies as a "worldwide model" via its networks.[25]

In its initial report opening the commission, CRAV identified its fundamental objective as promoting small and medium property ownership—in the form of both rural landholdings and the single-family home—arguing that this would foster initiative and personal responsibility, in turn increasing productivity, improving the standard of living, and stimulating the country's economic development. It emphasized the links between agrarian reform and urban housing, arguing that the best means of controlling the barriadas was to address their main cause—the rapidly increasing rate of rural-urban migration—by correcting imbalances in the distribution of economic activity, currently heavily concentrated in the capital to the detriment of rural and regional areas. Specific measures included facilitating access to cultivable land via agrarian reform and establishing strong regional centers to counterbalance the attraction of the capital.

In the end, while the commission's findings, presented in mid-1957 and published the following year, included some important and far-reaching innovations concerning housing, its approach to agrarian reform was retrograde, limited, and cautious, reflecting the conservative interests of large landowners among the Peruvian elite, such as Beltrán himself. Accordingly, it recommended expanding access to agricultural landholdings via irrigating marginally productive land, opening up remote regions of the Amazon, and reallocating unused public and private land—but not via arguably the most effective immediate solution, the redistribution of existing productive land. Just as "satellite nuclei" for low-income residents would be relegated to the urban fringe, agricultural sites for landless farmers would be carved out from the leftover spaces of the national territory, thereby avoiding significant disruption to existing property regimes.

Notably, although projects to tame and develop the Peruvian Amazon had been floated since the nineteenth century, the idea would receive a significant boost from Belaúnde, who proposed an infrastructure campaign of "road-colonization" to improve access to "exploitable lands . . . thereby alleviating demographic tensions in other regions"—particularly the capital, with its overburdened housing supply. In this way, the paisano invasion of Lima would be redeployed toward the conquest of the Peruvian interior. Once elected to the presidency, Belaúnde enacted this ambitious vision by initiating construction of the Carretera Marginal de la Selva (Forest-Edge Highway), projected to be 1,000 kilometers in length. Significantly, he conceived the project as obeying the "ancient custom of *cooperación popular* [cooperation by the people]"—a key element of his political platform—whereby rural communities would utilize local resources to initiate projects for their own economic development, thereby reviving "the old *minka* that made the [Inca] Empire great and whose vestiges still endure in the communities of today." On this model of regional development via mutual aid self-help, the government would construct the main artery, but each settlement was responsible for its own branch road. For Belaúnde, this scheme epitomized a key credo: "To help he who helps himself."[26]

In a memo accompanying CRAV's findings on housing, Beltrán similarly invoked a spirit of self-sufficient self-help, emphasizing that no extraordinary government funding would be needed to solve the housing problem. Rather, the Peruvian people's "ordinary powers, duly channeled and protected" could more than meet the challenge. Likewise, the problem of the barriadas could be solved through "technical assistance and financial cooperation"—taking care that these initiatives were framed in such a way that allowed prospective self-builders "to acquire their own dwellings [*su habitación propia*] through their own efforts [*su propio esfuerzo*] and with their own means, which is what they desire."[27]

In order to promote "financial cooperation" CRAV advocated establishing a system of savings and loans institutions to provide small-scale housing finance. This resulted in the Asociaciones Mutuales de Crédito para Vivienda (Savings and Loan Associations for Housing, 1957) and the Banco de la Vivienda (Housing Bank, 1962). The provision of technical assistance to self-builders was to be achieved through the creation of a national system of Oficinas de Asistencia Técnica (OATs, Technical Assistance Offices, 1957). The CRAV report argued that barriadas were a prime example of the potential of individual effort, at once providing effective shelter, creating the foundations for economic development, and cultivating the moral improvement of the individual character. However, a lack of competent direction had led to wasted efforts, with the selection of "unsuitable sites, materials, systems, and designs from the point of view of urbanism, architecture, and engineering. As a consequence of such errors this valiant collective contribution that could be translated into decent dwellings has produced a large part of the *tugurios* and of the *barrios marginales* that are found in the country."[28] In CRAV's view, the core issue was technical, not socioeconomic, in nature; self-built housing was deficient due to inept production, and could be remedied with the input of professional expertise. To this end, the OATs would advise barriada residents on the construction and financing of their housing, as well as urban design and infrastructure provision, property law, and the management of collective improvement projects. OATs were immediately established in Lima as well as the rapidly growing cities of Chimbote and Arequipa. The latter office, coordinated from mid-1957 by Turner, produced the earliest tangible successes of this new approach, while also encountering considerable resistance from residents.

According to CRAV's conception, the technical assistance programs would offer job training and contribute to improving Peruvians' "systems of communal life"; in practical terms, it particularly recommended the employment of *ayuda mutua dirigida*, through which, it was hoped, Peru's ancient tradition of communal building practices would compensate for its lack of capital and savings. The assistance came with the expectation that residents would work toward the "regularization" of their residential situation, and to this end the program established a process for eventual ownership of the lot, contingent upon timely construction of "at least a minimal dwelling." This was defined as a structure of at least thirty square meters, with a kitchen and a lavatory, sufficient bedrooms to house the family without overcrowding or the "promsicuity" of mixing genders, and construction "in a stable and permanent manner with suitable materials." Property title would only be granted once "the dwelling is totally finished and ready for occupation."[29]

Emphasis was also given to the "social aspects" to be addressed by the OATs: "It will be of little use to put at people's disposal suitable housing and the corresponding communal services if they do not know how to use them as they should be used, and if they don't form hygienic and orderly habits, and stimulate human improvement." This rhetoric recalled that of the unidad vecinal program, further intensified: managed self-help housing would serve as a training ground to prepare residents for their responsibilities as independent citizens, and as actors in the private market; it would foster "aware and progressive communities . . . utilizing the many or few resources at their disposal, without expecting everything from the government and the authorities." In order to achieve this ideal self-sufficiency, residents would be required to buy their properties at a price covering the original value of the land plus any improvements undertaken by the government, such as redrawing the urban layout, grading roadways, or installing services. As the commission's initial report had noted: "'Helping them to help themselves' should be the principal idea and the constant practice of this work"—offering everyone, no matter their situation, "the possibility of creating their well-being with their own effort [*esfuerzo propio*]."[30]

Adolfo Córdova's study for CRAV presented a very different perspective on the housing crisis, which in large part reflected the views of the MSP. Córdova argued that the most serious problem facing Peru was not housing but poverty—accordingly, raising the economic capacity of low-income families as part of a comprehensive program for national economic development was the only path to a sustainable solution. Córdova's detailed assessment established that in order to meet the current housing deficit (both quantitative and qualitative), it would be necessary to build a total of 728,700 new dwellings, and repair around 1,011,500—the latter figure representing over half of the country's existing housing stock. While the most acute housing shortage was in the largest metropolitan areas (Lima and Arequipa), overall the housing situation in rural areas was far worse, with 60 percent of housing needing repair and only 5 percent in good condition.[31]

To meet the housing deficit, Córdova envisaged a construction program to be carried out over thirty years. Taking into account the continued deterioration of existing housing stock as well as projected population growth, he argued that meeting the total housing deficit would require the annual construction of 81,570 new dwellings, and the rehabilitation of 33,720. Given that total housing production in Lima over the previous eight years averaged less than 6,000 units annually, the most optimistic estimate for housing construction nationally was 9,000 units annually—a fraction of that needed. Only a ninefold increase would meet the target, and—as Córdova noted—the investment required to carry this out would absorb half of the national budget. Nonetheless, he expressed the extraordinarily optimistic hope that if addressed as part of a "radical transformation" of the Peruvian economy through a long-term, wide-ranging development program, the housing deficit could certainly be reduced, though not eliminated. Notably, in an oblique reference to Beltrán and the enticing headlines of *La Prensa*, Córdova warned that there were no quick and simple solutions to this problem: "The offers of a *'casa propia* [a home of one's own or a proper home] for all Peruvians' that are made from time to time are fallacious and dangerous, evidently with obscure political aims or, in the best-case scenario, are due to complete ignorance of the situation." As appealing as this slogan might be, "it is not honest to play with it, because the economic capacity of the Peruvian family precludes it." Córdova also observed that the housing crisis had been aggravated by unrealistic expectations on the part of the authorities concerning what kind of housing should be provided, insisting on "high standards of construction and urban services [*urbanización*]" that led to inflated costs—a reference to Belaúnde and the CNV. It would be far better, he suggested, "to establish a balance between the cost of these dwellings and the economic capacity of the population" by adopting a more flexible approach to minimum standards.[32]

A contemporaneous evaluation of the unidad vecinal program underscored the urgency of a policy reappraisal. Over the period 1949–1956, while Lima's population had increased by 76,000 families, fewer than 46,000 new dwellings had been built, and only 5,476 by public agencies such as the CNV that targeted lower-income residents.[33] As a result, demand for CNV housing far outstripped supply, leading to a highly selective screening process, including income benchmarks and home visits to assess domestic habits, that tended to favor higher-income applicants. As one consequence, many of the workers actually building the unidad vecinal projects were unable to meet the requirements to live in them. Instead, the CNV "provided the most suitable solution, giving them land to build their houses"; that is, the state housing agency enabled their construction of unaided self-help dwellings "in a clandestine manner in the areas next to where they work." This account suggests that by the mid-1950s the CNV had already reconciled itself to shantytowns adjacent to its showcase projects as the best it could offer its own construction workers, leaving the unidades vecinales as isolated outposts in an increasingly improvised city (fig. 1.9). Furthermore, the unidad vecinal projects themselves quickly showed signs of strain, particularly due to overcrowding. By 1966 Unidad Vecinal No. 3, designed for 5,000 residents, had a population of 7,151; this was partly due to the demise of the superintendencia that had been responsible for regular inspections of apartments and (in

Figure 1.9. The *unidad vecinal* as isolated outpost in the improvised city: in the foreground is the Mendocita rental tenement, illegally constructed beginning in 1941; in the background is the CNV's Unidad Vecinal Matute (architect: Santiago Agurto, 1952). *Source*: Carlos Enrique Paz-Soldán, *Lima y sus suburbios* (Lima: Universidad Nacional de San Marcos, 1957).

theory) transferring families to larger units as they grew.[34] Moreover, the modifications that residents made to the dwellings to create additional living space—such as enclosing the patio and terrace areas—effectively reproduced the confined spaces of the tugurios, overriding the CNV's attempts at housing reform.

Efforts to devise an "economical system of urbanization and construction" for Peru's cities had resulted in contrasting responses: Belaúnde's conventional modernist reform housing, providing modest dwellings but failing to cut costs sufficiently to match the reality of low incomes; Agurto's "house that grows" hybrid, revolutionizing the issue of standards by cutting the house to its core but remaining at the level of an experiment with an uncertain fate in the housing marketplace; and the OAT's aided self-help approach, promising to uphold the principle of the "minimal" dwelling but as yet untested. Short of raising overall incomes, or the major structural reforms advocated by Córdova as the foundation for any lasting solution, the widespread provision of the affordable, modern house remained elusive. Meanwhile, the formation of new barriadas only intensified.

2

THE BARRIADA UNDER
THE MICROSCOPE,
1955–1957

While *barriadas* have been part of Lima's urban fabric since at least the 1920s, their rate of formation accelerated after 1940, the year the city was hit by a major earthquake, and intensified throughout the 1950s, making them a more prominent—and unsettling—aspect of the city. In *Squatters and Oligarchs*, his study of the symbiotic relationship sustaining clientelistic politics in Peru, David Collier observed that the formation of barriadas tended to follow three distinct patterns. First, the gradual, ad hoc occupation of a site, generally of little value due to difficult terrain, such as steep hillsides or river banks, leading to irregularly arranged lots. Second, invasion—an organized mass occupation involving hundreds and occasionally thousands of people, usually dues-paying members of a residents' association, who were often armed in advance with a site survey and would trace out a basic urban layout for their settlement. Typically these utilized vacant public land on the urban periphery that was unsuitable for farming, and whose open flat terrain facilitated an orderly grid layout. Eric Hobsbawm noted that Peru has a long tradition of rural land invasions, impelled by various motivations, the most germane in this context being the perception—echoing the Spanish colonial imperative to expand settlement—that unused land "belongs to him who cultivates it by means of his labour."[1] Similarly, in the logic of urban land invasions, the site belongs to those who "urbanize" it by means of their labor.

Prior to the regime of General Manuel Odría (1948–1956), the vast majority of barriadas were established through gradual occupation; invasion increased dramatically in the 1950s, along with the third means of formation identified by Collier: government authorization. Deploying clientelism to court the loyalty of low-income urban dwellers (an increasingly important constituency, particularly in the capital), and in any case lacking the resources to implement an effective slum-clearance policy, Odría acted as patron to numerous groups seeking land for housing, in anticipation of earning their electoral support. These settlements were fully authorized to occupy the land, thanks to the strategic benevolence of Odría, but were extralegal nonetheless, since they failed to meet established planning regulations. Like invasions, these tended to occupy large parcels of government-owned land, and were set out on a regular grid, and thus—from a bird's-eye view—resembled planned urban neighborhoods. At ground level, however, it was evident that they lacked standard infrastructure and facilities. The largest of these extralegal settlements, the 27 de Octubre in Lima, which received legal recognition in 1951, commemorated the date that Odría seized power in a military coup. Later renamed Urbanización San Martín de Porres, by 1960 it had a population of over fifty-seven thousand people.

This particular dynamic of land invasions is specific to Peru. A more usual pattern is seen in Brazil, for example, where favelas were typically formed through gradual occupation, and while forced removals were rare, the threat was real, leaving residents in "a state of perpetual ambiguity" of barely condoned extralegality. However, as in Peru, this constituency was too valuable for politicians to risk alienating altogether with outright repression; the result was "indefinite tolerance, forged from political convenience, logistical incapacity, and societal impasse."[2]

In his recent analysis of Lima barriadas, Julio Calderón Cockburn determined that of the 213 established before 1960, 41 percent were formed by invasion (placing Collier's "government authorization" barriadas in this group), 36 percent by gradual occupation, and—supplementing Collier's taxonomy—15.5 percent by contentious tenancy relationships, with the remainder of more diverse origin, such as official relocations that morphed from provisional to permanent.[3] According to Calderón, barriadas arising from tenancy relationships that detoured into legally questionable territory fell into two main types: in some cases, landowners directly rented out vacant sites, but conflicts with tenants led to rent strikes, effectively turning tenants into squatters; in others, *yanaconas* (sharecroppers) had contracted to cultivate agricultural land, but as urban development encroached upon the farmland they worked, they sold it illegally. Whether engendered by clientelism or by profit, barriadas would become a permanent feature of Peru's cities.

This chapter takes as its starting point the establishment of Ciudad de Dios on Lima's southern periphery, achieved through a large-scale invasion on Christmas Eve 1954. Although this method of establishing settlements had been normalized under Odría, this invasion was by far the largest to date, and as such tested the limits of the state's tolerance for improvised urban development. The chapter begins with a narration of the events as outlined in the (far from disinterested) account of Pedro G. Beltrán's newspaper, *La Prensa*. It then shifts to the perspective of anthropologist José Matos Mar, whose groundbreaking research on the barriadas led to insights into their social dynamics that would influence government policy and architectural and planning practice alike. Finally, it examines the unprecedented legislative measures—and the resulting, tentative urban projects—that were devised in response to the Ciudad de Dios invasion, as experts and politicians were forced to come to terms with the realities of this new urban landscape.

A City Overnight

While the front page of the Christmas Day 1954 edition of *La Prensa* featured the latest image of Beltrán's "casa barata" (low-cost house) initiative, the previous evening had seen eight thousand people occupy state-owned land on the *pampas* (treeless plains) 16 kilometers from Lima to found the new squatter settlement of Ciudad de Dios—City of God. The *pobladores* (settlers, the barriada residents' preferred name for themselves) gave their city this name because "it was born on the same night the Lord was born."[4] The date was no doubt carefully selected: land invasions frequently took place on religious or national holidays in order to emphasize the pious and patriotic sentiments of the citizen-settlers in mitigation for the threat raised by their mass law breaking; it also provided the invaders with a tactical advantage, since it took longer for the police or armed forces to organize an effective response on a public holiday.

En una Noche Nace una Ciudad en el Desierto

De improviso ha surgido en el desierto "La Ciudad de Dios", con sus enjambres de chozas de esteras y el movimiento intenso de una ciudad cualquiera. Hasta solo tres dias, en estas pampas de Atocongo no existia una sola vivienda.

Figure 2.1. "In one night, a city is born in the desert." *Source: La Prensa*, Dec. 28, 1954.

La Prensa's first mention of the event came on December 28, with a description of the would-be founders of the new "pueblo clandestino" (clandestine town) arriving by night carrying all their belongings, "like a group of refugees from some war, or a strange caravan of twentieth-century nomads." As soon as they arrived at the determined location, they selected their lots and set up shelters made of *esteras* (fig. 2.1). Those lacking even these basic materials simply "traced the boundaries of their lots with rows of small stones and lines made with chalk." The pobladores told the newspaper that the invasion had been organized by a registered association of some five thousand would-be homeowners, who had been petitioning the authorities for the right to occupy this site for some time. With their attempts to follow the lawful procedure frustrated by an unresponsive bureaucracy, they had been forced to take dramatic action and—"assisted by God"—decided to invade on Christmas Eve. According to an association official, they would soon begin looking for an engineer to trace out "the streets, the park, the market, and the church" of the new city, intending to carry out the physical work themselves in order "not to cause the state any expense."

The newspaper's coverage continued daily until mid-January, in sympathetic accounts that appeared to give tacit support to the invasion. (By contrast, the only mention of the events in *La Pren-*

sa's main rival, *El Comercio*, was a two-paragraph description of a meeting between President Odría and association leaders in early January.)[5] On December 29, *La Prensa* reported that two government officials, whom the pobladores wouldn't name, had "authorized them to occupy nine hectares of the pampas"; however, they had decided to take possession of substantially more land in order to accommodate all the association members. Meanwhile, some of the association leaders had been detained by the police for several hours, suspected of having ties to the outlawed Communist Party or Alianza Popular Revolucionaria Americana (APRA), accusations that they rejected. The pobladores had already started digging to secure a water supply, and the orderliness of the whole process impressed *La Prensa*; the threat of chaos (the specter of lawlessness raised by the invasion, the latent fear of massed crowds of urban poor) was set to rest as the community effectively policed itself. On December 30 the newspaper reported that the pobladores had been ordered to leave the site by January 3—however, the association leaders had already acted to circumvent this by writing directly to Odría and his wife (frequent patrons of such enterprises), asking for the land to be granted to them. In the meantime, the population had risen to ten thousand, and armed police were preventing trucks carrying construction materials from entering the site. Still, people continued walking toward the "promised city." *La Prensa* helpfully published a map showing its readers how to get there.

December 31 featured an extended interview with Alejandro López Agreda, president of the association. Described as "affable" and sparing but affecting with his words, López emphasized that they were ordinary people, essentially law-abiding and hardworking. Fed up with living in the *tugurios*, they had simply run out of options and elected to take action on their own rather than waiting for the state to solve their problems: "Should we have continued waiting? We decided no. We have strong arms and we can build our houses with our own effort [*nuestro propio esfuerzo*]. The people are no longer how they were before. The people now understand and assess and know a lot of things. The people now know how to make sacrifices and to save for a better life. The people understand unity, brotherhood, mutual aid [*ayuda mutua*], and that with this they can achieve a lot to improve their circumstances." López reiterated that all they wanted from the state was access to the land—they were even willing to purchase it, "provided that the prices are reasonable" and that the state establish some kind of loan system, "since we gave up trying to obtain any credit, because they don't lend money to us poor people." Beltrán's campaign for mortgage-financing reform, launched via *La Prensa* six months previously, could hardly have found a better advocate. As with López's apparent fluency in the current terminology used to describe aided self-help housing ("esfuerzo propio" and "ayuda mutua"), it is impossible to determine to what extent these were López's actual formulations or a verbal polish added by *La Prensa*.

On January 3 the newspaper duly reported on the visit of Odría and his wife to the settlement, where they were warmly welcomed by patriotic crowds. Two students from the Escuela Nacional de Ingenieros (one of whom, Luis Felipe Calle, later worked with John F. C. Turner in Arequipa) had completed their first sketch for the future "ciudad tipo popular" ("popular" or low-income city). Estimating that the 300-hectare site would be suitable for a population of thirty thousand, they planned a city with a civic and commercial center ringed by a residential zone, sustaining its own industrial sector on an adjacent site. According to the student architects, this constituted "a useful large-scale trial" that would demonstrate the viability of establishing "autonomous satellite cities of the *unidad vecinal* type" on various low-cost sites around Lima. In conclusion, they endorsed *La Prensa*'s "casa barata" as "ideal" for this kind of city, "because they have been planned by the *técnicos* especially for cases like this"—that is, for low-income neighborhoods. (The term *técnico*—a professional with specialized technical knowledge, such as an engineer, architect, or urban planner—was invoked in this period as a guarantee of authority.) That their planning concepts echoed those of Fernando Belaúnde Terry was no coincidence, since he was head of the architecture department at the Escuela Nacional de Ingenieros and led classes there on housing and urbanism.

By January 4 the eviction deadline had passed with no attempt to enforce the order; instead, the association leaders had been invited to meet Odría at the Palacio de Gobierno. The students were now overseeing the preparatory works for the construction of a small market, as the pobladores made good on their promise to build the city themselves. They also began to divide up the land, an act that *La Prensa* compared to conquistadors founding a new city. Meanwhile, a new set of invaders had arrived: an association of residents recently dislodged from their neighborhood, because—the newspaper noted pointedly—they had "invaded private property right in the urban center of Lima." Clearly, from *La Prensa*'s view-

Figure 2.2. "Visit of thanks to *La Prensa*." On the left, the leaders of Ciudad de Dios admire *La Prensa*'s low-cost house; on the right, the leaders meet their patron—seated center are Alejandro López Agreda (with cane) and Pedro G. Beltrán (gesturing). *Source: La Prensa*, Jan. 5, 1955.

point, the seizure of unused state land on the urban fringes could be sanctioned, even encouraged, but taking possession of privately owned real estate in the central city could not.

On January 5, the newspaper announced a significant development: the meeting with Odría had resulted in the promise of a "symbolic sale" of the Ciudad de Dios site to the pobladores, essentially granting them security of tenure. In addition, the Ministerio de Fomento y Obras Públicas (Ministry of Development and Public Works) was to set up an office on the site; its first task would be to carry out an *empadronamiento* (official registration of residents), creating a record of all those hoping to be granted a lot. At this point, the government was effectively committing its resources and its técnicos to the process of developing the new settlement, taking over official responsibility for its administration from the association leaders. Two photographs flanking the main story sought to illustrate the newspaper's key role in the happy resolution of the affair (fig. 2.2): one documented the leaders' meeting with Beltrán in the offices of *La Prensa*, expressing their gratitude for "the objective information" the newspaper had published about their settlement, while the other showed their visit to the "casa barata" building site, bestowing their seal of approval via "their enthusiasm for the layout of the houses and for their form of construction." In the accompanying interview, the settlement leaders claimed *La Prensa*'s campaign to promote low-cost housing as the point of inspiration for their invasion; it had demonstrated that "raising a *ciudad popular* with their own effort and with the help of the state and of private capital . . . was not impossible." The leaders also claimed high ambitions for their project: distancing themselves from the negative connotations of squatter housing, they were determined to build "a city with hygienic houses and perfectly organized, and not simply one more clandestine barriada, unhygienic, without electricity, water, or sewerage."

Gradually, more details emerged of the government's intentions concerning what it now termed "the authorized occupation of state land in the Pampas de Atocongo." In an effort to confront Lima's growing housing deficit, the government would develop a master plan for "Urbanizaciones de Tipo Popular" ("popular" or low-income urban settlements) utilizing state land "in selected zones bordering the city"—a plan apparently inspired by Belaúnde's 1954 proposal for the establishment of "self-sufficient satellite nuclei."[6] The reformulation of Ciudad de Dios as an *urbanización popular* would act as a pilot project: the state would replace the squatters' improvised efforts with solutions developed by its técnicos, and would provide a supplementary program of "technical assistance for the construction of houses" (presumably on the aided self-help model).

In *La Prensa*'s estimation, the state's proposed reforms would effectively reregulate improvised urban development, allowing it to guide the city's further evolution with the minimum outlay of public resources. The commitment of state assistance to the new urbanizaciones populares would attract law-abiding and hardworking pobladores. As an enforcement mechanism, "those who invade land in the future—even if it is state property" would be excluded from the official programs and face the full force of the law. *La Prensa* confidently predicted that "scenes such as Ciudad de Dios will not be repeated": after the steady drip of unauthorized occupations and mushrooming barriadas that had brought the housing issue to the forefront of public concern, in *La Prensa*'s view, Ciudad de Dios marked the invasion to end all invasions. Underscoring the newspaper's key role in resolving the crisis, the following day *La Prensa*'s front page featured residents of Ciudad de Dios learning details of the government's plans in the pages of *La Prensa*, neatly tying up the story's narrative arc.

The Anthropology of Improvement

A more complex account of Ciudad de Dios emerges in José Matos Mar's *Estudio de las barriadas limeñas*, which used the research and analytical methods of anthropology to produce the first comprehensive survey of the barriada phenomenon.

Anthropology was recognized as an academic discipline in Peru in 1946, with the establishment of the Instituto de Etnología y Arqueología at the Universidad Nacional Mayor de San Marcos in Lima under influential *indigenísta* Luis Valcárcel, and the launching of a similar program in Cuzco in the same year. Valcárcel's ambition for the Instituto was to promote anthropology as a scientific discipline whose specialist knowledge and techniques could be deployed beyond the academy, specifically by policymakers concerned with the "development and integration" of the indigenous population—that is, their reformation as productive citizens of a modern Peru. To this end, Valcárcel also became director of the Instituto Indigenista Peruana (IIP), a research and advisory body within the Ministerio de Justicia y Trabajo (Ministry of Justice and Labor) that had been modeled on a Mexican precedent. Despite Valcárcel's enthusiasm for the project, the IIP never achieved the same level of influence in national affairs as its counterpart in Mexico. Regardless, many of the first wave of San Marcos graduates were active in producing reports for the Ministerio de Justicia y Trabajo, and on its own account the Instituto de Etnología y Arqueología developed "more than forty research papers on indigenous communities and three projects of technical assistance and cultural promotion" in its first decade.[7] This work included the Huarochirí Project, led by Matos Mar while he was still in his early twenties and had yet to complete his doctorate.

The Huarochirí Project focused on a group of villages in the province of Huarochirí near Lima, involving multiple research visits beginning in 1952. As described by Matos Mar, the project shifted from its initial "purely ethnological character" to a planned "improvement project" in mid-1953, when a number of técnicos—a category that in this case included psychologists and doctors as well as design professionals such as Adolfo Córdova and Eduardo Neira—became interested in the work. The project was reframed as an experiment in applied ethnology, with a comprehensive plan of action drawn up, including proposals to establish a health post, support artisanal production, and improve agricultural yields. The researchers were to live in the community for two years, directing the projects and testing the results via "ethnological verifications"; eventually community members would be trained to manage the programs themselves. Meanwhile, sociologists and psychologists would study "the shape of the groups' reactions, their behavior and attitude toward change."[8] In short, scientific study would provide data for the técnicos to translate into culturally appropriate proposals for "social improvement": modern technical knowledge would be rallied to produce a better version of everyday life in the Peruvian hinterland. As one example, by 1955 architects had drawn up plans for improving village housing, using locally available materials combined with "modern construction techniques"; the designs were adapted to the conditions of the region, but included updated amenities, such as "functional, though rustic, furniture" and a reform kitchen where "the woman doesn't need to be bending over all the time."[9]

Though never implemented, the Huarochirí Project was typical of the applied anthropology programs that emerged as a tool of development professionals in this period.[10] It could even be seen as a self-conscious response to the long-running Vicos Project established by Cornell University's Allan Holmberg, centered on a hacienda in the northern Andes from 1952 to 1966. While Vicos was largely run by US graduate students, the Huarochirí Project was designed by a multidisciplinary group of Peruvian professionals—although it did receive funding from a US-based foundation, a reminder that such research, at once highly localized in its focus on remote communities, also operated within an international network of applied research and policymaking. It is not by chance, then, that Matos Mar elected to publish his first report on Huarochirí in a United Nations Educational, Scientific and Cultural Organisation (UNESCO) journal.

In 1955, Matos Mar completed a second major research project, presenting to the UN his *Estudio de las barriadas limeñas*, which shifted his focus from the underdevelopment of the countryside to the misdevelopment of the city. The two contexts were deeply interconnected, since an explosion in rural-urban migration had contributed to the proliferation of barriadas in key economic centers such as Lima, Arequipa, and Chimbote. Underscoring the urgency of the situation, Matos Mar pointed out that the population of the capital had doubled over the previous fifteen years to approximately 1.2 million; at the same time, the 1940 earthquake had eroded the supply of affordable housing, leaving around 10 percent of Lima's residents to make their homes in barriadas.

Matos Mar's report collated census data on Lima's thirty-nine recognized barriadas, tracing the economic and sociocultural factors underlying their increasing prevalence. He selected Ciudad de Dios for a detailed case study, mapping its urban configuration as well as sample house plans. Matos Mar noted that the overall layout followed a pattern familiar from any number of Peruvian towns—in keeping with the settlers' ambition to create a "perfectly organized" city—with an approximation of an urban grid that reserved space in the center for a Plaza de Armas. Around the plaza were located key public facilities: the association meeting hall—performing an analogous function to the traditional *cabildo* (municipal council)—along with "the infirmary, the first-aid station, the cinema, and some shops" as well as a chapel on a small hill that framed one edge of the plaza (figs. 2.3–2.4).[11] By mid-February 1955 the provisional Ciudad de Dios had ninety-four businesses serving residents. The selected house plans included documentation of this nascent economic activity, even among highly provisional structures. For example, a two-room dwelling with an earth floor and walls of esteras reserved the front room for a shop, while the crowded bedroom (with three beds) also housed a sewing machine to be used for outwork, and outside there was space to keep animals (fig. 2.5).

As with Huarochirí, the structure of the 1955 report clearly announced its interventionist approach: divided into two sections, "the problem" of the barriadas was first measured and assessed, laying the groundwork for scientifically derived "solutions"; once again, the report recommended further study by "teams of *técnicos*" (comprising an architect-urbanist, a geographer, an economist, and a social anthropologist). Matos Mar emphasized that while barriadas might resemble some tugurios, they were distinctive in being formed by squatters who "occupy fallow lands, pay no rent, and, on the contrary, try to become owners of the land that they

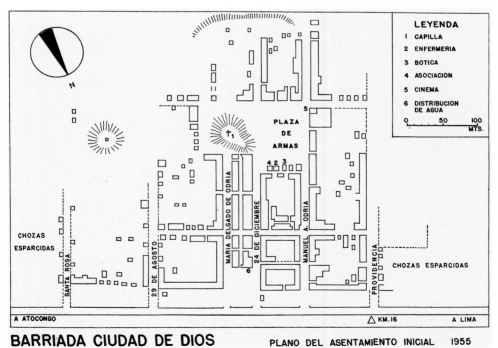

Figures 2.3 (*top*) and 2.4 (*bottom*). Ciudad de Dios, Lima, 1955: View and plan of the initial settlement. The schematic plan is an idealized version of the actual site conditions, which featured a more approximate version of an urban grid. *Source*: José Matos Mar, *Estudio de las barriadas limeñas* (Lima: Instituto de Estudios Peruanos, 1966).

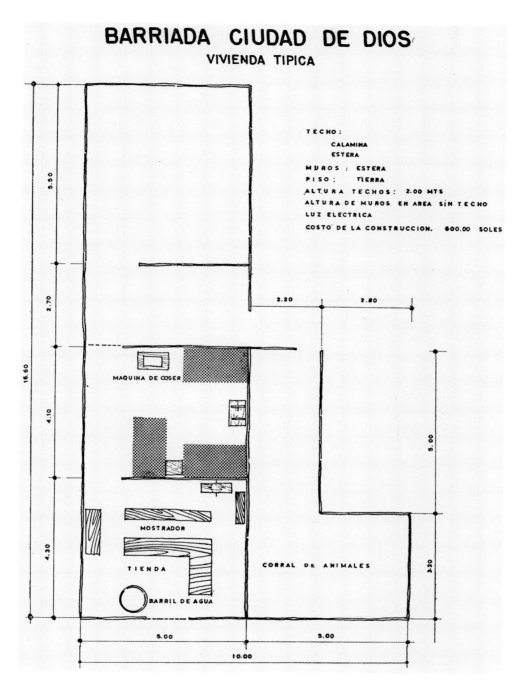

Figure 2.5. Ciudad de Dios, Lima, 1955. Two-room dwelling, within a *cerco* with a shop facing the street, a bedroom-workshop connected to a rear patio, and a space for keeping animals. *Source*: José Matos Mar, *Estudio de las barriadas limeñas* (Lima: Instituto de Estudios Peruanos, 1966).

occupy." Emerging as an "urban and local expression" of the "inefficient" socioeconomic structure of Peruvian society, real, long-term solutions to the barriadas would come only by stimulating economic development on a national level. Judging that Peru was not yet ready to take such action, Matos Mar recommended that, in the meantime, the shape and impact of the barriadas should be managed more assiduously. Barriadas develop "following a natural course and it is neither prudent nor advisable that this situation continue.... it is necessary to tackle the problem and try to channel it." The most powerful mechanism for "channeling" the barriadas would be to use legal recognition—granting or withholding property title—as leverage over residents: "This is the principal weapon that must be wielded and utilized effectively. We have already seen that the barriada *poblador* suffers a tremendous psychological anxiety . . . thinking that he can be evicted at any moment."[12] Given this fact, the authorities were in the position to mandate a series of behaviors in exchange for recognition: joining an official barriada association (under the control of "a state-run technical organization"), participating in running this group, making monthly payments to cover the cost of the granted property, and contributing to cooperative public works projects within the barriada. The principle articulated here of a coercive guiding hand, backed by the requirements of sweat equity, user-pays, and compliance with the rules, formed the Peruvian government's primary approach to barriadas in the late 1950s and into the 1960s.

For their part, Matos Mar warned, pobladores were vigorous and politically astute in their efforts to achieve de facto recognition for their situation, making constant and multifarious appeals to the authorities, with invitations to inauguration ceremonies for facilities they constructed, and arranging for visits by social workers, nurses, and school inspectors. They were also "attentive to changes of the authorities and alert to electoral processes and fluctuations in national politics"; one popular tactic was to name streets after the head of state, his wife, or other influential people "who have done or are thinking of doing something for them." They would even agree to pay property tax on all the lots that the barriada occupied—unthinkable under any other circumstances—if it were seen to bolster their position. Furthermore, Matos Mar viewed their cooperation with his own research as part of this larger campaign for recognition: "They give a full welcome to every person who comes to get information. We never had any difficulty in our fieldwork; on the contrary we were treated cordially and furnished with every type of information, even the most private."[13] Matos Mar's concern about settlers' lobbying skills seems to reflect an awareness that the authorities were not completely in control of the situation—or rather that the técnicos were not in control of the authorities, since certain officials were evidently quite vulnerable to the solicitations of the pobladores when it was to their own advantage. This aspect of the barriada "problem"—the symbiosis of extralegality between politician and poblador—could be observed with the finest scientific rigor, but any technocratic solution risked being outplayed by the forces of clientelism.

The flipside of the report's evident distrust of residents—in particular, of the power of residents left to their own devices—was that ultimately the solution to fixing the barriadas would come by taking advantage of the "marked communitarian spirit" that was one of their defining characteristics. In familiar terms, Matos Mar claimed that the Sunday *faenas* (work teams) regularly organized for building roads, cleaning streets, installing water reservoirs, and so on, were part of a "communitarian system, which corresponds to old Peruvian cultural patterns." The Huarochirí study had documented exactly such practices of cooperative work within rural indigenous communities, whose recognized members were required to contribute a designated amount of labor and/or building materials (such as handmade clay bricks) each year for communal improvement projects. Fostering this communitarian spirit in the barriadas could lead to significant results, provided that the state exercised proper control over residents' efforts through technical assistance programs. However, the extralegal initiatives of the pobladores in housing themselves could not be rewarded outright, and each resident should be required to pay what they owed for their dwelling: "It is necessary to iron out the difficulties for him, but not to make him a gift. Nothing for free."[14]

Underlying this entire discussion was the vexed question of the proper place of the provincial migrant in an increasingly urbanized world. As earlier articulated by Valcárcel, the traditional Andean village (*ayllu*) encapsulated the integrity of rural, indigenous culture: "The little Indian village forms spontaneously, grows and develops like the countryside trees, without subjection to any plan; the little houses group together like sheep in a herd." By contrast, from the colonial period onward, the city in Latin America has been coded as the redoubt of *criollo* (European-descended) civilization and power, set against the untamed territory of the *indio* (Indian) and the *paisano* (peasant)—with these two identifiers often treated as interchangeable. In the evocative formulation of literary critic Ángel Rama: "The [Spanish] conquest triumphantly imposed its cities on a vast and unknown hinterland, certifying and reiterating the Greek conception that contrasted the civilized inhabitants of the polis to the barbarous denizens of the country-side."[15] In this context, the indio-paisano was framed as utterly foreign to the city—in ethnicity, race, class, and frequently linguistic background. For many among the metropolitan elites, the waves of migration of the 1950s (even now known colloquially in Peru as "the era of the invasions") entailed a radical and disconcerting shift in the constitution of Lima, the Ciudad de los Reyes (City of Kings) and former center of the Spanish Empire in South America. The barriada—with its little houses often grouped "without subjection to any plan"—represented the invasion not just of unused real estate on the urban periphery but of the city as a whole, marking an assault on creole urbanity itself.

As for their residents, according to one government report, indigenous highlanders moving to coastal cities would inevitably suffer as "victims of climatic illness due to the change of altitudes"; they were likewise "ill-adapted for the socio-economic-cultural reality of urban areas" and thus unable "to compete on an equal footing with a capable workforce." In short, they constituted a substratum of citizens literally and figuratively unfit for urban life. Similarly, in a formulation that echoed theories of marginality, Valcárcel argued that the Indian transplanted to an urban setting could only become a degraded hybrid, irrevocably alienated from an original, essential identity yet unable to adapt to modern creole culture. For Valcárcel, the solution was local development programs to discourage rural-urban migration, improving the indio-paisano in situ, as at Huarochirí. An alternative position, articulated by cultural commentator Víctor Andrés Belaúnde (and shared by his nephew, Fernando Belaúnde Terry), regarded the city as a "source of social *mestizaje* [hybridity]" that operated as a civilizing mechanism: the Andean "invaders" could, with due care, be acclimatized to urban norms. The challenge, again echoing marginality theory, was to facilitate their integration while mitigating adverse effects. Along these lines, one influential study from the early 1960s employed "social psychiatry" to further research the emotional impacts of migration, noting with concern "the tragedy of a huge rural popu-

lation, experiencing transculturation, which does not always satisfy their expectations of social elevation." In this case, practices
of cooperative work and mutual aid were specifically singled out as
"unexpected integrative phenomena" that represented "stabilizing
factors for the individual and the group."[16] Such paternalistic and
highly charged assessments formed the deep background of later
government policies that promoted cooperative aided self-help
housing as part of efforts to eliminate the barriadas.

Reforming Ciudad de Dios

In the aftermath of the Ciudad de Dios invasion, the Odría government revised its tacit policy of tolerance toward extralegal urban
settlements, judging that this organized and willful flouting of
established property rights demanded a more proactive response.
Recognizing that it was not politically expedient to forcibly close
down the Ciudad de Dios settlement, Odría at once needed to confront the housing shortage exposed so dramatically by the invaders and to reassert control over processes of urban development.
Planning law offered the opportunity to broker a solution, if new
guidelines could be devised that would better accommodate—but
also more effectively regulate—these emerging urban forms.

Barriadas were extralegal in two distinct senses: being established through unauthorized occupation of land (in violation of
property law), and by failing to meet minimum standards in the
provision of urban services such as water, sewerage, electricity,
and roadways (in violation of planning law). With the legislative
reforms passed in 1955, in the wake of the Ciudad de Dios invasion,
the state endeavored to deploy the barriada residents' desire for
recognition under property law (and its inverse and complement,
the anxiety over eviction) as a "weapon" to demand conformity
with planning law—a strategy that Matos Mar's research suggested
would likely prove effective.

The first task was to define the new category of "urbanización de
tipo popular" that the Odría government had proposed as the basis
of a trial program to accommodate low-income families, beginning
with the residents of the improvised Ciudad de Dios. To this end,
the government announced revisions to the planning regulations
that had been in force since 1941. The new regulations established
two basic categories of residential subdivisions: standard subdivi-

sions (class B) entailed the provision of road, water, and sewerage infrastructure; the requirements for urbanizaciones de tipo popular (class C) were far less demanding, as the services to be provided would be determined on a case-by-case basis by a commission of planning experts. Additional measures would further reduce costs: smaller lots would be more affordable, and also discourage land speculation, since they would be too small to subdivide; the amount of open space within the urbanized area would be decreased; narrower streets with thinner or less-expensive surfacing material would be permitted; and the maximum length of the blocks would be extended from 100 to 300 meters—the resulting superblocks were intended to further reduce paving costs and also facilitate circulation. Any existing unregulated settlements would have to reformulate themselves in compliance with these new guidelines; those that failed "to regularize their situation will be declared 'clandestine' and as a consequence their elimination will be ordered."[17] Essentially, it was assumed that downgrading the minimum standards set by planning law—codifying the new officially substandard city—would be sufficient to "channel" future urban development. Those residents who were unable to afford basic services would at least be living within the law, if not within the norms followed by the rest of the city.

Putting this plan into practice, the Oficina Nacional de Planeamiento y Urbanismo (ONPU), the national planning agency, engaged architect Carlos Williams to draw up an urban design for a new Ciudad de Dios adjacent to the "clandestine" settlement; the preliminary studies were apparently carried out by Eduardo Neira.[18] Once the population was transferred to the planned site, the bulk of the housing was to be self-built by residents themselves, but to introduce variety into the urban scheme there would also be zones of multifamily housing constructed by conventional techniques. Around twenty thousand families had registered their interest in acquiring a lot in the future settlement, so the ONPU scheme envisaged a city of forty-five thousand to sixty thousand residents, with industrial zones, as well as areas of agricultural land so that the city could be self-sufficient in food production. This was to be a rationally organized and "self-sufficient satellite nuclei" as envisaged by Belaúnde, but governed by the standards of the urbanización de tipo popular.

According to Matos Mar's account, the residents' association and its president, Alejandro López Agreda, had devised their own ambitious plan for the settlement's development. Their plan even coincided with some aspects of the government's, since it also advocated the creation of a self-sufficient city, in this case to be based on "a group of supply services for housing construction." These were apparently intended to operate on a cooperative basis for the benefit of association members rather than as conventional businesses. First would be a brick works, established through members' financial contributions, loans, and "organized work"; then a factory for doors and windows, and another for the fabrication of glass, "taking advantage of the quality of the sand in the area." With these services in place, construction would be carried out in a highly organized fashion, with "teams of specialists who would build mass-produced housing, designed by architects and overseen by two engineers who were members of the [residents'] Association."[19]

The final Ciudad de Dios was entirely different in scale and scope from both of these schemes. Beginning construction only in 1957–1958 under the direction of the state housing agency, the Corporación Nacional de la Vivienda (CNV), the project comprised a little over 1,400 dwellings and was alternatively called "Urbanización Popular de Atocongo" or "Urbanización Popular Ciudad de Dios"; it retained an echo of the larger scheme developed by Williams, since the CNV described it as the "first stage of a project destined to furnish affordable housing to a population of 46,000 residents." This reformed Ciudad de Dios was located opposite the original improvised settlement and was "urbanized" to the extent of being provided with paved roads, water, and sewerage, but no electricity (fig. 2.6). According to Turner's account, the original goal had been "to treat the project as a social and economic unity, to build at a cost within the earning power of the wage earner and to use his own labour contribution"; however, these efforts to utilize self-help failed, "mainly due to the inexperience of the personnel involved; technicians, social workers, and administrators." Instead, the simple dwellings were constructed on a mass scale by the CNV, and offered to residents on the *alquiler-venta* system. According to *La Prensa*, the 1,400-odd houses were "based on the concept of 'progressive development'" and were available for purchase at different stages of growth, up to a maximum of four or five bedrooms (fig. 2.7). The more modest dwellings were designed to be extended via aided self-help on the owner's own schedule, "with his *propio esfuerzo* and the technical assistance that is provided to him."[20]

Figure 2.6. CNV (architects: Santiago Agurto, Luis Vasquez, and Manuel Valega). Ciudad de Dios, Lima, 1957–1958. *Source*: Servicio Aerofotográfico Nacional, Perú.

Santiago Agurto, the originator of the "growing house" within Peru, was the primary architect. Unlike Agurto's first "growing house" design in 1954, in this case the staging of the dwelling's evolution was reminiscent of barriada housing. House A, the most basic unit, consisted of a *cerco* (provided with two openings, allowing for the separation of formal and service entrances) and a *núcleo sanitario* (sanitary core) with kitchen and bathroom in one corner of the lot, making for a total roofed area of only 14 square meters. This replicated the typical construction pattern in Lima barriadas, where the almost complete absence of rainfall and a generally mild climate lessens the immediate need for a roof, so that a cerco demarcating territory and providing a basic level of privacy was generally completed before any permanent, enclosed spaces for living or sleeping. At the same time, house A provided the benefit of a functioning sanitary core connected from the outset to water and sewerage infrastructure, an element requiring a degree of technical expertise that would be difficult for untrained

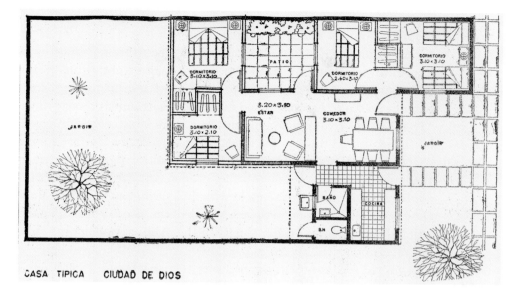

Figure 2.7. CNV (architects: Santiago Agurto et al). Typical house, Ciudad de Dios, Lima, 1957–1958. Black lines indicate the built section of House A, with *cerco* and sanitary core (*bottom right*); hatched lines indicate the walls forming the dining room, living room, and two bedrooms; clear lines indicate two additional bedrooms framing a patio. *Source: La Prensa*, Dec. 17, 1959.

self-builders to construct on their own. House B added a dining room at the front of the lot, and house C included a second, adjacent living space, for a total roofed area of 41 square meters. In the next stage, two bedrooms could be added at the front, followed in the final stage by another two bedrooms at the back, framing an interior patio. Once completed, the house covered a total built area of 95 square meters—around half of the 200-square-meter lot, leaving space for a large garden at the rear. Interestingly, according to the plan and description published in *La Prensa*, houses A, B, and C did not include a separate bedroom. It seems that the housing agency expected that the owner/resident of house A would build some kind of temporary shelter within the cerco, as was the practice in barriadas. In houses B and C, areas designated as the living or dining room could have been treated as multiuse spaces and used for sleeping, as would often be the case in incipient barriada dwellings, or in low-cost tenement housing.

At first glance the scale of this project seems completely inadequate given the many thousands of prospective residents who had made their way to the desert site. However, Matos Mar's survey, carried out in mid-February 1955, less than two months after the invasion, found a resident population of just 936 families, or 4,841 people. Many others had left due to the difficult living conditions. Especially challenging were the daily tasks of obtaining water and disposing of waste, as well as dealing with exposure to the elements. As *La Prensa* reported during the settlement's early days: "The families live huddled under their tents of *esteras*, suffocated by the sand and the sun during the day, and bitten by the intense desert cold at night. Since there is no electric light, sometimes the *pampas* wind blows out all the torches, and the town of 10,000 souls is left sunken in the most dreadful darkness, in which only the crying of children and the whistling of the wind is heard."[21] One can only assume that the majority of the original pobladores simply returned to the tugurios that they had hoped to leave behind, and waited for their next opportunity. Those who did remain, and who were deemed able to afford the CNV housing, were eventually transferred to the reformed Ciudad de Dios. The improvised settlement that had arisen from the invasion disappeared altogether in 1959.

Already by 1963 an article in *La Prensa* claimed that the new Ciudad de Dios—which the writer renamed "Caldera del Diablo" (Cauldron of the Devil)—was facing extreme overcrowding, since a large number of the original residents had sublet part of their properties to three or four other families, a practice facilitated by the large unbuilt space of the lot. This resulted in a total population of almost twenty thousand (if correct, this would mean an average of fourteen people per lot). Furthermore, a small but vocal number of residents "had given out the order not to pay rent to the government": those most up to date in their payments owed seven to ten months' rent; others owed thirty or more. Many were also refusing to pay for the cost of installing electricity. Yet they would not move out, as the alquiler-venta contracts stipulated for those in arrears, unless (according to *La Prensa*'s account of their position) "they give us back the lots we had before, along with the houses of *esteras* in which we lived." *La Prensa* concluded that the government's efforts had been wasted on "spoiled children" too accustomed to receiving "gifts"; according to the social assistants assigned to the settlement, the residents were suffering from "a collective psychosis of poverty" that led them to believe that the state was obliged to support them. The pobladores countered that they could not pay because they were too poor—and indeed both the extensive subletting and payment arrears suggest that residents were struggling to meet their obligations, and that ultimately the housing agency had overestimated their financial capacity.[22]

If it did not lead to better housing for its participants, what did the Ciudad de Dios invasion achieve? Matos Mar observed in 1966 that it "was planned and encouraged by powerful people and groups"; writing ten years later, he was more explicit, linking it to political struggles at the end of Odría's regime. This is confirmed by Collier: Beltrán had initially supported Odría's 1948 coup, but as his policies began to conflict with elite interests, Beltrán and others "became concerned with establishing a viable basis for opposing Odría" and seized on the issue of low-cost housing as a means of gaining popular support. According to this account, Beltrán effectively sponsored the Ciudad de Dios invasion in order to dramatize the housing problem and gain support for his solutions—hence a certain convergence between the invasion and the "growing house" giveaway in *La Prensa*'s coverage. In challenging Odría (the master of clientelistic politics), Beltrán sought to establish himself as a populist defender of the aspirational barriada resident: "He thus chose to fight Odría on his own ground by supporting settlement formation."[23] This dynamic is eloquently expressed in *La Prensa*'s self-reflexive coverage of the crowds in Ciudad de Dios reading in *La Prensa* of the government's promises of assistance for their new urbanización popular. In this context, Beltrán was not just the bearer of good news but a key agent in its creation.

As narrated by Matos Mar, plans for the invasion—seen, in part, as a performance to further Beltrán's agenda—had been percolating since 1939, when Alejandro López Agreda first visited a barriada nearby and with others began to consider the Pampas de San Juan as the possible site for an urban settlement based on an agricultural economy. As this idea matured, López carried out "a meticulous study" to determine the ownership of the site (it belonged to the Ministry of War) as well as transport options, the local availability of raw materials useful to construction, and the possibilities of irrigating the land. Equally importantly, "they thought about the repercussions and the effects that this type of invasion would have, not only within the country but internationally."[24] This certainly provides another dimension to López's observation that "the people now understand and assess and know a lot of things." Despite their organizational and political sophistication, however, ultimately the invasion was more successful in shifting the political terrain on

Beltrán's behalf than in securing significant, concrete assistance for all the would-be pobladores.

Beyond the reduced, reformed Ciudad de Dios, the revisions to planning law enacted in 1955 produced little in the way of concrete results. The government had downgraded its regulations in the hope of qualifying more low-income settlements as regularized, but it committed no more of its resources to constructing new urbanizaciones de tipo popular. For their part, residents of existing barriadas complained of the excessive costs of preparing the revised urban plans required "to regularize their situation" and as a consequence, by September 1957—two and a half years after the legislation was enacted—Urbanización Dolores in the southern city of Arequipa was apparently the only urbanización de tipo popular "recognized and authorized in all of Peru."[25]

The establishment of technical assistance offices in mid-1957, on the recommendation of the Comisión para la Reforma Agraria y la Vivienda (CRAV), was intended to facilitate this regularization process by providing the necessary expertise to barriadas. However, these new agencies faced their own challenges. In Lima, the technical assistance office was immediately responsible for 135 settlements with a combined population of over 180,000. The situation in Arequipa was more promising: an office of this kind had been in operation since 1952, and the city's relative isolation and insulation from the intense politicking in the capital around the issue of barriadas seemed to offer a more conducive working environment. As Turner took charge of this office in mid-1957, the growing body of scientific knowledge on barriadas and the recent innovations in planning legislation provided a solid platform for new efforts to tackle unregulated urban settlements, this time through exploring the potential of the aided self-help methodology. These explorations are the subject of the next chapter.

3

A PROFESSION
IN DEVELOPMENT,
1957–1960

On the cover of its August 1963 issue, *Architectural Design* presented a striking view of Lima, with recently formed *barriadas* dominating the foreground (fig. 3.1). Under the title of "Dwelling Resources in South America" (notably, not dwelling "problems"), the issue juxtaposed modernist mass-housing blocks with the resident-built housing of barriadas and aided self-help schemes, thereby positioning these heretofore marginal practices as equally viable solutions warranting serious consideration by a new vanguard of architects and planners. For guest editor John F. C. Turner, the aim was to shift the barriada and self-help housing away from the realm of technical reports and sensational reportage and into mainstream architectural discourse. At the ninth meeting of the Congrès Internationaux d'Architecture Moderne (CIAM) a decade earlier, architects based in Algiers and Morocco had introduced mass-scale urban informality to modern architecture, presenting studies of the self-built housing of the *bidonvilles* (shanty-towns) in North African cities, which, like Peru's barriadas, had emerged as a result of rural-urban migration. While these explorations framed the bidonville as an object of quasi-ethnographic study and aesthetic appreciation, its spare, function-driven forms sourced as local color for culturally appropriate modernist hous-

Figure 3.1. *Architectural Design* is introduced to the barriada: Pampa de Cueva (*foreground*) and El Ermitaño (*background*), with adjacent farmland, Lima. *Source*: *Architectural Design* 33, no. 8 (Aug. 1963), John F. C. Turner Archive.

ing, it was never viewed as a viable solution in itself that architects should replicate or preserve. By contrast, for Turner the squatter settlement was a valid urban form whose innately logical processes of evolution did not necessarily require reformulation by an outside expert. Despite its "apparent chaos" it was, as its residents saw it, "an achievement whose existence is self-justifying and whose appearance is irrelevant."[1]

At the same time, Turner suggested that a genuine engagement with these practices would require a revision of the very definition of the architect, raising the question of what, exactly, would be the profession's "functions and responsibilities" in this new mode of architectural production. Turner's own answer to this question evolved as he moved progressively further away from the conventional wisdoms of his education at the Architectural Association (AA) in the search for a different kind of architectural practice. This was only fully crystallized with his move to Peru in 1957, where he gained experience and a certain expertise in aided self-help housing, beginning with projects initiated following a devastating earthquake in the southern city of Arequipa in early 1958. Eventually he would abandon even this minimal approach as excessively interventionist, instead advocating what he termed "housing by people"—or user control over the production of housing—arguing that "who decides what for whom is the central issue."[2]

Although it may seem paradoxical to begin a discussion of self-help housing with the professional formation of one individual architect, it is through this singular figure that Peru and self-help housing—viewed as a marginal location and a marginal mode of practice—became legible to the larger world of architectural discourse. Though it seemed he emerged as if from nowhere, in fact Turner's metropolitan connections were crucial in providing the initial platform for his work, specifically through the aegis of Monica Pidgeon, the Chilean-born editor of *Architectural Design*, who had visited the barriadas with Turner on a visit to the continent.[3] Still, Turner's ideas were not formed in isolation, so this chapter also discusses the contributions of his key collaborators—in particular architect Eduardo Neira, who was pivotal in arranging Turner's migration to Peru and laid the groundwork for Turner's initial work in Arequipa.

Architecture, Anarchism, and the Artist-Technician

By his own account, Turner's education at the AA was significant less for the influence of the official curriculum than for discussions with fellow students. Turner first enrolled at the AA in 1944 at the age of seventeen, completing just one year before being drafted into the British army for two years of national service. This proved to be a seminal experience for an unlikely reason: Turner came across a copy of the anarchist newspaper *Freedom,* which had been left behind in his barracks, and was inspired to explore the philosophical underpinnings of the movement, reading the work of Peter Kropotkin, Herbert Read, and Eric Gill. Turner also had a close family connection to English radical thought through the figure of William Morris, since his maternal grandfather, Arthur Gaskin, had worked as an assistant to Morris, and Morris's daughter May was the godmother of Turner's mother.

From the outset the influence of anarchism is evident in Turner's approach to aided self-help, with his emphasis on self-generated community development and local action (an implicitly antistate position), and, echoing Kropotkin, the principle of mutual aid. Turner's enthusiasm for self-organizing groups of builders recalls Read's assessment of the contrasting models of social organization proposed by Kropotkin and Rousseau: "The anarchist recognizes the uniqueness of the person, and only allows for organization to the extent that the person seeks sympathy and mutual aid among his fellows. In reality, therefore, the anarchist replaces the *social* contract by the *functional* contract, and the authority of the contract only extends to the fulfilling of a specific function."[4] The fullest expression of Turner's interest in anarchist ideas appears in the distinction between "heteronomous" and "autonomous" approaches to housing provision outlined in *Housing by People* (1976), his most expansive theoretical text. While heteronomous systems (centrally administered and "other-determined") present a top-down dynamic familiar from traditional architectural practice, autonomous systems (locally self-governing and "self-determined") imply a network of end users making decisions for themselves, following the anarchist model. The collectively self-managed barriada presents an exemplary case—diametrically opposed to government-built mass public housing—but theoretically the principle of autonomy could be translated into other contexts, other modes of architectural production.

Turner returned to the AA in 1947, and early that year, in another fortuitous encounter, a neighbor who had been a personal friend of Patrick Geddes gave him a copy of *Town Planning towards City Development: A Report to the Durbar of Indore* (1918), along with sheaves of Geddes's handwritten notes. Already familiar with Geddes through the writings of Lewis Mumford, this discovery led Turner to several months of intense research as he focused on deciphering the notoriously complex elaborations of Geddes's "Notation of Life" diagram. Letters and notes of meetings in Turner's papers document exchanges with fellow AA students Paffard Keatinge-Clay and Bruce Martin as they discussed various iterations of the diagram and considered its applicability to their own studies. With the encouragement of Jaqueline Tyrwhitt, then preparing a new edition of Geddes's *Cities in Evolution*, Turner and Keatinge-Clay developed these ideas into a short paper, which Tyrwhitt then included as an appendix to the volume.

Although Geddes's Indore report has been credited as the first text to propose aided self-help housing, the paper is not concerned with this issue but rather celebrates the "new universality" offered by Geddes's synthetic approach, with its potential to reintegrate the fragmented and partial conceptions of reality resulting from the increasingly specialized forms of contemporary knowledge. While analysis (breaking apart phenomena into their constituent elements for closer, specialized study) is a necessary stage of thinking, a complete understanding of the "life-process" can only be achieved through synthesis (the "integration and coordination" of discrete observations into a holistic worldview). Geddes's Notation of Life diagram provides the paradigm for this "unitary form of thought": at its core is a three-by-three grid demonstrating the reciprocal actions of Place and Folk on each other via the medium of Work (elsewhere identified by Geddes as the actions of Environment and Organism via Function). Geddes proceeds to elaborate this field of nine relationships through the four interrelated "Chambers of Life" (designated Acts, Facts, Thoughts or Dreams, and Deeds), so that taken as a whole, the resulting thirty-six-square "thinking-machine" is seen as mapping an ecology of the vast complexities of human life. For Turner and Keatinge-Clay, the diagram is emphatically not an analytical tool; rather, its synthetic vision fulfills a longing for wholeness, relatedness, and universality—values that are repeatedly evoked throughout the text.[5]

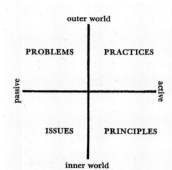

Fig. 28. *Four Elements of Action.* Following Patrick Geddes' interpretation of the classic and universal differentiation of inner and outer realities, and of active and passive modes of being, essential differences and complementarities of the elements of action are clarified. The most common confusions today are between general issues and particular problems, and between general principles and particular practices. When treated synonymously, issues and problems lead to useless generalizations or blindness to others' experience. When principle is confused with practice, action is locked into rigid programmes or it becomes incoherently empirical.

Figure 3.2. Geddesian diagrams illustrating the "four elements of action" and "the elements of change." *Source:* John F. C. Turner, *Housing by People: Towards Autonomy in Building Environments* (London: Marion Boyars, 1976).

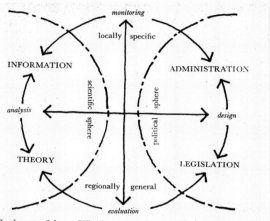

Fig. 40. *The elements of change.* Whether explicit or implicit, consciously recognized or not, action generates and is generated by the experience of previous action and administration, information, theory, and norms — which may be habits or customs or laws and regulations.

As a measure of the importance of the Geddes diagram to Turner, around this time he also made use of its basic structure to draw up a model for his own education in architecture, conceived as a "balance of four elements" echoing the Chambers of Life: Experience ("to be anchored in material reality"); Theory ("to be disciplined by factual truth"); Design ("to be energized by personal formulation"); and Practice ("to be humbled by personal expression"). The resulting program of study weaves together various facets of the four elements into an integrated curriculum culminating in a period of travel and practice. This diagramming of the "perception of a fourfold reality" recurs repeatedly throughout Turner's thinking: it appears as a holistic ideal in the explorations of the late 1940s; as a structuring device for his first program of works in Peru; and, in *Housing by People,* as a model to demonstrate the interconnected reality that must be grasped before informed and effective action can be undertaken (fig. 3.2).[6]

In early 1948 Turner's two key influences converged when he gave a lecture on Geddes at an anarchist meeting and published a short article on his work in *Freedom*. Turner argued that the bridge connecting Geddes and anarchism was their shared understanding of the "organic nature of society"—governed by the laws of nature, not the arbitrary rules of human institutions: "One can, in fact, attribute the failures of all political and philosophical systems to the use of inorganic or unbiological approaches." Geddes's broad synthetic approach, his ability to think across the disciplines of economics, "bio-sociology" (that is, a sociology informed by biology), and "the science of region and city" gave his work both intellectual authority and wide applicability.[7]

The clearest sense of how these intellectual influences translated into Turner's ideas on architecture emerges in the AA-based student journal *Plan* no. 6 (1949). Turner served on the editorial board for this and the next two issues with a group of close collaborators including Patrick Crooke, Andrew Derbyshire, and John Voelcker. While no individual writing credits are given, many of the ideas draw directly on Turner's reading list of the late 1940s: Mumford's *The Culture of Cities*, Read's *The Education of Free Men*, Kropotkin's *Fields, Factories, and Workshops*, L. L. Whyte's *The Next Development in Man*, and Sigfried Giedion's *Mechanization Takes Command*. More general cultural references include Karl Marx, William Blake, and the Bible. The issue consists of three parallel critiques aimed at the building industry, architectural practice, and childhood education, revolving around the themes of fragmentation, isolation, and the destruction of community. The potential for recuperation appears through an appeal to nature as holistic model, strongly recalling Geddes. The architectural heroes of the text are Peckham's Pioneer Health Centre (architect: Owen Williams, 1935) and the Hertfordshire schools program, on which both Turner and Crooke worked as students through their friend Bruce Martin. While conventional practice has left the architect isolated within a sea of facts, Peckham and Hertfordshire show the potential of an architecture attuned to human biology, industrial techniques, and the needs of the community. To realize such projects, this new architect (again reflecting Geddes) must learn to study "the relationship between man and environment—a study of a living process rather than a static form"; adopting the role of an "artist-technician" he must synthesize this knowledge into building.[8]

The discussion of the building industry negotiates a more complex path between a Marxist critique of work under contemporary capitalism and enthusiasm for the flexibility and variety offered by mass-produced prefabricated components. Most presciently, "building" is also considered in social terms, as a collaborative human activity grounded in everyday life: "If a man feels himself to belong to a community, he wants to work for that community." The connection to mutual aid self-help projects is explicit, as the demoralizing fragmentation of work is to be superseded by the "spontaneous formation of work teams" operating autonomously, their "actions . . . the result of collective control and responsibility." Examples are to be found in guildlike clock-making communities in rural France, decentralized Czech industries, Israeli settlements, and the English Midlands, where "fifty families . . . are building their own community—a work group building houses cooperatively in addition to their normal work in factories."[9]

Concurrently with this engagement with Geddes and anarchism, Turner maintained connections with CIAM-related projects and practitioners, attending the Bergamo and Hoddesdon conferences, touring the Unité d'Habitation construction site with Shadrach Woods, and undertaking a year's internship with the Italian architecture firm BBPR, at the end of which he traveled to Venice to attend the 1952 CIAM summer school. There Turner met the Peruvian architect and planner Eduardo Neira, who was fresh from his own pilgrimage to the Unité, and, as it turned out, also shared Turner's interest in Geddes, having translated the 1949 paper on the diagrams into Spanish. On the basis of this intellectual connection, Neira subsequently suggested that Turner move to Peru to practice architecture, an offer Turner readily accepted, since England presented few opportunities for the kind of work in community development that interested him. As Turner described the decision in 1972: "I felt that if I could get out from among the underbrush of technological innovations and intellectual formulations and into the much simpler situation described by Neira, I might be able to see my way." Whether the situation in Peru really was "much simpler" or its unfamiliarity just allowed Turner to view it as such, in the Eurocentric and elite cultural milieu of Peruvian architectural practice, Turner's metropolitan connections carried instant authority, and from Neira's perspective, would doubtless help to burnish any joint projects. Turner's entry into this world was facilitated by Neira's social connections within the Peruvian oligarchy: according to Turner's recollection, Neira's invitation was issued during Fernando Belaúnde Terry's 1956 presidential campaign, on the understanding that "there'd be plenty of work for the boys, jobs for the boys, if Fernando Belaúnde won."[10] All in all, Peru promised to be a receptive environment for a young, well-connected architect interested in exploring new ideas.

Toward a New Social Architecture

Eduardo Neira's own path to the meeting in Venice offers an interesting parallel to Turner's early career. Three years older than Turner, Neira studied architecture in Lima before traveling to England in the early 1950s to study urban and regional planning at the University of Liverpool. In 1947 he had been a founding member of Agrupación Espacio, a self-consciously vanguardist architectural group that also included in its membership artists, literary figures, and musicians.[11] Opposed to the eclecticism of mainstream architecture in Peru, where the "modern" was treated as just another style, deployed fluidly in alternation with the neocolonial, the group's key points of reference were CIAM and Le Corbusier; they were particularly vocal in their support for Town Planning Associates' projects for Chimbote (1946–1948) and Lima (1948). The group promoted its ideas through articles in the newspaper *El Comercio* (owned by the family of Luis Miró Quesada Garland, an architect and leading member of the group) as well as its own journal *Espacio*, which included Neira on its editorial board in the early 1950s. In 1955 those members interested in pursuing a more socially engaged practice (including Neira) precipitated a split in the group. This was apparently spurred by their involvement in the research project led by José Matos Mar to study the indigenous communities of Huarochirí, near Lima. This realignment of Neira's own architectural practice provided the impetus for the invitation he extended to Turner. Far from being the passive recipient of imported expertise, Neira solicited Turner's immigration as a likeminded colleague and a potential collaborator, apparently seeing in their shared interest in Geddes the potential to shift away from an architectural practice inspired by figures such as Le Corbusier, and to devise an alternative approach better suited to the social and economic conditions of postwar Peru.

After Neira returned from Europe, he joined the Ministerio de Fomento y Obras Públicas (Ministry of Development and Public Works) as the head of its Departamento de Urbanismo. In early 1954 he visited Arequipa to report on its problems of unregulated urban development. As the second-largest city in Peru, by the mid-1950s Arequipa had a population of around 125,000, and the area covered by its barriadas was larger than the planned city. While part of this urban expansion was due to newly arrived migrants, apparently much of it was caused by land speculation. In 1950 a commission established by the Ministerio had investigated 160 complaints related to illicit urban subdivisions—for commercial real estate developments as well as squatter settlements—most of which had been sanctioned by the mayor of a neighboring peri-urban district who was eager to capitalize on Arequipa's antici-pated future growth. In 1952 the Ministerio established a branch office, the Departamento de Inspección de Urbanizaciones y Obras Públicas de Arequipa (IUP), to bring some order to the situation, charging it with creating a register of land claimants, carrying out topographical surveys, and preparing and implementing develop-ment plans. However, a lack of resources and competent staff ren-dered this office completely ineffective. Neira's task in 1954 was to reassess the situation and to reorganize the IUP office.

Neira's initial report sought to clarify the distinction between two types of illicit settlements, the *urbanización popular* and the *urbanización clandestina* (clandestine urban settlement). The first emerged out of organized invasions of government-owned land by groups of *pobladores*, who then petitioned the authorities to grant them the site, while the second involved the illegal subdivision and sale of private land for profit. Neira argued that the government's purpose in establishing the IUP had been to assist the pobladores, who, he implied, acted outside the law out of desperation but were scrupulous in approaching the state postinvasion in order to regu-larize their situation. The second group simply flouted the law for personal gain, a problem that had been overlooked in the IUP's orig-inal brief. In any case, the need for intervention was clear: "It is pre-cisely a function of the state to protect and direct private invasions, especially in those groups of limited economic potential." Specifi-cally, there was "an official obligation" to ensure that settlements were established as economically as possible, on sites that were amenable to the installation of essential urban services, and free from competing legal claims requiring lengthy litigation.[12] Further, the pobladores needed to be kept safe from the predations of real estate speculators and self-seeking, manipulative barriada leaders.

This somewhat surprising approach—positioning the government as protector of the urbanizaciones populares rather than the agent of their removal—was absolutely congruent with the paternalism of President Manuel Odría and of the architectural profession alike. While Neira's interest in assisting the pobladores emerged from his socially committed and scientifically informed practice, and Odría's arose from pure political calculation, nonetheless their discordant motivations converged at the same reading of the situation, and at the same policies. It should also be noted that in this period of profound social inequality, when a literacy requirement prevented many low-income citizens from voting, paternalistic expressions of concern over the pobladores' childlike vulnerability to speculators and demagogues masked an unarticulated anxiety over their potential power as an organized force operating beyond elite control.

Neira recommended that the IUP begin by determining which households had the right to keep a lot—this being their only place of residence, occupied for at least a year and a day. Eligible residents should then be relocated from their existing "'nonconforming' *urbanización*" to a new settlement properly prepared by the state and provided with basic services; any remaining "nonconforming" constructions would be demolished. Neira judged that the office should endeavor to take advantage of the "enormous effort" that was evident in the squatters' self-built houses: with an "intelligently directed technical assistance" that was focused on *ayuda mutua*, residents could be shown how to work together as a group under the guidance of an appointed expert, constructing their houses as efficiently and economically as possible. Neira's final coauthored report provided additional details: lots would be offered to families in usufruct of extendable ninety-nine-year periods, granting the right to extended habitation but not the option to purchase the lot and become its legal owner—a measure that was intended to circumvent land speculation. This offer would be valid for a year, "within which time the benefiting family should commit itself to building their house"[13] or lose the option to the lot altogether. Although it does not appear that Neira had an active role in Arequipa following this report, these recommendations did result in a substantial reorientation of the IUP, giving it a more ambitious and assertive agenda that brought it into much closer contact with barriada residents.

Neira continued his interest in these issues, undertaking a study trip in 1955 under the auspices of the UN Technical Assistance Program that ranged from Europe and Algeria to Puerto Rico, where it seems that he met Luis Rivera Santos, director of a pioneering program in cooperative aided self-help housing begun in the 1940s.[14] In 1956 Neira published a long article on the housing crisis in Peru in Belaúnde's magazine *El Arquitecto Peruano*, in which—along with suggestions on dealing with the high cost of urban land, the difficulties of housing finance, and the dire state of the local construction industry—he argued that mutual aid was a "thousand-year-old tradition" in Peru that had great potential in combating the housing shortage, particularly in parts of the country "where the simplicity of the dwellings makes possible the employment of nonspecialized labor." He returned to the theme in a 1957 article published in Pedro G. Beltrán's *La Prensa*, advocating the adoption of technical assistance as a key element of national housing policy, viewing it as a realistic use of the country's limited resources, with a unique ability "to liberate the potential of collective action via the technical direction of communal effort." In this way, Neira argued, adapting a Corbusian phrase, it offered a path "toward a new social architecture." Once again Neira argued for the cultural appropriateness of techniques of ayuda mutua and *trabajo en común* (cooperative work) for Peru, "a country where for centuries no other form of work existed."[15] For Neira this was an organic and autochthonous form of building for Peruvians—yet he also identified the specialized practices of "aided" self-help as thoroughly modern, representing an emerging but well-regarded technique in the new field of community development that had been tested in a range of countries.

Neira was a key conduit for the importation of knowledge about aided self-help housing into Peru, passing on information about international trial projects to colleagues such as Turner, in addition to publishing articles on the topic. Furthermore, according to Neira's *La Prensa* article, the recommendation by the Comisión para la Reforma Agraria y la Vivienda (CRAV) to create technical assistance offices originated with a suggestion from the Ministerio de Fomento y Obras Públicas, where Neira worked; it may even have come from Neira himself, since he had made a similar suggestion in his 1954 report on Arequipa. The task of putting the idea into practice now fell to Turner.

Arequipa: The Ecology of Man and Environment

Turner arrived in Peru in early 1957, staying briefly in Lima, where he lectured on planning theory at the Instituto de Urbanismo in collaboration with Neira. From the extant notes it appears that Turner gave at least two lectures (on the "definition of planning" and "Geddes' basic theory") while Neira gave at least one lecture on Geddes. Turner's preparatory notes reveal a wide range of sources: assembled in a comparative table are quotes from Patrick Abercrombie's *Town and Country Planning*, Ludwig Hilberseimer's *The Human Environment*, Robert E. Dickinson's *City Region and Regionalism*, Percival and Paul Goodman's *Communitas*, and Geddes's Indore report. Despite the range of sources, the brief selected quotes all tend to reinforce a holistic, Geddesian outlook: thus in Turner's selection from Abercrombie, planning is "the accommodation of several units to make a complete but harmonious whole"; in Hilberseimer, its aim is "to bring about a harmonious relationship between man, technics, and nature"; and in Dickinson, it serves to create an ecological balance, "designing a pattern of human works ... which will bear harmonious relations to the underlying resources."[16]

Turner's own definition of planning closely followed Geddes: *"The science of planning is the* ECOLOGY *of Man and Environment"* where place, work, and folk operate in "an organic process of interaction." Expanding on the theme, he explained that planning was *"a process of ordering ... the physical environment* (in its present and future conditions and at all scales, from region to dwelling) *for the well-being of man* (at all scales, individual to collectivity)." Again reflecting Geddes, this was to be enacted through a dynamic four-phase process—survey, plan, administration, and "the plan in action"—before beginning the cycle again, as the "solution ... of PAST problems [is] *actually* the creation of new ones."[17] At first glance it is perhaps difficult to reconcile Turner's work with squatter settlements with this profound sense of order. Yet the fundamental equilibrium of a harmonious organic world is an important recurring element in Turner's thought, reflecting an inherent ambiguity of the Geddesian ecological worldview: conservative in its outlook, but pragmatic and even progressive in its practice. This conservative outlook is founded on the notion of an organic unity, whose fundamental structures and relationships do not change; in the closed system of a Geddesian world, every action is an interaction, modifying the exact content of a situation while maintaining its overall form and balance of elements. Its pragmatic practice is nonideological, suspicious of universal solutions, responsive to the local specificities of the situation, and predicated on the need to review and recalibrate action based on the outcomes of previous interventions.

Turner's initial impression of Peru was that the equilibrium of the everyday world was disturbed and in need of being righted through the interventions of the architect/planner. His lecture notes on Geddes's "Valley Section" express concerns about a violation of the harmonious relationship of village-town-city through the recent modernization of agriculture and manufacturing: *"The town is the urban reflection of the country. . . .* Overgrowth development of urban economy and attitudes produc[e] many of the contemporary problems planners are concerned with: the depopulation of the countryside and the cancerous growth of cities. . . . Conversion of Indian farmer into depressed industrial proletariat."[18] Recalling the horror of John Ruskin or William Blake at the distortions of the natural and human environments caused by Britain's industrial revolution (both were cited in *Plan* 6), the task of the planner was to manage the adverse effects of industrial and technological change, and reinstate a sense of order in the chaos of unplanned urban development. Though distinctive in its Geddesian references, Turner's diagnosis was not far from the consensus view of postwar urbanization experts (exemplified by the UN's 1959 Seminar on Urbanization Problems in Latin America) concerning the need for planned interventions to correct unbalanced development.

In June 1957 Turner took up a position in Arequipa with the government office responsible for regulating and improving urbanizaciones populares, which was then in a period of administrative flux: for the first few months he worked for the IUP, until it was reorganized as the Oficina de Asistencia Técnica de Arequipa (OATA). The situation in which Turner found himself was already highly charged, in sharp contrast to the "much simpler situation" that he evoked years later. As already noted, the recommendations in Neira's 1954 report had led to a substantial reorientation of the IUP office, bringing it into closer contact with the squatter settlements. Almost immediately it had become embroiled in political disputes with the residents' associations representing the twenty different settlements throughout the city. On the one hand, officials were engaged in a struggle for legitimacy, attempting to gain the trust of residents while lacking sufficient resources to respond to the real scale of the housing crisis. On the other hand, officials were wary of the association leaders, convinced that they were operating against the interests of ordinary residents by misappropriating association funds and inflating the real estate market. With all vacant land near the city effectively under their control, association leaders frequently assigned lots to multiple owners to create the illusion of scarcity while doing little to prevent speculators from accumulating lots that they had no intention of developing. Neira's 1954 report had recommended curtailing the power of the associations by eliminating the membership fees that funded their activities, and transferring responsibility for maintaining the *empadronamiento* (official register of residents) to the IUP; with this shift, the IUP would be positioned to demand residents' "obligatory cooperation" with its rules and regulations.[19] For the time being, however, the IUP lacked the effective power to carry out these measures.

The conflict came to a head in late 1956. With the IUP committed to suppressing the associations, its policy toward the urbanizaciones populares was now "to paralyse and prohibit all building activity" while it devised a comprehensive plan to regulate and normalize the settlements.[20] As soon as the associations became aware of this policy, they published a leaflet outlining their objections to it—and to the IUP itself—through their recently formed umbrella organization, the Asociación de Urbanizadores Populares de Arequipa (AUPA). Claiming to represent over thirty thousand families, the AUPA statement asserted residents' right to housing, their willingness to cooperate with authorities, and their competence in managing their own affairs. Through their own efforts and savings, they had selected suitable land for their settlements and had "engaged the necessary technical guidance and set out zones that were perfectly habitable." By contrast, they had expected much but had received nothing from the IUP, which was "squandering a good part of the national budget" supporting an inadequate and incompetent staff that had little understanding of the situation, as was evident in their efforts to hinder rather than assist construction in the urbanizaciones populares. Not just responsible citizens concerned over the waste of government money, AUPA members also claimed to be trustworthy partners ready to work toward resolving the housing crisis. AUPA stated that it "understands completely—because it is living it—the serious situation of the housing problem, and we are in favor of banishing the 'old paternalistic criteria of the state' and agree that our principal idea and constant practice should be 'Help-

107

ing them to help themselves' without expecting giveaways, that is why we have come together 'to obtain the cooperation of the state and this is ACTING BEFORE BEGGING.'" AUPA's declaration here directly referenced the preliminary CRAV report that had been released the previous month: "'Helping them to help themselves' should be the principal idea and the constant practice of this work. Nothing should be given away or imposed."[21] As resourceful in their politicking as they were in their building practices, the self-styled *urbanizadores* (urbanizers) salvaged and repurposed elements of the commission's classic liberal rhetoric in order to reinforce their claims for shelter.

The tactical sophistication of this media campaign reflects the force of need, but also demonstrates the organizational abilities and negotiating skills of the pobladores, which were needed to manage intracommunal affairs as much as to navigate the arenas of local and national politics. As indicated by census data and membership records from this period, residents typically came from a range of socioeconomic backgrounds, including some white-collar and public sector workers, even members of the police and military, as well as artisans, the self-employed, and itinerant and part-time workers. As Turner observed, contrary to frequent assumptions that barriada residents were helpless and "the most destitute section of the community . . . [i]t requires initiative, intelligence, and a little capital" to construct a house in a squatter settlement.[22]

The AUPA statement concluded with a demand for the removal of incompetent staff at the IUP and the hiring of a new team to work under its supervision. Further, the state should provide earthmoving equipment as well as the materials necessary for installing water and sewerage systems. A couple of years later, Turner noted that AUPA's demand for oversight "would be unacceptable to any Administration and also most unlikely to produce good results if it were tried." Still, he believed that the declaration was in general terms "sound and justified" and that an advisory board including AUPA "could do no harm." While more open to the participation of residents in decision-making roles than other officials, a certain distrust of popular power still remained. Turner was not yet ready to embrace full user control. For their part, AUPA's "implied willingness to collaborate with the Authorities"[23] did not in fact lead to any concrete cooperation, a situation that continued in the months following Turner's arrival.

Despite this contentious atmosphere, from the outset Turner projected an ambitious vision for the office. According to Turner's

"Confidential Report" written around September 1957 as he was preparing to take over the directorship, the office should not be blinkered by short-term goals but "must be orientated to the actual scale and the real nature of the problem and the first projects must be a conscious initiation of a process which may take a generation to mature."[24] Reflecting his Geddesian worldview, Turner's proposal consisted of a quartet of interrelated aspects that mirrored the "four chambers": survey, research, communication of information, and the design and execution of projects.

The first of these—diagnostic survey—was a key element of Geddes's planning methodology: following his medical analogy, a thorough scientific examination was essential for the accurate diagnosis of urban ills; only then could a suitable treatment of minimally invasive "conservative surgery" be planned and performed on the urban body.[25] In Arequipa, surveys of the physical and social aspects of the urbanizaciones populares were carried out by "social assistants" who had been trained to collect and analyze data for anthropological surveys. They determined whether a settlement had viable infrastructure and solid housing stock, assessed whether its community had a stable population and a well-established cooperative ethos, and tabulated residents' places of origin, income levels, and occupations, all in order to gauge the likely success of proposed programs—in short, whether there were "material and human resources ready to be utilized."[26] In addition, Turner noted that the office was collaborating with the US Geological Survey to identify nearby deposits of *sillar* (a white volcanic stone) and Roman cement, believing that efficient local production of such materials would considerably reduce building costs. As with Geddes, the city is conceived as embedded within the surrounding region, and the cataloguing of its resources in terms of both folk and place forms the basis of holistic urban planning (or in Turner's phrase, the "process of ordering . . . from region to dwelling").

Next, the functions of research and communication of information were targeted to make the most of limited resources. Though unable to implement large-scale projects, the office could still conduct research "into the organization and problems of cooperative work under technical assistance programs"[27] as well as direct experiments with new construction technologies, ensuring that the results were widely disseminated. Further, by building up an indexed library of relevant materials, the office would eventually be able to develop itself into the key housing research center in Peru.

Finally, the design and execution of projects would be necessarily constrained, focused on "prototypes or patterns for the bulk of the work which will be done by local groups with no more than occasional advice and supervision." Following the example of industrial product development, Turner envisaged an ongoing cycle of research and refinement, using "experimental and tentative" projects to reach an optimum solution that was ready to be deployed immediately, but could always be improved upon in the next round of testing. The various elements of these experimental projects ("walls, roofs, windows and doors—plots, the relationship of house to house and of houses to open space and roads") would in themselves function as prototypes, in order to devise the most appropriate design for production by self-builders.[28] Turner advocated standardization of components aimed at maximum variation and adaptability, thereby avoiding boilerplate house types and urban plans. Standardization also offered a way to economize not just on the construction site but in the design office, where a small architectural team had little time to work on individualized solutions.

Meanwhile, in practical terms Turner's first months in Arequipa were limited to small trial programs: developing remodeling projects for urbanizaciones populares and experimenting with the fabrication of soil-cement blocks by and for self-builders. The first of these programs involved redesigning existing urban plans to improve circulation, separate pedestrian and vehicular traffic, and provide additional green space. In the case of the Miramar association in the nearby port town of Mollendo, the modifications also addressed the character of the environment, as Turner suggested planting trees to mitigate the "monotonous regularity" of the half-built, gridded blocks that created "an aesthetically unsatisfying and even depressing character which . . . [would] discourage and to some extent frustrate the family and community life which is the purpose of any group of dwellings."[29] Thus aesthetics, while a secondary consideration, were nonetheless seen to have real effects in psychological terms on the quality of life. This program resulted in design proposals for two of the three urbanizaciones populares that were willing to work with the office at this stage.

The second program erupted in controversy in September 1957, only a few weeks after it had begun. Residents were skeptical of the cost savings of the method and the soundness of the blocks produced, and they aired their concerns vociferously via local newspapers: the blocks were "very fragile and flimsy" and therefore their money had been wasted "in [this] burdensome test." They also complained about the high cost of the block-making machine acquired for the project, and noted that while Turner and his colleague Luis Felipe Calle had told them they could produce a thousand blocks per day, using a small amount of cement mixed with local soil, in fact they were only able to produce a hundred, rendering the process completely uneconomical. The fracas then escalated as the residents threatened Turner and Calle with legal action for allegedly defaming the associations and their leaders, demanding that they provide evidence to support the office's habitual claims about questionable "selling and division of lots, misappropriations of funds, and all the allegations that they have made." The matter did not proceed beyond these initial threats. While there may indeed have been genuine outrage over imputations of corruption and problems with the soil cement blocks—at the time Turner argued that the residents weren't following the correct procedure, although he later acknowledged that the time and expense required to perfect experimental technologies were particularly burdensome for low-income residents—these controversies were completely enmeshed in a broader struggle triggered by the imminent introduction of a new national technical assistance program.[30]

Under the new operating guidelines, the renamed OATA would be given a greater role in the process of qualifying settlements as "regularized" urbanizaciones populares in accordance with the revised urban planning regulations instituted in 1955. The residents resented this concentration of power, and were concerned that since they lacked the resources to meet the stricter requirements for legalization, they would see their settlements disqualified and dismantled. Furthermore, the smaller maximum lot size of 250 square meters now stipulated would greatly disrupt existing settlement layouts. Playing on old resentments toward Lima, they claimed that this was designed for the conditions of the capital but could not be applied in Arequipa, where residents preferred "viviendas tipo granja" (dwellings of a farmstead type). Finally, while they wanted effective technical assistance from the state, the stipulated payment for this assistance was beyond their means, so it should instead be provided free.[31] While residents' calls for the repeal of the new guidelines were unsuccessful, in fact OATA had little power to implement them, so they had limited impact on the situation on the ground.

Toward the end of 1957, as the new technical assistance program was scheduled to take effect, Turner produced a study for

OATA containing detailed proposals for two new programs: a rehabilitation project for an existing settlement and a scheme for a satellite city. Together they offered a comprehensive strategy to curtail unplanned growth via "the control and integration of the barriadas with the city itself": first, established settlements that were "too deeply rooted to be transplanted" would be transformed into "healthy and modern districts"; second, incipient "irrational" urban development would be prevented, and the demand for new housing "channeled and concentrated to form a logical and appropriate extension of the city."[32]

Turner's approach in the first program explicitly followed Geddes's "conservative surgery" model, using a detailed survey as the basis for targeted interventions that minimized disruption to the urban fabric.[33] Focusing on the Mariano Melgar urbanización popular, a study of current densities was used to identify zones that already showed nascent consolidation; new construction would be channeled into these areas in order to speed up the process of eventual integration with the established city and thereby make the installation of services economically viable. The gridded urban layout was judged to have too much space devoted to circulation and not enough open space; in the rehabilitation plan, alternate transverse streets would be turned into parks, this having the added benefit of reducing the amount of roadway requiring the expense of paving. Pairs of photographs were keyed to the redrawn plan to demonstrate to residents the impact of the proposed improvements, the stark streetscapes transformed into tree-lined pedestrian thoroughfares, the disorderly street frontage remade into rows of whitewashed houses with quasi-Mediterranean vaulted roofs (figs. 3.3–3.4).

The satellite city program represented a more aggressive effort to control the direction of urban development. According to a report coauthored by Turner and Calle in September 1957, this was the "only solution" to the problem of the urbanizaciones populares. It was apparently first conceived some years earlier by Neira along with Hernán Bedoya, head of the southern region of the national planning agency, the Oficina Nacional de Planeamiento y Urbanismo (ONPU). To begin with, one or two residential zones would be drawn up into lots and provided with basic infrastructure; the pobladores would be required to leave their illegally constructed neighborhoods and offered a site in the new satellite city. Once the settlement's "human nucleus" had been established, OATA would begin to implement a housing program using *ayuda mutua dirigi-*

Figures 3.3 (*top*) and 3.4 (*bottom*). John F. C. Turner for OATA, Rehabilitation proposal for Mariano Melgar, Arequipa, 1957. *Source*: "Las Urbanizaciones Populares de Arequipa," 1957, John F. C. Turner Archive.

da, with residents building their own houses in teams under technical guidance; in the meantime they were presumably expected to erect their own provisional dwellings. In his study Turner argued that real estate speculation rather than actual housing need was responsible for many land claims, so Arequipa's true housing deficit could be met using "one seventh of the area actually invaded and solicited." Further, many existing settlements were sparsely populated and poorly consolidated, making them socially fragmented and uneconomical for the provision of even basic services. By contrast, a satellite city would be planned as "a logical and appropriate extension" from the outset, growing in stages as demand required.[34]

The project was to be kept secret for as long as possible: "Our campaign against speculation depends on publicizing such a plan widely and suddenly."[35] A site was selected to the south of the city, large enough to accommodate thirty thousand people, meeting Arequipa's housing needs for the next twenty-five years. Detailed drawings produced around 1958 by Bedoya depict a bucolic setting with tree-lined avenues and a wide range of communal buildings (schools, civic and commercial centers) that in practice would have been difficult to finance (fig. 3.5). This version of the satellite city was a model of decentralized urban development, clearly inspired by Belaúnde's concept of the *unidad vecinal*: framed by a wide greenbelt of agricultural land, it would function as a self-contained unit with its own commercial and industrial zones, as well as community facilities, most importantly the schools, which formed the center of each of the city's subzones.

Turner's response to this project was highly ambivalent. Some of his statements welcomed the idea as a way to sidestep the difficulties of dealing with ill-planned settlements and their combative leaders, while elsewhere he was highly critical, regarding its "evasion" of the real situation as misguided: "The idea of a new town is infinitely more attractive to us as architects and administrators but I have an uneasy feeling that it is an authoritarian and dictatorial solution which might destroy the incipient new communities (and therefore the basis of democracy), divide the population and, as a result, fail. Deservedly. I'm shocked and disturbed by Luis Felipe [Calle]'s calm assumption that we can create communities as easily as we can build houses. This kind of thinking is almost enough to convince me of the unsoundness of the whole idea."[36] Turner's unease suggests a discomfort with an urbanism based on the modernist ideal of the tabula rasa rather than a Geddesian examination

Figure 3.5. Hernán Bedoya for ONPU and OATA, Proposal for a satellite city, Arequipa, 1957. *Source*: "Las Urbanizaciones Populares de Arequipa," 1957, John F. C. Turner Archive.

of existing conditions. Despite Turner's reservations, however, the project remained on the agenda until at least the early 1960s.

By the end of 1957, with few concrete projects in hand, Turner was pessimistic about the future of OATA, writing that relations with the residents appeared to be deteriorating. With insufficient resources to carry out major projects, OATA was only succeeding in creating obstacles and introducing red tape. Writing at the end of his time in Arequipa, Turner observed that while the redevelopment process had worked well in some cases, in others it was counterproductive: the Miramar settlement had endured three sets of revisions to their official plans over nine years, and in the meantime, the residents wasted the money they would have invested in their own houses by paying rent for substandard accommodation. All in all, their experience underscored "the logic and economy of ignoring the regulations." A massive earthquake on January 15, 1958, dramatically changed the dynamic. As Turner observed, "besides providing the necessary credit the disaster predisposed everyone concerned to accept new ideas and methods."[37] With 1,647 dwellings destroyed and 3,407 badly damaged, OATA became the center for relief work.

Reconstruction in the Emergency Zone

The reconstruction effort involved the (not always harmonious) collaboration of a number of agencies. OATA's contribution focused on two new projects, the Rural House Construction Program and the emergency settlement of Ciudad Mi Trabajo ("My Work"), as well as the development of a third project, the Miraflores Pilot Program in Aided Self-Help, which built upon the existing remodeling plan for Miraflores.

Rural House Construction Program

With earthquake damage extending to a number of villages in the area around Arequipa, a US government aid agency—Servicio Cooperativo Inter-Americano de Producción de Alimentos (SCIPA, or Inter-American Cooperative Food Production Service)—oversaw the construction or repair of 385 houses over six months. OATA provided technical assistance in the form of plans for a simple "house nucleus" that could be further developed over time. Patrick Crooke, Turner's colleague from the AA, who had recently been working in Colombia, was assigned as OATA's supervising architect, and with the assistance of a dozen postgraduate agriculture students, he managed a group of four general foremen and eleven masons who helped each of the families to build their own house.[38] When the region suffered a second major earthquake on January 13, 1960, the houses performed well.

There was some difficulty getting residents to accept the layout and dimensions of the house nucleus, as it differed substantially from local patterns, which were based simply on "one large room with light and temporary partitions—sometimes only a curtain to divide the living and sleeping areas, or even humans and animals." As Turner later reported, OATA was "naturally anxious to improve the living standards" and produced a design with a few small rooms surrounding a patio, dividing the space according to function in line with the tenets of modernist reform housing. Yet, Turner added, with more time for "anthropological studies" the architects would have better appreciated the significance of the customary house form: "the large room has an important cultural function—the wake—which cannot be carried out in the patio. . . . Finally, a compromise solution was reached by the placing of a large opening, closed with doors, between the two small rooms."[39] Crooke's success with this program encouraged Turner to employ the method again, this time with teams of builders working together to construct their houses, creating the first managed cooperative aided self-help program in Peru. Still, while the logistics of the method were beginning to crystallize, the disjunction between expert knowledge and local custom, between the values of the architect and of the self-builder over the form and use of the house, remained unresolved.

Ciudad Mi Trabajo

In Arequipa, the first priority in the immediate aftermath of the earthquake was to establish an "emergency transit camp" for those left homeless. On the day following the disaster, OATA and ONPU jointly selected a site that was adjacent to the area already set aside for the proposed satellite city, on the theory that the new emergency settlement could act as a "base camp" for its construction, providing temporary housing for residents as they worked on their future permanent homes. Construction began the same day. Shortly afterward, Turner noted approvingly that the project had been able "to take advantage of the unique opportunity of clearing a large section of the slums" in Arequipa. The greatest challenge in developing the new city would be to prevent the transitional settlement from becoming permanent. Accordingly, all constructions were made of provisional materials, and the site was selected with a view to discouraging permanence: "The value of the site as agricultural land . . . must always be greater than the loss involved in moving people and materials." No equity would be built up, no real investment made. Ciudad Mi Trabajo was to function as a dedicated camp for a series of transitory populations, providing a necessary service to those displaced, while at the same time operating as "a place of study and readaptation of the people, so that during their stay in it the betterment of their economic, moral, and cultural level, and of their family organization, is secured, to facilitate their transfer to new zones." In part this would be achieved through programs of economic development, "to rehabilitate such families (by forming small cooperative workshops for instance)." With its ready population and controlled environment, the camp could also function "as a field of experimentation, for studies of a social and medical character"; OATA, for example, could conduct studies into the community organization aspect of cooperative aided self-help projects.[40] The approach here strongly recalls Matos Mar's planned "improvement project" at Huarochirí.

Toward the end of 1958, OATA ran into funding problems and the project was left without direction. As one newspaper complained, "the *pobladores* of Ciudad Mi Trabajo are victims of administrative irresponsibility, they live in a nonexistent town, without electricity, water, police, and are forming a clandestine barriada" that had effectively been established by OATA itself. In October 1960, some time after Turner had left Arequipa, a former colleague reported to him on plans for remodeling the "city" now that it had indeed become a permanent settlement. Progress had stalled due to conflicts between two groups of pobladores: "the old ones say that the victims of the last earthquake [in January 1960] have invaded the zone that they currently occupy, which had been destined for the expansion of Ciudad Mi Trabajo."[41] Both groups eventually agreed that they would live in the remodeled settlement, but each insisted on being rehoused in their own separate area. A year later the residents had finally approved a definitive lot plan, after the architects resorted to subterfuge in order to proceed with a reduced lot size: a dummy plan with extremely small lots was created expressly for the purpose of being rejected in order to give the pobladores the illusion of having successfully negotiated an increase.

Around the same time, a representative of the newly instituted Peace Corps visited Arequipa to meet with residents of Ciudad Mi Trabajo (now numbering 350 families) and a "citizens' committee" that was dedicated to the realization of the project. The committee had secured a S/.550,000 donation for earthquake relief from the American Society in Lima (whose members were primarily US businesses operating in Peru), and another S/.200,000 from a local body, which they hoped would push the project forward, using aided self-help to build a total of two hundred houses.[42] The committee requested that the Peace Corps provide a variety of support personnel, and Peace Corps officials viewed the project favorably, seeing its combination of self-help and community development as a "model of alleviation" for the barriadas. They also framed it as a trial for a national aided self-help housing program that the Peruvian government hoped to implement with US assistance and funding from the Inter-American Development Bank (IDB), reporting: "Possibilities similar projects limitless once Government program under way." In January 1962 the Peace Corps confirmed that it would send eleven of its volunteers, ranging from "plumbers, electricians, carpenters . . . [to] nurses and social workers."[43] Four years after the initial earthquake, it appeared that the human and financial resources required to complete the project would finally be forthcoming.

Miraflores: Pilot Program in Aided Self-Help

The project in Miraflores proposed that residents should be moved from Arequipa's crowded inner-city *tugurios* (where the earthquake damage was the worst) to Miraflores, a legally recognized self-built district on the edge of the city selected because it already had a high level of consolidation. From the outset it was intended to employ managed cooperative aided self-help: Turner initially proposed this method in March 1958, believing that it would reduce costs by 30–50 percent, allowing for more units to be built with the available reconstruction funds. The program began with 150 families, but a number were forced to withdraw because they were unable to cover the costs. In the end, 141 houses were completed for the estimated cost of 100 contractor-built houses. The costs were shared by the participants and the sponsoring agencies. The Comisión de Ayuda a la Zona Afectada por el Sismo (CAZAS, Commission for Aid to the Zone Affected by the Earthquake), an agency set up to oversee the use of reconstruction funds donated by national and international organizations, was responsible for purchasing the materials, which it then provided to the participants via low-interest loans. The administrative expenses were shared by OATA and CAZAS, and thus were not included in Turner's estimate for the cost of the house.

In an evaluation report written for the UN—commissioned by Ernest Weissmann of the UN Centre for Housing, Building and Planning, who had visited Arequipa while in Peru for the Second Inter-American Technical Meeting on Housing and Planning—Turner outlined the process of developing the design. The first phase was focused on temporary housing, in order to achieve tangible results quickly. This "provisional minimum dwelling" featured two divisible rooms on either side of a patio space, built with reusable materials, and sited at the back of the lot, leaving the street-facing edge free for the later construction of the permanent dwelling (fig. 3.6). This scheme proved unpopular, as participants saw little value in expending their efforts on provisional construction. Instead they devised their own adaptations to make these structures permanent, fortifying the foundations and adding ce-

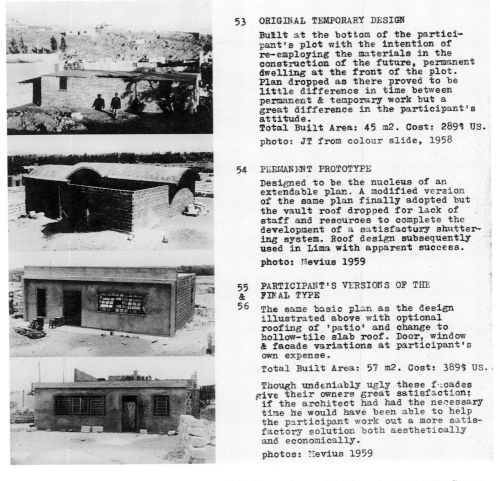

53   ORIGINAL TEMPORARY DESIGN

Built at the bottom of the participant's plot with the intention of
re-employing the materials in the
construction of the future, permanent
dwelling at the front of the plot.
Plan dropped as there proved to be
little difference in time between
permanent & temporary work but a
great difference in the participant's
attitude.
Total Built Area: 45 m2. Cost: 289$ US.

photo: JT from colour slide, 1958

54   PERMANENT PROTOTYPE

Designed to be the nucleus of an
extendable plan. A modified version
of the same plan finally adopted but
the vault roof dropped for lack of
staff and resources to complete the
development of a satisfactory shutter-
ing system. Roof design subsequently
used in Lima with apparent success.

photo: Mevius 1959

55   PARTICIPANT'S VERSIONS OF THE
&   FINAL TYPE
56
The same basic plan as the design
illustrated above with optional
roofing of 'patio' and change to
hollow-tile slab roof. Door, window
& facade variations at participant's
own expense.

Total Built Area: 57 m2. Cost: 389$ US.

Though undeniably ugly these facades
give their owners great satisfaction;
if the architect had had the necessary
time he would have been able to help
the participant work out a more satisfactory solution both aesthetically
and economically.

photos: Mevius 1959

Figure 3.6. The evolving design of a dwelling built by directed mutual aid, Arequipa, 1958–1959. *Source*: John F. C. Turner, "The Housing and Planning Problems of Arequipa, Peru," ca. 1959–1960, John F. C. Turner Archive.

ment to the composition of the mortar. Once OATA recognized this, it revised the program and produced a new design for a permanent dwelling. This design, developed by assistant architect Federico Mevius, focused on the need for flexibility within standardization (fig. 3.7), using a fixed basic module with variable internal parti- tions for the "nucleus" of the house so the space could be subdivided into two or three rooms according to each family's needs; the plan envisaged the addition of further modules as family circumstances changed. Since Miraflores was not connected to the city's water or

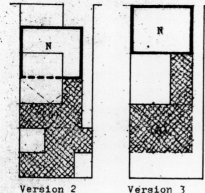

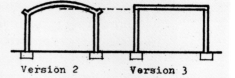

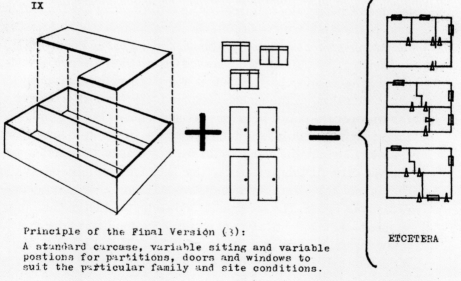

Figure 3.7. Federico Mevius for OATA, Design of a dwelling built by directed mutual aid, Arequipa, 1959. Above: Two versions of the dwelling, with the "nucleus" (outlined in black) and possible future extensions (shaded). Below: The "standard carcass" of the dwelling, with variable placement of doors, windows, and internal partitions. *Source*: John F. C. Turner, "The Housing and Planning Problems of Arequipa, Peru," ca. 1959–1960, John F. C. Turner Archive.

sewerage infrastructure, the nucleus did not include any plumbing fixtures; latrines and "a small hygienic water cistern" were proposed, but not completed in the initial construction phase.[44] The dimensions of the module were determined by the standard span of the structure's vaulted concrete roof. The vaulted roof (which had previously appeared in Turner's redrawn version of Mariano Melgar) was apparently favored by the architects on aesthetic as well as structural grounds, but from a practical point of view it would have greatly complicated horizontal extensions, which would have to conform to the dimensions of the set module, or the addition of a second story. For this reason, self-builders generally preferred an *azotea* (flat roof), which allowed rooms to be added in more variable configurations and could be used as additional work or living space. In any case, OATA experienced technical problems with the construction of the vaults, so the final design featured an azotea.

The lots at Miraflores were dispersed and irregular (a consequence of its development out of an earlier rural settlement), so despite the standardized design, an architect had to visit each participating family to advise on the best siting of the house nucleus on their lot (fig. 3.8). Turner observed that in their discussions with the architects, most participants proposed carrying out exactly the same alteration to the house, declaring "their future intention of roofing over the patio" in order to create a larger living room. Furthermore, "after duly admiring the model (made to demonstrate the way in which the house could grow by stages) the participants showed little further interest in the designed plan." He concluded that it was unlikely that residents would follow the recommended extensions either. The architects again adapted their design in response to the residents' evident preferences, modifying the plan "to allow for the roofing over of the 'patio'": while the original design reflected their adherence to the modernist dictum of maximizing light and air (here embodied by the culturally appropriate form of the patio), this revision showed a willingness to accommodate the residents' desire to maximize their usable living space.[45]

The participants were divided into six groups, each group having an average of four participants each workday, plus a bricklayer. Social assistants were responsible for interviewing prospective participants to select the best candidates, based on their cooperative attitude and demographic profile (being a stable nuclear family, and having sufficient income to cover costs associated with the

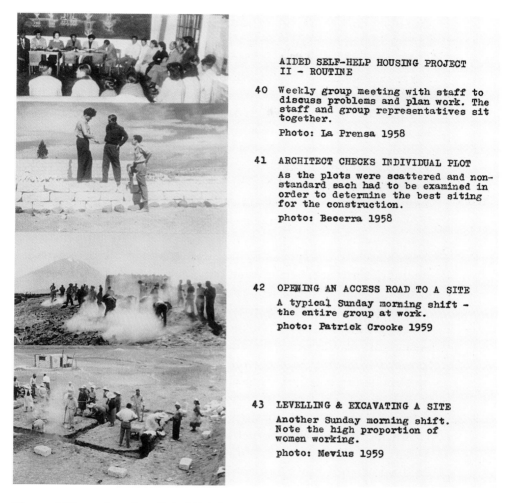

AIDED SELF-HELP HOUSING PROJECT
II - ROUTINE

40 Weekly group meeting with staff to
discuss problems and plan work. The
staff and group representatives sit
together.

Photo: La Prensa 1958

41 ARCHITECT CHECKS INDIVIDUAL PLOT

As the plots were scattered and non-
standard each had to be examined in
order to determine the best siting
for the construction.

photo: Becerra 1958

42 OPENING AN ACCESS ROAD TO A SITE

A typical Sunday morning shift -
the entire group at work.

photo: Patrick Crooke 1959

43 LEVELLING & EXCAVATING A SITE

Another Sunday morning shift.
Note the high proportion of
women working.

photo: Mevius 1959

Figure 3.8. The routines of an aided self-help housing project (detail). *Source*: John F. C. Turner, "The Housing and Planning Problems of Arequipa, Peru," ca. 1959–1960, John F. C. Turner Archive.

project); they also organized the work teams and managed their social dynamics throughout the project. The first houses took around twenty days to build; this later dropped to ten days (the "record" being six days). A high proportion of women provided manual labor, working both on scheduled shifts and extra days as volunteers, despite the initial objections of some men. Again it seems that the emergency situation worked in favor of an unconventional solution, as women's contributions were too valuable to exclude. Furthermore, Turner noted that "the enthusiasm and seriousness displayed by the women participants—who obviously enjoyed their day out"

led OATA staff to consider the option of basing future schemes on women's labor alone.[46]

In his evaluation report Turner noted that the organization of the project followed the guidelines set out in the manual produced by the Centro Interamericano de Vivienda (CINVA) based on Puerto Rican trial projects, which had been given to him by Neira, but it was "impossible to follow all the recommendations" because of differences between the two contexts. Still, in Arequipa as in Puerto Rico, the administrative requirements were substantial, generating a staff of some thirty-eight people, along with a series of forms to manage the program—keeping track of the hours worked by each participant, the progress of construction, and the price and whereabouts of construction materials. At the head of the team was an architect responsible for framing the overall program, producing designs, inspecting each individual lot, and attending weekly meetings with the project participants. In addition to educating participants on technical matters, these meetings served to promote good citizenship: as Turner stated, "for many it was their first experience of democracy."[47] As one concrete example, the rules governing the conduct of the cooperative work groups—the required work hours, attendance at meetings, fees to cover shared expenses, and the fines to be imposed on wayward members—were developed in consultation with the first group to participate in the program.

Turner's later writings, such as *Housing by People*, minimize the issue of conflicting interests within communities of self-builders: in line with an anarchist model of society, autonomous or locally self-governing groups are characterized as egalitarian and organically balanced, as the needs of one person are limited by the needs of another, producing equilibrium, stability, and efficiency. They do not appear to be vulnerable to manipulation or distortion by their more powerful members. Rather, throwing off governance by outside bodies leads to a kind of benign laissez-faire system where each receives his "fair share" thanks to the network's self-regulating mechanisms. In a marked contrast, the Arequipa report discusses at length the problems of internal political disputes, corruption, and speculation by settlement leaders. This critique—which Turner would subsequently attribute to his own "liberal authoritarianism"—was used to emphasize the "importance of government intervention" to advocate for the interests of ordinary residents against settlement leaders, and to demonstrate that the leadership of the architect-organizer was a necessary corrective

STAGES OF SQUATTER SETTLEMENT
GROWTH:

15   A - LAYOUTS

'Urbanización Pachacutec' 1948,
the first stage: boundary walls
of loose tufa blocks later to
be used in building the house —
already started in a few cases.
Note earlier layout which can
be seen in the foreground.

photos: JT from colour slides
        1957

16   B - SCATTERED DEVELOPMENT

'Urbanización Gráficos' 1949,
considerable individual building
activity with a small proportion
of finished, unfinished and
provisional dwellings occupied.
Enormous physical effort is put
into levelling terraces and
making roads in the particularly
broken terrain of this development. The city centre can be
seen in the distance. A ground
level view of this area is
shown in 10.

17   C - CONSOLIDATION

'Urbanización Santa Rosa' and
a part of 'san Martín' & 'Mariano Melgar'1950 & before 1948.
A still later stage of development, most plots have some construction under way and many are
occupied (about 20%). The blocks
in the foreground are of the
earlier SS as shown by the
established eucalyptus trees.

18   D - Legal INTEGRATION

'Urbanización La Libertad' 1932,
the oldest established SS, now
an officially recognised District which includes the original
rural village of Cerro Colorado
seen in the top left hand corner. Note that the original
plan with its civic and market
squares respected (the latter
originally intended as a foot-
ball pitch).

Figure 3.9. Stages of squatter settlement growth. *Source*: John F. C. Turner, "The Housing and Planning Problems of Arequipa, Peru," ca. 1959–1960, John F. C. Turner Archive.

to imbalances within the group; he is an engineer who recalibrates discordant dynamics to ensure the smooth functioning of the social organism.[48]

In his evaluation report, Turner wrote that in essence the squatter settlements were a "normal" pattern of urban development ("physically indistinguishable" from "typical incipient towns"), as he demonstrated via a series of images that traced their evolution and integration into the established city (fig. 3.9) He concluded that "it is only the exaggerated scale of the whole taken together which is really abnormal." However, the barriadas also revealed the state's failure to provide "appropriate popular housing"—a situation that had forced ordinary people to operate outside the law. On a more fundamental level, Turner viewed the barriadas as the symptom of an emerging, undefined social disorder, in a Geddesian interpretation predicated on the reciprocal actions of environment and organism: "If, as archaeologists, many historians and most architect-planners believe, the city is the shape of the social order (or its shell, as it were, which is both formed by and forms the social structure) then the future product of the spreading chaos is as dangerous as its present cause." Since the Peruvian government was evidently "unable to contain this movement by force"—due both to its scale and to clientelistic reliance on the urban poor for electoral support—the answer therefore lay in "the voluntary collaboration of the people and the state." In this context, the value of the Arequipa project was not in the houses built or even the people housed but "in the proof of the administration's ability to build the vital bridge between the people and the state across which the complementary forces of coordinated government planning and mobilized local action can freely pass."[49] From this decidedly unequal encounter, initiated from above and outside (despite Turner's anarchist leanings, it is the state that builds the bridge), Turner expressed the hope that an equitable collaboration would emerge—a view that took little account of the political realities facing marginalized low-income citizens in negotiating with their governments.

The report ended with a consideration of the role of international agencies such as the UN in resolving the problems facing cities like Arequipa. Turner concluded that along with providing advisors, their most significant contribution would be "the orientation and stabilization of government policy"—that is, using targeted financial aid to ensure administrative continuity for housing programs, allowing them to "be independent of established institutions and have the protection necessary for any scientific experiment." In this scenario, the role of the international agency was to establish proper laboratory conditions within the host country, insulating the trial project and its supervising foreign expert from the contaminations of shifting local politics. In fact, Turner himself had suffered the consequences of such shifts: despite the successes of the pilot project, OATA lost most of its staff in a political shakeup in late 1958, and Turner himself was forced to leave. According to the official account, OATA was closed to avoid duplication of services. According to Turner, inopportune comments by Weissmann in support of Turner's work at OATA had created a backlash within the government and the housing bureaucracy, which resulted in Turner's firing; Weissmann then offered him the opportunity to write the Arequipa report for the UN both as recompense and as a vote of confidence in the aided self-help methodology. Weissmann also wrote a memorandum to President Manuel Prado (1956–1962) in an effort to convince him of the need to continue the work of OATA, arguing that the office should be afforded the opportunity "to prepare the personnel necessary to extend such programs to the entire country."[50]

Following Turner's departure, Mevius took over the job of directing the programs in part from October 1958, and in full from January 1959; at this time OATA itself was closed down, and its programs (along with Mevius) were transferred to CAZAS. The work shut down entirely at the end of 1959 when CAZAS used up the last of its funds. Writing in mid-1959, with the closure of the office all but confirmed, Mevius reported that there was growing interest from barriada associations in its aided self-help programs, with calls for another earthquake reconstruction agency to take up OATA's initiatives. Subsequently, some ten years after the 1958 earthquake, this agency reported that it had built 1,319 houses throughout twenty different barriadas using the self-help system, hailing this as its most successful program due to "its social importance, its low cost, and the revitalization of a thousand-year-old Peruvian tradition of working together."[51] In this sense OATA's program did have an ongoing legacy, yet with some five thousand houses badly damaged or destroyed in the earthquake—not to mention the thirty thousand families that AUPA had claimed as members—many families were left without adequate housing.

Systematizing Self-Help

Among housing experts in Peru the work of OATA was soon recognized as groundbreaking, representing "the most important experiment in the country, not just in terms of size but also the method used."[52] Immediately after leaving Arequipa, Turner worked on developing a self-help housing project for quite a different context: the US-owned W. R. Grace and Company sugar-processing factory in Paramonga in northern Peru, whose workers were housed in an overcrowded company town (fig. 3.10). This provided the opportunity for refining techniques used in Arequipa, now making greater use of anthropological data, with an extensive social survey conducted by anthropologist Eduardo Soler (previously involved with Matos Mar's Huarochirí project), complemented by a physical survey of sample housing layouts by Turner, using photographs and drawings.

Similar to the Huarochirí project, this undertaking was framed as a "community development pilot project": the goal was to "promote the community's economic self-sufficiency and so reduce the participants' dependence on the Company." This alluded to the fact that many workers lived in company housing rather than their own homes, and also to the presence of unemployed members of the workers' extended families, perceived as burdensome hangers-on who had followed a relative to the town but were unable to find work in its limited economy. The project aimed to develop new employment opportunities within the community, while also "prepar[ing] the participants for their adjustment to new conditions"—apparently a reference both to the new economic conditions of an imposed self-sufficiency and to the new cultural conditions of urbanity for recent rural migrants. With these goals in mind, the aided self-help methodology promised not only to provide lower-cost housing but also to support the project's larger aims of fostering "the participant's sense of responsibility."[53]

The preparatory report by Soler and Turner noted that Paramonga's residents were a mix of *paisanos* (peasants), *criollos* (urban dwellers), and *acriollados* (those in the process of becoming acculturated to urban life), with each group having distinctive domestic patterns. Turner had acknowledged that in Arequipa "there was insufficient knowledge of family living patterns and requirements when the prototype was designed." In Paramonga, this insight led to in-depth research into sociocultural differences in the use of

Figure 3.10. Worker housing at W. R. Grace and Company, with a collective standpipe (*foreground*) and latrine (*background right*), Paramonga, ca. 1960. *Source*: John F. C. Turner Archive.

the house. Turner's drawings, cataloguing furniture and belongings, conveyed detailed information about social spaces, sleeping arrangements, and food storage and preparation. This research revealed that the paisano dwelling "is more open and less differentiated" in terms of function, while the criollo dwelling will tend to "have more but smaller rooms" with clearly defined usages; to this end, the criollo household "demands a fully enclosed 'sala' or parlor [for receiving guests] where the family's status will be shown by their furniture, radio, etc. . . . even if they only have two or three rooms for a large family one will be sacrificed to make the parlor."[54] These patterns can be seen in two of the households Turner documented, both of which lived in barrackslike company housing with windowless rooms, the only light and air coming from roof vents and a semiroofed rear patio, which in most cases residents enclosed with lightweight roofing materials, such as *esteras*. The two-room dwelling of Gregorio Pomajulca (fig. 3.11), defined as acriollado, housed eight family members, sharing one bedroom (with four cots) and a kitchen-dining room (with pens for guinea pigs and chickens). The three-room dwelling of Bartolomé Rodríguez (fig. 3.12), defined as criollo, housed seven family members, again

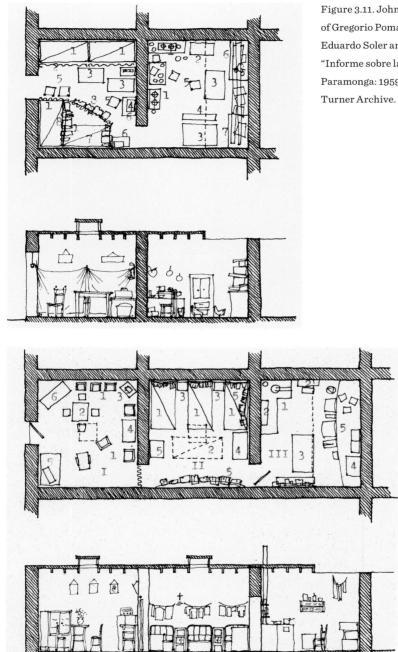

Figure 3.11. John F. C. Turner, House of Gregorio Pomajulca (detail). *Source*: Eduardo Soler and John F. C. Turner, "Informe sobre la vivienda urbana en Paramonga: 1959–1960," John F. C. Turner Archive.

Figure 3.12. John F. C. Turner, House of Bartolomé Rodríguez (detail). *Source*: Eduardo Soler and John F. C. Turner, "Informe sobre la vivienda urbana en Paramonga: 1959–1960," John F. C. Turner Archive.

sharing one bedroom (with three cots and a mattress), while their sala was reserved for several items of furniture, including a vitrine, a recliner, a corner table with a radio, and pictures on the wall. The only animal in this household was a cat.

On the basis of this survey, Turner developed two distinctive plans for Paramonga, one for paisanos and one for criollos, working in collaboration with architect Diego Robles. Robles, who was Afro-Peruvian and from a modest economic background within a profession that was still dominated by the European-descended elite, had studied painting and drawing at the Escuela Nacional de Bellas Artes, before gravitating toward architecture as a bridge between his artistic interests and "issues of low-income housing, of the city that is often not seen as the city." Robles had himself grown up in a *barrio popular* in Lima, and while studying architecture at the Escuela Nacional de Ingenieros in the late 1950s, he observed land invasions taking place nearby, and joined other students in volunteering to assist the pobladores by drawing up basic urban plans. Robles met Turner after he gave a talk at the architecture school, and they first worked together on a project for a community-built school, before collaborating at Paramonga.[55]

Both plans for Paramonga followed the growing house model and shared the same basic footprint and framework, despite their different layouts (figs. 3.13–3.14). The primary difference between the two was that the paisano dwelling featured a grouping of rooms (including the two bedrooms) at the front of the lot, leaving space at the back to accommodate a *huerta* (kitchen garden) and a *corral* (livestock enclosure), while in the criollo dwelling the rooms were grouped around a central patio, with the bedrooms separated from the social spaces of the house, sited on the far side of the patio. The spaces of the paisano dwelling were designed to be much more open: entry was via an *alar* (verandah) with access on two sides, leading directly into the kitchen-living room, a large space running the width of the house. By contrast, in the criollo dwelling, entry was via an enclosed sala, which connected to the family living room and the patio but was clearly separated from the service space of the kitchen. Finally, while the criollo dwelling featured a patio as additional social space and a decorative front garden (which could later be transformed into additional rooms), the paisano dwelling utilized all the open areas as productive spaces, whether for gardening or raising animals. The design's focus on flexibility within standardization reflected the perceived needs of a population that was in transition:

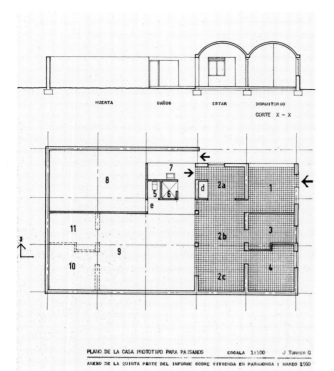

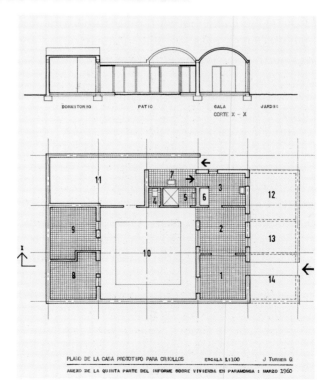

Figures 3.13 (*left*) and 3.14 (*below*). John F. C. Turner and Diego Robles, Plans of the prototype houses for *paisanos* (*left*) and *criollos* (*below*), Paramonga, 1960. Source: Eduardo Soler and John F. C. Turner, "Informe sobre la vivienda urbana en Paramonga: 1959–1960," John F. C. Turner Archive.

"It is important that the peasant type should be easily convertible into the mestizo [or *criollo*] type, also that certain 'creole' features can be included in the basic peasant type and vice versa."[56] For example, in the paisano dwelling, part of the huerta in the backyard area could be converted into two bedrooms framing a small patio, following the lead of the criollo dwelling. Conversely, the criollo dwelling had a small corral in the back corner of the lot, for those households that continued this rural tradition. This growing house could be transformed not only as the household increased but also to reflect its shifting cultural identity as it urbanized over time.

Turner and Soler submitted their report to Grace in 1960, and the company decided to proceed with a trial project of sixty self-built houses. In all, the program was to include six hundred self-built and four hundred contractor-built houses. A massive publicity campaign was mounted to convince the workers—who would have to take out loans in addition to building their own houses—to participate in the aided self-help program: posters, radio coverage, a promotional newspaper, a print run of five thousand leaflets, informational flyers inserted into the worker's weekly pay packets, and a film on construction through mutual aid that screened on four occasions, attracting around seven hundred people each time. Scale models with movable pieces were employed to help prospective participants visualize the possibilities of the growing house (fig. 3.15), followed later by full-scale demonstration houses. This was not an emergency situation as in Arequipa—the workers would have to be persuaded that the benefits of the program warranted their efforts and their resources.

The first phase went ahead with a group of fifteen families, starting construction in March 1961 under Turner's supervision. However, from July 1961 he was only able to continue as a part-time advisor, since he had taken on a position with a new housing agency, the Instituto de la Vivienda (INVI, or Housing Institute), which required him to work in Lima. In December 1961, Turner left for Lima permanently, and was replaced in Paramonga by another architect. In October 1961 an audit of the project raised concerns about lax accounting practices, especially the lack of control over cash disbursements, noting that supervision from Turner had been wanting due to his frequent travel. This was followed a year later by a highly critical report, which had been commissioned in order to investigate the misappropriation of funds by the project's bookkeeper, but in the process also uncovered evidence of massive

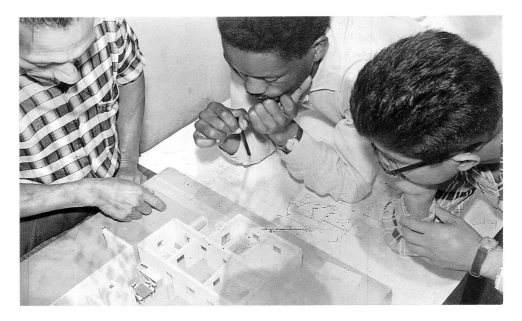

Figure 3.15. Architect Diego Robles (*center*) explaining the model of a self-build "growing" house to prospective residents, Paramonga, ca. 1960. *Source*: John F. C. Turner Archive.

cost overruns on the housing itself. The first fifteen houses had been completed in July 1962 at 500 percent of the estimated budget. The basic house nucleus had been projected to cost the resident S/.20,000; in fact, they cost S/.100,000 each, paid for by the Grace Company, which then sold them on to workers for S/.35,000.[57]

As a result, the self-help approach was abandoned, and in mid-1962 Grace and the unions representing the Paramonga workers decided to complete the remaining forty-five houses of the pilot project using conventional construction. They requested bids from two US-based real estate development companies that were beginning to establish themselves in the low-cost housing market in Peru: Nelson Rockefeller's International Basic Economy Corporation and the Wichita-based Hogares Peruanos. However, after union elections, the new leadership rejected the project "of privately owned homes and . . . demanded that Grace build houses and give them to the workers as has been traditionally done."[58] Although it is difficult to confirm the reasons for the cost overruns—the report speculated that a major factor was "a marked lack of on the spot planning and leadership before and during the executing of this project"—it seems quite possible that there was a general lack of enthusiasm for the entire project, which was in essence an effort to shift responsibility for housing from the company to the workers. In a 1975 interview, Turner frankly acknowledged that Paramonga "turn[ed] into a disastrous attempt to transfer the relatively successful Arequipa experience to a totally different and, as it turned out, wholly unsuitable context."[59] While Grace may have assumed that the security of owning a home would naturally appeal to its workers, the scale and intensity of the marketing campaign suggests that there was considerable resistance to the idea of purchasing housing when it was customarily provided by the employer, especially in the case of migrant workers who lived only temporarily in Paramonga, a small company town that offered few other economic opportunities. Grace put the entire project on hold in December 1962 following riots directed against a US-owned mining company in La Oroyo, concerned that the violence would spread to Paramonga. The project appears to have stalled permanently shortly afterward.

Back in Lima, from late 1961 Turner was engaged in preparations for the implementation of a nationwide, two-year program of aided self-help projects planned for 1962–1963. Turner was part of the team that had presented this program to the IDB for funding, and would now be responsible for overseeing it through his new position at INVI. However, midway through this program, in August 1963, Turner left official employment at the housing agency—now reorganized as the Junta Nacional de la Vivienda (JNV, or National Housing Board)—after his status as a foreign national employed by the Peruvian civil service was called into question, causing a minor political stir. Nonetheless he continued to work for the JNV as an advisor, now contracted through the British Government's overseas aid office, the Department of Technical Cooperation. His work no longer dealt with designing on-the-ground projects, but developing theoretical proposals. These frequently drew upon Turner's detailed observations of the resident-directed processes of founding and consolidating barriadas.

Turner continued to explore his interest in standardization, modularity, and prototypes, which gives some insight into his evolving view of the role of the architect in the production of self-help housing. In 1963 Turner developed a proposal for "a system of design" for low-cost housing for the JNV, arguing that because poor design and construction were wasting much of the resources invested in housing, it was "essential to establish and make general a modern tradition that responds to the actual needs and to those of the next generations."[60] As in the "Confidential Report" of 1957, this "modern tradition" would make use of standardization via the development of a modular system made up of a small number of components; this would allow a great deal of flexibility and variety in the assembly of the individual house. In a second proposal for the JNV in 1965, Turner extended the question of standards and prototypes to consider three scales: the individual dwelling, the group of dwellings (or the street), and the locality. Using Christopher Alexander and Serge Chermayeff's *Community and Privacy* (1963) as a point of reference, Turner's proposal emphasized the importance of balancing public-private space at each level, since the dearth of public space was a particular problem in squatter settlements. As in the 1963 paper, the rationale for the "systematization of designs" was to facilitate the development of improved prototypes, since "neither the popular traditions nor the [housing] agencies' projects provide what is required": self-builders simply imitated the poor housing models they had absorbed from their own experience (whether substandard rural shelters or tugurios), while none of the many designs developed by government architects had yet managed to produce a solution worthy of widespread reproduction. The problems resulting from this failure resonated on a number of levels: "The value of a viable tradition in the design of the environment is not, of course, a merely aesthetic value though the results of such a tradition will, almost certainly, be aesthetically satisfactory. The present lack of a tradition—its substitution by the habitual repetition of inappropriate forms—is extremely damaging to personal, social, and economic health and it produces ugly shapes."[61]

This concern with the aesthetic dimension is perhaps unexpected, and it is by no means at the core of Turner's later writings on self-help housing; this persistence of a concern with the architectural object could be understood as an intermediary step in the shift from conventional architectural production to conceiving "housing as a verb" (as Turner would write in 1972). Tellingly, the first article in the issue of *Architectural Design* that Turner edited, preceding the introduction, presented the pristine forms of a "Village Artisan's Self-Built House" that evoked the figures of the bidonville and the vernacular Mediterranean village that had by now been established as objects of modernist admiration (fig. 3.16). The house, built by Pedro Vizcarra near Arequipa, demonstrated "how far, given the opportunity, one man's skill and resource will

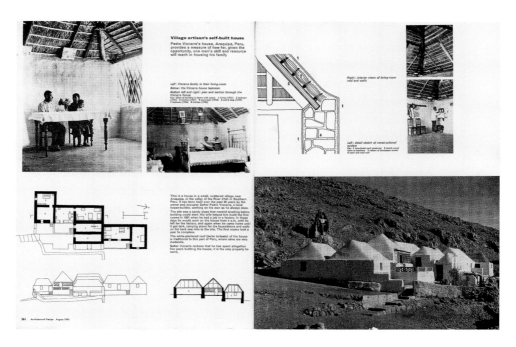

Figure 3.16. House of Pedro Vizcarra, Arequipa. *Source*: Patrick Crooke, "Village Artisan's Self-Built House," *Architectural Design* 33, no. 8 (Aug. 1963), John F. C. Turner Archive.

reach in housing his family."[62] Its accomplishment was testament to Turner's sense of an aesthetics of self-building that was also an ethics—a certain integrity inherent to self-build construction, arising from the pure potential of what people could achieve on their own, a stance that also reflected his anarcho-Geddesian understanding of the organic order of things in their natural state.

This house had earlier been featured in a 1958 article by Eduardo Neira in *El Arquitecto Peruano*. According to Neira, Vizcarra's house—with its "plastic and pure forms"—was not an isolated example. Channeling Le Corbusier's *Vers une architecture*, Neira argued that "it is only the best, more than the prototype, it is the archetype, a product of selection, as the Parthenon is nothing but the archetype of the Greek temple of the Age of Pericles." A 1957 article by Neira on aided self-help housing provides some insight into the nature and significance of this "archetype": while the main focus is on the economic benefits of the self-help methodology, in the final section—given the Corbusian subtitle "Toward a New Social Architecture"—Neira envisages the "interminable monotony" of social housing projects being replaced by a new vernacular architecture, where the architect as technical assistant cultivates both a revival and an updating of native creativity. Here emerges "a way to overcome the current stagnation, to revive using modern terms the plastic and functional qualities of the cheerful little towns of the past where the popular spirit created pleasant and fitting environments for a simple and direct life."[63] A fusion of the traditional and the modern, and a return to the authentically Peruvian, appear within reach even as the forces of modernization intensify.

Shortly after arriving in Arequipa, Turner observed with concern that in the barriadas, money and labor "are being misspent by the poorest people to create unhealthy and disorganized environments." He argued that it was essential to convince residents that their efforts at "providing themselves with some sort of home of their own is against their own interests and to convince them to wait for alternatives to be put forward by us." On leaving Arequipa, his viewpoint had changed little: "The only possible way of ordering city development is through the harnessing of the blind but powerful forces of spontaneous popular urban expansion to planned development programs."[64] A decade later, in an influential paper written for the UN, "Uncontrolled Urban Settlement: Problems and Policies" (first presented 1966, published 1968), his position had shifted to some degree. On the one hand, there was still a role for the architect's professional training and expertise, particularly in addressing the wastefulness of poorly designed and constructed housing, and poorly conceived and sited urban plans, which suffered from excessive density and "built-in blight." On the other hand, Turner now called for governments to respond to "the real needs and resources of the governed" by focusing on providing elements that were beyond the scope of individual citizens—large-scale infrastructure, legislative guidelines, and technical assistance: "The crucial difference between 'working with' and 'working for' must be understood by anyone who wishes to 'mobilize the resources of the common people.' The paternalist concept of the State as a provider has to give way to the concept of the State as the servant—providing tools."[65] In this formulation, the state (and the architect) no longer need to exercise control over ordering urban development by "harnessing blind but powerful forces"; rather, their role was to mitigate the "problems of uncontrol" by complementing and facilitating the self-generated initiative of ordinary citizens—"working with" rather than "working for" people.

Looking back on his work in Peru, Turner wrote that the experience of trying to manage aided self-help programs had soon convinced him that the extensive "administrative superstructure" they required was too expensive and inefficient. Rather than attempting "to find and train the army of dedicated field workers and local program administrators"[66] that such schemes required, he now advocated simply providing construction funds to individual house-builders, with only basic oversight to ensure that dwellings were built to acceptable standards. Individuals and locally controlled groups could more effectively direct their own development without the encumbrance of outside professionals: in the terminology of his later writings, the forces of autonomous (self-determined) building did not need harnessing by heteronomous (other-determined) organizations in order to produce decent housing.

After considering but then declining an offer to join Constantinos A. Doxiadis at the Athens Centre of Ekistics, Turner left Peru in September 1965 to take up a fellowship at the Harvard-MIT Joint Center on Urban Studies.[67] His work as an advisor to the JNV had already prepared the way for this segue into the role of researcher, writer, and teacher. As Turner continued to refine his ideas on user control in housing, he diverged progressively further from mainstream self-help projects with their emphasis on sites-and-services provision and leveraging resident labor to lower costs. For Turner, the key point was, rather, to facilitate the resident's control "of the design, construction, and management of his own home."[68] This was not an economic argument, but a political—or rather, ethical—vision of how groups of people could work together to house themselves and develop their own communities. In this sense, Turner's later writings on "housing by people"—on "autonomous" modes of building, under local control—strongly evoke the "work teams" envisaged in *Plan* 6 (1949). "Uncontrolled Urban Settlement" marks the end point of Turner's gradual move away from conventional architectural practice: from the architect as "artist-technician" advocated in *Plan* 6 to the architect as technician-administrator of managed aided self-help, and finally to the architect as advocate-facilitator of unaided self-help or "autonomous" building. Yet the progressiveness of Turner's position was still limited by the positioning of authority and expertise with the professional; it is only in his writings of the 1970s that a full appreciation of the contribution of local knowledge and the importance of dweller control becomes apparent.

If Turner had now answered his own query as to the architect's "functions and responsibilities" in aided self-help, the position of the self-builder remained in flux—at once active participant and unequal partner, client, beneficiary, and unremunerated laborer. Meanwhile, the relationship between the two figures would continue to shift between the collaborative and the conflictual.

4

MEDIATING INFORMALITY, 1961–1963

I n mid-1957, following the recommendation of the Comisión para la Reforma Agraria y la Vivienda (CRAV), a national system of technical assistance offices was created, with the intention of providing *barriada* residents with the necessary guidance to regularize and rehabilitate their settlements, and to improve the condition of their housing. Soon after, with the support of the Oficina de Asistencia Técnica de Arequipa (OATA), organized groups of self-builders completed 141 dwellings in a trial reconstruction project, demonstrating the viability of the aided self-help methodology within constrained budgets. By late 1959 the agency responsible for administering the technical assistance offices, the Fondo Nacional de Salud y Bienestar Social (FNSBS), had two additional projects under way—Andrés Avelino Cáceres in Lima and 21 de Abril in Chimbote—and was planning similar projects elsewhere in Lima and in five additional cities. Yet the number and size of barriadas continued to increase, particularly in Lima, where the high concentration of barriadas along the Río Rímac in the city center intensified and the areas of Comas (to the north) and Surco (to the south) were now being urbanized by invasion (plate 1). It was evident that the technical assistance offices would not in themselves be sufficient to control the insurgent settlements.

Thus, in February 1961, more than three years after CRAV had delivered its report, and following prolonged debate, the government enacted the most innovative and far-reaching initiative to emerge from its recommendations: Law no. 13517, for the "Remodeling, *Saneamiento* [sanitation, regulation, or regularization], and Legalization of *barrios marginales*" (hereafter Law 13517). The reforms to urban planning regulations that had been introduced in 1955 following the Ciudad de Dios invasion had included some important measures—notably, the codification of a new category of urban settlement, the *urbanización de tipo popular*, which allowed for urban services to be built to a lesser standard in low-income neighborhoods. Law 13517 advanced a more comprehensive legislative framework to tackle unregulated urbanization, outlining a process for upgrading and eventually legalizing existing squatter settlements, as well as instituting measures to discourage the formation of new ones, in order to regain control over future urban growth. The modernist imperative to shape urban space—epitomized in earlier years by the Plan Piloto for Lima and Fernando Belaúnde Terry's *unidad vecinal* projects—was now expressed through alternative strategies, as the new law began to outline a radically different approach to understanding and directing the evolution of the self-built city. While conventional urban planning techniques had failed, Law 13517 reflected a confidence that once they were recalibrated in line with this revised regulatory framework, planning professionals could again deliver rational and effective solutions to manage urban growth. This chapter begins with an overview of FNSBS technical assistance initiatives prior to Law 13517, then examines the principles and the underlying logic of the new law, and assesses how efforts to implement it were developed and how they fared in practice.

Trials in Technical Assistance

For the first year following the creation of the technical assistance offices, only three were in operation—in Lima, Chimbote, and Arequipa, the latter functioning with a considerable degree of autonomy. In mid-1958 the nascent program was incorporated into the FNSBS, the social welfare agency, and reorganized as the División de Asistencia Técnica a la Vivienda (DATV, Division of Technical Assistance to Housing). The DATV began to build a new administrative infrastructure, defining four subdepartments to support what it termed the technical assistance methodology: Planning, Legal, Development of the Family and Community Economy, and Social Technical Assistance. The last two speak to the prevalence of development theory within the technical assistance worldview. For example, initiatives to promote the economic development of participant communities included proposals for occupational training or stimulating craft production to boost family incomes, while "social" technical assistance encompassed preparatory community liaison and mobilization throughout the project, with the larger goal of "awakening, maintaining, and developing the confidence of the *pobladores* in their own possibilities, . . . progressively giving them the moral and material responsibility for community improvement projects, bearing in mind their future self-sufficiency." The planning department framed its mission in similar terms, envisaging not only a solution to the housing problem but also a path toward far-reaching development, all while drawing upon indigenous practices of mutual aid: "the traditional form of work in Peru, *Ayne* [or *ayni*, the Quechua term for reciprocity or mutualism] . . . is nothing other than the communal effort of human groups." By refining *ayni* via technical assistance, the DATV hoped to amplify the deeper effects of this communal work, "affording individuals better opportunities for their personal development, creating a civic conscience, at the same time as preparing them to participate in larger projects of community benefit."[1]

More concretely, in addition to overseeing the work of OATA at a remove, the DATV began to develop its own trial aided self-help housing projects. In November 1958 the DATV reported that it was soon to begin construction on Urbanización Andrés Avelino Cáceres, a neighborhood of forty houses in Lima, and that preparatory work for a much larger project, 21 de Abril in Chimbote, was already under way. The *técnicos* needed to direct the latter program were currently "training in Arequipa" with OATA, and further down the line they were to be supplemented by others who would gain on-the-ground experience by implementing Andrés Avelino Cáceres. However, following the Arequipa training trip of two DATV personnel, John F. C. Turner wrote to César Solis, the head of the DATV planning department, expressing his concern that the three weeks they had spent there were insufficient to gain adequate experience in aided self-help; rather, at least three months were needed. Suggesting that the lack of adequately trained personnel would compromise the effectiveness of aided self-help programs, Turner employed an organic, Geddesian metaphor to underscore the need to carefully nurture their development: "It is impossible to make a plant grow more quickly than its environment allows."[2]

Despite Turner's reservations, the DATV pressed ahead with its plans, signing a "technical assistance contract" with prospective residents of Andrés Avelino Cáceres in mid-1959. The participants seem to have been ideally suited for a trial project: they were all employees of the Cemento Portland factory, earning modest but regular incomes, and they had already worked together to pool their savings through a self-organized housing association that would help to coordinate the project. The FNSBS provided access to loans as well as a site in southern Lima, adjacent to Ciudad de Dios and near the Cemento Portland factory. The contract stipulated that residents were to pay for this land, as well as the construction of streets and sidewalks, water and sewerage infrastructure, building materials, and administrative expenses. For its part, since this was a trial project, the DATV would cover the cost of an engineer, social assistant, and other key staff. *La Prensa* reported that representatives of each household were organized into four work teams; as a supplementary workforce, the project's social assistant prepared a plan to employ the participants' children during the school holidays.[3] Construction was completed within eighteen months.

The DATV's design for the basic house featured two bedrooms, a living-dining room, kitchen, bathroom, and *cerco* for a total roofed area of 44 square meters on a 10-by-20-meter lot; the plan envisaged the possible addition of two more bedrooms and a separate dining room, while still leaving generous space for a patio and a garden (figs. 4.1–4.2). The design experimented with Catalan vaults for the roofing, employed for their low cost and antiseismic qualities. These set the basic module for the design: a trio of 3-meter-span vaults ran across the width of the lot, with the remaining space providing a passageway leading to the back patio. Two vaulted sections at the front of the lot, slightly recessed from the street, housed the bedrooms and living space, while the third section housing the kitchen was set some meters further back; this created a small entry courtyard, with separate doorways to the formal and functional spaces of the house (respectively, the living room and the kitchen). As noted in the earlier discussion of OATA's original model house, the use of a vaulted roof would virtually preclude vertical additions, and would greatly constrain any horizontal extensions, since

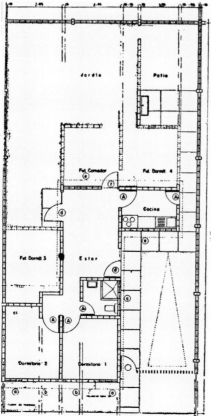

Figure 4.1 (*above*). FNSBS, Urbanización Andrés Avelino Cáceres, Lima, 1959–1960. Two houses built with aided self-help, sharing a party wall. In order to differentiate their home from that of the neighbors, the household on the right has personalized the design by erecting a wall to demarcate the front yard, adding decorative grilles under the vaulting, and replacing the original windows. *Source*: John F. C. Turner Archive.

Figure 4.2 (*left*). FNSBS, Urbanización Andrés Avelino Cáceres, Lima, 1959–1960. A trio of 3-meter-span Catalan vaults sets the basic module. The two vaulted sections at the front house the bedrooms and living space, while the third section housing the kitchen is set some meters further back, creating a small entry courtyard. *Source*: *La Prensa*, December 31, 1959.

they would need to accommodate the set module, as well as the specialized (if low-technology) vault construction technique, which was not common in Lima and would therefore require supervision to be carried out successfully. In fact, the technical assistance contract insisted that the DATV would oversee all future modifications, stipulating that any residents who wanted to make additions were to organize themselves into groups of four "who seek the same extension" and sign an additional contract for this work with the DATV. It added a warning that "the breach of this clause could cause the revocation of the [original] contract" with the errant resident, effectively ending their participation in the program and with it their chance to own the house.[4]

In tandem with this small-scale trial project, work had begun on 21 de Abril in Chimbote. A few months after CRAV had released its findings, Solis wrote a memorandum on the housing situation in Chimbote; echoing one of CRAV's principle themes, he observed that the city's "disordered and uncontrollable" growth was in large part due to the lack of a coordinated approach to regional development to effectively channel migratory flows. In the absence of such plans, migrants had flooded Chimbote looking for work, far outstripping growth projections. The result was an estimated housing deficit of 8,000 dwellings in a city with a population of 43,000. Solis observed that constructing conventional housing on this scale was beyond the means of the government and would in any case likely encourage further migration to Chimbote, thus intensifying the problem. Accordingly, he proposed that the DATV oversee the "construction of the dwellings by their own residents, the head of the family and family members, a principle . . . frequently used by our ancestors (the *ayni*) as well as currently by many sectors [of society] in a precarious economic condition." The proposal was to establish a neighborhood of 1,416 lots, accommodating up to 8,400 residents. Solis noted that the "appropriate selection of a community to carry out a program of *ayuda mutua* is fundamental"; in Chimbote this prerequisite was somewhat compromised because "it has been necessary to accept as a fact working with the [barriada] communities of El Zanjón and El Acero, since continuous fires (Acero) [and] floods (Zanjón) oblige immediate attention" to their needs. Fortunately, initial outreach to these residents suggested some receptiveness to the aided self-help approach.[5]

On April 21, 1958, President Manuel Prado laid the first stone, giving the new neighborhood its name. Participants were to pay for the installation of services and all materials, but the land, on the site of the old airport, was donated by the state. By October 1960 most of the services (water, sewerage, paving) were completed and ninety-eight houses were underway. By June 1961 steady progress had been made, with 300 houses finished and another 300 under construction; it was now estimated that the project would be finished in six years. The contract that residents had signed with the FNSBS in 1958 on being assigned their lots seemed to anticipate this protracted construction schedule, stating that while waiting for their aided self-help houses to be completed, participants could erect temporary dwellings at the rear of their lots, provided that they leave ten meters free for the permanent dwelling.[6]

In these early projects, it seems that the FNSBS was trying to find its way in aided self-help housing, seizing opportunities when they arose and tailoring its response accordingly. At Andrés Avelino Cáceres, a boutique project initiated by self-motivated and socially cohesive participants, the FNSBS saw an opportunity to foreground experimentation in design and construction. By contrast, 21 de Abril was a mass-scale project, accommodating vulnerable barriada residents, many of whom had lost their possessions to fire or flood. Here, the emphasis was on straightforward plans and construction methods in order to test the wider applicability of aided self-help techniques.

Following these ad hoc efforts, in October 1960 the FNSBS presented a more proactive plan of work, outlining a proposal for a national program of aided self-help housing for barriada residents, covering six cities: Lima, Ilo, Iquitos, Piura, Tacna, and Trujillo. These had been selected as priority locations based on a combination of three factors: the physical state of existing housing, likely participants' economic capacity, and "the intensity of the problem, reflected in social unrest" (the latter being ranked on a scale from "normal" to "highly subversive"). The size of the program was determined by an FNSBS estimate of its capacity to produce aided self-help housing: based on the experience of the trial projects, it believed it could build a total of 3,180 houses over three to six years. On the other side of the ledger, it calculated that over 70,000 households were living in barriadas in the selected cities, with 62,000 in Lima alone. Balancing the need against the available resources, the program aimed to provide 30 percent of the dwellings needed to rehouse barriada residents in each city, except the capital. In Lima, the FNSBS proposed to build less than 1 percent of the needed housing, or six hundred dwellings, to be located in San Juan, a new low-income settlement adjacent to Ciudad de Dios. The rationale for this deliberate restraint was twofold. Firstly, the FNSBS was concerned that conspicuously generous state assistance for housing in the capital—in the form of "land, credit, and technical assistance"—would only exacerbate the pull of migration. Secondly, in an effort to curb the push toward migration, the FNSBS proposed that the self-help housing program be coordinated with a plan for rural development, providing economic opportunities closer to home in order "to cut off the human supply of the barriadas"; the successful implementation of such a plan would necessarily curtail the demand for housing in Lima.[7]

As an indication of the importance FNSBS planners gave to this parallel initiative, the proposal included the outline of a plan for nationwide economic development broadly in line with CRAV's recommendations. This would unfold on two fronts, as explicated in an accompanying map, making explicit the national dimensions of the problem of access to land (fig. 4.3). The Andean region—"the vertebra of Peru"—was subject to "demographic instability" due to "a continuous exodus" of migrants, primarily toward the coastal cities (particularly Lima, dramatized by nine arrows converging on the capital). To counter this tendency, the proposal called for "a DEVELOPMENT OF STABILIZATION along the Andes"—this should be based on agrarian reform to expand access to agricultural land, supplemented with small-scale industrialization connected to rural production, as well as pockets of mining activity. With these measures in place, "then we will have fixed man to the land." Simultaneously, and perpendicular to this front, there should be "a DEVELOPMENT OF INTEGRATION" via road networks improving commerce and communication between the coastal, Andean, and Amazon regions. Finally, the migratory currents heading east toward "small colonizing nuclei" in the Amazon should be better managed via "properly conceived colonization plans" (potentially this could include Belaúnde's proposal for "road-colonization" that would be concretized with construction of the Forest-Edge Highway). By contrast, the planners viewed the recent departure of fifty families from the San Martín de Porres barriada in Lima—established under the patronage of General Manuel Odría—in order to establish the Amazon colony of La Morada, as an "adventure" that was "only explicable by desperation at continuing to live in the barriada."[8]

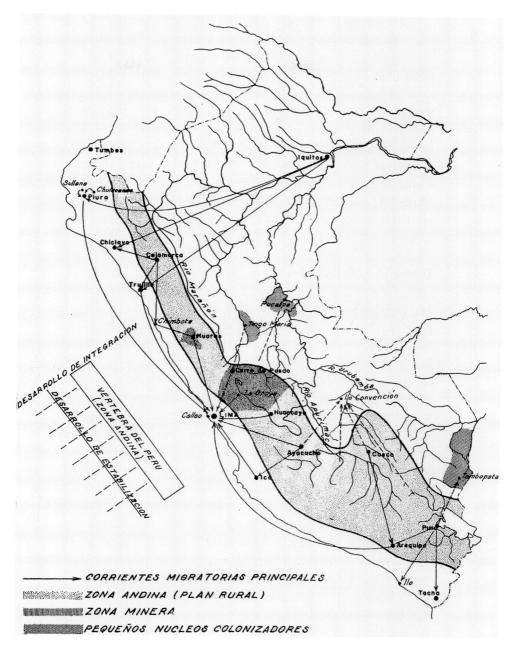

Figure 4.3. A plan for the development of Peru that lays the groundwork for an aided self-help housing program: fostering stabilization and integration will promote growth poles and moderate migratory flows, thereby preventing barriada formation. *Source*: FNSBS, *Anteproyecto de construcción de viviendas por ayuda mutua en la República* (Lima: FNSBS, 1960).

This national program in aided self-help housing was carefully planned, its targets calibrated in relation to the available human resources and the observed rate of construction in the trial projects. Nonetheless, in the view of FNSBS experts, achieving the program's most fundamental goal—substantially reducing the barriadas—would be impossible without parallel efforts to develop economic opportunities in rural and regional areas. In the end, this program never materialized—although in a sense it set the stage for a more ambitious nationwide program of aided self-help housing, backed by a large loan from the Inter-American Development Bank (IDB), the Perú-BID Plan Bienal 1962–1963. In the meantime, the invasions continued. It was clear that an alternative approach was needed.

Dwelling on the Margins

In 1958 the DATV legal department reported that "barrios marginales" (marginal neighborhoods, defined as being "structured at the margins of the law") were undermining official property registers because so many ad hoc occupations of state land had not been properly recorded. Likewise, in cases involving private property, the extralegal transfer of title by leaseholders (without the owner's knowledge or permission) was blurring the threshold between fully authorized occupants and those who had gained residency through "irregular, violent, or clandestine tenancy." Continued inaction by the state would only lend legitimacy to this situation, since over time, these "marginal" arrangements would gain some legal protections, inevitably leading toward "the conversion of barriada property holders [*poseedores*] into property owners [*propietarios*]." Allowing this increasingly porous boundary—between legally owning land and merely occupying it—to dissolve altogether "would mean giving legality to chaos and abuse."[9]

While squatter settlements had been tolerated (even cultivated) under various political regimes, the state now believed that these illegal occupations could not be allowed to become the norm. The framework of Law 13517, passed in February 1961, proposed two parallel approaches to reforming this landscape of irregularities. First, all barriadas established prior to September 1960 would be given the opportunity to legalize their status, on the condition that their urban services were upgraded and that individual dwellings were rehabilitated to acceptable standards as defined by the law.

Second, no new barriadas would be tolerated; instead, the government would establish a new kind of housing project—the "Urbanización Popular de Interés Social" (UPIS, "popular" or low-income urban settlement of social housing)—where dwellings would once again be self-built by residents, but construction would be closely supervised by architects and conform to an approved urban plan. Both solutions involved technical assistance, the difference being that the intervention of architects and planners occurred at different stages of the process: the first case would employ a Geddes-like "conservative surgery" approach to remodel the barriada after occupation and building had commenced, while the UPIS would establish a framework for self-build construction to develop within, allowing architects to control the process from the outset.

Not surprisingly, the new law raised concerns among residents likely to be affected. One such group, a self-described "Committee for the Defense of the Urbanizaciones Populares" took out advertisements in *La Prensa* to publicize their objections while the law was being debated. First, they drew a distinction between their settlements and barriadas per se (dismissed as "a set of huts"), because they had built their dwellings with "materiales nobles" (permanent materials), had paid various municipal fees and taxes, and should therefore be exempt from the law. As a second line of defense, they asserted their rights as property owners of their self-built houses, if not of the settlements where they resided: "The land may belong to the state or a private party, etc., but the construction belongs to whoever made it." To ignore this fact "is to follow the Cuban example" into the wholesale negation of private property.[10] Clearly the pobladores would rally to protect their hard-won investment in a home by any means at their disposal.

On signing the law, President Manuel Prado described it as "a work of public good, leading toward strengthening the family unit, reinforcing work habits, and securing a decent existence for our people."[11] Two key measures would ensure that this "public good" would be realized with maximum economy of means on the part of the state: making use of residents' self-help labor, as well as insisting that they cover the costs of technical assistance, urban upgrading, and purchasing their lots. With all expenses recuperated from the participants themselves, the projects would be self-sufficient, in keeping with the philosophy of self-help underlying Law 13517, and with Prado's promise that it would not become a financial burden on the taxpayers.

While most countries continued to regard slum clearance as the preferred response to unauthorized urban development, Law 13517 proposed an entirely different approach to directing urban growth—one that attempted to negotiate between improvised, self-generated construction (which provided low-income families with much-needed housing) and the dictates of official plans (which offered the benefits of coordinated urban development, with zoning guidelines, efficient circulation routes, the provision of green space, and suitable public facilities). With this legislation the drive to shape urban space was not abandoned altogether, but rather found an alternative expression in these hybrid modes of urbanism, on the one hand capping and reforming existing improvised construction, and on the other managing new self-built—but architect-conceived—construction.

The law transferred primary responsibility for the barriadas from the FNSBS to the Corporación Nacional de la Vivienda (CNV), shifting the focus of the government's response from the social welfare agency to the housing agency. Previously focused on the production of conventional housing blocks, the CNV would now oversee the translation of the new law into policies and programs. Reflecting on this period, Manuel Valega, head of the CNV in the early 1960s, described Law 13517 as marking a fundamental shift in how the agency's técnicos understood the housing problem: the approach of the unidad vecinal program had been to focus on the design and construction of housing projects, and then find suitable residents to inhabit them; now it was "to study the socioeconomic situation of the people and to give them what they could pay for."[12]

Prior to preparing any urban planning projects, the CNV needed to develop a deeper and more fine-grained knowledge of the situation in the barrios marginales. The FNSBS had laid the groundwork with its study *Barriadas de Lima Metropolitana* (1960). This was the first systematic survey of barriadas in the capital, building on the precedent of José Matos Mar's fieldwork (completed in 1955, though not published in detail until 1966) and Adolfo Córdova's survey for CRAV, *La vivienda en el Perú* (1958). The FNSBS carried out an *empadronamiento* and a detailed census collecting demographic data, as well as compiling basic information about the physical condition of the settlements themselves: their location, age, size, population density, topography, and the quality of land occupied—whether cultivated, uncultivated, or "basurales" (rubbish dumps). The FNSBS estimated that it had completed a full

Figure 4.4. Social assistants "prepare the community": "On identifying a dwelling with the corresponding letters and numbers, it remains to register the dwelling as well as the head of the household"; "After registration, data are collected as indicated by the census form." *Source*: FNSBS, *Barriadas de Lima Metropolitana* (Lima: FNSBS, 1960).

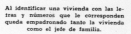

Al identificar una vivienda con las letras y números que le corresponden queda empadronado tanto la vivienda como el jefe de familia.

Después de·haber empadronado se procede a recolectar los datos que indica la ficha de censo.

TRABAJOS DE LABORATORIO

Los datos recolectados son:

1) Concentrados y clasificados.

2) Tabulados y convertidos en cuadros estadísticos.

3) Archivados.

Figure 4.5. The barriada is brought to order: "Laboratory work: The collected data are: 1. Compiled and classified; 2. Tabulated and converted into statistical tables; 3. Archived." *Source*: FNSBS, *Barriadas de Lima Metropolitana* (Lima: FNSBS, 1960).

census on roughly half of the capital's 64,231 barriada households, and had registered and numbered 45,617 dwellings, a first step toward formal acknowledgment of their presence in the city (fig. 4.4). The next phase of this resource-intensive work of data collection and management was to transfer information gathered in the field into the filing system in the FNSBS office-cum-"laboratory" (fig. 4.5). This unprecedented process of integrating the marginal into the bureaucratic machinery of the state had been facilitated by employing IBM data processing equipment, requiring special training for agency personnel.

Once responsibility for overseeing the barriadas was transferred to the CNV, it began its new responsibilities by undertaking a nationwide survey of all potential or suspected barrios marginales. Completed in early 1962, the survey resulted in the declaration of 271 barrios marginales across Peru, 123 of them in greater Lima. In addition, 41 groupings of substandard housing (33 of them in Lima) were found to be outside of Law 13517. For example, clusters of *corralones* (shanty housing) were physically indistinguishable from barriadas—both lacked urban services and utilized provisional construction materials—but corralones were erected on land that had been rented rather than squatted and claimed, and therefore were not eligible for the processes of upgrading and legal recognition that Law 13517 promised. Once declared eligible, each settlement was to be classified as suitable for eradication or rehabilitation. Since rehabilitation would involve not only physical improvements but also resolving disputes over the ownership of the settlement site and of individual lots, future viability would be determined by a panel of four experts: a public health professional, an urban planner, a sanitary engineer, and a lawyer. Eradication would be mandatory when the settlement was adversely affecting "the normal growth of the city"; when it was too expensive or technically challenging to provide services; when the site was vulnerable to landslides or river erosion; or when the value of the land "does not justify building low-cost housing on it."[13] These guidelines created a conundrum: on the one hand, residents were to be expelled from vulnerable or difficult sites rightly deemed unsuitable for development, but which they had been able to occupy in the first place precisely because of their marginal economic value; on the other hand, sites that were more suitable from a technical standpoint risked being ruled out on economic grounds, their greater value not "justifying" the accommodation of low-income households. Here technical considerations were confronted with the profit motive of capitalist urban development, raising questions about the right to use or to exploit urban land that could not be easily resolved.

In the case of barriadas set for rehabilitation, the guidelines stipulated the provision of passable roadways, water and sewerage infrastructure, and a wide range of urban facilities, to be determined by the settlement's size, location, and population. At a minimum this meant schools, medical posts, churches, parks, and sports fields, but it could also include workshops for small-scale industries and commercial centers. This approach was influenced by the CRAV report, which had presented an expanded definition of housing: "The dwelling embraces not only the house itself, but also the neighborhood and the community, and generally the environment as a whole or habitat where man and his family develop their usual activities." This definition consequently entailed a higher benchmark for an adequate "dwelling"—now conceptualized as being integrated into a well-appointed neighborhood. The 1958 DATV legal department report had condemned the barriada not simply for its poor-quality housing but more seriously because of its limited economic opportunities and inability to meet its own food supply; this revealed it to be "a parasite city [*ciudad parásito*], which is reflected in the high cost of housing."[14] By contrast, the reformed neighborhoods envisaged under Law 13517 would be self-sufficient and fully functional, emulating Belaúnde's unidad vecinal.

The detailed workings of the rehabilitation process emerge in a report on a project for the San Martín de Porres area undertaken in May 1961. This remodeling project covered eighteen barriadas in central Lima and proposed an ambitious series of programs to be coordinated with various government agencies: the health ministry was to provide a medical post, while the education ministry would build schools—an urgent requirement, given that around ten thousand children in the area were not attending school. However, before any of these programs could begin, it was necessary to fulfill the requirements of Law 13157 for establishing rightful residency to the lot, an arduous five-part process. First, the empadronamiento—creating a register of residents, confirming their status as property holders, without conceding them property ownership. Second, the *catastro* (cadastral survey)—drawing up detailed plans of the settlements in order to determine the boundaries of each lot. Third, the "cleaning-up of the empadronamiento"—identifying unoccupied or unclaimed lots, which would be turned over to the CNV to be used as sites for public facilities or reassigned to other residents. Fourth, studying existing provisions for water and sewerage lines. Fifth, developing plans to remodel individual lots that were too large, too small, or irregular in shape. Following this, provisional title would be granted—nontransferrable, nonmonetizable title, in order to counter land speculation—with residents given seven years to finish their dwellings to acceptable standards and to complete payments for their individual lots, as well as for their share of any upgrading costs for the settlement as a whole. Only at the end of this process would residents gain full title to the property.[15]

The logic behind this elaborate procedure was governed by the need to reinforce the existing property regime, underscoring the threshold between those who owned property and those who had possession—or had taken possession—of it without proper authority. In the process, the legislation also reasserted the state's right to police this boundary, to grant (or refuse) title, to legitimate possession. The aim was not to facilitate, or speed up, the process of gaining title but to clearly outline the requirements to pass from property "holder" to property "owner"—and to establish them as arduous, emphasizing the fact that ownership was not a universal right but a privilege to be earned. In this case, possession was not nine-tenths of the law but merely the first rung on the bureaucratic ladder to recognized legal ownership. For the poseedor who did not have the means to purchase land through conventional property markets, the law stipulated a series of complementary investments: compliance with bureaucracy, expenditure of self-help labor, and at least a nominal payment.

A vast amount of data was required to ascertain the nature and condition of each "marginal" settlement—or the precise degree of each settlement's marginality—in sufficient detail to be able to determine its fate with professional exactitude. With 271 barriadas nationwide and an estimated population of 105,781 households, this was never going to be a fast process. Furthermore, when set against the reality of the improvised city, the law faced a series of challenges that sharply defined the limits of its efficacy.

As one instance, the tangled histories of those barriadas where the mandated studies were actually carried out demonstrated that the implementation of the law would be far less straightforward than the guidelines had suggested. Replacing the official maps that had included the barriadas as indeterminate outbreaks of red dots amid the planned city, the new survey plans delineating roadways and blocks of housing (if not yet the individual lots of a full cadastral survey) were decades ahead of other countries in rendering these patterns of urban settlement legible and thereby extending them the most basic level of recognition. Yet their theodolized precision masked competing claims of ownership and occupation that were complex and opaque, with invasions and illegalities by tenants equally matched by questionable acts on the part of landowners and real estate developers, and further confused by poor record keeping and uneven enforcement by the authorities.

For example, the neighboring sites of El Altillo and Tarma Chico (figs. 4.6–4.7) both occupied state land, but while the first (on an undesirable, difficult-to-develop hillside site) was quickly recognized under the law, the residents of the second (on a flat site in between the folds of the hill) were evicted to accommodate a shooting club, then allowed to return on the condition of paying land tax in lieu of rent. However, seeing that their neighbors on the hillside paid nothing, the residents of Tarma Chico stopped paying, leaving their legal situation tenuous. 28 de Julio had begun as a disorderly *ranchería* (shanty settlement) established by a brick factory for its laborers. Following the factory's closure, the workers continued living on the site, paying rent to their former employer; however, the settlement subsequently expanded as other families established themselves on adjacent sites, paying nothing. At Gonzales Prada the residents had been paying rent through an agreement with a private owner, but the local municipality now ruled this invalid, arguing that this "landlord" had no right to lease out the land since it actually belonged to the state. Finally, Ramon Castilla Baja was situated within a private subdivision, whose developer had been authorized to sell lots once services had been installed; nevertheless, the developer had also sold lots that lacked services and furthermore had been earmarked for a public works project. These illegally established sections evolved through the letting and subletting of lots and the gradual invasion of any remaining open spaces. Eventually, the tenants "had refused to continue paying rent, availing themselves of the benefits of Law 13517."[16]

In this way the law revealed another of its limits: while the legislation vowed to enforce a cutoff date to benefit existing settlements and to criminalize the establishment of new ones, the slightest hope of securing decent, affordable housing inevitably intensified unauthorized construction. In the Río Rímac area in central Lima, between 1959 and 1961 the population grew from 50,000 to

Figure 4.6. Survey plan of the barriada of El Altillo in Lima, bordering on Tarma Chico, as indicated at the bottom right of the plan. *Source*: JNV, *Datos estadisticos de los Barrios Marginales de Lima: Distrito del Rímac* (Lima: JNV, 1963).

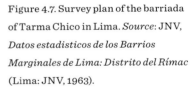

Figure 4.7. Survey plan of the barriada of Tarma Chico in Lima. *Source*: JNV, *Datos estadisticos de los Barrios Marginales de Lima: Distrito del Rímac* (Lima: JNV, 1963).

120,000—the increase being attributed to the promulgation of the new law, "since under the promise of a prompt attainment of property title, those who were living in other places in the urban area came to occupy its vacant lots."[17] The law operated as a system of solids and voids, creating the conditions for its evasion, as requirements and restrictions in one area created loopholes and incentives in another.

Constructing Law 13517

As the new survey plans revealed, diverse forms emerged from the intersections of history and topography behind each barriada. With some highly irregular, and others shaped by an approximation of gridded layouts, the resulting urban fabric would test any plan for regularization. Furthermore, the improvised city was by definition constantly evolving, as pobladores continued to establish and consolidate their neighborhoods, independently of what planners envisaged for them. Despite these challenges, by early 1962 plans for the first remodeling projects and UPIS schemes were being drawn up.

Barriada Remodeling: Plan Río Rímac

The CNV began by dividing Lima—and its 123 barrios marginales—into several zones, each of which would require a master plan. One of the first to be developed was the Plan Río Rímac, covering an area close to the historic center of the city and comprising over thirty barriadas on both sides of the Rímac river with a combined population of 120,000 (including the 57,000 residents of San Martín de Porres, founded a decade earlier) (plate 2). The Plan Río Rímac called for rationalizing the existing barriadas into ten sectors—termed unidades vecinales—in preparation for their redevelopment, and the construction of two UPIS projects: Condevilla Señor (on a site within the newly designated Unidad Vecinal No. 1) and Valdiviezo (on adjacent unbuilt land). The existing barriadas had been formed by various independent settlement associations, in an ad hoc process that ignored "the physical and human realities that enable a rational delimitation" of neighorhood boundaries.[18] This had resulted in large differences in population density throughout the area, ranging from 233 to 450 residents per hectare, an issue that planners also sought to address. However, any efforts at overriding the existing boundaries—no matter how "irrational"—would have to contend with the specific histories of the barriadas and the social connections within (or tensions between) the different groups of residents.

The unidades vecinales of the Plan Río Rímac, each with a population of ten thousand to twelve thousand people, shared no formal or material qualities with the modernist housing projects of Belaúnde's vision, but the planning documents defined them in exactly the same terms, as "Unidades de barrio [neighborhood units] self-sufficient in their primary needs"[19]—as if the linguistic gesture of extending the category to include the reformed barriada in itself contributed to its integration into the norms of urban development. Yet this approach was also a faithful realization of the 1947 resolution on the unidad vecinal sponsored by Belaúnde, which had argued that this model could also be applied in urban renewal projects, as the provision of comprehensive facilities could transform "parasite" neighborhoods into ideal "self-sufficient" urban units.[20] Accordingly, the Plan Río Rímac listed facilities to be provided at the level of the unidad vecinal and others for the entire zone. Each unidad vecinal should have its own markets, neighborhood civic center, and health post, while a commercial area, civic center, and a hospital were planned to serve the whole zone. In addition, fifty-seven kindergartens, twenty-six primary schools, and four secondary or technical schools would be distributed throughout.

Ironically, the physical proximity of the plan area to the CNV's first unidad vecinal projects—the largest of which, Unidad Vecinal No. 3, comprised 1,112 housing units and a population of roughly half of one of the Plan Río Rímac unidades—only underscored the limitations of the earlier program. Inaugurated just twelve years before and projected to solve the deficit of affordable housing, these unidad vecinal projects were now dwarfed by the proposed unidades vecinales of the Plan Río Rímac; placed on greenfield sites to decentralize urban growth, they were now close to being absorbed within the fabric of the improvised city.

The Plan Río Rímac proposed a series of measures to rehabilitate the area's barriadas: better integration with existing public facilities; detailed—but minimally invasive—remodeling projects; and the "eradication" of housing when deemed necessary. As one example, all existing construction within the new Unidad Vecinal No. 10 would be demolished, since it was chaotic and overcrowded, and its location on the eastern edge of the site, near the city center,

Figure 4.8. CNV, Remodeling of Unidad No. 6, Plan Río Rímac, Lima, 1962. Condition of existing construction: for conservation (black), for rehabilitation (grey), empty (with dot), for demolition (white). *Source*: CNV, *Plan Río Rímac: Remodelación de la Zona* (Lima: CNV, 1962).

Figure 4.9. Remodeling of Unidad No. 6, Plan Río Rímac, Lima, 1962. Remodeling proposal. *Source*: CNV, *Plan Río Rímac: Remodelación de la Zona* (Lima: CNV, 1962).

demanded high-density housing as a more appropriate use of the land. Families affected by these demolitions were to be rehoused in one of the two new UPIS projects that were included in the plan.

The detailed plans for Unidad Vecinal No. 6 of the Plan Río Rí-mac area provide an insight into how the rehabilitation approach would be applied. Employing a lot-by-lot cadastral survey, the existing housing was divided into three categories based on the quality of construction, the building materials, and the appropriateness of the functional layout in terms of avoiding the "promiscuity" of mixed uses (especially in relation to sleeping arrangements). An initial survey found that roughly 20 percent of the dwellings were conservable, with 60 percent suitable for rehabilitation, and 17 percent requiring demolition (fig. 4.8). On the urban level, two-thirds of the lots required remodeling because they were outside the stipulated size of 70 to 250 square meters or were irregularly shaped. In total, only 1,000 households would be able to remain on the same lot, while 395 were to be relocated and 803 "eradicated"—a measure required both to reduce the overall population density and to provide space for the additional facilities needed to convert the zone into a self-sufficient unidad vecinal (fig. 4.9). Specifically, the newly free space would be used for the construction of two schools (the key structuring element of the classic neighborhood unit), with adjacent green space. After calculating the costs per square meter of the remodeling, the CNV determined that the project was viable—that is, the estimated monthly payment to be levied from each family, at 10 percent of the average income, could be covered by the residents.[21]

In summary: one unidad vecinal consisting of six barriadas out of a total of 123 in greater Lima required a vast amount of detailed research and planning—carrying out the project, and convincing residents of its value, would be even more arduous. Furthermore, the amount of rehabilitation needed would likely be far higher in other areas: Unidad Vecinal No. 6 was selected as an ideal site for a trial project because it had a relatively stable workforce earning decent incomes, including barriadas formed by public sector employees from the Ministerio de Fomento y Obras Públicas (Ministry of Development and Public Works) and the police force.

Satellite Cities: San Juan

The concept of the satellite city predated Law 13517, as did the initial planning of the four satellite cities proposed for Lima—Ventanilla, Canto Grande, Vitarte, and San Juan—but they were an integral part of the CNV's overall approach to low-cost housing, and were easily folded into the UPIS initiative since they were essentially the UPIS in expanded form: an urban-scale framework for self-build construction (or, in the words of one *La Prensa* headline, the "city that will be built by its residents"). Of the four, all but Vitarte were realized in some form, to varying degrees of success. The concept owed a debt to Belaúnde's 1954 proposal for "self-sufficient satellite nuclei" to frame Lima, and although Ventanilla and San Juan lay outside of the 15-kilometer radius Belaúnde specified, a promised road system would bring them within fifteen minutes of the city center. The program was announced in mid-1960, with the satellite cities projected to be "self-sufficient" in key facilities (with schools, churches, medical posts, and markets), in economic activity (with adjacent industrial zones providing job opportunities), and in food production (with the técnicos considering a trial of dwellings with vegetable gardens to promote small-scale agriculture, and perhaps even supplement the capital's food supply).[22]

The first to be implemented (and the most successful) was San Juan, announced in March 1960. Situated on the other side of the highway from the CNV's Ciudad de Dios project, and in part occupying the site of the original Ciudad de Dios invasion, San Juan was rooted in an earlier proposal to build an urbanización popular of forty-five to sixty thousand people in response to that invasion, and the extensive public facilities planned for San Juan were to serve both settlements. The CNV reportedly viewed San Juan as an effort "to initiate the solution to the problem of the formation of new barriadas, in accordance with realistic methods and systems." To this end, the urbanized land would be sold at cost to residents, with access to favorable credit packages and assistance in building basic dwellings: "the obligatory *núcleo de vivienda mínima* [minimum dwelling core] . . . only comprises a *cerco*, sanitary unit (bathroom and kitchen), and a room built with *materiales nobles*, with the freedom to erect other rooms with cheaper materials." Although the residents would be given support, these houses would not "rain from the sky": they would be realized via "the only formula" that planners regarded as feasible—"with the participants' *esfuerzo propio.*"[23]

By the time construction was ready to begin in early 1961, the CNV's plans had become more concrete: San Juan would be an urbanización popular of 8,000 lots, to be built in stages. The first 2,000 lots would be allocated to prospective residents in August; by mid-January the CNV had already received 23,000 expressions of interest, with 4,000 completed applications. San Juan offered residents a comprehensive program on the "suelo-servicio" (sites-and-services) model (fig. 4.10): the CNV installed basic services (water,

Cinco unidades de vivienda, dotadas de servicios propios

Figure 4.10. CNV, Urbanización San Juan, Lima, 1962. The "city that will be built by its residents" awaits occupation. *Source: La Prensa*, January 14, 1962.

sewerage, electricity, paving) and provided technical assistance in self-help construction, along with a range of "typical plans of low-cost dwellings" on the "growing house" model. These were simple, compact houses (though much more substantial than the *núcleo de vivienda mínima* described in 1960), comprising a single-story dwelling with a bedroom, living-dining room, bathroom, and kitchen. Some models offered the possibility of adding a second story accommodating up to four additional bedrooms, all while leaving much of the 8-by-20-meter lot open for patio space (fig. 4.11). The construction plans were available to residents for around S/.10 (for comparison, the daily edition of *La Prensa* cost S/.1.50), and included plans for the installation of residential water, sewerage, and electricity lines, as well as the built structure.[24]

According to one account, most owners made use of these plans, and a well-organized "local field office served to educate and advise participants, inspect and maintain standards, and expedite paperwork." Due to the large number of applicants, the CNV was able to select a group of well-qualified residents. This contributed in large part to the success of the project—although this came at the expense of lower-income applicants, since "the selection process seemed to favor a group that was almost middle class."[25] San Juan proved that with coordinated technical assistance this approach

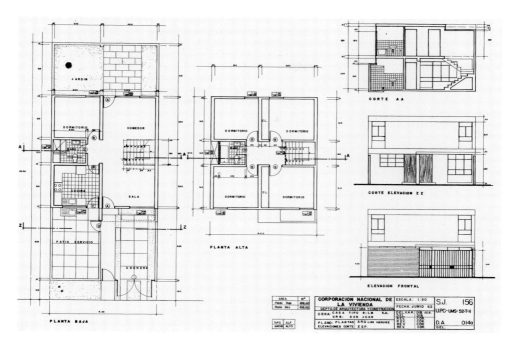

Figure 4.11. One of a set of five plans for a dwelling to be self-built at San Juan. *Source*: CNV (architect: Luis Vasquez), Casa Tipo 8-LM, Urbanización San Juan, Lima, June 1962.

to the provision of low-cost housing could be highly effective, but perhaps only with the upper tier of low-income households, who had reasonable resources to draw upon and could consolidate their dwellings fairly rapidly. However, in the absence of the projected industrial zone, trials in small-scale farming, or other initiatives to support itself as a self-sufficient city, San Juan essentially functioned as a large suburb.

UPIS in the Central City: Valdiviezo and Caja de Agua

The first projects to be realized under the UPIS name were those rehousing families "eradicated" by remodeling in the Plan Río Rímac area: Condevilla Señor, with 2,000 lots, and Valdiviezo, with 557 lots, would each become a new unidad vecinal within the Plan Río Rímac. Once again, the key structuring element of each urban plan was the location of the various schools, sited to minimize the distance children would have to walk. In order to reduce costs, initially the settlements were provided with only basic services, with no electricity, and no domestic water or sewerage connections;

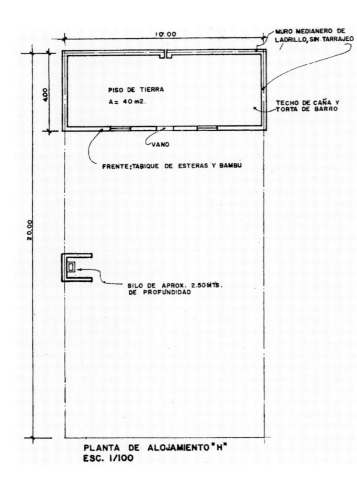

Figure 4.12. CNV, Urbanización Valdiviezo, Lima, 1962. Plan of the basic "Plan H" dwelling. *Source*: MVC, "Evaluación técnica y social del programa 'Alojamiento H'" (Lima: MVC, ca. 1981).

instead, residents accessed drinking water via communal standpipes, and disposed of waste via silos installed on each lot. Full services were installed a couple of years later, organized and financed by the residents themselves.

Construction was underway by early 1962, and the first lots were allocated later that year. Only very basic shelters were provided, aligned back-to-back in long rows (an arrangement that the CNV called "Plan H"). Located at the back of each 10-by-20-meter lot, a single room with an earthen floor was constructed measuring 10 by 4 meters, with party walls of brick at the back and on each side; the front of the dwelling was a *tabique* (partition wall) of *esteras* on a framework of bamboo poles; the roof was of cane and clay (fig. 4.12). The tabique was developed by the CNV as an improved version of a familiar low-cost building material (fig. 4.13):[26] provisional barriada housing generally employed esteras attached to a loosely assembled

Figure 4.13. CNV, Urbanización Valdiviezo, Lima 1962. The *tabique* (partition wall) developed for the basic "Plan H" dwelling. *Source*: *La Prensa*, February 24, 1962.

skeleton of wooden poles (see, for example, plates 7–8), while the tabique offered a much more solid structure, which some residents immediately reinforced with a layer of whitewash (plate 3). Residents were expected to gradually develop their houses, following set plans provided by the housing agency, moving toward the front of the lot. Eventually, the provisional roofing and the tabique were to be demolished, leaving a rear patio framed by the original brick walls.

An evaluation report of Valdiviezo after twenty years of occupancy found that 45 percent of residents had completed their dwellings,

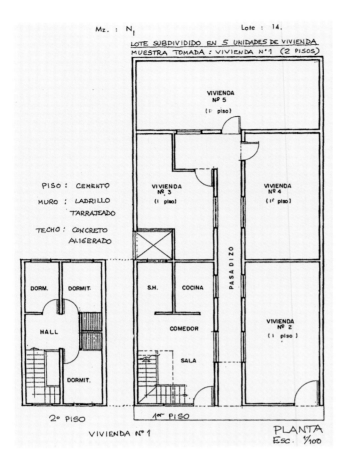

Figure 4.14. CNV, Urbanización Valdiviezo, Lima, 1962. A "Plan H" dwelling developed from the basic unit, subdivided into five dwellings. *Source*: MVC, "Evaluación técnica y social del programa 'Alojamiento H'" (Lima: MVC, ca. 1981).

building three or more bedrooms to house an average family of eight. A third of the lots had either added space for a business or workshop or built a second residence to house family members or to rent for supplementary income. In one case, the lot had been subdivided into five small dwellings, four of them consisting of one room with no kitchen or bathroom amenities, and the fifth, with a footprint of approximately 8 by 4 meters, extending to a second story. However, many other households were still in the process of building (figs. 4.14–4.15). Since the program had been structured for the acquisition of the dwelling through the *alquiler-venta* system, all the residents became property owners after ten years. Although each household had apparently been provided with full construction plans for a permanent dwelling considered to be suitable for their needs, few if any residents had used them, at least in part because they had not been given any postoccupancy technical assistance. Instead, most had built a house "in accordance with their particular criteria and

Figure 4.15. CNV, Urbanización Valdiviezo, Lima, 1962. A "Plan H" dwelling developed from the basic unit by simply enclosing the sanitary unit. *Source*: MVC, "Evaluación técnica y social del programa 'Alojamiento H'" (Lima: MVC, ca. 1981).

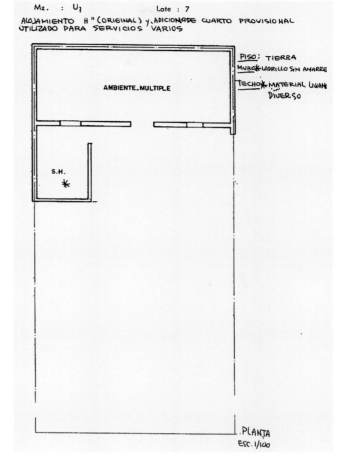

needs." The report concluded that technical assistance was essential to this kind of project, in order "to better channel the resources and potentialities of the population"; in the absence of such guidance, it estimated that at least 28 percent of the resources invested had led to poor results.[27] For example, one family had built windowless rooms to serve as the living space and the bedroom, and many others had decided to eliminate a patio in favor of additional living space.

In its conclusions, the evaluation report recommended a revised layout for future use in similar projects: in the original design, the built walls of each pair of back-to-back lots formed a wide *H*; the revised plan proposed an elongated *U* sited perpendicular to the back of the lot in order to avoid the use of party walls and thereby allow each family greater independence from their neighbor to the rear (fig. 4.16).[28] This was a small innovation, but in a context where

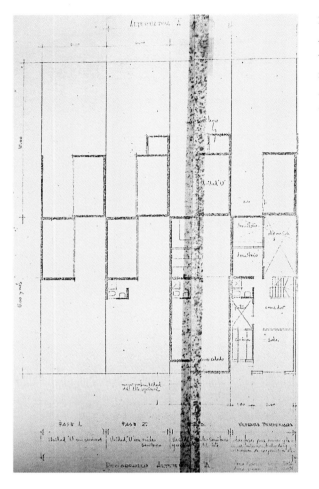

Figure 4.16. MVC, "Plan U" (Alternative A), ca. 1981. Realigning three brick walls offers the possibility of greater independence. *Source*: MVC, "Evaluación técnica y social del programa 'Alojamiento H'" (Lima: MVC, ca. 1981).

few residents had funds readily available to radically alter a misconceived plan, small design decisions could have an outsized impact. It is not clear where or how widely these revised plans were employed.

In the August 1963 issue of *Architectural Design*, which he edited, Turner offered a generally positive assessment of Valdiviezo and Condevilla Señor, with reservations about the design of the provisional dwelling. Turner concluded that the advantage of such "planned squatter settlements" was that they reflected "the traditional and economically logical process of the barriadas themselves" but with the benefit of superior urban layouts and basic service provision. Over the long term, these benefits would become even clearer, as the eventual installation of full services could be carried out more economically, "thanks to proper initial planning." Further, he anticipated that the residents' investment

Figure 4.17. John F. C. Turner, The first two stages of a schematic design responding to the drawbacks of the "Plan H" dwelling, 1963 (detail). *Source: Architectural Design* 33, no. 8 (Aug. 1963), John F. C. Turner Archive.

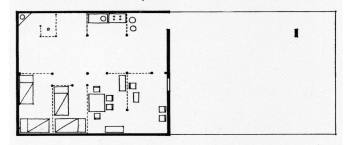

Stage 1
At first a permanent masonry enclosing wall is built by the financing agency, together with public drinking-water standpipes and, if possible, electric light (for security and night-time building work as well as to satisfy the demand for this service which is stronger, very often, than for a laid-on water supply). Within the enclosure the family can erect, at very little cost and in a few hours, a minimum shelter from cane mats and bamboo poles.

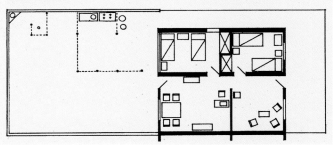

Stage 2
Once installed in its provisional dwelling the family can proceed to build the first stage of its permanent house; being on-site the able-bodied members can lend a hand in any spare time they may have and the family can supervise any hired labour constantly. In this way the family is free to make a maximum contribution in the building of the simplest parts of the construction itself—an advantage lost with the 'shell' house solution.

of money, time, and labor in their houses would be "guaranteed by the planning and controls exercised by the agency"—although as already noted, in the end the CNV did not provide this oversight. For Turner, the main deficiency of the Plan H dwelling was its failure to achieve the CNV's original intention of ensuring completed dwellings with back-to-back patios instead of back-to-back living space. As an alternative, he developed a schematic design that rejected the use of a provisional dwelling altogether, observing that it almost invariably became permanent, since "the owners are loath to part with what is . . . a better structure than they have ever lived in before, and for which they have paid, for them, a large sum of money."[29] Instead, he proposed a cerco enclosing the back half of the lot, where the residents could erect a provisional shelter (fig. 4.17). The half cerco provided a subtle push to direct construction

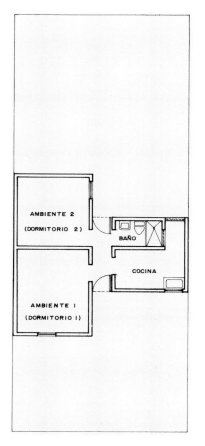

Figure 4.18. JNV, Plan for Núcleo No. 2, UPIS Caja de Agua, Lima, 1964. *Source*: MV, *Evaluación de un proyecto de vivienda* (Lima: MV, 1970),

toward the front, since the self-builder would likely prioritize completing the wall. As a result, there was a better chance of avoiding back-to-back living space. Turner did not propose a particular layout for the permanent construction—rather, his captioned plans describe what the self-builder aims for and achieves in each phase, as if anticipating a diversity of individual solutions, with the success of each one (he hoped) to be "guaranteed by the planning and controls" of the CNV.

Other UPIS projects offered a more substantial minimum unit. UPIS Caja de Agua was a relocation settlement for residents of the Cantagallo barriada, which had arisen on a private estate bordering the Rímac in central Lima. Since most households could not afford a finished dwelling, they would be allocated a "lote con servicios" (a serviced site). Even so, 103 families were disqualified from the project because they failed to meet the minimum income requirements. Instead, they were offered esteras and lots at Collique, an unserviced site far from the center of the city, to construct their provisional shelters anew. Many of these families decided to leave their allocated lots for other parts of the city; at the same time, this government-organized mass transfer triggered an uncontrolled invasion of the Collique site.

In late 1961 the government had initiated a nationwide aided self-help housing program, supported by the IDB, which brought new funds for projects fulfilling Law 13157. Following the terms of the loan, the Cantagallo relocation project was initially planned to employ self-help construction of a basic dwelling; soon afterward, the loan was revised, now favoring conventional construction. Accordingly, the final project offered residents a completed minimum unit, which could be extended using self-help labor, following the housing agency's plans. Whether or not this was the most appropriate approach, given the residents' financial resources, this was the solution for which the agency could secure funding.

The Caja de Agua site and a neighboring property, Chacarilla de Otero, allowed for a total of 2,361 dwellings, provided with basic services. Residents were offered the choice of two houses, sited in the center of an 8-by-20-meter lot: Núcleo 1 (31.5 square meters) comprised a single multipurpose room separated by a short corridor from the service core, with a small kitchen and bathroom; Núcleo 2 (43.75 square meters) added to this a second multipurpose room (fig. 4.18). The housing agency's recommended plan for the completed house foresaw a *sala*-dining room adjacent to the kitchen, a front garden, a generous garden patio, and two additional bedrooms at the rear (fig. 4.19). In the end, as at Valdiviezo, due to the lack of technical assistance, "the development of the house was left to the complete initiative of the recipient."[30] However, in many cases the initial short corridor did function as a guide for future construction, with owners building a series of rooms leading off a central passageway. Within five years, 94 percent of residents had begun to make additions, the majority adding between four and six rooms. This was achieved by sacrificing the planned open spaces, incorporating the intended front setback into the body of the house, or even extending beyond the property line to appropriate adjacent public space (figs. 4.20–4.21). In other cases the núcleo had barely been modified decades later, leaving the dwelling isolated behind a huge setback (plate 4).[31] Although far better than the conditions in Cantagallo, these were not the improved dwellings envisaged in Law 13517.

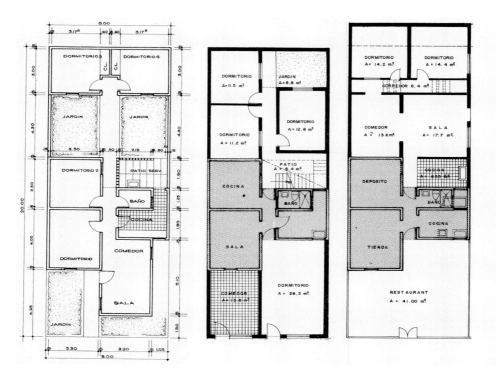

Figure 4.19 (*above left*). JNV, Plan for completed dwelling, UPIS Caja de Agua, Lima, 1964. *Source*: MV, *Evaluación de un proyecto de vivienda* (Lima: MV, 1970).

Figure 4.20 (*above middle*). JNV, UPIS Caja de Agua, Lima. A developed Núcleo 2 dwelling (original built area shaded in grey): a four-bedroom house, with stairs in the patio indicating the intention to add a second story. *Source*: MV, *Evaluación de un proyecto de vivienda* (Lima: MV, 1970).

Figure 4.21 (*above right*). JNV, UPIS Caja de Agua, Lima. A developed Núcleo 2 dwelling (original built area shaded in grey): a two-bedroom house with an open-air restaurant and shop at the front, and construction extending beyond the rear property line. *Source*: MV, *Evaluación de un proyecto de vivienda* (Lima: MV, 1970).

UPIS in the Northern Cone: Plan Carabayllo

While the Plan Río Rímac covered longstanding low-income areas close to the city center, other CNV plans responded to the ongoing expansion of Lima to the south and the north. Law 13517 had excluded any barriadas established after September 1960 from its benefits, hoping to stop further unauthorized settlements. However, the invasions continued unabated: those in the Comas area (northern cone) had begun around 1958; by 1963 there were half a dozen bar-

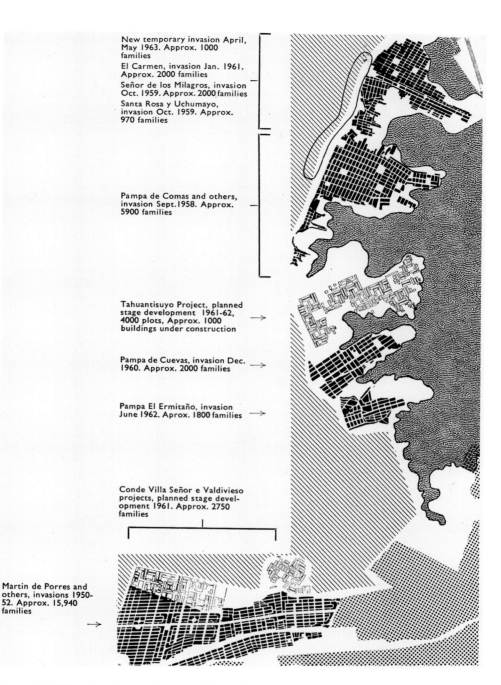

New temporary invasion April,
May 1963. Approx. 1000
families

El Carmen, invasion Jan. 1961.
Approx. 2000 families

Señor de los Milagros, invasion
Oct. 1959. Approx. 2000 families

Santa Rosa y Uchumayo,
invasion Oct. 1959. Approx.
970 families

Pampa de Comas and others,
invasion Sept. 1958. Approx.
5900 families

Tahuantisuyo Project, planned
stage development 1961-62,
4000 plots, Approx. 1000
buildings under construction

Pampa de Cuevas, invasion Dec.
1960. Approx. 2000 families

Pampa El Ermitaño, invasion
June 1962. Aprox. 1800 families

Conde Villa Señor e Valdivieso
projects, planned stage development 1961. Approx. 2750
families

Martin de Porres and
others, invasions 1950-
52. Approx. 15,940
families

Figure 4.22. "Map of barriadas to the north of Lima showing age and population of each." San Martín de Porres is located at the bottom, with Condevilla Señor and Valdiviezo just above; Tahuantinsuyo, Pampa de Cueva, and El Ermitaño are in the center. *Source*: *Architectural Design* 33, no. 8 (Aug. 1963), John F. C. Turner Archive.

riadas in the area, located in a series of reentrant valleys between the foothills of the Andes (fig. 4.22). In October 1961 the CNV produced the Plan Carabayllo, a master plan for the entire zone, extending from El Ermitaño to Señor de los Milagros, projecting a total population of 135,000. This plan outlined a comprehensive zoning scheme, dividing the area into five districts, setting aside areas for multifamily housing, and siting heavy and light industry along major roadways. The remainder of the space would be dedicated to low-rise, single- or two-family housing. The CNV also developed individual remodeling schemes for some of the incipient barriadas, hoping that with early intervention they could be transformed into UPIS projects. This would require negotiating with residents' associations, which were often in the process of developing their own urban plans and distributing lots to their members. Convincing them to cooperate would require skills that were more political than technical in nature. Devising urban plans for sites that had recently been occupied by invasion, or were likely an imminent target of one, presented particular challenges, examined here via three case studies: Pampa de Cueva, El Ermitaño, and Tahuantinsuyo.

The initial invasion of Pampa de Cueva occurred in mid-November 1960—after Law 13517, with its September 1960 cutoff date, had been publicized, but before it was promulgated, putting the would-be pobladores in an "enviably ambiguous and flexible legal position." Predictably, this invasion—a provocative test case for the new law—generated a show of force from the government, and the pobladores were quickly evicted by heavily armed assault troops. However, three hundred families refused to leave the area, camping out at a disused railway line nearby, and with some patience they managed to exhaust the government's will to enforce the letter of the law. On Christmas Eve, the authorities allowed these families to establish a "temporary camp" in one corner of Pampa de Cueva, while a longer-term solution was devised. Rather than waiting for this to arrive, "the squatters contracted for the planning and setting-out of the entire site" with some engineering students.[32] Within a couple of months, they had laid out the site and allocated the lots, and the families had moved their esteras onto their designated plots (fig. 4.23).

In January 1962 the CNV completed its plan for the Urbanización Popular de la Pampa de Cueva. The proposal noted that "there currently exists an *anteproyecto* [preliminary plan] presented by the *pobladores*" for the site, which suffered from a number of faults: 90 percent of the lots were less than 150 square meters; excessive space

CUEVAS: INCIPIENT SETTLEMENT
Progressive self-improvement, fired by
hope, unhampered by built-in blight, has
lead to an evolving, modern settlement.

1961 - Dense provisional encampment at
lower right houses settlers while planning
occupation of invaded site.

1962 - Incipient settlement developing.
Note school in allocated area.

1963 - Settlement consolidating in masonry.
New school, lining with settlement plan,
replaces aborted attempt, built without
technical guidance.

Figure 4.23. The evolution of Pampa de Cueva, Lima, from 1961 to 1963. *Source*: John F. C. Turner, "Three Barriadas in Lima, Peru, and a Tentative Typology," 1968, John F. C. Turner Archive.

was given to streets, while there was insufficient park space; and the communal facilities, such as markets and schools, were inadequate for the population. In fact, the pobladores' urban plan was much more than an anteproyecto, since they had enacted it months earlier (albeit largely with provisional structures). In any case, the CNV proposal took these existing site conditions as the basis for its plan, retaining the basic layout of the housing blocks as well as the pedestrian promenade running through the center of the site. It differed from the existing layout in its ambitions to create "the character of an Urbanización Popular de Interés Social" by carving out space for community facilities and parks, relocating some dwellings to realize its vision if necessary.[33] The pobladores had constructed a suitable urban framework to guide the orderly development of their settlement, but by the CNV's measure it would never function as a truly self-sufficient unidad vecinal. In the end, the on-the-ground reality proved stronger than the hopes of CNV planners: the pobladores' version of the settlement—securing each of the residents a lot rather than providing them with public space—prevailed.

In the conclusion to its Pampa de Cueva proposal, the CNV noted that it was imperative to begin studies of the neighboring site of Pampa El Ermitaño, in order to produce a coordinated plan for the integrated development of the two settlements. However, in mid-1962, before the CNV could complete its proposal, the El Ermitaño site was invaded. Officials from the Instituto de la Vivienda (INVI) visited the site in early July. In addition to recording observations about the settlement, the INVI report on this visit includes an account of exchanges between Turner, representing INVI, and the president of the residents' association, identified as Mr. López. Once the INVI group was allowed through the self-policed entrance to the settlement, the housing officials were taken to meet López. Turner began by introducing the group as a "disinterested party" curious to observe "the initial phase of the development of a squatter settlement." López's response—filtered through the report's writing and its subsequent translation into English, apparently by aid officials at the US Embassy—described in some detail the legal history of the land they aimed to secure, evincing a sophisticated understanding of the laws framing their actions. According to López, the basis for their occupation was "a Supreme Decree issued in 1945 which had reserved the area for 'urban development' for popular communities"; the association had requested permission from the authorities to establish themselves on the site on that basis, but received no response. They believed this silence was because "a well-to-do family carrying a foreign name" had claimed this parcel of state land in order to cultivate it. However, the claimants had not complied with the requirement to irrigate the land within a year, and López maintained that through this lapse, they had forfeited any right to it. Consequently, the association members had decided to settle the site for themselves, and—López claimed—they had already begun implementing improvements, installing "a reservoir, a motor and a canal system" in order to develop one section for agriculture. They believed that this investment proved that they had acted in good faith, and should not be "accused of unlawful action . . . since they had made their invasion in defense of the law."[34] This claim—to be acting in defense of the law—effectively aligned the pobladores with the state as a de facto partner in realizing its unfulfilled plans for an "urban development for popular communities" in the face of spurious land claims.

Turner queried López about the residents' need for assistance with "housing and 'community development'"; López replied that they could not afford to pay the CNV to prepare an urban plan, so "friends who were engineering students and some other professionals" would assist them in devising one. He added that they were considering building their dwellings "through the aided self-help method." Following this exchange, the INVI visitors were led on a tour by the head of the community-organized police force. Turner's photographs of El Ermitaño from this period document dwellings under construction, entrepreneurs setting up stalls to sell food or offer services, and community-organized enterprises such as a school and a special women's police force (its tasks: "to take care of the children and the sick; control to see that no new invaders get in; and register the people already admitted")[35] (plates 5–10). Some pobladores had begun to mark out their plots in chalk or rows of stones, while others were using esteras to frame the lot, providing the family with a degree of privacy even though they had yet to erect a roof. Visiting communities such as El Ermitaño year after year, observing the arduous process of settlement and consolidation, was key to Turner's deepening understanding of the barriada.

A little over a year after this first visit to El Ermitaño, in the August 1963 issue of *Architectural Design*, Turner's article "Lima Barriadas Today" preceded those on the remodeling and UPIS projects emerging from Law 13517. Turner concluded this article with this assessment: "Socially and quantitatively, even if not architec-

Figure 4.24. CNV, El Ermitaño, Lima, ca. 1965. Ten rectangular blocks of housing that were established according to the *pobladores'* plan are in the southwest sector of the original site, to the right of the irrigation ditch (indicated in black). *Source*: John F. C. Turner Archive.

turally speaking, the barriadas are, undoubtedly, the most effective solution yet offered to the problem of urbanization in Peru." Yet he began the following article with an acknowledgment of the limits of this approach, observing that the series of invasions in the Comas area were an example of "unaided or help-yourself methods" that had emerged from the Peruvian government's "laissez-faire urban development policy"; here, he argued that this mode of urbanization needed to be tempered by the guidance of planning professionals, "if there is not to be a total collapse of organized city development."[36]

At Pampa de Cueva, the CNV's proposal had arrived too late to be implemented, even in its modest efforts to reframe the pobladores' urban plan as a UPIS. At El Ermitaño, the pobladores appeared to be similarly poised to enact their version of an urbanism for "popular communities" independently of the CNV. However, internal disputes arose as it became clear that there was insufficient space for all of the would-be pobladores. The CNV intervened to resolve the situation, enlarging the site by expropriating adjacent land across an irrigation ditch on the western edge of the original invasion site. In September 1962 it presented a new urban plan for the area as a whole, aiming to maximize the number of residential lots, while creating a UPIS by providing ample community facilities and green space.[37] The process of remodeling and redistributing plots began in mid-1963. The realized urban layout was an accommodation between the ambitions of the CNV's plan, with a substantial amount of public space, and the existing conditions on the ground—specifically, it retained ten blocks of housing that had been established according to the pobladores' plan, in the southwest sector of the original site (fig. 4.24).[38] Once again, making a tabula rasa of the site to set out an ideal urban plan was not an option, given the political dynamic and the agency's limited resources. This was not the "total collapse of organized city development" foreshadowed by Turner, but a slow and steady undermining of coordinated planning, with the housing agency forced into a permanent defensive position.

In his 1963 assessment Turner offered as a more successful model the CNV's project for Urbanización Popular Tahuantinsuyo, just north of Pampa de Cueva, and initially invaded around the same time. In the zoning scheme for Plan Carabayllo, this site had been set aside for multifamily housing, but under pressure to produce a fast and inexpensive mass-housing solution, the CNV now proposed four thousand single-family lots. With early intervention, the CNV "managed to control the invasion" and convinced the pobladores to accept official oversight of the settlement's planning and growth, including the requirement that they build their dwellings "only to the approved plans and specifications." Yet as Turner's description demonstrates, having the CNV's assistance brought drawbacks as well as opportunities for prospective residents. The Tahuantinsuyo layout had the advantage of ample space for communal facilities, and would guarantee the economical installation of utilities. Construction proceeded quickly on the dwellings, "all of them to adequate standards and most of them well designed—thanks to the admirable work of the agencies' architects who set up a site office and centre for technical assistance." For Turner, the project's only disadvantage was the slow rate of occupation. This had emerged as a consequence of "forcing the economic level of the participant families too high"; generally, only the poorest pobladores—those unable to keep paying rent elsewhere in the city—would occupy their lots immediately. At Tahuantinsuyo, the selected households, "used to relatively high standards, preferred to wait until services had been installed before moving in."[39] This points to a second disadvantage: like San Juan, the success of Tahuantinsuyo rested on the exclusion of the lowest-income applicants. A project with this level of direction and oversight suited only those who could afford to delay occupation of the lot and to build according to the "approved plans" and "adequate standards" set by the agency.

Reflecting on the effectiveness of the various programs he had observed, Turner suggested that the state's role should be "to direct and coordinate existing forces and resources (and not to abandon them to create havoc or attempt to replace them)." Under this criterion, Turner believed that Tahuantinsuyo offered the blueprint for a new housing policy that was a natural extension of the UPIS approach: "acquiring land on the necessary scale and allowing its occupancy with an absolute minimum of utilities and then following up with the full set once the occupiers are well enough established."[40] Although he would later articulate a more ambivalent position on the sites-and-services approach, here Turner was advocating for a systematic program along those lines: setting up the conditions for aided self-helpers to establish viable settlements, redirecting their resources rather than supplanting them. However, in the case of Lima, such a program would only be workable if the state acted immediately and on a massive scale to secure attractive sites close to the urban core, in advance of either invasion or development by private entrepreneurs. While a technical solution to this challenge was within the grasp of housing officials, the larger obstacles would be part political and part financial in nature.

Space, Time, and Aided Self-Help Architecture

The satellite cities program had solved the problem of securing sites for low-cost housing in Lima by using low-value, peripheral locations, which in the case of San Juan and Ventanilla already belonged to the government. In mid-1963 Federico Mevius, Turner's colleague from Arequipa, headed a team that prepared a three-year spending plan for housing in Lima for the state housing agency—by this stage reorganized as the Junta Nacional de la Vivienda (JNV). The plan noted that in response to the hopes raised by Law 13517, as of mid-1963—just two years after its passage—over 35,000 low-income families in Lima had applied to the JNV for housing, with the expectation that the total would rise to 65,000 by the end of 1963, and 149,000 by the end of 1965. If these needs were not met in a timely manner, the JNV warned of continued invasions. The most realistic solution—given the limited economic capacity of these applicants—

would be to invest in a program of serviced sites with access to cred-it plans, thereby keeping the legal option attractive and stemming the drift toward the barriadas. In contrast to the UPIS approach at Valdiviezo and Caja de Agua, no *núcleo básico* would be provid-ed. Instead, the focus was on securing suitable sites and install-ing basic services, envisaging residents' eventual, stage-by-stage construction of a house with some degree of technical assistance.

The spending plan proposed expropriating up to ten sites located on minimally productive agricultural land, selected so as not to in-terfere with any private initiatives in low-cost housing, and located near existing "nuclei of demographic pressure" (such as Comas) so they would be attractive to potential residents (fig. 4.25). Although few of the selected sites were near the urban center, they were at least on or near major roadways leading into the city. In essence, this was a global plan for new low-income settlements, anticipating the provision of tens of thousands of basic lots in an effort to come to terms with the scale of Lima's housing shortage. Initially, the pro-posal envisaged the expropriation of 2,460 hectares over a period of three years, along with the necessary work to prepare the sites for occupation. The program would go into effect in 1964, with the acquisition of 1,770 hectares to accommodate 55,250 households at the level of an *obrero bajo* (low-income blue-collar worker); in 1965 an additional 500 hectares would be acquired, for 15,500 *obrero* (blue-collar) households. Beginning in 1966 sites for *empleado* (white-collar) families would be included in the program; the plan-ners argued that serving these applicants could be safely postponed for a couple of years, because higher-income families were less likely to invade "for cultural reasons."[41] The proposal envisaged the ongoing acquisition of sites for the foreseeable future: 190 hectares in 1966, 290 in 1967, 300 annually from 1968 to 1974, and 150 annu-ally from 1975 onward. Beginning in 1965 the program would also offer loans to families that had been granted lots, in order to speed up construction of their dwellings. The JNV estimated that on this schedule, the accumulated housing deficit for obreros would be met in 1967 and that of empleados in 1974. The budget for the first year of operation—covering the acquisition and preparation of 1,770 hect-ares—was S/.325 million, which the JNV believed could be covered by the government, possibly supplemented by funding from the IDB.

In January 1963 the brief military government of General Ricar-do Pérez Godoy (1962–1963) had bolstered this approach by passing a law facilitating expropriations in order to promote the establish-

Figure 4.25. JNV, Plan for expropriations in metropolitan Lima, 1963. Ten sites slated for expropriation are indicated in grey (labeled A to J). The largest single site is to the north in Comas, a "nucleus of demographic pressure" targeted by recent invasions. *Source*: JNV, "Plan trienal de inversiones en viviendas nuevas en Lima metropolitana" (Lima: JNV, July 1963).

ment of low-cost urbanizaciones. Counterbalancing this support, opposition to the proposed expropriations from landowners was, predictably, rapid and forceful. In June 1963 *La Prensa* reported on their assertion that vacant sites unsuitable for farming should be used instead of any agricultural land, however unproductive. Manuel Valega, now the head of the JNV, responded that the only such sites in Lima were in areas unsuitable for urban development. Valega underscored the importance of executing the expropriations policy, arguing that the agency would be "applying a life-saving law that will drive away the specter of communism from the country." Further, he suggested that many of those protesting had no intention of preserving farmland, but were in fact "interested in making *urbanizaciones privadas* on a commercial basis." This accusation was not unfounded. According to Julio Calderón Cockburn, by 1955 most of the land in Lima—31,456 hectares in all—was controlled by only sixty-five landowners; between 1950 and 1972, forty-one of these landowners established their own real estate operations, consisting of around 150 companies developing new subdivisions.[42]

In the end, the housing agency was forced to abandon its plan for expropriations, due to insufficient funds as well as continued opposition from landowners. If the expropriations had been implemented, it would have marked a fundamental cultural shift, placing the right of access to urban land over the right to speculate in urban land. However, it is not clear what the JNV could have offered to these seventy thousand new households beyond the land itself. Absent a significant increase in its budget and trained staff, developing urban plans and installing basic services on this number of lots would have presented an enormous logistical challenge—likely leaving the pobladores, once again, to rely on obliging engineering students and their own initiative.

In any case, the JNV's 1963 spending plan judged that even a minimum unit might be beyond the capacity of many applicants. According to its estimates, roughly 3 percent could pay for a completed house, while 85 percent could afford a serviced site (on which half of them could eventually build at least a basic dwelling), and the final 12 percent could afford nothing at all. This represented a major shift from the position of the DATV in late 1960, which—following the OATA precedent—had proposed the aided self-help construction of basic dwellings from the ground up, under close on-site supervision. The early UPIS projects had moved to the "growing house" model, with the provision of a contractor-built minimum unit, to be extended via aided self-help, according to plans developed by the housing agency and with its technical assistance. The JNV now proposed accommodating the middle 85 percent of its applicants by simply providing a lot on which a dwelling could be built in stages, over an unspecified time period (fig. 4.26). Stage one offered basic services to the settlement, and a standpipe in the middle of the lot, but no built structure. Stage two consisted of "the necessary works for the completion of a partial definitive dwelling":

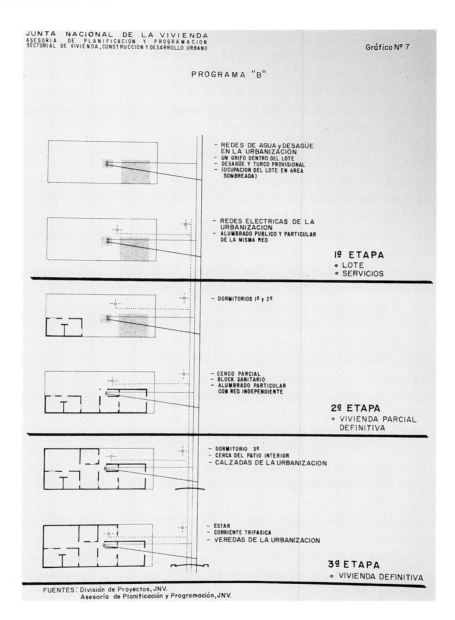

Figure 4.26. JNV, Experimental Program B, 1963. Stage 1. Serviced site; Stage 2. Partial definitive dwelling; Stage 3. Definitive dwelling. *Source*: JNV, "Plan trienal de inversiones en viviendas nuevas en Lima metropolitana" (Lima: JNV, July 1963).

this would begin with a two-bedroom unit, followed by a sanitary block, living area, and a partial cerco. Finally, the "definitive dwelling" would fill out the lot, leaving space for an interior patio. While the costs were relatively modest, a surcharge of 15 percent was to be added at each stage to cover the technical assistance provided by the JNV, including fees for architects and planners, as well as for financial advice regarding loan applications.[43] For homeowners who would begin their residence with nothing more than street lighting, a standpipe on their lot, and provisional sewerage service, an investment of 15 percent in mandatory "assistance" represented a substantial expenditure, and it is likely that the JNV would have faced a considerable challenge in convincing applicants of its value.

The JNV's decision not to attach a time frame to its outline for the evolving dwelling reflected the unpredictable temporality of aided self-help projects, with construction undertaken in fits and starts, in response to the ebb and flow of material resources. This complicates the traditional timeline of architectural production, which draws a clear boundary between the construction and post-occupancy phases. Writing in 1963, Turner observed that it was unclear "how long the average barriada dweller takes to build his house." The pobladores' own estimate was ten years, without credit or technical assistance; with credit but only "minimum or no technical assistance" a house could be completed in six months, or "the typical half-completed structure in two or three months."[44] Assuming that participants were in a position to take on loans, and that Turner's estimate of two to six months was accurate, aided self-help in the form of ongoing postoccupancy technical assistance could be achievable with a dedicated site office (as at San Juan and Tahuantinsuyo). However, rates of construction and consolidation varied greatly from one household to another, suggesting that for the majority these estimates were far too optimistic. Once post-occupancy technical assistance was stretched into a long-term endeavor, its viability was greatly compromised; unless established on a firm institutional foundation, it would be highly vulnerable to the impacts of changing governments, policies, and funding priorities.

In a sense, Law 13517 was at once too ambitious, given the financial and human resources that would be required to properly implement it, and not ambitious enough, since it risked being overwhelmed by the pace of unauthorized urbanization. It was also hampered by questionable assumptions concerning the level of financial contribution that residents could manage, the length of time required for construction, and the ease of organizing such projects on the human as well as the technical level. This was especially true with rehabilitation projects such as Unidad Vecinal No. 6, which do not seem to have progressed far beyond the preliminary planning stage—perhaps inevitable given the difficulties of convincing settled residents of the program's merits versus the disruptions and expenses of mandatory upgrading, or "eradication" and relocation. The tabula rasa of the UPIS was theoretically easier to implement, and in the first couple of years of the new legislation the CNV did initiate a number of projects, but it also faced serious difficulties in acquiring the necessary land, particularly in Lima.

The 13517 program faced an uncertain future, with the challenge of assembling sufficient human and financial resources to fulfill the promise of the projected settlements. However, there was also some reason for optimism, from a source that could not have been anticipated at the time the law was passed. By late 1961 the economic and social development of Peru—including its efforts to improve housing provision for low-income families—had become an issue of concern for President John F. Kennedy, in the context of the Alliance for Progress, the core element of his new Cold War strategy for Latin America. The regional superpower's new interest in supporting initiatives promising bold socioeconomic change gave the Peruvian government access to unprecedented financial resources to fund its programs, primarily in the form of subsidized loans. The outcome of this intervention on the policies that had emerged from Law 13517 is the subject of the next chapter.

COLOR PLATES

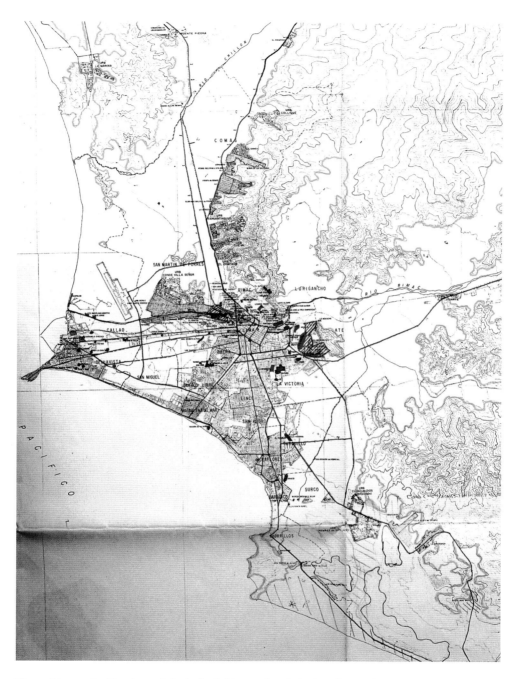

Plate 1. Lima, 1962. The planned city is shaded in grey, barriadas in yellow, and *tugurios* in red. While the highest concentration of barriadas is still along the Río Rímac in central Lima, the areas of Comas (northern cone) and Surco (southern cone) are starting to be settled. *Source*: CNV, "Mapa Regional de Lima: Barrios Marginales y Urbanizaciones Populares," October 1962.

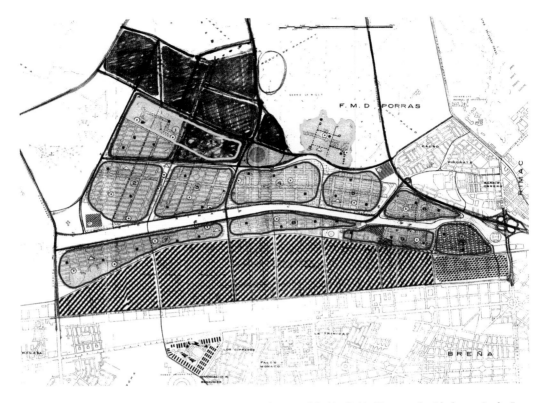

Plate 2. CNV, Plan Río Rímac, Lima, 1962. The area to be remodeled is divided into ten "unidades vecinales" (outlined in blue, and numbered left to right): San Martín de Porres covers half of Unidad Vecinal no. 1 and all of nos. 2, 3, 4, and 5; Condevilla Señor and Valdiviezo are to the north (outlined in yellow); Belaúnde's Unidad Vecinal No. 3 is the inverted triangle at the bottom of the plan. *Source*: CNV, *Plan Río Rímac: Memoria Descriptiva* (Lima: CNV, 1962).

Plate 3 (*above*). CNV, Urbanización Valdiviezo, Lima, 1962. Back-to-back basic "Plan H" dwellings in the process of being extended by residents; the San Martín de Porres barriada (established 1951) is in the background. *Source*: John F. C. Turner Archive.

Plate 4 (*right*). JNV, UPIS Caja de Agua, Lima, ca. 2010. Two of the JNV houses, which appear to be in almost original condition. *Source*: © Gustavoc, Panoramio.

Plate 5. El Ermitaño, Lima, 1962. Invaders' camp with flag and plots marked out with chalk lines or with stones, continuing onto the hillside. *Source*: John F. C. Turner Archive.

Plate 6. El Ermitaño, Lima, 1962. Setting up house. *Source*: John F. C. Turner Archive.

Plate 7. El Ermitaño, Lima, 1962. Constructing a provisional dwelling, using a framework of wooden poles that will support *esteras*. *Source*: John F. C. Turner Archive.

Plate 8. El Ermitaño, Lima, 1962. Interior of a first-stage provisional dwelling. *Source*: John F. C. Turner Archive.

Plate 9. El Ermitaño, Lima, 1962. Informal commerce. *Source*: John F. C. Turner Archive.

Plate 10. El Ermitaño, Lima, 1965. Ongoing consolidation of dwellings, proceeding at varying rates: three years after the invasion, some dwellings are still of *esteras*. *Source*: John F. C. Turner Archive.

Plate 11. Hogares Peruanos, Brochure for Sol de Oro, Lima, ca. 1962. The site plan shows the proximity of Sol de Oro and Villa Los Angeles; the Alliance for Progress logo appears to the left. English translations have been overlaid for the benefit of the World Homes head office in Wichita. *Source*: Jean and Willard Garvey World Homes Collection, Wichita State University Libraries, Special Collections and University Archives.

Plate 12. Hogares Peruanos, Brochure for Sol de Oro, Lima, ca. 1962. The four model houses: Discoverer, Polaris, Atlas, and Explorer. *Source*: Jean and Willard Garvey World Homes Collection, Wichita State University Libraries, Special Collections and University Archives.

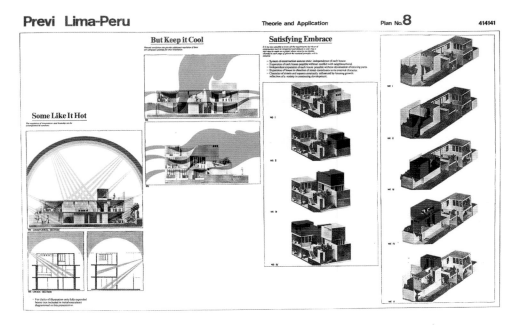

Plate 13. Atelier 5, PREVI PP1 I-4, 1969. Light and ventilation diagrams; models showing the progressive development of the houses. *Source*: Atelier 5, "International Competition for an Experimental Housing Project in Lima, Peru" (ca. 1969).

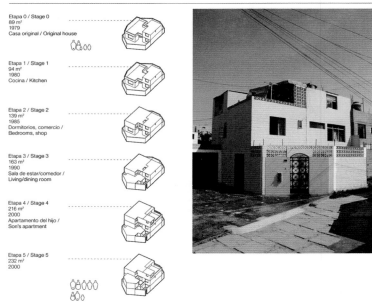

Plate 14. PREVI PP1, Lima, 1979–2000. Evolution of a house designed by Aldo van Eyck and modified by the Villegas family. *Source*: Fernando García-Huidobro et al., *¡El tiempo construye! [Time Builds!]* (Barcelona: Gustavo Gili, 2008).

5

WORLD INVESTMENTS, PRODUCTIVE HOMES, 1961–1967

On April 3, 1962, David Rockefeller hosted a one-day symposium on Latin American housing at the headquarters of the Chase Manhattan Bank in New York. The event featured speakers from nine Latin American countries, the US Department of State and Department of Commerce, the Federal Housing Commission, the Export-Import Bank, the Inter-American Development Bank (IDB), and the United States Agency for International Development (USAID), as well as the founding director of the Centro Interamericano de Vivienda (CINVA) in Bogotá, Leonard J. Currie. In the audience were investment bankers, construction material manufacturers, US corporations with interests in the region, and housing developers such as Wichita-based World Homes and Nelson Rockefeller's International Basic Economy Corporation, as well as Ogden Tanner of *Architectural Forum*, and four attendees from Skidmore, Owings & Merrill, including Gordon Bunshaft.

This was not (entirely) a philanthropic exercise. As one speaker observed of the current situation in Latin America, "it is in the slums of the cities where the battle of democracy will be fought"; as the spoils of victory, the symposium presented the tantalizing prospect of "a vast lower middle-class market, once financing mechanisms are developed." Most immediately, improving the living conditions of the

Figure 5.1. The singular, entrepreneurial self-help home builder. The caption on the inside cover reads: "Home construction in progress at Ciudad de Dios, near Lima, Peru." Source: Chase Manhattan Bank, *Housing in Latin America* (New York: Chase Manhattan Bank, 1962).

rapidly increasing ranks of the urban underclass offered insurance against political radicalism; from a broader perspective, upgrading housing stock would bring construction jobs, along with a stimulus to the production of building materials, and to the market for furnishings and appliances. Improving housing—understood as a "productive investment" with benefits far beyond the simple provision of shelter— would pay dividends in economic development and social stability, along the way shaping new opportunities for US business. According to the symposium organizers, government had its role to play, "yet it is recognized that the problem must be solved principally by private enterprise."[1] Since the state could not build housing on the massive scale required, it should instead focus on providing incentives for entrepreneurs to commit their resources to the housing sector. Specifically, by facilitating access to mortgage credit and fostering deeper reservoirs of personal savings, the state could develop a market of consumers with sufficient funds to undertake the purchase of a house.

The private enterprise of each individual family, actualized through the self-help construction of their own homes, would also play an important role and was endorsed by many speakers on economic as well as moral grounds: self-help lowered the cost of the house while increasing the self-sufficiency and initiative of the participants. Teodoro Moscoso of USAID noted that President John F. Kennedy's Alliance for Progress, a recently instituted initiative for the economic and social development of Latin America, favored such programs precisely because they embodied "two fundamental ideals of the Alliance: direct, tangible assistance to the underprivileged combined with rigorous self-help." As opposed to charity, this form of aid would operate as a bracing tonic to strengthen the beneficiary through its demands. Moreover, the promotion of individual property ownership and self-improvement through work were implicitly opposed to the "handouts" and latent socialism of public housing. For his part, T. Graydon Upton of the IDB was at once pragmatic but idealistic in his concluding assessment: "Although the monetary returns from direct sales or local investment may be quite limited, the return in terms of US relations with Latin America and self-satisfaction at having made a valuable contribution to a major hemisphere problem, may be tremendous."[2] Not entirely philanthropy then, but not pure business either.

Above the familiar logo of the Chase Manhattan Bank a man labors with a trowel and roughly formed bricks, carefully building up the walls of a simple house (fig. 5.1): with this image the cover of the symposium report offers a perfect illustration of the hoped-for alliance of rustic workman and international finance that is presented within. The photograph—captioned "Home construction in progress at Ciudad de Dios"—alludes to events that transformed the direction of housing policy in Peru: the Ciudad de Dios invasion on Christmas Eve 1954, which brought national focus to the crisis of affordable housing, leading to a government commission, headed by conservative economist and newspaper proprietor Pedro G. Beltrán, which recommended the promotion of individual home-ownership, to be achieved through a combination of self-help construction and expanded availability of mortgage credit. This promarket position was perfectly in line with the priorities of US development policy, and as a result, from the late 1950s Peru became a major recipient of US aid for housing through various channels.[3] The largest single loan (approved in late 1961) was $22.8 million from the IDB to establish a national program of aided self-help housing. A number of smaller loans—by 1969 totaling more than $24 million—were allocated to support a system of *mutuales* (savings and loans associations) aimed at giving lower-middle-income consumers easier access to housing finance. Although in later years international agencies such as the UN and the World Bank would become involved in the sponsorship of housing programs, the earliest aid for housing in Peru came exclusively from the United States.

Underneath the surface of this image, then, is the issue of how the dynamics of on-the-ground events, the circumstances of local and national politics, converged with the wider frame of US government development programs at this specific moment—how US aid agencies seeking to sponsor housing programs within Peru, to reinforce policies amenable to their aims, were able to gain traction due to the synergy between their outlook and the positions of key actors in Peru. Beginning with a discussion of the establishment of new financing mechanisms for housing in Peru, this chapter explores two key projects that emerged out of this convergence of finance, geopolitics, aid, need, and architecture, examining the disparate collection of actors involved in their production and their often unlikely partnerships. First, the operations of real estate developer World Homes—on a self-appointed mission to universalize the "American dream" in fulfillment of its credo: "Home Ownership—The Free World's Unused Weapon"—focusing on its endeavors to organize and finance Villa Los Angeles in Lima. Second, the development and implementation of the Perú-BID Plan Bienal 1962–1963 (BID being the IDB's Spanish acronym), an ambitious program that aimed to mobilize self-help labor for housing construction in cities throughout Peru. Both projects were funded through US government aid programs, and both involved John F. C. Turner, who was emerging as an influential voice on aided self-help housing, as a consultant. Turner—a Western-trained, Anglophone *técnico* with the benefit of local, on-the-ground, hands-on expertise—can be seen as a translator between US development professionals, housing developers, and the Peruvian government, and between architecture and social policy. At the same time, he was developing his own practice as a housing expert and theorist, absorbing the outcomes of each project into a more ambivalent understanding of the self-help methodology.

The Money Miracle

The first substantial US aid programs in Peru emerged during the Second World War. Framed as technical assistance projects and funded jointly by the United States and Peru, they were largely motivated by US national interest rather than altruism, focusing on the production of materials needed for the war effort. Apart from the practical benefits of such programs to the United States, their strategic aim was to foster hemispheric solidarity against the Axis powers; following the war, the model was redeployed to ensure "mutual security" in the region by encouraging the incorporation of Latin American countries into the Western Bloc rather than the Communist order. In the wake of the Cuban Revolution, this would take on added urgency.

Under President Harry S. Truman these ad hoc efforts coalesced into the Point Four Program, which established technical assistance as a key tool of US foreign policy. Originally focused on health, agriculture, education, and industrial productivity, by the late 1950s it had expanded to encompass entrepreneurial skills such as marketing and management, as well as community development and housing. In the case of Peru, it included guidance for the establishment of a system of mutuales via US experts assigned to the Comisión para la Reforma Agraria y la Vivienda (CRAV). President Dwight D. Eisenhower's foreign assistance program initially focused on promoting private enterprise in beneficiary nations, favoring projects that married public- and private-sector funding. In 1957, he established a new lending institution, the Development Loan Fund (DLF), with greater flexibility in its lending practices than existing bodies, allowing it to support nontraditional development projects such as the mutuales. Following the Cuban Revolution, social development became a greater priority, seen as a cost-effective way to defuse political discontent. To this end, in September 1960, the US signed the Act of Bogotá with Latin American governments, committing $500 million for initiatives in agrarian reform, public health, education, and housing. Kennedy's Alliance for Progress, announced in March 1961, supercharged US support for such projects with a $20 billion budget over ten years.

In parallel, US-based Christian missions had long operated in Latin America and beyond, blending religious and more pragmatic uplift. Particularly significant in postwar Peru was the contribution of the Catholic Maryknoll Fathers. As characterized by one contemporary account, the Maryknoll Mission operated under the belief that "the only way to help a man spiritually is first to help him materially" and it generally gave its missionaries "wide latitude in the choice of projects into which they may channel their energies."[4] Noted for their particular success were Father Robert Kerns, who founded a series of indigenous-language radio schools in the southern city of Puno, and Father Daniel McLellan, who established a credit union in his Puno parish in early 1955. Providing modest loans for personal use (family emergencies, medical expenses, funerals, and minor home repairs) or small-scale business ventures, the credit union grew quickly, finding a ready constituency among the vast numbers of ordinary people excluded from conventional bank loans.

Following McLellan's lead, 1956 saw the creation of five more credit cooperatives throughout Peru; by 1960 there were 207. Of these, the largest group (almost 40 percent) was coordinated through the Catholic church at the parish level, with others organized through various workplace or community groups. McLellan remarked on the importance of the leadership of the Catholic church—and of the Maryknoll Mission in particular—in this effort: "The Protestants and other groups would like to move in but the people want the Church to guide them and it is true that through this material aid they come to look more for the spiritual guidance of the Church."[5] Raising the standard of living solidified the authority of the church in the lives of its parishioners, effectively leveraging faith in the credit union to maintain denominational market share. Evidently Maryknoll considered this work to be of great value: in January 1958, McLellan was released from his pastoral duties to focus on it full-time; the following year he began teaching workshops on the management of credit cooperatives through the Universidad Nacional Mayor de San Marcos in Lima.

By fostering the values of private initiative and personal responsibility, and providing an opportunity for self-sustaining material advancement, the credit cooperatives were also working to construct a bulwark against communist influence, the mutual enemy of capital and the church. The dangers of ideological infiltration were acute, however, and McLellan issued a vehement warning concerning the need to remain vigilant: "Communism is always deploying efforts to take control vis-à-vis cooperatives. Publications come to us from Prague, and they solicit the exchange of ideas with us and with our affiliates. These publications are a great danger, since they try to use the word cooperative, with aims foreign to it, in order to then twist it according to their own interests." As emphasized in a number of articles about McLellan's efforts, although it was founded on mutualist principles, the credit union was very definitely a protocapitalist venture, offering "a form of self-help assistance that lets the proud individual keep his pride, and that develops the managers and risk-takers for a free, modern society." Initiating its members into the operations of the credit market, the cooperative would transform Andean peasants—cast as "backward, distrustful, and a severe drag on Peru's economic structure"—into model entrepreneurs. As McLellan once stated: "The French have their worker priests. Well, I am a capitalist priest."[6]

McLellan's original organization, the Puno Parish Credit Union, soon addressed itself to the housing problem, and approached the government of President Manuel Prado (1956–1962) for assistance. A loan of S/.450,000 was arranged to facilitate the purchase of land for a model housing scheme, which would be developed under the guidance of the government housing agency, the Corporación Nacional de la Vivienda (CNV). (A significant missed connection: some years later, Turner recalled that his work in Peru "included a rather abortive effort to build cooperative houses in Puno for Daniel McLellan.") The seventy-two dwellings were to be sold to members of the credit union, to be paid for with six- or seven-year loans. In line with the Maryknoll worldview, McLellan argued that "Christian family life can hardly exist in a mud hut." In addition to Prado's government, the credit union also impressed the US embassy and the "Point 4 people": the latter extended their supervised credit program to Puno, and granted the manager of the Puno credit union a "Point 4 scholarship . . . for study in Puerto Rico"[7]—then in the midst of Operation Bootstrap, a massive, federally funded economic development program. The US embassy provided further support in the form of publicity, apparently including a film about the credit union's achievements.

Despite these successes, McLellan was initially reluctant to become involved in the savings and loans business. Unlike the revolving short-term loans of the credit unions, long-term, high-value home financing would require a substantial reserve of funds in order to commence lending—far more than could be raised through deposits alone. Instead, it was Beltrán who organized the first *mutual*. After recommending their creation in the CRAV report and helping to devise their founding legislation, Beltrán established Mutual El Perú in September 1958. It was quickly granted $2 million from Eisenhower's new lending agency, the DLF, to support its initial capitalization; however, by the end of 1960 Mutual El Perú had made few loans. A second institution, the Mutual Lima, was in operation for only a brief period before being forced into liquidation as a result of poor management. The combined effect of these abortive efforts was to bring the entire initiative into disrepute. Hoping to salvage the program by association with his stellar reputation, the Peruvian government and the US experts providing it with assistance turned to McLellan. At their urging, in late 1960 McLellan agreed to establish a *mutual*, once assured of legislative support (from Peru) and financial support (from the United States). McLellan's Mutual El Pueblo began operations on March 1, 1961.

Meanwhile, in September 1959 President Prado had appointed Beltrán as prime minister and minister of finance, positions he held until April 1961. As prime minister, Beltrán—who in the past had used his newspapers to influence housing policy—was now able to push for the implementation of his own favored projects. However, his approach was not uncontested. In late 1960, as Beltrán's Mutual El Perú was facing criticism for its lack of progress in establishing lending operations, *El Comercio*—a main rival of Beltrán's *La Prensa*—began to publish a series of articles questioning his policy priorities, especially his outsized support for the mutuales. These progressive critics—partisans of the Movimiento Social Progresista (MSP), including Adolfo Córdova, Germán Tito Gutiérrez, Sebastián Salazar Bondy, and Luis Miró Quesada Garland—argued that the mutuales were not the panacea promised by Beltrán, but could only address the needs of the middle-income market. Further, since the loans could also be used to improve an existing dwelling or refinance a mortgage (all the while providing costly tax breaks), they would not actually help to build many more houses. Most damningly, while supporters of the mutuales claimed the heritage of the US Federal Savings and Loans system, critics responded that they were a counterfeit of this prestigious model, since the US associations were far better regulated and better armed to prevent the distorting influence of speculative investors. Elsewhere, Beltrán was condemned for using his newspaper to orchestrate support for the mutuales in general, and his own Mutual El Perú in particular ("as if it had special virtues that the others lack"). Further, his promise that by investing in mutuales the poor would become homeowners was dismissed as "a marvel similar to the multiplication of the loaves and the fishes"; and finally, an editorial pointedly endorsed Córdova's critique—expressed in his *La vivienda en el Perú* (1958)—of the easy appeal but ultimate mendacity of Beltrán's promise to bestow a "casa propia" on all Peruvians.[8]

Despite these critiques, in February 1961 Prado's government moved ahead with a comprehensive series of policy initiatives, including both Law 13517 and the establishment of the Banco de la Vivienda (Housing Bank) to oversee the operations of the newly founded mutuales. The following month, Kennedy announced to the US Congress his intention to forge an "alliance for progress" with Latin American nations. The funding committed to cement this alliance promised a bright future for Peru's development agenda.

In order to promote the *mutual* concept—still unfamiliar to many of its readers—in a February 1961 editorial, *La Prensa* cited Father McLellan in order to draw parallels with credit cooperatives: both were "Christian solutions" that drew on "the ancient communitarian roots, so characteristic of the psychology of this country . . . practiced since the Inca Empire." A promotional magazine produced by the Banco de la Vivienda—titled simply *Vivienda* (Dwelling)—continued the campaign in every issue, reporting on the stories of "modest families" who had managed to attain their dream homes, even though in many cases they had done so via winning promotional lotteries organized by the mutuales rather than purchasing the house themselves. It was relatively easy to join the *mutual*: prospective homeowners could open an account with as little as S/.50, and as their deposits reached S/.250 they would begin to receive interest. Once they could "demonstrate a real will to save" the *mutual* would lend up to 90 percent of the cost of a house. However, with dwellings at one project defined as "social interest housing" costing S/.280,000 (in 1968), reaching the requisite 10 percent deposit still represented a considerable challenge for the vast majority of households. Indeed, the residents of this development were identified as "white-collar workers, teachers, *técnicos*, experts in middle management"[9]—all clearly middle-income occupations.

Nonetheless, the mutuales were also required to set aside 12.5 percent of their loanable funds for upgrading projects. In one case, with their local priest as intermediary, twenty-eight families living in the San Martín de Porres *barriada* in Lima undertook small loans of approximately S/.3,000 each in order to pay for the installation of electricity in their homes as well as street lighting. One resident noted that as soon as the money was repaid, they were planning to apply for "another loan to build a good paved footpath and to complete the houses." McLellan objected to the requirement that mutuales support such projects, on the grounds that within a couple of years of operation, his Mutual El Pueblo "had made 85.77 percent of these loans in the Lima-Callao area, and . . . given the three-year maximum terms allowed by the Housing Bank (which put these loans far out of the reach of those who needed them the most), the market was saturated."[10] As a consequence, McLellan estimated that $1 million in *mutual* funds were sitting idle waiting for borrowers who would not appear.

More usually, the mutuales sponsored new housing developments—whether organized by housing cooperatives established to serve government employees, built by the state housing agencies themselves, or promoted as for-profit ventures by private developers. The *mutual* funding was particularly crucial to this last group, since they could not count on a pool of dedicated buyers (as with cooperative projects) or access to government resources (as with state housing). A case in point was the Wichita-based firm Hogares Peruanos, whose customers received some of the first loans granted by Mutual El Pueblo.

"Every Man A Homeowner": The Wichita-Lima Axis

According to his own account, World Homes founder Willard Garvey first became interested in establishing an international home-building corporation in 1958. His father, R. H. Garvey, had been an agribusiness pioneer, starting with a mortgage investment firm, and then amassing extensive landholdings to form his Wichita-based grain empire. Willard was particularly involved with the family's real estate concerns, beginning with the construction of grain elevators. The Garveys diversified into housing in 1941, as Wichita's population swiftly doubled with the influx of wartime workers to staff the area's aircraft factories. Writing two decades later, Garvey recalled their first development: twenty houses selling for $350 each, on a site "outside the city limits on gravel roads" and with only provisional services—"a WPA [Works Progress Administration] outdoor toilet, pitcher pump for water and city electricity." (There is a surface similarity here with the initial situation of squatter settlements, with the substantial difference that since the latter lack economic resources and secure tenure, they remain in this provisional state for much longer.) By 1946, when Garvey returned from his wartime service in Europe, the development was incorporated into the city: "paved streets, sewers, modern plumbing, wings, annexes, fences, porches, and shrubbery had been added. I was struck with the basic principle of the motivation provided by pride of homeownership. . . . [which] causes a man who had property to help himself to exercise his own enlightened self interest. . . . It separates him with an iron curtain from the non-homeowner just as the free world is separated from the communist world."[11]

Willard Garvey was deeply engaged with the question of US influence in the international sphere, in line with his fellow Kansas Republican Dwight D. Eisenhower. Garvey had served in the Allied Komendatura in Berlin, and—as he recalled—"stood 45 feet away from Stalin" at the Potsdam conference, experiences that evidently left him with a heightened awareness of Cold War geopolitics.[12] In 1958 Garvey became involved in supporting another Wichita-based entrepreneur, Bill Graham, and his associates, in their efforts to develop low-cost housing internationally, operating under the name Private Enterprise Inc. Following a meeting between a member of this group and Eisenhower (apparently arranged at the president's request to discuss "developing the individual—'the basic soldier'—abroad"), Garvey helped to write a précis "on how best to help people to help themselves." This text—titled "Every Man a Capitalist" as a riposte to Nikita Krushchev's "every man a communist"—warned that communism "has tripled in 10 years and may gain 100% of the world in 10 more"; in response, the United

States needed a straightforward and appealing "master plan" to reach "the little man" being targeted for communist recruitment. The strategy should be to focus on basic human needs: shelter, food, and clothing. Of these, "shelter, or home, has most appeal. It is the 'little man's' best chance to be a capitalist or a property owner." To implement this plan, the US government itself should act as housing developer on a trial project, tapping its various international aid programs for interim financing. If successful, the program could be repeated, with some involvement from the private sector, in perpetuity. The short-term goal was "ten million new private homes this year"; the intermediate goal one hundred million homes; and eventually, "every man a home owner." Rather than earning any wages, the construction worker should be remunerated in kind: "Perhaps surplus flour ("food") in sacks ("clothing") could be taken by [the] construction worker to pay one half his labor and the other half taken as downpayment or equity in a house (100 workers build 100 houses, move in, then hire another 100 workers?)."[13] In this highly efficient operation, simultaneously targeting all basic needs, the worker—reframed as an involuntary self-help home-builder—becomes the (captive) market for his own product, and is instantly unemployed to make way for the next batch of workers.

Two months later Garvey expanded on these thoughts in a presentation to the Committee on Foreign Economic Practices, an advisory body of the Commerce Department. By this time he was himself investigating the possibility of building low-cost housing overseas, in Nicaragua. Garvey recommended that the United States focus its efforts where it clearly had the upper hand over the Soviet Union: "Let's hit them where they live, housing and food." Specifically, through the Public Law 480 program (or PL 480, also known as "Food for Peace"), established under Eisenhower in 1954 to dispose of surplus agricultural products in the form of overseas aid, the United States should "lend" its food surplus to developing countries with repayment scheduled on a long-term, low-interest basis. The proceeds of these transactions (which could not be converted into US dollars and repatriated) should then be reinvested in the purchasing country "as long-term mortgage financing on low-cost privately owned homes."[14] As titans of agriculture, the Garvey family was receiving around $15 million a year in government subsidies to grow grain, to not grow grain (thanks to the federal soil bank program), and to store grain.[15] Under this new proposal, when surplus grain was sold overseas, Garvey would access the proceeds to fund his housing ventures.

Garvey pointed out that as of late 1958, $89 million in PL 480 funds were awaiting reinvestment in a range of countries. Since the money had not yet been committed to specific projects, he suggested that it should be earmarked for housing. After receiving in-principle support from the Export-Import Bank—responsible for distributing PL 480 funds—Garvey asked the bank to recommend where to start his operations (since by this stage his Nicaraguan prospect had fallen through). They advised him that "the real demand" was "in the Eastern hemisphere, Pakistan, India, etc." but suggested mounting a trial program closer to home for ease of supervision. Only three countries in the region still had funds available—Colombia, Ecuador, and Peru—so in February 1959 Garvey undertook a research trip to determine how his plan would be received by the prospective hosts. Apparently he found greatest encouragement in Peru, where he met with government officials, bankers, and entrepreneurs who were generally enthusiastic about the scheme. Beltrán—who had established his Mutual El Perú only a few months earlier and no doubt welcomed the prospect of additional business—made a particularly good impression on Garvey for the manner in which he used his newspaper to forward his ideas on the housing problem: "Most of the newspapers in this country have lost your crusading zeal, much to my regret." This favorable opinion was apparently shared by Stanley Baruch, a senior US aid official who was reported to have described Beltrán as "one of the strongest advocates of private housing in the entire world." Milton Eisenhower, the president's brother, went further, citing Beltrán's pleas as the inspiration for his own advocacy of US aid to Latin America.[16]

By August 1959 Garvey had established the World Homes headquarters in Wichita, and the following month the Export-Import Bank approved a loan of $140,000 in PL 480 funds as partial financing for a project of seventy-two houses in Peru. In October, manager Howard Wenzel arrived in Lima to set up World Homes' first office: Hogares Peruanos, or Peruvian Homes (code name: Operation Guinea Pig). In April 1960 the inaugural Hogares Peruanos model house opened to the public (fig. 5.2), and by the end of the year the firm had completed its first group of houses, financed using PL 480 funds. (Meanwhile, the initial model house had been paid for with a loan from the University of Wichita—Garvey's alma mater—which it was apparently expected to classify as an overseas research venture.)[17] As with most Hogares Peruanos projects, the design followed the "growing house" model. Beginning with a minimal core unit, the

Figure 5.2. Ernesto Aramburú for Hogares Peruanos, inaugural model house, Lima, 1960. Howard Wenzel (*center right*) courts prospective buyers. *Source*: Jean and Willard Garvey World Homes Collection, Wichita State University Libraries, Special Collections and University Archives.

dwelling would evolve over time as the family's needs and resources changed, extending horizontally into the garden and vertically with an additional story, facilitated by a flat roof. All the while the pattern of expansion would follow the original plans set out by the architect, which would be provided to the buyers with their purchase. As Wenzel described the rationale: "It is the desire of most middle-class Peruvians to own a two-story house. For this reason most one-floor houses constructed in the low and middle cost range in Lima are prepared for second-floor construction. The buying public insists on it."[18]

In accordance with its innovative business model, Hogares Peruanos now pursued various sources of development aid to finance its next projects—applying for a second round of PL 480 funds, as well as loans from the IDB, and a housing investment guaranty from USAID. Its next two projects were located on adjacent sites, but aimed at quite different markets: Sol de Oro would be developed as a speculative venture with the houses sold on the open market, while Villa Los Angeles had been initiated by members of a housing cooperative who had approached Hogares Peruanos to be their developer after visiting the model house.

Sol de Oro (meaning both "golden sun" and "golden sol"—the Peruvian currency) was promoted using a sophisticated marketing campaign that played on the popular appeal of the US space program, with its streets named after planets, stars, and astronomers. The naming of the four model houses continued this theme, with some misalignments—perhaps an inevitable byproduct of Cold War ambiguities: Explorer and Discoverer were known as space research programs, though the latter actually performed CIA reconnaissance; Atlas was a space launch rocket that doubled as an intercontinental ballistic missile; Polaris was a nuclear missile pure and simple. The housing was presented as modern and sophisticated, the single-family dwellings with cars in the driveway evoking an imagined Americana suburbia—although these flat-roofed houses would never have appeared in a US subdivision (plates 11–12). With funds from the Alliance for Progress backing the mortgages available to buyers, Hogares Peruanos made a point of using the organization's logo on the publicity materials, betting on the added cachet of Kennedy's new program.

On paper at least, Villa Los Angeles would seem to be a less profitable venture, but its suitability to the broader Hogares Peruanos mission—and to the priorities of funding agencies, which "wanted to reach lower down the income scale"—offered other incentives for the firm to take on the project. More than a business, Hogares Peruanos operated as a philanthropic-ideological-entrepreneurial conglomerate with multinational ambitions, endeavoring to proselytize free market values wherever US aid funding led it, under the dual objectives of making "a fair profit" and advancing its motto, "Every Man a Home Owner." This ideological commitment was not just a public relations posture. As becomes evident in the company's internal memos, business decisions were never simply financial in nature but guided in large part by considerations of their strategic impact in furthering the cause. Wenzel reported on the culture shock he experienced in real estate negotiations with wealthy *limeños* on discovering that this ideological commitment was not shared: "The Peruvian rich love to talk about the social problem of housing and how the 'revolution' may come unless they do something about it but when money is involved the social conscience goes out the window." For the Peruvian elite, there was no question of making concessions on a business level to forward a particular agenda—profit trumped altruism or ideology—whereas for Hogares Peruanos, promoting the procapitalist message was part of the company's core business. To this end, the five hundred members of the Villa Los Angeles cooperative—many of them low-income families—had been paying small weekly fees over several years to build up sufficient funds to buy the land for their housing project. As Wenzel observed, it was more usual for such cooperatives to acquire land through invasion, "then claiming the land . . . under squatters' rights."[19] Wenzel argued that by respecting private property and abiding by the law, this group had set a positive example that deserved to be endorsed via aid support.

Since purchasing the land for the Villa Los Angeles development would likely exhaust the savings of many families, it was anticipated that they would complete their houses through self-help labor. Wenzel expressed great enthusiasm about the potential of this model: "Self-help offers the real long-run solution to the housing problem in the developing countries and if a private company can develop a system for profitably working in this field the market is unlimited. Not to mention the tremendous social contribution that will be made and the propaganda in the struggle with Communism." Having committed the firm to the self-help model, Wenzel recommended Turner to coordinate the project. In general, the preferred Hogares Peruanos modus operandi was to find an investment partner to share the financial risks of its projects. In this case, Wenzel reported that Turner lacked the funds for such an arrangement (he had been "unemployed during 1958 and part of 1959 since there was little doing in Self-Help here"), but he was prepared to work for out-of-pocket expenses until the financing came through.[20] More importantly, Wenzel argued that Turner's expertise was invaluable, and he enthusiastically recommended Turner's Arequipa report to officials at World Homes.[21] For its part, the company would act as "technical and financial consultants" for the project, offering their services for 10 percent of the net construction costs.[22] Although the cooperative agreed to this deal, the IDB—providing mortgage financing to the Villa Los Angeles association members en bloc, since they had all been persuaded to join McLellan's *mutual*—objected, arguing that 2 percent was the usual fee; in the end, they settled on 5 percent. At such times, its heavy reliance on US government aid funds presented particular challenges to the company's efforts at profitability.

At Villa Los Angeles Turner began by commissioning "an exhaustive market research study" of prospective residents, carried out by anthropologist Eduardo Soler, who had previously worked with Turner at Paramonga. It soon became evident that the major-

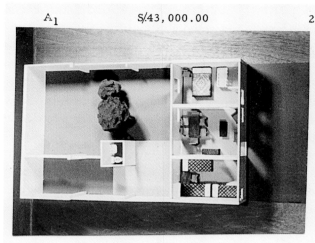

A₁   S/.43,000.00   2 Dormitorios
Sala–Comedor
Cocina Ramada
Baño
Jardín
House unfinished.
Original shell includes
Four walls, water, sewer,
light connections.
Finishing done by owner
on basis of sided self-
help.

Figure 5.3. John F. C. Turner for Hogares Peruanos, House Type A1, Villa Los Angeles, Lima, 1961. *Source*: "Application for a Loan to the Inter-American Development Bank, Asoc. Pro Vivienda Propia Villa Los Angeles," Aug. 1961, Jean and Willard Garvey World Homes Collection, Wichita State University Libraries, Special Collections and University Archives.

ity preferred to pay for contractor-built houses and had sufficient means to undertake a mortgage. However, many could only afford an unfinished "minimum house": provided with the bare structure and basic plumbing connections, self-help labor would take care of installing partitions and sanitary fixtures, plastering, flooring, and painting. The remaining 25 percent of residents would have access to no resources but their own labor. Turner now prepared the initial plans for the urban layout and for the various house types required to accommodate the different budgets. The trapezoidal site plan was defined by preexisting boundaries and, in accordance with planning regulations, 40 percent of the land was set aside for park space. In order to reduce paving costs—and since few residents would have cars—the passageways between the lots were no wider than double sidewalks. The effect was to create multiple points of pedestrian access to the central spine of green space, while limiting cars to parking areas at the center and at either end of the development. The most basic house consisted of two bedrooms, a living-dining room, an outside toilet, a *cocina ramada* (an outside kitchen protected with a roof of *esteras*), and an area in the backyard "to keep chickens and other animals."[23] With extensions and a second story the house could include up to five bedrooms (fig. 5.3).

Each house was available in finished or unfinished states—the latter, "minimum" house being considerably less expensive. Proceeding in this way, residents of the minimum dwelling could move in as soon as basic construction was completed. According to Turner, by living on site, they could work on their houses "in their spare time"; without this option, since the development was on the urban periphery and most worked in central Lima, they would only be able to work on Sundays, likely leading to a protracted construction period that would adversely affect neighborhood cohesion. In an additional effort to accommodate the lower-income residents, Turner envisaged the establishment of a cement block factory on-site to provide well-paying local jobs, a gesture in the direction of holistic community development.

Estimates of the time needed for construction were unduly optimistic: less than a year for the installation of services, and the completion of all contractor-built houses, and eighteen months for the self-build housing. In fact, work was repeatedly delayed by the process of preparing aid applications, waiting for approvals, and arranging for money to travel through the bureaucracies of US funders and Peruvian housing agencies. As a solution to this problem, Hogares Peruanos seriously considered the possibility of taking over an existing *mutual* or establishing its own, or even becoming a wheat broker—selling grain directly to Peru, and using the profits to establish a "revolving fund" for mortgage financing that would be directly controlled by the company or its associated businesses.[24] None of these projects came to fruition, leaving the company tied to the agendas and procedures of the development agencies.

In the meantime, Wenzel began to explore alternative proposals for the housing. In March 1962 engineer Leonard Oboler submitted two designs for consideration: a standard three-bedroom house, and a "paraboloid roof house" consisting of "a simple shell roof, middle column and cement floor with one enclosed bathroom." This second design was to serve as the core of a self-build house: once enclosed with exterior walls, the space could be divided into a series of rooms with distinct functions; the kitchen would be located behind this unit, framed by a half-wall, as in the cocina ramada of Turner's design (figs. 5.4–5.5). Within a few weeks, Wenzel was investigating using this "shell home" more widely in an "urban renewal project." In September, having received provisional approval from the new housing agency, Instituto de la Vivienda (INVI), Wen-

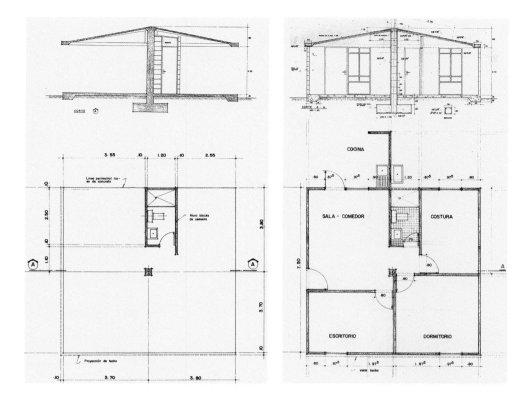

Figure 5.4 (*above left*). Leonard Oboler Engineers SA for Hogares Peruanos, Paraboloid Roof House, 1962. The "Shell Home" as the core for a self-build house: in stage one, a concrete roof, central column, concrete slab floor, and enclosed toilet. *Source*: Jean and Willard Garvey World Homes Collection, Wichita State University Libraries, Special Collections and University Archives.

Figure 5.5 (*above right*). Leonard Oboler Engineers SA for Hogares Peruanos, Paraboloid Roof House, 1962. The "Shell Home" as the core for a self-build house: in the final stage, four enclosed rooms. *Source*: Jean and Willard Garvey World Homes Collection, Wichita State University Libraries, Special Collections and University Archives.

zel reported: "We are now doing a brief market study of 4 different slum areas to see just how ma[n]y units we can expect to sell." As a result of this survey, Wenzel determined that there were "over 5000 buyers qualified."[25] According to Wenzel, INVI approved a first group of 250 houses, with the possibility of extending the program up to 1,000 units. In this context the "shell home" (fig. 5.6) seems to have been envisaged as an addition to a minimal dwelling that had been offered for sale by the CNV only a year or so before in Urbanización Popular de Interés Social (UPIS) Valdiviezo (see

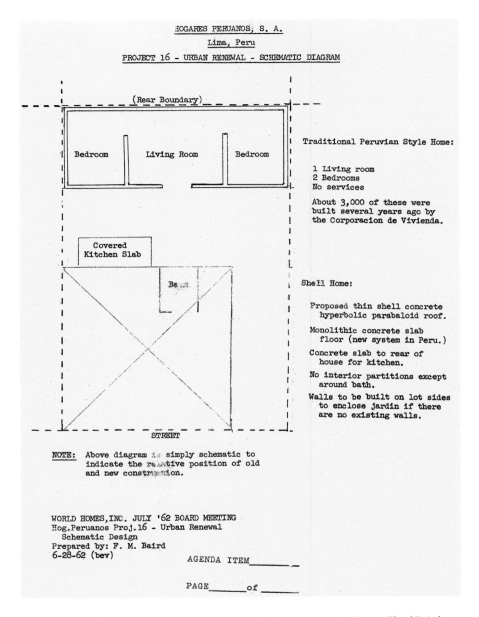

Figure 5.6. The "Shell Home" as a complement to a CNV basic core unit. *Source*: Floyd Baird, "Project 16: Urban Renewal—Schematic Diagram," June 28, 1962, Jean and Willard Garvey World Homes Collection, Wichita State University Libraries, Special Collections and University Archives.

fig. 4.12). Consisting of a small, single room at the back of the lot, and constructed with a mix of permanent and provisional materials, residents would gradually construct their houses to fill the lot.

With the addition of the "shell home" the lot would now contain two provisional, expandable shelter units, which did not quite add up to a house.

While the initial proposal anticipated delegating the organizational aspects of the self-help program to an outside body such as the Peace Corps, Wenzel subsequently reported that INVI had recommended that Hogares Peruanos take charge of all aspects, "including the self-help phase of the project in the provision of materials and technical assistance as well as constructing the shell unit." While the firm had no prior experience in this area, Wenzel judged that "if handled properly the supplying of materials for the self-help phase could be very profitable." Shortly after this report, Wenzel's notes on the project end, indicating that it did not proceed any further as an "urban renewal" solution or as a model for Villa Los Angeles. Indeed, at Villa Los Angeles the self-help component of the project disappeared entirely by early 1963, and Turner's involvement came to an end. Wenzel had become aware that the Paramonga project had failed due to massive cost overruns and he lost faith in the self-help model: "Self-help housing is a nice text book solution sort of like Utopia, the early Utopian Socialists, but it just doesn't work in practice. Sounds wonderful when you read it in a book but it takes too many technicians and too much administration. . . . If it isn't done properly, the people gradually lose interest and the whole thing falls on its face."[26] Rather than a magic ticket to an "unlimited" market, aided self-help housing presented complex challenges of its own, and proved resistant to successful for-profit production.

Villa Los Angeles did progress, but at a much slower rate than initially projected. Actual construction began around 1964 and continued into the early 1970s (fig. 5.7). Hogares Peruanos reached agreements with three architectural firms to present new model houses to the cooperative and within a couple of years, residents began moving into their homes. Although the self-help component disappeared from the first stage of construction, it was certainly made use of in postoccupancy extensions, with the addition of a second, third, or fourth story, or as little as a parapet wall to enclose the *azotea* (fig. 5.8).

Considering the scale of the housing deficit and the limited financial capacity of most Peruvian families, from the outset critics such as Adolfo Córdova and others from the MSP had questioned the viability of broad-based homeownership as a solution. In any

Figure 5.7. Villa Los Angeles, Lima, ca. March 1965. *Source*: Jean and Willard Garvey World Homes Collection, Wichita State University Libraries, Special Collections and University Archives.

Figure 5.8. Self-build construction as an ongoing process at Villa Los Angeles, Lima, 1990. *Source*: Photograph by Hans Harms.

case, the government-to-government and government-to-business partnerships cultivated in the early 1960s to enact this policy quickly showed signs of strain, fatally compromising the Hogares Peruanos mission. Following a military coup in 1962—staged to stabilize the country after inconclusive election results—the United States suspended diplomatic relations as well as aid funding, making it difficult for the firm to conduct business. Wenzel hoped that they would soon resume operations with continued—if reduced—US support, but sensed that the coup would have broader repercussions: "Peru was to have been the example for South America" and this unwelcome turn in its domestic affairs brought US policy toward the entire region into question.[27] Soon after, US aid was again restricted, this time in retaliation for the government's efforts to renegotiate the terms of its contract with a subsidiary of Standard Oil of New Jersey. As a final blow, the 1968 military coup initiating the (short-lived) Peruvian Revolution created a climate hostile toward foreign-owned businesses, while a declining economy hurt the firm's core market of lower-middle-income families. In the early 1970s Hogares Peruanos wound up operations altogether, after completing 450 of the 500 houses planned for Villa Los Angeles. Converted into a gated community in response to increasing insecurity, but with its green corridor intact, the development remains under permanent construction—almost as envisaged by Turner, but self-built by default rather than by design.

Development through Self-Help

In a sense, Hogares Peruanos was an Eisenhower-era project that subsequently adjusted itself to Kennedy-era funding opportunities. By contrast, Perú-BID Plan Bienal 1962–1963 (hereafter Perú-BID) was much more closely shaped by Kennedy's vision for Latin America.

The United States considered support for aided self-help housing in Latin America as early as 1954, following the Tenth Inter-American Conference held in Caracas in March of that year. Jacob L. Crane, director of international operations for the Housing and Home Finance Agency (HHFA), was among the US attendees, and reported to the State Department on the US delegation's cool reception of various ambitious proposals by Latin American nations; these included the establishment of an Inter-American Bank, an Inter-American Housing Institute, and additional Inter-American Housing Centers, to complement CINVA in Bogotá. The United States countered with a proposal to develop opportunities for technical cooperation, with a particular emphasis on "aided self-help shelter improvement."[28] A memo on this subject written in March 1954 indicated that officials were already discussing the potential for such projects with a number of countries: "A total of 15,000 houses might be produced in such aided self-help demonstrations in Latin America during the next year or two."[29] Crane provided more details: a trial would take place across fifteen countries, with 1,000 houses constructed in each, "at a cost to [the United States] of about $200 per house." The advantage of the aided self-help approach would be to maximize Latin American output for minimum US input, since the monetary value of the labor invested "would total at least $25,000,000, or five times the [US] participation."[30]

A few months later, another US housing official floated an alternative proposal for "an 'impact' program in housing": the mass-scale provision of technical assistance, "at the rate of one technician for every 10,000 families" in Latin America, totaling 200 US experts to be deployed over a ten-year period. In addition, the participating countries would establish training centers for local "aided self-help technicians"; the goal was to produce experts "at the rate of 1 per 100 dwelling units" or 20,000 in total, their salaries paid by the United States. Calculating that "about half of roughly 40,000,000 families in Latin America" were in need of their assistance, the 20,000 technicians could oversee the production of 20,000,000 houses over a decade, at the rate of 2,000,000 per year.[31]

While neither of these schemes came close to being realized, the new emphasis given to housing at the conference in Caracas did have an impact on how the US viewed housing within its international aid agenda. At the end of 1954 aid officials circulated a new housing policy, recognizing "that shelter for the working forces is a necessary and productive investment: the house is as important economically as the barn; the industrial worker's home is as important as the factory or mine." The new policy stressed the role of US technical cooperation in improving housing provision, while the implementation of any projects "must be wholly from internal resources of host countries" rather than relying on US funding.[32] Fostering the housing finance system would be one key measure to achieve this, along with aided self-help.

In the case of Peru, one outcome of this policy shift was the provision of US experts to CRAV in 1956, brokered by Stanley Baruch, Latin American branch chief of the housing division of the International Cooperation Administration (ICA, a precursor agency to USAID). The technical assistance to CRAV was initially focused on the establishment of mutuales; discussions over similar support for aided self-help housing began in late 1960. In September, Baruch wrote to a US aid official in Lima, noting that the United States was working with

Peru "in the encouragement of private home ownership throughout the country"—a goal that could be furthered by the promotion of aided self-help. To this end, "an aid program on a crash basis and assistance from the US in an amount of from 7 to 10 million dollars will serve the purpose." He recommended that the US mission in Peru hire two US experts to set up and supervise the program, assisted by "at least four" Peruvians who would receive three months of training in Puerto Rico, Chile, Guatemala, and Nicaragua—locations where US agencies had already assisted with such programs.[33]

A month later, the head of the ICA housing division in Washington contacted the director of the US mission in Peru to underscore the importance of this initiative: "All of a sudden some of the top brass in State have decided that we should start aided self-help housing programs all over South America, beginning last week. Particular emphasis is being given to Peru."[34] The problem was securing funding: the US ambassador reported to Beltrán (then prime minister and minister of finance) that the DLF (which had funded Beltrán's Mutual El Perú) was unwilling to back aided self-help projects, and that it might be necessary to postpone plans until the following year, "when we hope substantial funds will be available under the new Latin American program" (that is, the $500 million committed under the Act of Bogotá). He reassured Beltrán that he had been advocating for the funding, and acknowledged Beltrán's personal commitment to the initiative, specifically his "desire to start six projects as quickly as possible."[35] (This was apparently a reference to the proposal by the Fondo Nacional de Salud y Bienestar Social to implement projects in six cities across Peru, which, though unrealized, in a sense laid the groundwork for Perú-BID.)[36] Shortly afterward Baruch reported that Beltrán was continuing to lobby for a major program, and suggested offering the services of a US self-help housing expert, George A. Speer, who could visit Peru for two months to help frame the program that Beltrán envisaged.

On his visit, Speer met a range of figures involved in low-cost housing, including Father McLellan, Hernán Bedoya (identified as the architect of Ciudad Mi Trabajo in Arequipa), three representatives of Hogares Peruanos (Wenzel, Turner, and Soler), as well as senior staff from W. R. Grace and Company in Paramonga. In January 1961 Speer prepared a draft of a proposed aided self-help project, to be submitted to the ICA for funding. Significantly, Speer suggested the utilization of two distinctive modes of aided self-help—individual and collective. The first option "includes the formal provision of developed land, a construction loan, and technical assistance to ingenious and resourceful low income individuals. In return, they shrewdly purchase much of their own building materials, employ labor, direct and participate in the construction of their own home. . . . Others, unable, for one reason or another, to accept the responsibilities outlined above, would be organized into groups to help each other build a group of houses under the direction of the sponsoring agency." Significantly, the first option resonates with the HHFA's identification of "family aided self-help" as a preferred program for US assistance, viewed as fulfilling the goal that the housing policies of beneficiary nations reflect the pro-private-enterprise principles of the US Housing Act of 1949.[37] Speer stressed that both types of self-helpers—the ingenious as well as the marginally responsible—were to cover all project costs via low-interest loans, "without subsidy": "The program should develop desirable personal habits of enterprise and thrift, a vital factor in economic growth in a free society."[38]

These recommendations carried over, in slightly modified form, to the terms of a loan agreement between the ICA and Peru, signed at the end of June 1961. This loan covered $500,000 for a pilot project in aided self-help to be carried out in Lima and Chimbote, with a total of 840 houses (later revised to $475,000 for 798 houses). Both project locations would provide "on-site training of personnel" for a national program in aided self-help housing, and would educate the public about the benefits of the method, in order to "stimulate favorable public response to the efforts of the Government to advance public welfare." The project was carefully structured to gradually foster the participants' personal development. In stage one, the site would be prepared and the participants could "build any type of provisional shelter" provided it was at the rear of the lot, so as not to interfere with the permanent dwelling. In stage two, aided self-help labor would be employed to build "permanent nuclei" of expandable houses, sited at the front. Stage three entailed the expansion of the nuclei via individual loans to each family, managing the work on its own schedule. As the family's residence improved—"from emergency shelters to minimum permanent sanitary housing and finally . . . to expanded, adequate homes"—they would be "introduced to increasing responsibility for their own advancement with each step, as the Government's role shifts from active to passive."[39] In this way, the project would acculturate the participants into the "personal habits of enterprise and thrift" envisaged by Speer, as supervised, "aided" self-help gave way to self-managed self-help. Since site preparation was already under way, it was estimated that construction of the nuclei would begin in September 1961, with completion in twenty months. In addition to lending funds, the US would provide technical assistance via "a housing generalist" and an aided self-help specialist, along with training for eight Peruvian staff.

Although framed as a pilot project, this was launched only a couple of months before the IDB approved Perú-BID. Effectively, the two programs were run concurrently, with little opportunity for the pilot project to provide feedback for the larger program, in order to refine or reorient its approach. It seems that the imperative to get an "impact" program under way—both to satisfy the "top brass in State" and to "stimulate favorable public response" in Peru—contributed to the decision to push forward with Perú-BID before the pilot project was completed.

In March 1961 Kennedy announced the Alliance for Progress; the Declaration of Punta del Este, adopted in August, identified steps beneficiary nations should undertake in exchange for the promised assistance. As articulated in a USAID memorandum: "For its part the United States has agreed to help those countries which help themselves." Latin American participants were to foster their own social development by enacting a series of "self-help and reform measures": improvements to education, government administration, and the tax system, the encouragement of private enterprise, and the formulation of long-range development plans.[40] Peru fulfilled this last requirement by producing its *Plan nacional de desarrollo económico y social del Perú, 1962–1971* (National plan for the economic and social development of Peru, hereafter *Plan nacional*). Constructed specifically to meet the criteria set by the Alliance concerning administrative reform, this plan formalized Peru as a modern, technocratic society, articulating a vision for its own "development" and setting out a process to fulfill it by disciplining the ad hoc workings of government into articulated targets, budgets, and evaluated outcomes. Parallel to cultivating the squatter home builder's enterprise and thrift via self-help labor, the Alliance prescribed the subject-formation of a democratic nation-state via self-help efforts in administrative transparency, efficiency, and accountability.

In October 1961 the IDB approved funding for Perú-BID, providing $22.8 million for low-income housing, primarily to be constructed using aided self-help. Turner was part of the Peruvian delegation that went to Washington, along with Luis Marcial, an architect and senior official at INVI. Turner recalled that in advance of the meeting, the IDB "made known that [they] would be prepared to consider funding a national program of self-build"; following the group's presentation, "the bank's board was delighted" and immediately doubled the amount of the loan.[41] (Beltrán's long-cultivated relationships and persistent behind-the-scenes correspondence with US officials no doubt also played a major part.) Alliance projects were to be jointly funded by the United States and the participating government, so Peru committed $20.9 million to the program (around 20 percent being "the estimated value of beneficiaries' labor"), giving it a total budget of $43.7 million.[42]

The *Plan nacional* was completed a year after the Perú-BID loan was approved, its purpose being to situate that program within the larger landscape of housing needs, and to coordinate the housing program with the overall plan for national development. It determined that over ten years the state needed to build a staggering 671,350 new dwellings and rehabilitate an additional 343,800. However, the *Plan nacional* stressed that "these figures are nothing but indications of the need" and that the actual targets would have to be negotiated against other spending priorities. Accordingly, the concrete projects it outlined for the immediate term were more modest: the construction of 22,000 dwellings by the newly established INVI, and a series of upgrading projects by the existing housing agency, the CNV. The latter would focus on four areas related to the implementation of Law 13517: "urbanistic remodeling" of barriadas, provision of basic infrastructure, formalizing property titles, and granting 12,500 loans for "the improvement, completion, or construction of dwellings" in barriadas.[43] In addition, sites-and-services programs run jointly by the CNV and INVI would furnish 25,000 lots, and land would be secured for future projects.

Under the original loan agreement, Perú-BID was to fund the construction of 17,350 new dwellings using aided self-help and 5,350 using conventional construction (via INVI), along with 12,500 loans for the improvement or completion of barriada dwellings using self-managed self-help (via the CNV), for a total of 35,200 households assisted. In September 1963, two months before the Perú-BID program was due to be completed, the contract was renegotiated, extending the deadline by two years, significantly increasing the allowable maximum cost per house, and altering the primary construction system from "auto-ayuda" (self-help) to "indefinido" (undefined). According to the documentation explicating this shift, by May 1963 only 1,050 aided self-help dwellings had been completed, compared to 3,750 in conventional construction. In addition, only 700 loans had been granted for the completion of barriada dwellings, while a further 4,150 households had been served by "barriada eradication" projects, defined as providing a minimally serviced site with a *núcleo inicial de vivienda* (initial core dwelling) to residents "eradicated" from their homes as a consequence of urban remodeling. The revised contract maintained the overall goal of 35,200, and the amount of conventional construction, but dramatically reduced the aided self-help component to only 7,950, and dropped the completion of barriada dwellings to 6,980, while increasing the allocation for "barriada eradication" to 14,920 households.[44]

Overall, given that the numbers are not consistent across the various sources, the best estimate is that Perú-BID eventually assisted 38,698 households. There were 4,106 new dwellings built with aided self-help and 8,895 with direct construction, with the remaining number a mixture of infrastructure provision to barriada households and the completion of individual barriada dwellings. This represents a precipitous decline in the expectations for aided self-help housing. Initially, 17,350 dwellings were to be completed over two years; then, 7,950 within an additional two years; the eventual total was 4,106 built over four years. Although the extant documentation is slight, it is possible to outline the problems emerging from Perú-BID through the field reports of architects working to implement the program, and the assessments of US aid officials stationed in Peru.

The Architects' View

The focus here will be on Chimbote, since this represents the most extensive set of documentation. Sited on the coast a few hours north of Lima, in the 1940s Chimbote had been selected as the site of a regional development scheme connected to a hydroelectric project on the nearby Santa River. However, by the early 1960s the influx of migrants hopeful for work had vastly exceeded projections, resulting in astronomical unplanned urban growth. INVI's Perú-BID projects in Chimbote represented a remediation effort against the effects of this rampant industrial modernization. They fell into two categories. First, upgrading existing barriadas, including the provision of technical assistance and loans in the tuído por todos los gastos documentados que se hayan efectuado en su vivienda por concepto de materiales, Ayuda Técnica y Administrativa.

MONTO DEL CREDITO

Los préstamos otorgados en esta forma se harán sobre un promedio de $. 20,000.00 y en ningún caso podrán ser menores de $. 5,000.00 incluyéndose en estas cifras el costo del programa de saneamiento (agua, desagüe luz).

INTERESES

El interés será del 5 y ½ % anual al rebatir.

COMO OBTENER EL CREDITO

Para obtención de un crédito en las condiciones señaladas, el interesado acudirá a las oficinas del INVI, en donde se le facilitará la información complementaria sobre el Programa a desarrollarse y se le entregará un formulario de solicitud, Este deberá llenarse cuidadosamente con la ayuda de sus familiares y deberá ser devuelto a la oficina, en la fecha que se le indique.

ESFUERZO PROPIO: La familia participante ha recibido los materiales para ampliar su vivienda

Para obtener dicho formulario sólo será necesario la presentación de la libreta Electoral o Militar. En caso de analfabetos la partida de nacimiento o bautismo legalizada.

PARTICIPACION DEL INTERESADO

Si el INVI, encuentra apta la solicitud presentada, se dispondrá de inmediato la Ayuda Técnica, planos, materiales y la orientación debida previa firma del convenio y/o contrato.

La familia tiene dos alternativas para construir su casa.

1.–POR ESFUERZO PROPIO: En este caso la familia se encarga de la construcción de su casa propia personalmente ó contrata la mano de obra, recibiendo el asesoramiento técnico: materiales y equipo de construcción necesarios.

2 –POR AYUDA MUTUA.–En este caso un grupo de familias organizadas por el INVI, sumando las contribuciones individuales de sus miembros y con la instrucción, asesoramiento técnico, materiales y equipos de construcción proporcionado por el INVI, construye las casas de cada familia de su grupo al costo más bajo posible,

AYUDA MUTUA: Un grupo de familias en una tarea Dominical

Figure 5.9. Brochure promoting Perú-BID's barriada upgrading program in Chimbote: "*Esfuerzo propio*: The participating family has received materials to extend its dwelling"; "*Ayuda mutua*: A group of families in a Sunday working bee." *Source*: INVI, "Programa para las barriadas en Chimbote: construir, terminar, mejorar, ampliar, rehabilitar," 1962.

form of building materials to individual families in order to facilitate housing construction (fig. 5.9). Second, the construction of a new neighborhood: Urbanización El Trapecio would consist of 773 residential lots for single-family houses on the *núcleo básico* model and 288 apartments, with a comprehensive range of urban amenities and areas for light industry. In both programs, INVI offered two aided self-help options, described in a promotional brochure as *esfuerzo propio* (whereby "the family takes care of the construction of its *casa propia*") and *ayuda mutua* (whereby "a group of families . . . constructs the houses of each family in the group"). In contrast to Speer's moral hierarchy of individual over collective self-help, INVI's brochure framed the two options as equivalent, suggesting that both represented a modernized version of a familiar Peruvian system, offering the modest family "that traditionally builds its house with its own initiative and efforts, the necessary elements to build it rapidly and economically with the essential services for a healthy life."[45]

Some indications of the difficulties that emerged with the implementation of these projects can be found in the small number of extant field reports prepared for the head office in Lima, dating from 1963. At El Trapecio, after a year and a half of work, the first stage consisting of 530 núcleo básico dwellings had been completed. The housing agency had distributed a total of 1,400 application forms to prospective residents, but only 804 were actually submitted, and of these only 524 were declared to be suitable for the program. Meanwhile, approximately 5,000 families in the city were renting, and should theoretically have been attracted to this opportunity to own their own homes. The report concluded that El Trapecio "hasn't had the reception that was hoped for" because it did not correspond to the priorities of residents, which began with securing tenure for their lot. Furthermore, its location far from the center of the city lessened its appeal, particularly since it was adjacent to "the only group of *casas de diversión* [bars and gambling halls]" in the city, which, according to the housing office's own rules, made it a "dangerous and undesirable neighborhood" for families. Finally, it was still not possible to hand over the houses to residents because administrative delays had left work on the infrastructure "practically paralyzed" and key urban amenities, such as the school and the market, were not yet completed. As a consequence, "with the discouragement of the current, qualified concerned [applicants], one is running the risk of giving free rein to opponents' attacks."[46]

The most powerful of these opponents, according to housing officials, were the *pobladores* of the El Acero barriada, which had two rival residents' associations, with leaders who were hostile toward the authorities and found it to be in their interest to intimidate residents into withdrawing from the Perú-BID programs. However, it was evidently not difficult to sow dissent against the housing agency among the pobladores since "they have been the object of many surveys and have received few concrete results."[47] For their part, the reports' authors complained that there had not been enough time to carry out preparatory surveys—instead of the few days allotted, a month was necessary to build rapport with the pobladores and thus collect accurate information. Furthermore, there were few existing studies to use as a foundation, and to compound the problem, a high turnover of staff in the local offices meant that there was little continuity of institutional knowledge, and little consistency in interactions with the barriada residents.

More generally, the complaints underscored the disjunction

between the situation on the ground and officials' expectations. For example, the qualification rules (apparently determined by the IDB) specified an ideal candidate—married, healthy, with full and correct documentation—when in reality cohabitation was more common than matrimony, poverty and unsanitary environments compromised health, and acquiring certificates of birth, baptism, and property represented a considerable expense to most prospective residents. As a result, it was often difficult to muster sufficient qualified participants to carry out the projects. In the barriada La Libertad, for example, the housing agency had been building a relationship with the community over the course of a year, and remodeling plans had proceeded well in eighteen of the twenty blocks. However, a time limit had been set on the project, and the residents' lack of interest in signing up for the associated loans meant that it would be hard to enroll the target numbers by the deadline. By contrast, the upgrading program at 21 de Abril (established as an aided self-help project in 1958) promised to be easier to implement, since it was sponsored by USAID rather than the IDB and thus had fewer restrictive guidelines. At an even deeper level, there was a fundamental disjunction between the range and scope of the projects offered through Perú-BID and the actual needs of the intended beneficiaries, since the focus on the dwelling per se was not in keeping with residents' priorities, which were securing tenure for their lot, the installation of basic services, and communal amenities such as schools, markets, and health posts.

The Aid Officials' View

Meanwhile, US aid officials were already fielding concerns from INVI executives in September 1961, before the Perú-BID loan had even been signed. The pilot project for eight-hundred-odd houses in Lima and Chimbote was due to begin, and it seemed that the agency lacked sufficient trained personnel to carry it out. The problem was a shortage not of architects or planners but of administrators to oversee the program, statisticians to offer training in demographic survey techniques, and social assistants to select participants and manage the projects' dynamics. INVI requested IDB funds to train more Peruvian staff, and to hire six US experts in the fields of social anthropology, community development, industrial engineering, financial administration, public administration, and construction management. In theory, US aid officials supported the provision of such technical assistance, but they faced challenges recruiting qualified staff. As a result, the US mission in Peru relied heavily on the support of Peace Corps volunteers: eighteen were assigned to assist with the aided self-help pilot project in Chimbote, including "architects, engineers, skilled tradesmen, social workers, and nurses." At least another thirty were assigned to projects in Lima, Piura, and Arequipa (specifically, Ciudad Mi Trabajo).[48]

In early 1963 Teodoro Moscoso, then a senior USAID official in Washington, wrote in frustration to the director of USAID in Peru that the lack of adequate personnel was emerging as a widespread problem with Alliance projects, and that developing "leadership and technical capabilities among Latin Americans" would be crucial to the ultimate success of the Alliance. The problem was less a scarcity of specialists than one of a broader technocratic class: "It is ... painfully clear that approved projects very often don't get implemented properly and sometimes not at all for the one simple reason that there are no administrators to manage them."[49] In Peru this problem was compounded by the decision to manage Perú-BID via a new housing agency, whose very existence, for many observers, was redundant, or worse, counterproductive. The Prado government attempted to position INVI as fulfilling a new and distinct mission, complementing the CNV. In fact, it seems that operational efficiency played far less of a role in its establishment than interpersonal dynamics: according to one observer, INVI had been "created by Beltrán since he didn't get along with" the CNV director.[50] Because of this bureaucratic power struggle, the challenges of implementing a complex and extensive housing program were exacerbated by handing its execution to two competing agencies, one of which was completely untested. In early 1963 the two agencies were merged as the Junta Nacional de la Vivienda (JNV) in an effort to streamline the housing bureaucracy.

Other issues to beset the program ranged from spiraling costs to poor oversight of material and financial resources, opening the door to misappropriation. On the first issue, in August 1962 a US housing advisor based in Lima reported to Washington that work on Perú-BID was "anywhere from fifteen days to three months behind schedule" and the "actual cost of projects has averaged about 30% over estimates." This had an impact on all the subprograms, but the largest delays were in the aided self-help projects, "where very little has been accomplished."[51] On the second issue, memos between the controller of USAID Peru and the JNV concerning missing and/or misused sheets of plywood—300 in Chimbote and a further 454 in Lima—are one materialization of the traces of corruption that surely undermined the projects at multiple levels. According to the IDB's own internal evaluation, administrative deficiencies at the JNV resulted in the "absence of adequate controls over financial administration, construction materials, documents in the portfolio, bank accounts, etc."[52]

The IDB also identified poor coordination between the JNV and outside agencies as a major problem. In many cases, the state or municipal authorities that were responsible for preparing the site or installing urban services failed to complete the work in a timely manner or to an acceptable standard. As a result, construction schedules were delayed and budgets ran over, as the JNV was forced to take on these tasks in addition to its designated work of design and construction. This seems to have been a particular challenge in Chimbote: the El Carmen project was funded through the pilot program that began in September 1961, but in November 1965 a USAID official reported that the water and electricity systems were still being installed. In March 1966 "the water lines have been installed in all of the houses, but water is not available due to the failure of the city to complete the supply system."[53] By February 1967 the water supply was adequate but the electricity company was refusing to serve the neighborhood, because a number of high-tension poles were too close to roadways recently completed by the JNV; the poles would need to be relocated before electricity would be provided.

More fundamentally, a review of Perú-BID undertaken by the IDB in the process of evaluating a new JNV loan application suggested that there had been mistaken assumptions, based on incomplete data, as to the economic viability of aided self-help housing. In framing the new loan, the IDB recommended "thoroughly analyzing the real costs of housing in the country, as well as the real income levels of families with scarce resources" in order to set more realistic benchmarks for the cost of the dwelling and the maximum allowable income of potential participants.[54] In May 1966 a USAID official based Lima reported to the mission director that the Perú-BID projects were now "essentially completed" but were "unlikely to be extended"; they had been valuable in serving lower-income brackets that were not covered by the mutuales or by most government-funded housing projects, but they had faced serious challenges in their execution. He argued for a shift in focus for future projects, concluding that "USAID should not have a major program in housing." Instead, he pointed to the barriadas in Lima as "a priority opportunity for urbanization"—that is, upgrading infrastructure—but not housing. Simply put: "The magnitude of the need for housing in Peru is so great that the greater part of it cannot be met under any circumstances."[55]

The Value of "Aided" Self-Help

In mid-1967 the IDB completed its first evaluation of the initial round of housing programs it had funded, comparing the outcomes in four countries—Costa Rica, Colombia, Chile, and Peru. Arguing that it was essential for IDB-sponsored programs to become self-sufficient by mobilizing domestic resources for sustained growth in the housing sector, the evaluation took note of the repayment rates on its various loans. Primary borrowing institutions (such as national housing agencies) negotiated the terms of the loan and its repayment with the IDB, and then employed the funds to grant loans to individual homebuyers. Low recovery rates from these borrowers to the housing agencies would severely affect not just their ability to repay the IDB but potentially their overall financial stability.

In Peru, the two institutional borrowers were the JNV (funding four subprograms) and Father McLellan's Mutual El Pueblo. The latter had given out a total of more than four thousand mortgages, as well as eight hundred smaller loans for upgrading. For the IDB-backed mortgages, 95 percent of its borrowers were up to date with their payments, and only 3.6 percent were more than three payments behind—generally in cases where borrowers had experienced unemployment or unanticipated family crises. At the JNV, however, the repayment rates varied dramatically among its subprograms: in direct construction 61.5 percent were up to date, in rehabilitation only 19.6 percent were, while in self-help and barriada eradication programs no borrowers were up to date and 74 percent were more than three payments in arrears. According to the IDB, the primary reason for the lack of repayment was "political": opportunistic candidates had curried favor with residents by encouraging them to stop payment, offering vague promises of a better deal. (This is confirmed by a field report from Chimbote, which observed that a contentious election campaign contributed to the lackluster participation in the Perú-BID programs, as candidates "make large promises and the people anticipate the benefits that could follow"—for example, one candidate was encouraging residents to demand interest-free loans from the JNV instead of the 5.5 percent rate on offer.[56]) For its part, the JNV lacked the will or the means to evict delinquent tenants, giving others the courage to follow suit. The report concluded that this problem was ultimately due to the fact that many of the selected families had insufficient or erratic incomes and probably should not have been given loans in the first place.

The report identified two subprograms as problematic across the four countries surveyed: núcleo básico houses and aided self-help programs. With aided self-help programs, the report argued that success was highly dependent on the adequacy (or not) of the organized assistance, and recommended a more critical assessment of the capacity of housing agencies to carry them out. Even when well managed, the projects tended to be very drawn out, taking eighteen months to complete as opposed to four months for direct construction, since work was limited to three nights a week and a half day on Sunday (which would nonetheless represent a substantial time commitment for working families). In addition to the actual mechanics of managing construction and financing, aided self-help programs required a great deal of retraining of residents in the good use and maintenance of their dwellings—a costly exercise, but failure to carry this out could jeopardize the entire investment. Housing agencies needed to provide "a real school where families can 'learn to live'" and become motivated "for a change toward a better system, inculcating in them at the same time the need to fulfill the social and financial obligations imposed by their new 'status' as *propietarios* [owners] of a dwelling."[57] The missionary tenor of the enterprise was unmistakable: this represented not simply the provision of a house but a new socioeconomic identity as homeowner and borrower.

In its conclusions, the report noted that the IDB's initial programs had been organized without having "great experience in international financing for housing programs." In July 1966, with the benefit of some experience, the agency had produced a memorandum recommending a change in direction. The IDB's paramount goal should be to provide "seed capital" for housing, not endless funding, and thus it needed to achieve a reasonable return on its initial investments. It was now clear that núcleo básico and aided self-help housing could not meet this benchmark, and that furthermore, "there is a socioeconomic group that cannot be helped in the attainment of their dwelling except through high subsidies." These would-be homeowners needed to be provided with an alternative solution of a "global character": that is, "a job and decent wages."[58] This was an acknowledgment that in the absence of economic security, an improved living environment meant little; in actuality, the worker's home was not as important as the barn, factory, or mine providing an income. Finally, for those households with sufficient funds to be assisted, the report advised a focus on lowering costs via technological innovations in materials and construction systems.

Turner's critique of the Perú-BID program led him to a different conclusion. As Turner had the responsibility of overseeing the aided self-help component of the program, he soon began to feel that the whole enterprise was heading in the wrong direction: pressures from the sponsors to implement projects within a strict schedule led to quick solutions that were less than ideal. In particular, there was insufficient time to properly organize the participants—or, more precisely, to assist them to organize themselves. At the same time, Turner had the opportunity to work on a smaller project in parallel with the main Perú-BID program. Initiated by his INVI colleague Luis Marcial, this trial project at the Huascarán barriada in Lima explored an alternative approach to aided self-help: supervised credit. The eighteen participating families were provided with plans and specifications for the houses they would build, and a building inspector was assigned to explain the plans and ensure that each stage of construction was completed to an acceptable standard. Initially, credit was issued in the form of construction materials, but the administrative requirements for acquiring, distributing, and keeping track of the materials proved to be prohibitive. Under the revised project, participants were given a series of small advances to cover the cost of each stage of construction—foundations, walls, basic shell of the dwelling, roof—with money for the subsequent stage disbursed as the scheduled work was finished and approved. A similar approach was used at the Comas and San Martín de Porres barriadas, where Perú-BID loans allowed pobladores to complete or upgrade their dwellings with minimal supervision.

In an assessment published in 1964, Turner noted that although the approach at Huascarán was initially treated with some skepticism by officials concerned by ceding so much control, the participants demonstrated that self-builders "use their resources more economically and to greater benefit" than housing agency administrators, who are never personally affected by wasteful expenditures. Further, the administrative costs were substantially lower than other Perú-BID projects, as "executive responsibility passed to the borrowers" and trained staff played a correspondingly smaller role. By streamlining the contributions of técnicos in this way, supervised credit offered a solution to the problem of scaling up aided self-help housing. Turner argued that by using this method, fifty thousand dwellings could be self-built annually with existing resources, matching the quality of housing agency projects for far less money.[59]

A contemporaneous assessment by the World Bank reached a similar conclusion. The Peruvian government faced the urgent task of organizing "some type of orderly and controlled settlements" for those unable to acquire conventional housing. Supervised credit had proven to be a highly cost-effective approach to housing provision, at its most successful "where the barriada was in a reasonably well organized and viable condition"; in such cases, the pobladores' loaned funds helped to speed up the consolidation of an essentially sound urban settlement.[60] This success could be replicated at a larger scale by formulating a comprehensive plan for urban development, based on well-designed lower-income neighborhoods to be built using supervised credit.

Apparently, the JNV also recognized the effectiveness of this method: its outline for a second IDB loan application, prepared in July 1966, emphasized the role of sites-and-services projects to be executed by supervised credit instead of more resource-intensive aided self-help techniques.[61] In the end, however, the IDB approved this loan in the form of funding for mortgages to be distributed via the Banco de la Vivienda and the mutuales—a more secure investment, since it served more financially stable participants. Theoretically, the aided self-help methodology remained part of the JNV's repertoire, but in practice official support for it had begun to wane soon after the Perú-BID contract was signed, as political shifts brought dramatic changes in the direction of housing policy. The question of how much could have been achieved with more government support—whether the challenges of running the projects could have been resolved, approaches modified as more experience was gained—is impossible to answer.

While the IDB, Turner, and the JNV were reassessing the value of technical assistance for self-help housing, a 1967 survey of pobladores in Lima indicated that self-builders themselves were quite skeptical of its benefits. From their perspective, participa-

tion in aided self-help projects represented a considerable investment of time and financial resources, and the consequences of any
mistakes or inefficiencies would have enormous repercussions for
them—far greater than for the housing agency or its international
funders. According to the survey, official efforts seemed to have
had little impact generally, since almost half those surveyed had
no knowledge of the main housing agency, the JNV, and another
quarter knew of it but not its work; only 8 percent found its work to
be very useful, while 18 percent believed that "it did not carry out
any work." Relatively few expressed dissatisfaction with the JNV's
technical assistance programs: "In most cases this was because
they had not used such facilities and did not regard them as important."[62] Only 11 percent had used assistance in the construction of
their dwelling; while 30 percent would have liked assistance, 31
percent were ambivalent, and 28 percent would have refused it if
offered. When asked what kind of technical assistance they would
like, 33 percent nominated building materials (and 7 percent "instruction in use of materials"), 30 percent plans or designs (which
they would presumably execute on their own), but only 12 percent
wanted "engineers" ("architects" was not included as an option).
When respondents were asked to list the services that they considered to be a priority, they overwhelmingly nominated infrastructure provision and property title rather than assistance in building
their houses.

In the face of various challenges to its implementation, Perú-
BID funds dedicated to aided self-help housing contributed to the
construction of a total of 4,106 housing units in nine projects located in seven cities across Peru, ranging in size from 56 to 900 units.
In addition, through the barriada-upgrading programs, Perú-BID
funds contributed to realizing aided self-help projects developed
under the umbrella of Law 13517, such as UPIS Valdiviezo and UPIS
Caja de Agua. The Alliance for Progress could claim some success
in these efforts in the provision of affordable housing, but it was far
from what had been initially planned. Despite the hopes that had
been placed in them, aided self-help housing programs were facing
skepticism from would-be allies (Hogares Peruanos), from within
(JNV), from above (IDB), and from below (residents). This was not
a profitable undertaking for venture capital, not an economically
sustainable solution for state agencies, not a productive investment
for development funding, and not an easy route for self-builders
themselves. International funding had been instrumental in ex-

panding these programs to a national scale, but in the light of their ambivalent results it was unlikely this funding would continue, and in the absence of domestic political support to sustain them, these trials would be short-lived.

The Architect of a New Peru

In the half decade following passage of Law 13517, government policies toward the barriadas and aided self-help housing underwent radical shifts. In the 1962 presidential election, Fernando Belaúnde Terry ran a strong campaign, with housing as a core issue: posing as "the architect of a new Peru" in front of *unidad vecinal* blocks, Belaúnde invited voters to envisage the "thousands of houses" he would provide as president, promising a bold expansion of the programs undertaken by the CNV in the late 1940s and early 1950s (fig. 5.10). However, with a field of six candidates, the 1962 elections produced no clear winner, and on July 18, 1962, a few days before the end of Prado's term, the military staged a prophylactic coup in order to circumvent the efforts of Alianza Popular Revolucionaria Americana (APRA), a party it considered to be too radical, to form a coalition government. During its brief period in power (it had agreed to hold elections within a year) the military government carried out the important reform of merging the CNV and INVI into the JNV, and reaffirmed the importance of the UPIS as a means of developing well-ordered and affordable urban settlements.

One year later, the rerun presidential election was won by Belaúnde and his Acción Popular party in a reformist coalition with the Partido Demócrata Cristiano. The Belaúnde government (1963–1968) unequivocally steered housing policy in another direction. With little tolerance for self-help construction, let alone the idea that architects should facilitate such efforts, Belaúnde's response to the demand for affordable housing in the ever-expanding cities was to direct government resources back into conventional mass-housing schemes, now projected on a larger scale than ever before, including Conjunto Habitacional Palomino (architect: Luis Miró Quesada Garland et al., 1964–1967) and Residencial San Felipe (architect: Enrique Ciriani et al., 1962–1969), both in Lima. Increasingly sophisticated in design and construction methods, they were likewise increasingly beyond the means of low-income citi-

BELAUNDE ARQUITECTO DE UN NUEVO PERU

MILES DE CASAS
CON BELAUNDE TERRY

EL PROBLEMA

Aparte del déficit habitacional del momento, cada año 300 mil peruanos necesitan techo, o sea 50 mil nuevas viviendas anuales.

SOLUCION

Ataque en tres frentes:

- Construcciones estatales, con inversiones públicas y financiamiento del exterior. (Aumentar a un mínimo de mil millones de soles anuales las inversiones para vivienda y reagrupar los diversos organismos técnicos gubernamentales de vivienda bajo una sola entidad, para evitar duplicidad de funciones y desorientación de las inversiones y de los préstamos del exterior)

- Construcciones privadas, orientando los ahorros hacia la construcción de tipo popular y no suntuario. (Ley de Seguros y Vivienda Popular).

- Construcciones por cooperación popular. (Ley de Cooperación popular y Ley de Barriadas)

NOTA: El problema de la vivienda no puede ser considerado como problema independiente sino colateral al subdesarrollo (bajos ingresos para el sector mayoritario de la población y baja productividad), por lo que está comprendido dentro del plan integral de desarrollo nacional.

- HOY tenemos un millón sesenta mil casas por reparar y setecientos ochenta mil casas por construir.

- 38 de cada cien peruanos viven en tugurios que no son casas.

- 51 de cada cien peruanos viven en casas que deben ser reparadas y sólo 11 de cada cien peruanos viven decentemente.

¿Quién mejor que Fernando Belaúnde Terry, arquitecto, para dar solución técnica al problema de la casa propia? El, que hizo la Facultad de Arquitectura de la Universidad de Ingeniería y que construyó la primera Unidad Vecinal en el Perú, él, que creó la Corporación Nacional de la Vivienda, ha preparado con los técnicos de Acción Popular un vasto plan nacional de casas de alquiler-venta que se empezará a ejecutar **A LAS 24 HORAS DE SU ASCENSO AL GOBIERNO.**

Votar por Belaúnde Terry y las listas parlamentarias de Acción Popular significa casa decente para todos los peruanos ... ¡PARA UD.!

BELAUNDE LO HIZO... BELAUNDE LO HARA
ACCION POPULAR

Figure 5.10. "Belaúnde, Architect of a New Peru" photographed at Unidad Vecinal No. 3, Lima: "Thousands of Houses with Belaúnde Terry; Belaúnde Did It . . . Belaúnde Will Do It: Acción Popular." *Source*: Election advertisement, *La Prensa*, June 7, 1962.

zens. According to the IDB's own internal assessment, the decision to divert the JNV's resources toward housing projects that "due to their cost and objectives, could well have been developed by private enterprise" harmed the agency's ability to implement Perú-BID.[63] In parallel, Belaúnde promoted internal colonization via large-scale infrastructure projects—irrigation schemes, the Forest-Edge Highway—in order to stimulate regional development, seen as the key to discouraging rural-urban migration, the ultimate cause of the barriadas. But Belaúnde's unwillingness to countenance the unconventional measures proposed by Law 13517 left a vacuum; initiatives such as Valdiviezo and Tahuantinsuyo, regarded by Turner as promising, were left to languish. In fact, Turner's August 1963 issue of *Architectural Design* was published only a few weeks after Belaúnde took office, marking the beginning of the end for the innovative aided self-help housing projects that it depicted with such enthusiasm; it represented a catalogue of past achievements rather than a vision of the future. In 1966 the JNV office overseeing aided self-help housing was dismantled altogether.

Still, Belaúnde did not repeal Law 13517 (he acknowledged that it had introduced important measures to regularize property title, for example[64]). Moreover, toward the end of his presidency, under the threat of large-scale street protests from pobladores, his government eased some aspects of the law's implementation. First, in June 1967, in a law focused on the agglomeration of barriadas in San Martín de Porres, the state transferred ownership of the land and responsibility for overseeing upgrading from the JNV to the local district municipality. On paper the upgrading requirements did not change; however, they were no longer policed by housing officials but rather by local politicians with close ties to the pobladores, and with greater interest in extending title to their constituents than in enforcing planning regulations that were clearly beyond the means of most. Second, in July 1968 revised guidelines for Law 13517 recommended that it was now "advisable to facilitate the granting of property titles"—in part because it was hoped that the newly legalized neighborhoods would generate tax income for local municipalities. The new decree claimed to be upholding the essence of the earlier law, while systematically undermining it. On the one hand, it insisted that the provisions of Law 13517 prohibiting new barriadas and mandating rehabilitation of existing ones remained in force; on the other, it allowed property titles to be granted without the provision of basic services as long as "studies and an urban layout" had been completed.[65] In practice, the state committed no additional resources for upgrading, but simply transferred these responsibilities to the local municipalities and public utility companies. As a result, Belaúnde—the architect of a new Peru—effectively oversaw the inexorable downgrading of minimum standards and the relaxation of enforcement efforts.

As late as 1966 Belaúnde was proposing the mass demolition of the *tugurios* in Lima he had been campaigning against since the 1940s, envisaging in their place vast modern housing projects. However, with rapidly mounting foreign debt, due in large part to his spending on infrastructure and construction projects, it became clear that this strategy toward housing provision was economically unsustainable. Although unwilling to endorse self-build construction, Belaúnde recognized that there was a pressing need to investigate alternatives. In the spirit of the 1967 IDB evaluation that recommended exploring technological solutions, Belaúnde found an ideal venture to support in the ambitiously conceived PREVI (Proyecto Experimental de Vivienda), which is the focus of the next chapter.

6

BUILDING A
BETTER BARRIADA,
1968–1975

I n the nine months between August 2010 and May 2011, three prominent international architecture magazines featured articles on a medium-scale housing development built in Lima in the early 1970s: PREVI (Proyecto Experimental de Vivienda). Labeled variously a "metabolist utopia" and the apex of "Peru's modern project" by their authors, in these accounts PREVI appears as the long-lost solution to the problem of low-cost housing in the developing world—or it would have become so, if only its lessons had been heeded.[1] This renewal of interest seems to have been sparked by two sources: a detailed postoccupancy study produced by three Chilean architects (beginning their research in 2003, culminating in a book in 2008), and Alejandro Aravena's identification of PREVI as a key precedent for the Quinta Monroy housing project in Iquique, Chile (2004), built by his Elemental partnership, a lineage given critical weight by Kenneth Frampton in the 2007 edition of *Modern Architecture: A Critical History.* For Aravena, the roster of high-profile, international architects involved with PREVI evokes the legacy of the Weißenhofsiedlung in Stuttgart, and together these two projects represent the most "important moments in the history of social housing" (while Elemental aims "to write the third chapter").[2] This association has been encouraged by Peter Land, a

British-born architect who played a key role in initiating PREVI, while a more ambivalent reading of the pairing appears in commentary by the architectural collective Supersudaca, who observed: "If the Weißenhofsiedlung is the natural childbirth of social housing in the industrialized world, PREVI is the coitus interruptus of social housing in the Third World."[3] Here the comparison evokes the sense of a destiny thwarted, a Latin American failure to reproduce European modernism. Yet there is perhaps another, more uncomfortable truth in this recurring trope of PREVI as Weißenhofsiedlung redux, which PREVI's boosters would prefer to overlook: that is, not that PREVI failed to equal the example of the earlier project but that it equaled it only too well in its chief (and often unacknowledged) flaw—the fact that few of the architects at Stuttgart met the goal of providing realistic, repeatable models for low-cost housing (with the notable exception of J. J. P. Oud), constructing instead a competitive showcase of the new architecture.[4]

This chapter outlines the history of PREVI, and examines the source of its mythology: its assemblage of an impressive cross-section of the architectural avant-garde at the end of the 1960s to focus on the elusive modernist ideal of fusing social engagement, new technologies, and radical form making, now within the arena of the developing world. It considers the strategies and solutions that PREVI proposed, discusses postoccupancy evaluations of its outcomes, and finally, reconsiders its place in the history of social housing, in particular addressing the notion that it represents a "third way" able to move beyond the limitations of the entirely planned housing project and the entirely unplanned informal settlement, and thus offers a viable, underexplored alternative for the provision of low-cost housing.

A Peruvian Weißenhofsiedlung

According to Land's account, he first proposed the concept of an experimental housing project to President Fernando Belaúnde Terry in 1966. Trained at the Architectural Association in London, Land subsequently undertook postgraduate study at Yale University, which led to his appointment as director of the Inter-American Graduate Program in Urban and Regional Planning at the Universidad Nacional de Ingeniería in Lima (1960–1964). In 1965 he accepted an advisory position with the Banco de la Vivienda

243

(Housing Bank), inspecting projects throughout Peru that were under consideration for funding through the *mutuales*, such as Sol de Oro. Given Belaúnde's background as an architect with a long-term interest in affordable housing and his developmentalist ambitions, Land recalled: "I realized this was a unique opportunity to do something special with an international splash."[5]

In mid-1966 Peru presented the project to the United Nations Development Program (UNDP) for funding, and it was approved a year later; the official contract between Peru and the UNDP was signed in June 1968, specifying the realization of the entire project within three years. As originally conceived, PREVI consisted of three complementary "pilot projects" developed in response to the main factors identified as contributing to the nation's urban housing crisis: a quantitative housing deficit due to growing urban populations; a qualitative deficit due to the deterioration of existing housing stock into slum conditions; and the formation of squatter settlements. To meet these varied challenges, the pilot projects employed three parallel strategies: Proyecto Piloto 1 (PP1) addressed the quantitative deficit by focusing on lowering per-unit costs via innovations in design and construction, which would be tested in a model neighborhood of 1,500 housing units; PP2 addressed the qualitative deficit by developing techniques to rehabilitate compromised housing stock; and PP3 addressed the *barriada* issue by providing "sites-and-services for new settlement areas" with aided self-help to guide their development[6]—an approach reminiscent of the Urbanización Popular de Interés Social (UPIS) projects of the early 1960s. With this tripartite exploration, it was hoped that PREVI would generate a range of prototypes that could be replicated en masse to address Lima's severe housing shortage, and—as signaled by the UNDP's involvement—would also be transferrable to other developing countries. Following a devastating earthquake in May 1970 centered in the Ancash region north of Lima, a fourth project was added: PP4 was framed as a trial reconstruction program based on aided self-help housing. Although a comparative evaluation of the various approaches was a key element of the "experimental housing project" as originally conceived, most discussions reduce PREVI to the international contributions in PP1, thereby sidelining the less spectacular pilot projects, along with the Peruvian architects who were involved in PP1.

As preparatory planning documents make clear, while all the pilot projects were intended for low-income groups, they were pitched at different income brackets within that category, officially defined as socioeconomic levels I, II, and III. PP1 was geared toward those "with incomes that allow, through a monthly saving, the acquisition of a dwelling with long-term financing" (corresponding to levels II and III), while PP3 was intended "for families of very limited financial resources" (levels I and II).[7] Aimed at the upper end of the low-income spectrum, the stated goal of PP1 was "to demonstrate advanced ideas in housing design and economical construction"—balancing the imperative to keep costs low with the desire for innovation and quality design solutions. By contrast, PP3 included a strong "community development" element, making use of *autoconstrucción* and *ayuda mutua* in order "to guide the people in making better places in which to live: by helping them to help themselves."[8] Finally, PP2 would straddle all three socioeconomic levels, and therefore proposed that participating families construct their homes with a mixture of financing and self-help labor.

The financing of PREVI PP1 and PP2 was to be arranged through the Caja de Pensiones del Seguro Social del Empleado (White-Collar Workers' Social Security Pension Fund)—an organization serving office workers, government employees, and similar groups, who identified as middle class.[9] Accordingly, an entry to the PREVI PP1 competition by Peruvian architects Juan Gunther and Mario Seminario that proposed communal kitchens shared between households rather than a kitchen in each house was rejected early in the judging process, presumably because it evoked a working-class lifestyle rather than one appropriate to the *empleado*. Similarly, although some entries included plans for very basic core houses, when it came to the construction phase, the Caja selected dwellings of two, three, and four bedrooms as suitable for its members, "taking into account . . . the living patterns of these families"; the resulting dwellings would be within the means of only a quarter of Lima's residents.[10] These houses were to be aspirational, not minimal.

Project organizers solicited designs for PREVI PP1 via an architectural competition that was open to all Peruvian architects, as well as thirteen invited international teams. Peter Land, who represented the UN in the first stages of PREVI's development (March 1968–April 1973), traveled personally to issue the invitations, and the range of countries included reflected the desire to present "a truly global selection" in keeping with the UN sponsorship of the project:[11] the Eastern Bloc was represented by Poland (Oskar Hansen and Svein Hatløy), Asia by Japan (Kiyonori Kikutake, Fumihiko

Maki, Noriaki Kurokawa) and India (Charles Correa), the Americas by Colombia (Esguerra, Saenz, Urdaneta, Samper) and the United States (Christopher Alexander and the Center for Environmental Structure, with Sandy Hirshen). Nonetheless, the majority of the participants were from Western Europe: the United Kingdom (James Stirling), Denmark (Knud Svenssons), Switzerland (Atelier Five), Finland (Toivo Korhonen), West Germany (Herbert Ohl), Spain (J. L. Iñiguez de Onzoño, A. Vázquez de Castro), the Netherlands (Aldo van Eyck), and France (Candilis, Josic, Woods). Six winning projects (three international, three Peruvian) were to be selected for construction, with 250 examples of each to make up a total of 1,500 units; the overall design of the neighborhood would be devised by the PP1 working group assembled from architects and planners at various Peruvian government agencies, along with Land.

In March 1969 the international architects attended a mandatory ten-day briefing in Lima in order to familiarize themselves with the city's "terrain, population, climate, construction materials and methods" as well as seismic issues; they visited the project site, low-cost housing projects, and other residential areas. The project brief specified dwellings of 60 to 120 square meters, on a plot of at least 80 square meters, and no more than three stories high, creating a low-rise, high-density urban scheme. Since the costs of high-rise housing were prohibitive, it would not even be considered as a solution. The *unidad comunal* (community unit) of 1,500 houses, accommodating approximately 10,000 people, was to ensure the clear separation of vehicular and pedestrian routes, and would include a range of facilities to create a fully functioning neighborhood—schools, sports grounds, community centers, commercial areas, parks. The stated intention was to build on the experience of Belaúnde's *unidad vecinal* model using "contemporary ideas and experiences of other countries."[12]

The individual dwellings were to provide for a household of four increasing to sixteen members, taking into account the "socioeconomic mobility" of the prospective residents, who were imagined as a young family, adding rooms with the arrival of new children, then subdividing the space to accommodate adult married children (viewed as "an emergency measure" until the young couple could afford their own home). In this way, the house would develop from its initial nucleus as the circumstances of the owner allowed: "The dwelling should not be considered as a fixed and unchangeable unit, but as a structure with a cycle of evolution." Accordingly, each architect was to present a twofold design—a core housing unit to be constructed by professional contractors and taking advantage of the economies of mass production, and a blueprint for gradual horizontal and/or vertical extension of the house over time by self-help, contractors, or a combination of the two. The architects were to facilitate the dwelling's incremental construction by incorporating the increased loading requirements of any additional stories into the initial structural calculations for the core unit, and by providing designs for standardized building components that could be mass produced on site and thereby made available to residents at low cost. The rationalization of construction, in particular the use of modular coordination, was to be based on the guidelines of existing UN publications. Here, one aim was to modernize the Peruvian construction industry, improving efficiency and productivity. In addition, as the project brief explained, "in the past self-help methods have often been identified with improvisation and with primitive construction materials and methods." Now, due to technological advances bringing "simplicity, ease of assembly, and reduction in weight" to the building site, the results of self-help labor could be significantly improved and refined, and the method could "be identified with a more advanced technology" and thereby "extend its application."[13] This approach was in line with the UN's *Manual on Self-Help Housing* (1964), which had advocated the use of modular coordination on the grounds that it saved labor, materials, money, and the time required for training and supervising the self-helpers.

Despite claims made for PREVI PP1's originality—such as Land's assertion that "in the areas of expansion, flexibility, and adaptation, PREVI [PP1] broke new ground"[14]—its hybrid model was less a radical innovation than a deeper exploration of existing approaches. The UN's *Manual on Self-Help Housing* had already argued for the importance of "expandable" houses, and within Peru the concept of the "growing house" had been employed since the late 1950s in housing agency projects at Ciudad de Dios, Urbanización Valdiviezo, and elsewhere, and by private developers such as Hogares Peruanos to appeal to buyers with modest incomes. Such projects borrowed and systematized the techniques of barriada housing—progressive development, resident participation in construction—but aimed to circumvent ad hoc building through technical assistance and carefully conceived expansion plans. PREVI PP1's innovation was to transfer these techniques into the realm of high architecture and "advanced ideas" in order to refine the results still further.

Forty-one projects were submitted to PREVI PP1 (thirteen international and twenty-eight Peruvian). The winners were a diverse group: Atelier Five; Herbert Ohl; Kikutake, Maki, and Kurokawa; Elsa Mazzarri and Manuel Llanos; Fernando Chaparro, Víctor Ramírez, Víctor Smirnoff, and Víctor Wyszkowski; and Jacques Crousse, Jorge Páez, and Ricardo Pérez León. The selection of the international winners was not unanimous: in a minority report, two jury members vehemently condemned the entry by Ohl (then director of the Institute of Industrialized Building at the Hochschule für Gestaltung, Ulm) as "a regimented project and an expensive solution. . . . We believe that it is inhuman." Conversely, they commended the entry by the Center for Environmental Structure (CES) as "a milestone" in the design of low-cost housing and advised the UN "to publish this project now in its current form" as a matter of urgency.[15] The official competition report reiterated that the intention was to construct the six winning designs, but also suggested that due to the valuable ideas proposed by other projects, their best elements should be further explored. It therefore recommended that the next stage should be to "build and test certain housing types in a small number . . . before deciding which should be built in a larger number." An imagined affinity with the Weißenhofsiedlung was already evident in the organizers' vision of the pilot project as "being used as a permanent exhibition of low-cost housing for Peruvian and foreign specialists."[16]

In early 1970 the PREVI PP1 working group decided to develop prototypes of twenty additional projects (the remaining ten invited international entries and ten selected Peruvian entries), constructing a smaller number of each design. The organizers now planned for the completion of preparatory work by the end of 1972, and of construction by the end of 1975. In the end, only twenty-four of the twenty-six prototypes would be realized, with approximately twenty examples of each constructed, creating a neighborhood of 467 houses; Ohl's project was "left for a later stage" due to technical difficulties, along with that of one of the Peruvian teams.[17] The overall design for this trial neighborhood, on a site 8 kilometers north of the center of Lima, was developed by the PP1 working group, including Land (fig. 6.1). It emerged as a patchwork of the disparate competition proposals, loosely structured around a narrow central walkway. Allocated only a small number of units, none of the architects were able to fully realize their original plans for the residential groupings, seriously compromising the integrity of the realized designs.

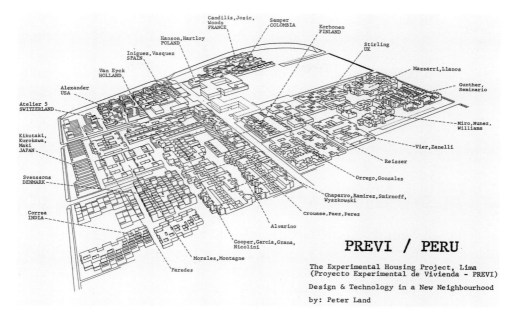

Figure 6.1. PREVI PP1 working group, site plan for PREVI PP1, Lima, completed 1975. *Source*: Drawing © Peter Land.

Following the completion of this abbreviated version of PREVI PP1, no additional housing units were ever constructed. Consequently, in a very real sense the unrealized competition proposals offer richer ground for discussion than the project as built—representing interpretations of, and responses to, practices of self-help construction as read through different strands of late-1960s architecture. The first challenge was how to frame the marriage of "advanced technology" and self-help; the second was how to incorporate the imperative to design for future adaptation, balancing the architect's management of the complete lifecycle of the structure against the possibilities of improvised transformation. In the process, certain limitations of this collaboration between architect and self-builder become evident.

The discussion here will focus on a selection of the international projects; unfortunately, the Peruvian projects have not been published in the same level of detail, precluding their inclusion. To make a virtue out of necessity, this offers an opportunity to view the Peruvian situation from the outside, foregrounding the question of whether strategies developed elsewhere were transferrable to this context. Of particular importance was the modernist belief that innovative design combined with technological advances—new construction materials, standardization and modular coordination, mass production, the reorganization of the building site—could significantly lower the costs of minimum-standard affordable housing. The proposal devised by Christopher Alexander and the CES represents the most comprehensive effort to rethink mass housing provision that was generated by PREVI PP1, and thus provides an appropriate starting point for the discussion.

Houses Generated by Architects

A central tenet of the CES proposal was to promote enhanced user input in a context where this was not easily incorporated—a low-cost mass housing project—by streamlining the unwieldy process of participatory design into a manageable form. The CES had been formally established in 1967 with the aim of developing a set of principles that would constitute a systematic language of design. Its experiments along these lines had begun a couple of years earlier with commissions to produce conceptual designs for the San Francisco Bay Area Rapid Transit system (1964–1965), and for the Hunts Point Multi-Service Center (1967–1968), where it first used the terminology of the "pattern language" to describe its design process.[18] In 1969 PREVI PP1 became the largest CES project to date to use the pattern language system, and the first in which the CES was engaged directly rather than acting as a consultant. The projects for San Francisco and Hunts Point had emerged from a detailed analysis of the operational needs of the proposed program, as well as observations of people's behavior in the environments under study. For PREVI PP1, this quasi-ethnographic approach was greatly expanded, as Alexander and three other members of the CES—Shlomo Angel, Christie Coffin, and Sara Ishikawa—each spent a month in Lima before the official competition briefing, living with low-income families as participant-observers to document how they inhabited their houses. San Francisco–based architect Sandy Hirshen joined them for a shorter period in order to research local construction techniques. The photographs and drawings of everyday life in Lima that accompanied their PREVI PP1 proposal provide a vivid record of this research period.

The CES proposal was a conceptual blueprint for "houses generated by patterns": less architectural plans than general principles,

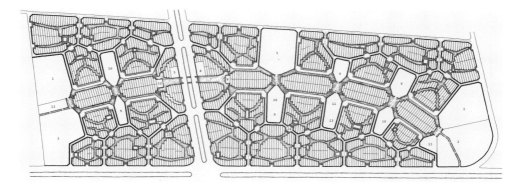

Figure 6.2. Center for Environmental Structure, PREVI PP1 I-13, 1969. Site plan. *Source*: CES, *Houses Generated by Patterns* (Berkeley: CES, 1969).

the patterns identified various "problems" that would need to be addressed for the successful design of the house or the neighborhood, proposing spatial, technical, or constructive "solutions" for each issue. Falling into three basic categories—community, house, and construction patterns—the ambition was to document the sociospatial specificities of the Peruvian context and to translate these observations into a design lexicon. Accordingly, many of the sixty-seven patterns referenced or replicated traditional spatial forms. For example, the main structuring device of the site plan, the free-form "paseo" (a central spine of paired pathways linking the various communal facilities) was loosely inspired by Latin American pedestrian promenades (fig. 6.2). For the house itself, "front door recesses" would facilitate the traditionally close social interface between the house and the street (fig. 6.3); a "mirador" with a built-in seat for watching the street emulated the enclosed balconies of colonial Lima; and a secure "perimeter wall" for each house replicated the *cerco* that was typically the first permanent element to be constructed in barriada dwellings. (Significantly, the CES's description of this pattern referenced an article by John F. C. Turner from the August 1963 issue of *Architectural Design* that he edited.)[19]

The house patterns fell into two broad categories. On the one hand, patterns deriving from environmental factors—such as a north-south orientation and open-air patios at front and back to maximize cross-ventilation—were to be applied universally, in every version of the house. On the other hand, patterns expressing the social functioning of each household were variable, and would

FRONT DOOR RECESSES

IN THE PROYECTO EXPERIMENTAL
HOUSE, each front door is
surrounded on the outside by
one or more deep recesses,
according to the exact position of the entrance with
respect to other houses.
The front doors are of the
dutch door type.

THE GENERAL PATTERN IS:

Context:

Any Peruvian house which
has a front door opening
directly off a public path.

Solution:

The front door is surrounded, on both sides, by deep
recesses, each at least 50 cm deep – if possible by double
recesses. The effect of the recesses is helped by an opening in the door, or a dutch door.

-170-

Problem:

"Hanging out" is a standard part of Latin culture. People
like to watch the street. But people do not always want the
same degree of involvement with the street. The process of
hanging out requires a continuum of degrees of involvement
with the street, ranging all the way from the most private
kind, to the most public kind. A young girl watching the

-171-

Figure 6.3. Center for Environmental Structure, PREVI PP1 I-13, 1969. Front door recesses. *Source*: CES, *Houses Generated by Patterns* (Berkeley: CES, 1969).

determine the individual character of each dwelling. The very form of the plan—the "long thin house"—was intended to facilitate internal differentiation between various types of spaces, maintaining privacy and reducing the sense of overcrowding by ensuring that even within the most constrained footprint, "the mean distance between rooms is as high as possible." The clear separation of public and private zones was translated into a pattern called "intimacy gradient" (fig. 6.4). Reflecting the layout of the traditional Peruvian house, passage into the more private spaces of the house was staged in a strict sequence: entry–*sala*–family room–kitchen–bedrooms. The entry marked the physical threshold between inside and outside, but it was the sala that demarcated the transition between public and private zones within the dwelling, setting a limit for visitors. In more affluent Peruvian households, the sala was a formal space reserved for prized furnishings and ornaments, but the CES provided even the most modest version of the house with a symbolic sala in the form of "a tiny receiving alcove immediately inside the front door."[20]

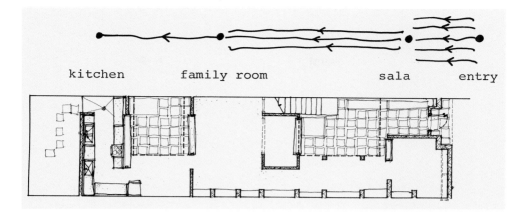

Figure 6.4. Center for Environmental Structure, PREVI PP1 I-13, 1969. Intimacy gradient. *Source*: CES, *Houses Generated by Patterns* (Berkeley: CES, 1969).

In the construction patterns the aim was to facilitate future modifications by establishing a simple structural system based on easily produced elements requiring no specialized skills or technologies, responding to the existing state of the Peruvian construction industry rather than revolutionizing it. The intention was to rely primarily on manual labor, even in the first phase of construction, with some mechanical assistance for heavier tasks such as laying concrete slabs. According to Hirshen, the rest of the structure was to be extremely lightweight, achieved through the development of new, vernacular-inflected materials such as floor planks and roof beams fabricated from bamboo stalks and sulfur (or urethane) foam (fig. 6.5). In Peru bamboo was regarded as a low-prestige material—seen in the *esteras* commonly employed in provisional barriada housing—but Ishikawa had visited a local resort that used sophisticated bamboo construction techniques for exotic effect, suggesting the value of further experiments. The concrete blocks were also innovative, designed to stack easily in an interlocking system that would not require specialized labor. Their formal qualities were also a consideration: as Hirshen described the decision to finish the surface with sulfur coating, "we were all attuned to the idea of making these traditional materials more aesthetically pleasing."[21] In the end, fabrication of these materials proved to be too costly, so in the construction phase the PREVI PP1 working group made the decision to use mass-produced concrete elements instead, against the wishes of the CES.

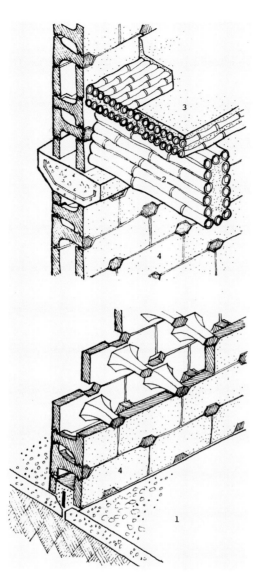

Figure 6.5. Center for Environmental Structure with Sandy Hirschen, PREVI PP1 I-13, 1969. Bamboo-urethane foam plank and beam; mortarless block cavity wall. *Source*: CES, *Houses Generated by Patterns* (Berkeley: CES, 1969).

The CES proposal made clear that the application of the patterns was not to be subject to the creative whims of the designer but would be responsive to each family for its own house, and to each group of residents for its neighborhood. To make this workable for the stipulated population of 1,500 households, Alexander and his collaborators devised a method of streamlining the participatory element of the design process via a six-page "Family Choice Sheet" that would be translated into usable plans via a twenty-step guided design template. Prospective residents were to choose how much space they wanted for each room of the house, and where their house should be located within the site. The questionnaire provided pricing for each option, so that residents could tabulate the financial impact of each improvement to their domestic comfort: a small kitchen cost S/.13,000, a large one S/.22,000; a center lot with a secondary rear entrance was S/.2,000, while a corner lot with a secondary side entrance and a rental space was S/.10,000. Other options were free of charge, but personalized the design by asking residents to specify which facilities they would like to be near (market, clinic, church), and whether they preferred a quiet or a busy area.

With this information at hand, the first step was to assign the house to an appropriate area within the site. Next, the dimensions of the house were set, with a uniform width of 5.2 meters, and the length varying from 13 to 27 meters. The patio openings were the first architectural element to be positioned, followed by the front door, and so on for the rest of the rooms and various custom features. The process could almost be reduced to a binary code of 0–1 options for each element, as if presenting a prototype for computer-aided design. Indeed, the CES argued that the "rules of the combination process" were "almost mechanical": *The low cost of the houses cannot support any individual design time. We estimate that a trained draftsman will need about one hour per house, to translate the family choice sheet into a set of working drawings and specifications for the contractor."*[22] No reference was made, however, to how much additional time would be required for the fabrication of these made-to-measure houses. Offering a larger number of options than tract homes, and more fundamental modulations—not just finishes and fittings, but the size of every single one of the various rooms—the production phase would arguably be the most complicated part of the entire process. Furthermore, building individualized row houses, as opposed to freestanding homes, would present additional difficulties, requiring customization at the level of every housing block.

Alexander and his team were confident that their fieldwork had allowed them to develop a sourcebook of practical design solutions that reflected local needs and could serve as a resource for local architects and builders: "In this sense, these patterns may begin to define a new indigenous architecture for Peru." In opposition to a modernist universalizing approach to design, the CES emphasized a responsiveness to the specificities of the context. However, while their patterns emerged from close observation of low-income households, they were not developed in consultation with them; it is therefore legitimate to ask whether the CES was projecting its own vision onto prospective residents. Along these lines, some jurors argued that the CES proposal reflected outdated cultural models— it "tended to reinforce customs and traditions, some of which had already changed, rather than adapting itself to a process of change and improvement of family life, as incomes increase."[23] Without accepting the assumptions of modernizing "improvement" expressed in this statement, it is important to acknowledge the implicit nostalgia underlying much of the CES proposal, exemplified by the invented handmade vernacular of the construction system.

Finally, an exchange that Ishikawa had with the family hosting her in Lima provides an insight into the competing visions cultivated by the architects and their potential clients. When asked what they imagined for a future home:

> Four of them at the same time said, "I want an *I Love Lucy* house! ... It's so BIG"—and the mother said, "and it has a BIG kitchen." I said, "Yeah, but you know, the kitchen is wide open to the living areas, so that if you were cooking there, all the smells would drift into the rest." And she said, "Oh! that's no good." So it was good that they knew at least, once they identified a house, that there were some problems with it—you know, for them, just given the way they lived.[24]

Needless to say, this account does not appear in the CES publications on the project. It does, however, suggest that Lima families were not always as attached to traditional elements as the CES architects were, and raises the question of whether actual resident participation in the development of the patterns would have produced a significantly different outcome.

Other proposals by international participants, while rarely outlining as comprehensive a vision as the CES, nonetheless presented distinctive responses to the challenges raised by the project, marking the encounter of each architect's practice with the logic and processes of aided self-help, set to work in partnership with advanced technology. Many of the proposals focused on the construction system, particularly the requirement that it accommodate both conventional and aided self-help building techniques.

At one extreme, Herbert Ohl's proposal focused exclusively on technological innovation and its promises of efficiency. The design

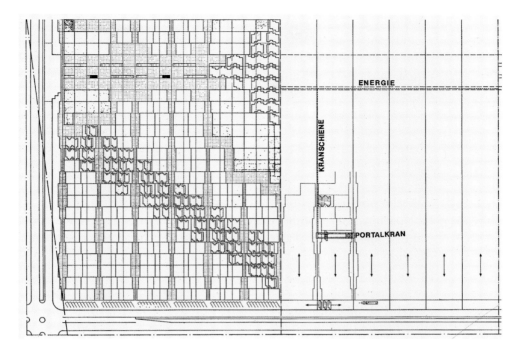

Figure 6.6. Herbert Ohl, PREVI PP1 I-6, 1969. Site layout with moving crane (detail). *Source: Baumeister* 67 (1970).

was based on the progressive combination of dimensional modules to generate the house, the neighborhood, and the urban plan. The fundamental unit was set at 30 centimeters, which could be broken down for "more refined dimensional areas"; multiplied by four, it produced the "basic planning module" of 1.2 meters. This in turn determined the dimensions of the main building component: rectangular, ring-shaped "building frame sections" in precast concrete, measuring 1.2 by 7.2 meters (or six basic modules).[25] Each housing lot was 9.6 by 9.6 meters (eight basic modules), allowing for the building frame sections to be shifted laterally by one or two grid squares to produce more complex internal volumes; eight building frame sections would fill the lot, creating a roughly 60-square-meter dwelling.

At the next level, the residential zones were laid out in a grid of housing lots framed by parallel walkways spaced 28.8 meters apart (equal to three 9.6-meter-wide lots); these walkways held tracks to convey a massive movable crane system that would be used to position the building frame sections (fig. 6.6). Ohl claimed that the mobile crane could be deployed at any stage throughout the life of the neighborhood to carry out alterations, additions, or the "replacement and modernization of individual units"; in this way the system would allow "a combination of high density with considerable formal flexibility impossible to achieve by traditional methods."[26]

In an attempt to adapt an industrialized building system to the socioeconomic context of Peru, Ohl proposed the independent fabrication of frame and fittings, with the "continuous production of highly-finished three-dimensional building frame sections" and the "on-site manufacture of housing elements" to finish the dwelling—the one focused on quality and efficiency, the other on local fabrication and responsiveness to shifts in demand, since it did not require specialized plant and machinery. This exterior-interior division was comparable to N. J. Habraken's contemporaneous proposal for the mass production of housing units in two distinct parts: the standardized "support" (or housing "superstructure") and the "detachable units" (all the finishings, furnishings, and fixtures) to be purchased and installed by the occupant individually. Like Habraken's proposal, Ohl's thoroughly rationalized construction system was in effect a practical critique of the inefficiencies and distorted marketing fantasies of capitalist housing production. This reflected Ohl's affiliation with the Hochschule für Gestaltung, Ulm, which emphasized the designer's responsibility to educate the consumer, producing superior design in order to elevate the level of aesthetic discernment within the marketplace. For Ohl, creating an open structure of the simplest possible form would maximize individual expression within the unit. However, while the austerity of the concrete building frame sections could be modified by the overlays of habitation, it would be impossible to overcome their rigidity to make any structural adjustments, circumscribing any spatial intervention. Ohl believed that the "basic order" of the system would "establish a democratic interchange between human and technological factors."[27] In practice, the technological governed the possibilities of the human: at the level of the house, through the intractable building frame sections; at the level of the site, through the crane tracks guiding the urban plan. The dissenting jurors' verdict of "inhuman" does not seem excessive. Still, it is telling of a prevailing faith in technological solutions that this project was placed second.

Diametrically opposed to Ohl's approach was Toivo Korhonen's proposal, which borrowed closely from the growth patterns of bar-

Figure 6.7. Toivo Korhonen, PREVI PP1 I-5, 1969. Dimensional system for the house; various growth patterns for the house, beginning from type A1. *Source*: Toivo Korhonen.

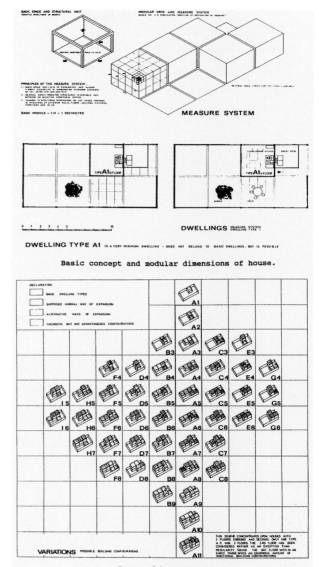

riada housing, but rationalized the form (fig. 6.7). Korhonen devised a very basic dwelling nucleus (type A1), offering considerably less than the minimum specified by the competition: following the barriada model, it consisted of a cerco and a single multipurpose room, with water and drainage in a service patio "which at the outset would serve as kitchen." The proposed structure could be built with a range of materials, from timber to light concrete, allowing both conventional and self-built construction. The simplicity of the proposed form—basically dividing the lot into a grid of eight standard modules—allowed the owner-builder to make additions in multiple horizontal and/or vertical configurations. Korhonen considered some to be more "advantageous" than others, and recommended the functional separation of service, living, and sleeping zones, but ultimately he believed that each family should have the freedom to "determine the form of its own immediate surroundings." Likewise, Korhonen imagined that the use of barriada-inspired collective self-help labor on public works for the site—specifically, digging the irrigation channel required to water the park—would promote residents' sense of agency: "This kind of work, improving the level of the environment, could be a way of increasing social contact, and getting the inhabitants to feel that they belong to their neighbourhood, and that their neighbourhood belongs to them."[28]

The remainder of the projects found a middle way between Ohl and Korhonen. For example, Charles Correa's proposal made use of specialized prefabricated components (such as reinforced concrete planks) within a construction system that was simple enough to be executed by self-builders if supplemented with skilled labor for certain tasks, such as casting concrete in situ for the floor and roof. The interlocking row houses, with alternating wide and narrow sections, avoided the potential monotony of the row house form by creating a variety of internal spaces, with the widest sections reserved for a living-dining space with an adjacent interior patio (fig. 6.8). Concerned that heterogeneous self-made modifications would produce a discordant effect, Correa argued that the "very narrow frontage" of the row houses had the benefit of "ensur[ing] that the facade to be 'controlled' is very small and set well back into the porch."[29] By minimizing the facade's visual impact in this way, the design obviated the need to police or otherwise "control" future self-built construction. Through this design decision, the necessary balance between the individual autonomy of each household and the creation of a visually cohesive streetscape would be achieved with minimal social friction.

For Atelier 5, the economic and technological particularities of the Peruvian context were key in designing a construction system. The small number of skilled workers available necessitated the careful division of tasks: "operations of a precise and complex nature" required to fabricate the building components would be closely supervised in an on-site workshop, while construction itself could be carried out by unskilled workers using a minimum

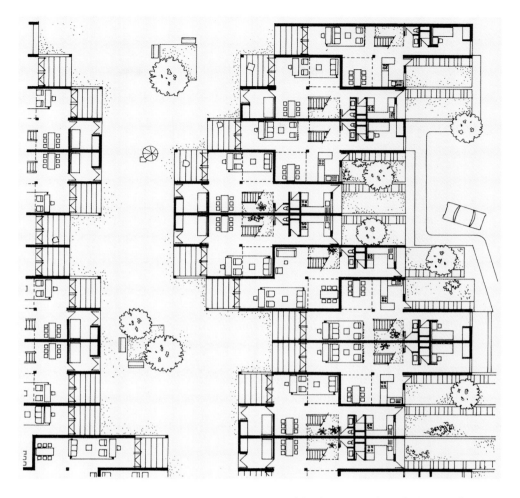

Figure 6.8. Charles Correa, PREVI PP1 I-7, 1969. Grouping of the three types of interlocking row houses, facing onto the community spine. *Source*: Charles Correa Associates.

of mechanized equipment. Just two precast concrete components would be required for erecting load-bearing walls, ceilings, and roofs; these were compact and lightweight, so they could be moved around the site by forklift and easily installed by self-builders. Atelier 5 anticipated that their careful organization of the entire process would foster a self-sustaining system: "The assembly and handling of these elements must be easy enough that the residents are persuaded to use them. . . . In this way these elements will constantly be produced, assuring their continuing availability."[30]

The houses began as two-story dwellings enclosed by a cerco, with privacy established by a walled garden area and service patio

Figure 6.9. Atelier 5, PREVI PP1 I-4, 1969. Model showing the street frontage of houses in various stages of development. *Source*: Atelier 5, "International Competition for an Experimental Housing Project in Lima, Peru" (ca. 1969).

sharing the street frontage (plate 13). The two-story layout allowed for a generous amount of open space, with an upper-floor terrace supplementing the garden and patio. The plans for growth maintained this basic organizational principle, with new bedrooms and living space added without compromising any of the open spaces or the sun exposure and ventilation that they guaranteed. With their walled gardens and setback volumes, the houses presented a dynamic street frontage; the process of extending the house—adding one box after another—would be easily incorporated into this lively collage (fig. 6.9). In contrast to Correa, who felt compelled to disguise the houses' continually evolving facades, according to Atelier 5's understanding of progressive development, the growth of each house should be clearly visible from the street, since it carried a strong performative, public element: "The individual is aware that when he adds to his house he adds to the community; that his house is a building block of the whole environment." Atelier 5 believed that the order of the underlying structural system would provide an overall sense of unity, as each house would "serve primarily . . . as a unit in a recognizable whole, and only secondarily as the expression of the home's individuality." Because the phased growth of the house was integral to the design concept, each household could make modifications without compromising the integrity of adjacent units, or the coherence of the neighborhood as a whole.[31]

James Stirling's PREVI PP1 house proposed a two-phase construction system: initially, the load-bearing perimeter walls, formed of precast concrete panels (incorporating parapets, windows, or doors, as needed), would be installed by crane, while the components for subsequent extensions would be lightweight enough to allow self-help construction. The floor plan was defined

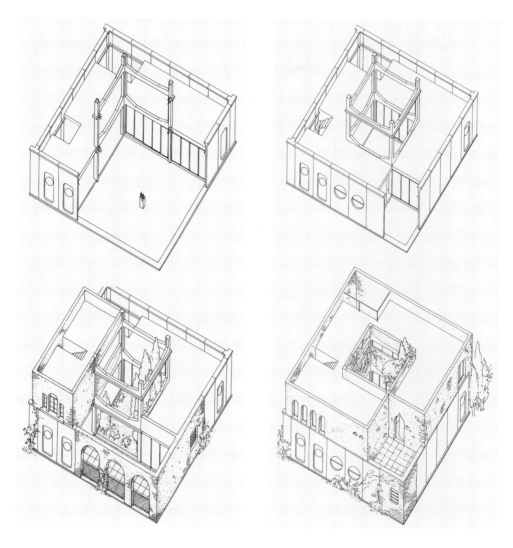

Figures 6.10 (*above left*) and 6.11 (*above right*). James Stirling, PREVI PP1 I-1, 1969. Minimum and large houses as built by contractor in stage one and as developed by occupants. *Source*: James Stirling/ Michael Wilford fonds, Collection Centre Canadien d'Architecture/Canadian Centre for Architecture, Montréal.

by a modified three-by-three structural grid, its slightly enlarged central square designated as a "patio de estar" (living patio) for social exchanges (figs. 6.10–6.11). The form recalls Stirling's Stiff Dom-ino Housing (1951), an homage to Le Corbusier based on an evenly measured three-by-three grid, and his Expandable House (with James Gowan, 1957), based on a two-by-two grid.

The smallest version of Stirling's PREVI PP1 house formed an L-shape around the structural frame of the patio; as it grew, it would fill out the rest of the grid, enclosing the patio. As the drawings indicate, it was anticipated that the order of the initial layout would begin to collapse as the house extended to an upper level, perhaps even developing into an entirely separate dwelling accessed via an exterior stair. The axionometric drawings of this process (executed by Leon Krier) celebrated this formal dissolution, not only in variations to the layout but also in the eclecticism of materials, detailing, and stylistic references. In a 1969 interview, Stirling described a six-year-old housing project he had visited in Lima that was suffused with such alterations, the outcome of a "tremendous free-for-all among house owners and builders" that left "only one house in every thirty like the original, and even that was barely recognizable." Stirling continued: "They always seem to change the architect's windows, they put up wrought iron work, they paint them different colours. One might extend in concrete, another brick. It has its own very extraordinary quality.... We have to allow for this, and organize it into something less uncontrolled. In a way, it is restrictive not to build for some kind of change and adaptation."[32]

Although Stirling's emphatic use of porthole windows and curved-corner doors could be seen as an attempt to maintain his signature throughout subsequent overlays—in fact, they remain one of the few recognizable features of the entire PREVI PP1 neighborhood—he viewed self-building as complementary, rather than antagonistic, to his own design. Furthermore, the role that residents would play in the project's evolution was essential to its success: "The pride and sense of ownership achieved through self building must be retained and the inventiveness and variety of environment which this produces is to be encouraged and is considered essential for a dynamic community."[33] Fundamentally, Stirling's project sought to organize this self-built "inventiveness and variety" within an overarching structure—specifically, the grid form and the central patio. As seen in a cross-section through the streetscape, the patio's skeletal framework protrudes above the roofs of growing dwellings, setting out a clear pathway for future additions (fig. 6.12). While leaving plenty of latitude for residents' customization, the evolution that Stirling foresaw would be "something less uncontrolled" than purely improvised construction.

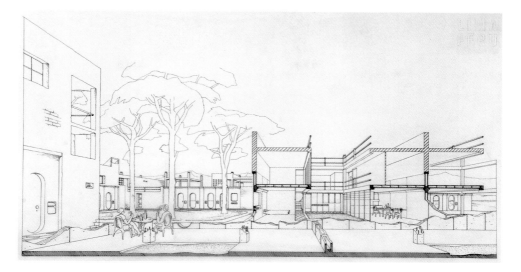

Figure 6.12. James Stirling, PREVI PP1 I-1, 1969. Self-built streetscape as a work in progress. *Source*: James Stirling/Michael Wilford fonds, Collection Centre Canadien d'Architecture/Canadian Centre for Architecture, Montréal.

The Colombian team of Esguerra, Saenz, Urdaneta, Samper were the only architects among the international entrants to have had experience in aided self-help construction: Germán Samper designed Barrio La Fragua in Bogotá (1958–1962), and the entire team collaborated on the Sidauto neighborhood, also in Bogotá (1968). La Fragua, one of the first aided self-help housing projects in Colombia, featured one-story semidetached (or two-family) houses with small gardens at the front and rear. Observing residents' postoccupancy transformations to the dwellings, Samper learned—in the words of one recent assessment—that "the urban structure is what endures, not the house." This insight clearly informed the approach at Sidauto, where the design dispensed with siting the house in the middle of the lot in favor of a dwelling framed by a perimeter wall. At La Fragua, the visual disorder of improvised construction had often overtaken the front garden spaces; at Sidauto, with the perimeter walls erecting a continuous street frontage, any self-built modifications were kept out of view. In addition, the selection of a square lot brought inherent constraints that made it more successful in "programming the possible transformations" of the dwelling, thereby giving the neighborhood greater visual coherence.[34]

In their PREVI PP1 project, Esguerra, Saenz, Urdaneta, Samper again utilized a square lot framed by a cerco, generating twenty

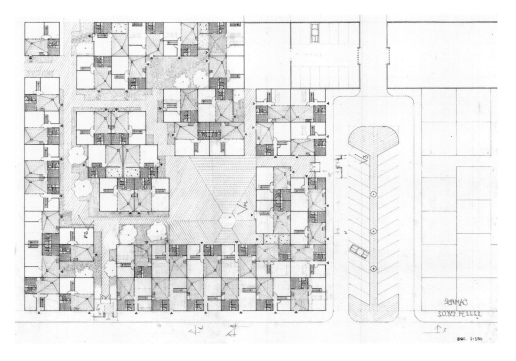

Figure 6.13. Esguerra, Saenz, Urdaneta, Samper, PREVI PP1 I-3, 1969. Residential grouping of fifty families, with shared green space. *Source*: Germán Samper/Archivo de Bogotá.

variations of the basic plan by shifting the position of elements such as the stairway to the upper story. Recognizing that the appearance of the dwellings would be diverse and continually changing, the emphasis was on preserving the quality of the neighborhood as a whole and the public spaces formed by the arrangement of houses. The key design element was the *agrupación residencial* (residential grouping), a pedestrian-only neighborhood housing around fifty families (fig. 6.13). The architects adapted its form from the Spanish colonial urban grid, claiming it was the most cost-efficient layout for installing infrastructure. While the outer edge of the agrupación residencial presented an orderly street frontage, the clustering of houses in the center—framing a series of plazas and walkways—was diverse and dynamic.

In their site design, the agrupaciones residenciales were aggregated into groups of ten to form superblocks of approximately five hundred families, with centrally located "subcenters" housing local facilities (schools, sports centers, community halls). A conceptual plan for a larger neighborhood of sixteen superblocks (or

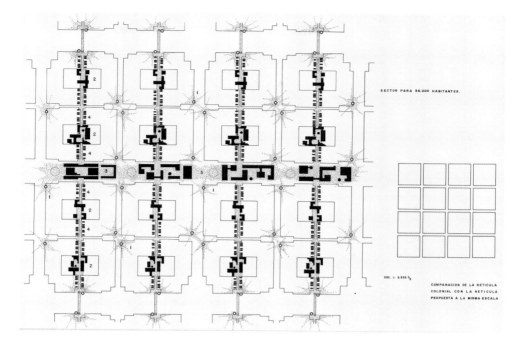

Figure 6.14. Esguerra, Saenz, Urdaneta, Samper, PREVI PP1 I-3, 1969. Diagram of "the city as a dynamic organism" (detail), with scalar comparison to the standard Spanish American colonial grid. *Source*: Germán Samper/Archivo de Bogotá.

fifty-six thousand residents) envisaged the agrupación residencial as a building block for the design of a "city as a dynamic organism" (fig. 6.14). The plan offered an overall framework that was flexible enough to accommodate variation and evolution, with "planned elements" and "elements of spontaneous origin" woven together. In the first category were the superblock "subcenters" as well as larger community centers with major public facilities (church, cinema, market) assembled in one continuous band running east-west across the middle of the site. The "subcenters" were then linked together by long walkways running north-south, intended to house shops and workshops established by local entrepreneurs that would be spontaneous in their particular formation, emerging out of a "natural dynamic" that the architects hoped to set in motion. With time, the architects anticipated that these walkways would become "the real nerve centers of the sector, places of social encounter, a modern version of the 'paseo' [or] the 'alameda' of the colonial era."[35] With this hybrid urban organism, the architects aimed to establish a structure robust enough to accommodate the impro-

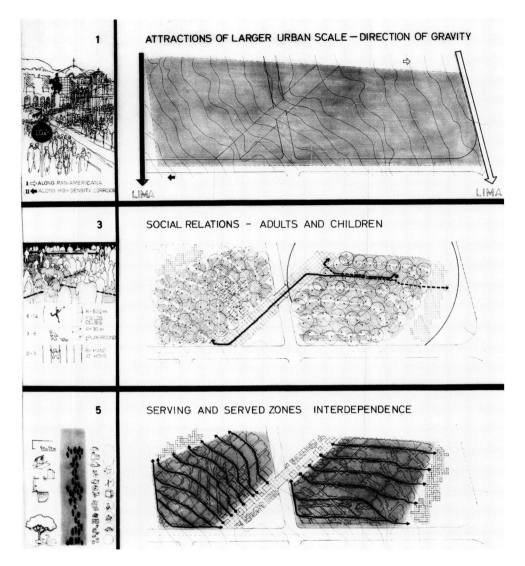

Figure 6.15. Oskar Hansen and Svein Hatløy, PREVI PP1 I-10, 1969. Components of an urban system (detail). *Source*: Zofia and Oskar Hansen Foundation, Warsaw.

visations of private enterprise and everyday interaction, while preserving a legible hierarchy of major and minor public spaces. This urban structure was designed to endure, while residents were free to shape and reshape their self-built houses.

By contrast, the urban scheme presented by Oskar Hansen and Svein Hatløy rejected any predetermined organizational framework for community life. In concert with Hansen's concept of "open form"—first presented, in collaboration with Zofia Hansen, at the CIAM '59 meeting in Otterlo—interconnections between groups of dwellings at PREVI PP1 would be determined by the residents themselves as the relationships between neighbors evolved. The architects approached the overall planning of the project via a multi-faceted analysis of the designated site, ranging from environmental factors (trade winds, water provision, available shade, the impact of noise from nearby roadways) to the performance of the site as a social space (fig. 6.15). The latter focused on the experience of the neighborhood at a personal level, whether measured as the "direction of gravity" that pulled residents toward the city center, or the ideal walking range from dwelling to public space, or the maximum acceptable distance between parents and children of various ages (diagrammed as overlapping circles of "social relations"). Responding to both environmental and social criteria, the architects proposed a site layout in broad strokes, with large residential zones on either side of the roadway dividing the site, a band of public facilities forming a bridge connecting the two halves, and supplementary areas of recreational space at either end of the site.

Within the residential zones, the architects aimed "to minimize hierarchical structures in favor of parallel opportunities for all inhabitants" (fig. 6.16). In essence, they sought to promote unstructured social interactions, arranging the dwellings in groups that framed small-scale open-air gathering places, sheltered with trees to encourage lingering, but without "fixed paths" so that pedestrians could establish their own lines of movement. Described as "private open spaces" rather than public spaces, these were highly localized, belonging to the immediate neighborhood—yet through daily usage, they would become organically linked into "chains" of free-form pathways crossing the entire site, offering multiple routes for residents to access the service and recreation zones.[36] Over time, preferred routes would become consolidated, while others would fade into disuse. In this way, spatial form would not direct community interaction, but community interaction would direct spatial form.

Finally, the proposal by Aldo van Eyck expressed a deep ambivalence over the relationship between the architect's design and the resident's input. At the urban level, van Eyck emphasized a nonhierarchical approach: the main public facilities, such as schools and parks, were not concentrated along a central strip but were placed throughout the site. There was no designated commercial zone with all the expense of its associated infrastructure; rather, van

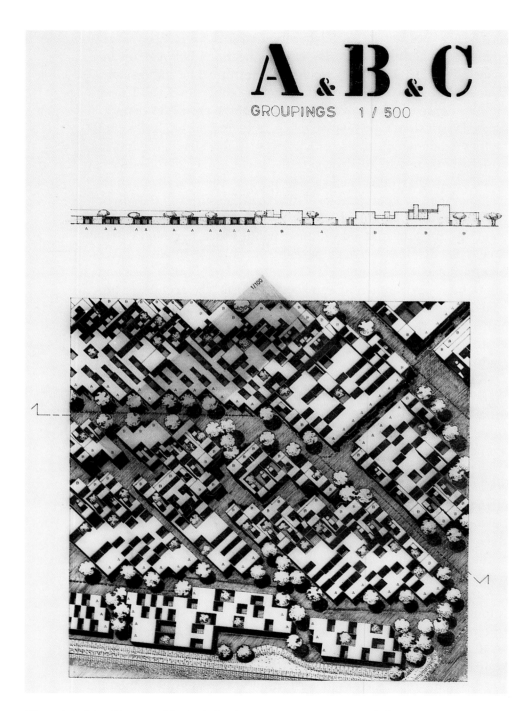

Figure 6.16. Oskar Hansen and Svein Hatløy, PREVI PP1 I-10, 1969. A, B, and C houses grouped together, with deviating pathways through the residential fabric (detail). *Source*: Zofia and Oskar Hansen Foundation, Warsaw.

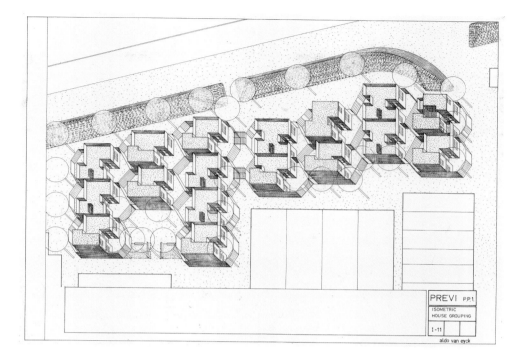

Figure 6.17. Aldo van Eyck, PREVI PP1 I-11, 1969. Grouping of houses. *Source*: Aldo + Hannie van Eyck Stichting.

Eyck hoped "that small home-based businesses will develop spontaneously along the principal *avenida*" to create a dynamic mixture of amenities.[37]

In the design of the house, van Eyck aimed to exercise more control over postoccupancy usage. The polygonal residential lots were oriented to take advantage of the prevailing winds, and offset laterally to facilitate the movement of air. The dense honeycomb of lots was punctuated at frequent intervals by small, irregularly shaped parks, forming communal spaces shared by micro-neighborhoods of six to twelve dwellings (fig. 6.17). A sketch by van Eyck of a Lima streetscape depicts the urban context to which this scheme responded: tightly packed houses built right up to the property line, straining to absorb all usable space (fig. 6.18). While van Eyck's urban fabric suggested a similarly high density, the house itself was intended to occupy no more than 60 percent of the lot, so the layout was much more open than it first appeared. The house was set within a square in the middle of the lot, the kitchen in the center, and patios at the front and rear in order to maximize light and air

271

Figure 6.18. Aldo van Eyck, Lima streetscape, 1969 (detail). *Source*: Aldo + Hannie van Eyck Stichting.

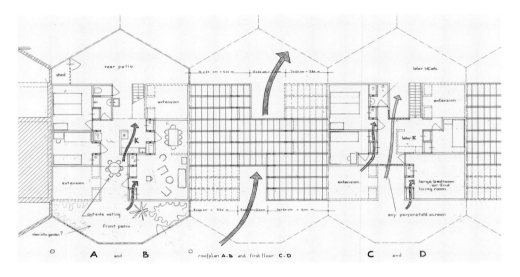

Figure 6.19. Aldo van Eyck, PREVI PP1 I-11, 1969. House type A, ground floor plan. *Source*: Aldo + Hannie van Eyck Stichting.

(fig. 6.19). The unusual geometry of the front and rear walls, with their 30°- or 60°-angle corners, gave the patios an awkward shape, which was precisely calibrated to deter postoccupancy construction that would result in their enclosure. Van Eyck explained that the use of "saw-tooth, non-loadbearing yard walls" was deployed as an additional disincentive for "expansion outside the house's maximum orthogonal perimeter." Such expansions would reduce the light and air available to the house—elements deemed the sine qua non of modernist reform housing—and eliminate its sense of openness: "In a sense the houses are designed so that further free development cannot work against the best interests of the occupants."[38] In effect, van Eyck made a self-defensive architecture of the house itself in order to protect the integrity of its design from self-builders, thereby protecting them from themselves. Instead, progressive development was expected to follow the architect's own designs, which employed a low-technology construction system well suited to self-building, using only materials, methods, and equipment that were currently in use in Peru.

While van Eyck aimed to prevent substantial changes to the form of the dwelling, his writings suggest that he anticipated, even welcomed, interventions at the decorative level, and he was disparaging about the decision to finish the neighborhood uniformly, effectively dismissing any aspirations to emulate early modernist housing: "Painting the houses should have been left to the people: literally dipped in white it looked like a postwar Weißenhofsiedlung." He expressed approval when residents employed other surface treatments (such as tile), leaving none of the walls "looking like the original material . . . , which is customary in Peru and very effective."[39] It is as if van Eyck imagined his houses being absorbed into the existing urban fabric, camouflaging the differences between the city as it was and his own reformed version of a Lima neighborhood.

In summary, for many of the international architects, the key to a successful partnership of aided self-help and advanced technology would begin with the construction system, whether through the design of lightweight and easy-to-assemble elements (CES and Stirling), dividing skilled and unskilled tasks (Correa and Atelier 5), or greatly simplifying both the form and the structure (Korhenen). Most seem to have taken for granted that the basic form of the house would follow a plan of evolution outlined by the architect, with owner-builders guided via the promised technical assistance. However, Correa and the Colombian team had some appreciation that the future form of the house might well evade their rules and designs, and set about accommodating this reality by strategies to minimize the resultant visual disorder—whether by a slender, recessed facade (Correa) or keeping self-built modifications behind a continuous street frontage (Esguerra, Saenz, Urdaneta, Samper). Others regarded the potentially unruly visual effects of self-building from a somewhat more positive perspective, with Stirling's imaginative embrace of the dissolution of uniformity into individualism (while retaining his signature porthole windows) and Atelier 5's strategic employment of a dynamic street frontage built to accommodate constant change. Van Eyck's position was more ambivalent, allowing resident input only within clearly defined limits: the surface of the house was open to improvisation, but not its essential form. Finally, both Hansen and Hatløy and the Colombian team were particularly engaged with the role that self-determined elements could play in the evolution of urban or neighborhood form, whether by opening urban form to being shaped by the patterns of everyday life (Hansen and Hatløy), or by setting a framework for the harmonious intertwining of the planned and unplanned (Esguerra, Saenz, Urdaneta, Samper).

When the international PREVI PP1 proposals were published in *Architectural Design* in 1970, the introductory section outlining the project's aims ended with a brief text that van Eyck had submitted with his competition entry, asking: "Who are we building for, and why?" In van Eyck's view, the "who" were equally likely to be residents of "pre-designed and partially constructed settlement[s]" (such as the UPIS projects), or the *pobladores* "who go to the barriadas to build from scratch both their own house and the community they have initiated themselves." Since the barriadas already offered "an emphatic testimony" of what these pobladores aspired to achieve, van Eyck questioned whether PREVI PP1—as another "pre-designed and partially constructed" project—was help or hindrance, because it could easily "counteract the growth and development of the barriada idea and practice, instead of stimulating it through the erection of improved dwelling types, construction systems, and overall community planning."[40] If PREVI PP1 failed to produce such improvements—along with lower construction costs and higher productivity—then the "why" would remain an open question.

Van Eyck's unsettled assessment was in many ways prescient, but its presentation inadvertently revealed the limits of the international architects' brief exposure to on-the-ground conditions in Lima: it was illustrated by the outline of the PREVI PP1 site superimposed over an aerial photograph of the Ciudad de Dios barriada—yet the photograph dated from 1957, not long before it was demolished to be replaced by a "pre-designed and partially constructed" neighborhood. Hovering somewhere between van Eyck's question and the ghost barriada was the answer to whether these architects' rich speculative explorations of aided self-help offered a real contribution to housing provision in Peru.

PREVI and the "National Reality"

In each case, the implementation of the four PREVI pilot projects proved to be protracted and difficult. None of the projects progressed beyond the initial trial stage, and none succeeded in completing the number of dwellings originally planned. As already noted, while PP1 was projected for 1,500 dwellings, only 467 were built. For PP2, preparatory surveys were undertaken in sixteen different areas of the city at the behest of the funder, the Caja, in an effort to locate a site suitable for urban renewal that also housed representatives of its membership. Once it became evident that empleados neither lived in nor aspired to own such housing, the Caja withdrew its support from the project. Eventually a site was selected in Barranco, which was "not qualified as highly blighted" but had the advantage that the local municipality and most residents supported the project.[41] Although 292 families were initially surveyed, renovation work was completed on only twenty-six houses: factors included difficulties financing the project (less attractive to lenders than new construction), and legal complications arising from the fact that most deteriorated housing was rented, not owned, and thus required addressing the interests of landlords as well as tenants.[42] PP3 (discussed in greater detail below) was planned as a sites-and-services project of 1,000 lots furnished with communal services, but actually resulted in 286 contractor-built dwellings, with self-building left for future extensions. In total, then, the three pilot projects within Lima resulted in 779 dwellings.

Outside of Lima, PP4 was developed in response to the May 1970 earthquake, which had left seventy thousand dead and 1.5 million homeless. This project focused on two towns in the Ancash region: Casma (on the coast), with 127 lots, and Catac (in the Andes), with 200. In this case, the construction system was revised from the initial proposal of contractor-built housing to *ayuda mutua dirigida* in order to accommodate residents' limited financial resources. One key aim was to lower costs by combining self-help labor with rationalized designs in order "to incorporate new technology into traditional local construction systems"—this included prefabricating lightweight elements with standardized dimensions in order to facilitate modular coordination. However, a postoccupancy study of Catac expressed concern that "due to ignorance and lack of follow-up technical assistance" these improved techniques were not utilized in the self-built extensions. While overall PP4 was judged to be a successful demonstration of the aided self-help methodology, questions remained about the economic viability of such projects beyond the trial phase: Catac had utilized donated funds, and therefore "established precedents impossible to repeat in other programs"; Casma "would not bear an economic analysis" if all the administrative expenses had been included in the cost of the house.

There was, however, some optimism that per-unit costs could be reduced if a followup program were undertaken on a larger scale.[43]

Beyond the various logistical challenges, one key factor compromising PREVI's effective implementation was the unstable political climate. In October 1968 Belaúnde was overthrown in a coup; the leftist military government that replaced him continued with PREVI but without Belaúnde's enthusiasm for it. (Similarly, Belaúnde had inherited the Perú-BID Plan Bienal 1962–1963 negotiated under President Prado, with little enthusiasm for its promotion of aided self-help housing.) The devastating May 1970 earthquake placed additional strain on the government's financial and organizational resources. Furthermore, economic pressures adversely affected all of the pilot projects. In the case of PREVI PP1, according to an evaluation report prepared for the UN in 1976, the total construction costs per house (including land and services) were initially fixed at S/.78,000–S/.164,000, within reach of families with a monthly income of S/.2,800–S/.5,800, estimated at a quarter of Lima's households. As the project dragged on, rising construction costs and the doubling of interest rates began to outpace family incomes. By January 1975, the actual cost per house was S/.275,000–S/.425,000, with financing charges adding another 15 percent. This left the houses accessible to families with a monthly income of S/.15,000–S/.24,000, or "only 12 percent of socioeconomic level II" of Lima households, representing a small subset of the city's total population. By the time the houses were put on the market, in 1977–1978, they were priced at around S/.1,000,000, and required a 30 percent deposit; a concurrent inflationary crisis further lowered their affordability.[44]

While the cost overruns were in large measure due to external factors beyond the control of PREVI PP1 organizers, a couple of key decisions made early in the process greatly exacerbated the problem. First, the Caja's decision to reject minimum houses in favor of dwellings it deemed more suitable for its membership raised overall costs. Second, the expansion of the construction program from six winning projects to over twenty greatly complicated implementation, causing delays and further increasing costs. In this way, the ambitions of the Caja for the status and comfort of its members and the ambitions of PREVI PP1 planners for the project's public profile undermined its ability to perform as low-cost housing. In short, organizers' aspirations acted at cross-purposes to housing need.

This disjunction is vividly illustrated by Atelier 5's account of how the expanded trial inevitably overstretched available resources: "The UN (whose agile architect Peter Land . . . had always seen in PREVI [PP1] a kind of Latin American Weißenhofsiedlung) was obviously asking too much. At the gigantic, empty site, first 26 types of stairs were finished and erected as a test. 26 different staircases, outside the city, that rose up into the sky . . . a grotesque sight, that only made clear how here time and energy would be frittered away."[45] In this parable, the skyward-gazing staircases expressed the misguided impulses of an experiment derailed by questionable priorities—in particular, the desire to invoke the pantheon of modernist housing by creating a Peruvian Weißenhofsiedlung. As a consequence, the project was reduced to the arcane exercise of producing variations on a single architectural element abstracted from its function, rather than building livable housing. This was not simply an issue of poor implementation; rather, this landscape of staircases raises questions about the overall assumptions behind PREVI PP1—the value of "advanced ideas" in design and construction in providing low-cost housing in this context—and thus the viability of the whole enterprise, irrespective of the competence of its realization.

In making this larger assessment of PREVI PP1, it is important to acknowledge that the project as realized—in line with its shaping by the Caja—was squarely aimed at the upper tier of the low-income sector: families that were able to access loans to finance the legal purchase of a modest house, which they would extend over time. This financial requirement effectively excluded the significant number of Lima residents who lacked secure, well-paid employment. These upper-tier low-income families were a coveted demographic, being less of a financial risk than lower-income applicants, and as a result, a high percentage of housing agency projects were already targeted at them. The housing shortage in Lima was so acute that many still had difficulty securing decent affordable housing, but they were only a minority of those requiring assistance. Given this context, the characterization of PREVI PP1 as "low-cost" can be quite misleading. One recent article counted among the project's "successes" the fact that "people didn't move out as their financial situations improved. Residents stayed, and turned a housing estate into what feels like a middle-class community." In fact, PREVI PP1 was planned and built as a "middle-class community" of homeowners, not as public housing, and the "low-cost" solution that it offered—as originally (and most optimistically) framed, before the impact of rising costs—was beyond the means of three-quarters of Lima households. Theoretically, a lower-cost version of PREVI PP1 could have been built: for example, the UN's 1976 report proposed constructing more modest versions of the houses—utilizing *viviendas tipo "casco"* ("shell" dwellings) to be completed via self-help labor.[46] However, it is not clear how much cheaper these "shell" dwellings would have had to be in order to accommodate a significant percentage of lower-income Lima households.

Regardless of which particular sector of low-income residents it served, PREVI PP1's original premise was "to demonstrate advanced ideas in housing design and economical construction": to lower costs by introducing new materials and methods into the local building industry, thereby improving productivity, and increasing the overall provision of affordable housing. There is little evidence that it met these goals. The UN's 1976 report found that the cost of developing the site was slightly lower than comparable housing agency projects, the key factor being the low-rise, high-density layout: the average lot size of 100 square meters, compared to 160 or 200 square meters for standard housing agency projects, lowered the overall expenses of land acquisition and site preparation. A provisional assessment of the houses, based on about half the housing types, found that on average, the per-square-meter costs were 5 percent lower than conventional projects (with a broad range in performance for the various types, from -20 to +10 percent). It also suggested that a second phase of construction focusing on the more cost-effective types and taking advantage of the economies of scale could have lowered costs a further 10 to 15 percent. This did not convince the leftist military government, who instead proposed completing the PREVI PP1 neighborhood with a lower-income population in mind: revising the standards of urban services to meet "the national reality and the available resources"; and utilizing "the direct participation of the community" via the *autoconstrucción* of dwellings, and *autofabricación* (self-fabrication) of building components such as soil-cement blocks.[47] However, these changes were never implemented, since PREVI PP1 ended with the trial phase.

Similarly, the performance of the actual houses does not make a strong case for the effectiveness of the promised advances. A postoccupancy study from 1985, based on a small sample (twenty households), included socioeconomic profiles of the owner-builders, along with their qualitative assessments of their houses, and notes on the changes they had made. In most cases the owners were empleados, and the majority (fourteen) held public sector jobs (three of them at the Banco de la Vivienda, raising questions about the fairness of the adjudication process). The main reasons given for the choice of a particular house were its location within the site, size, cost, or perceived ease of adaptation, rather than the design per se. Almost all owners had undertaken modifications—often enlarging rooms, since in most of the house types surveyed they were perceived to be small and hot. None had used their own labor; instead they had hired contractors, or drawn upon the expertise of family members with some knowledge of engineering or construction. Most surprisingly, a total of four families did not have legal title to the house, two of them because they were unaware of the process and two because they had received the dwelling extralegally (one family had exchanged an apartment in central Lima for their house; the other had received theirs through a relative working at the Banco de la Vivienda).[48]

A second survey with a somewhat larger sample (fifty-six households), published in 1991, confirmed that 70 percent of the owners were empleados, primarily working in public sector jobs. By this stage, two-thirds had made extensions to their houses, in particular enclosing the patios. In an apparent reference to the van Eyck houses, the survey noted that "in the dwellings of irregular form, they have invaded the setbacks, enclosing them in an effort to align them with the streets." Almost a quarter of the residents complained that the houses were too small, perhaps a response to the fact that the lots were more compact than the norm. This report also noted that the innovative construction systems and materials had little impact, because the owners had no knowledge of "the technical characteristics of the houses that they occupy, although they have extended and modified them, putting the stability of the structure at risk." (As early as 1984, Alfredo Montagne, the Peruvian site architect for Atelier 5, observed that technical support for residents had been nonexistent, rendering extensions according to the architects' original plans impossible.) Most damningly, the report suggested that in practice, for all the expense and expertise invested in it, PREVI PP1 as lived had minimal impact on day-to-day experience: "For the resident population this project does not differ from others in terms of the quality of life and of functionality."[49]

The most recent evaluation of PREVI PP1 documented in detail the phased transformations of fourteen households over thirty-five years of occupation (1978–2003), setting aside socioeconomic questions altogether (plate 14). This research once again confirmed that instead of following architects' plans for progressive development, residents improvised their own solutions. For example, the Villegas family, owner-builders of a house designed by van Eyck, in essence "totally rejected the two postulates inherent in the design": first, after one year of residence, they enlarged the kitchen and moved it from its original central location to the front passageway in order to take advantage of cross-ventilation; and a decade later, they enclosed the polygonal back patio to create additional living space.[50] They later added a third story, taking the total enclosed area to 232 square meters. In general, the surveyed dwellings far exceeded the maximum surface area of 120 square meters mandated by the original specifications, ranging from 172 to 352 square meters, and as a consequence retained less openness, light, and air than the architects had envisaged. By and large, their "advanced ideas" were subsumed within the ongoing life of the house.

Assessed more broadly, PREVI PP1's effectiveness in producing low-cost housing is questionable: it promised a dynamic partnership of technology and aided self-help to provide a viable alternative for the provision of low-cost housing, yet each half of the equation was founded on flawed assumptions. First, there was a misplaced faith in the power of innovative building technologies to lower costs, as well as insufficient consideration of the challenges of introducing such technologies into the Peruvian construction industry. Consequently, a number of the projects proposed construction methods that were too expensive or technologically complex to be realized: Ohl's project was cut altogether, while those by Stirling, Hansen and Hatløy, and the CES had to be fundamentally modified in order to keep them within budget. A brief report on a site visit in September 1973 described slow progress, with workers voicing complaints that they were not paid during the training period necessary to learn the new techniques, and that "the project required more specialized skill than most workers in Lima have, and that not even the engineers were very clear about the system."[51] Here PREVI PP1's technocratic vision of a modernized building site met the reality that even well-designed technological innovations, attuned to the capabilities of Peru's construction industry, would incur considerable startup costs.

Second, project organizers seem to have regarded the aided self-help component as self-evident, its techniques requiring no elaboration, rethinking, or refinement. Nowhere in the competition brief, judges' report, or the UN's 1976 evaluation was this dimension of the project's implementation discussed in any detail. Aided self-help seems to have been included as a necessary tool to lower the costs of producing a standard modern dwelling, not because of any commitment to the practice, or insights into how it could benefit from "advanced ideas" and new technologies to become more economical or effective. In particular, the competition brief asserted that technical assistance would be available to oversee self-built extensions according to the architects' plans, evincing no awareness of the challenges of providing such assistance. Yet by 1968 there was ample evidence that few of the earlier generation of aided self-help housing projects had managed to meet this need, and PREVI PP1 proposed no initiatives to guarantee its provision here. Without the resource of an on-site architect to offer advice or to advocate for the value of the original design, there would be little to distinguish this project from other Lima neighborhoods.

As a point of contrast, it is worth reviewing the framework of PREVI PP3 in some detail, since it was primarily concerned with innovation in aided self-help, while PREVI PP1 only considered the method as a supplementary technique. PREVI PP3 was led by Federico Mevius, who had worked with Turner in Arequipa in the late 1950s. It recalled aspects of housing policy in place in the early 1960s, specifically the UPIS projects, which were conceived as planned low-cost settlements offering an alternative to the barriada, with a minimum dwelling built using aided self-help either in the initial construction or subsequent extensions. Aided self-help had fallen out of favor following Belaúnde's election to the presidency in late 1963, but was revived under the military government, beginning with a new development policy announced at the end of 1968 that underlined the importance of "family efforts in the construction of their own dwellings." Mevius was a key contributor to a policy document produced in late 1970 that sought to reassert the role of autoconstrucción in housing policy, recommending a new agency to study, execute, and evaluate projects, to improve professional training in its specialized practices, and to implement a "program of experimentation" to determine the most effective methods.[52] PREVI PP3 presented Mevius with the opportunity to undertake precisely this kind of experimental program. Beginning in 1971 Mevius spent eighteen months developing thirty-odd innovations in seven areas: site selection, *urbanización* (urban planning

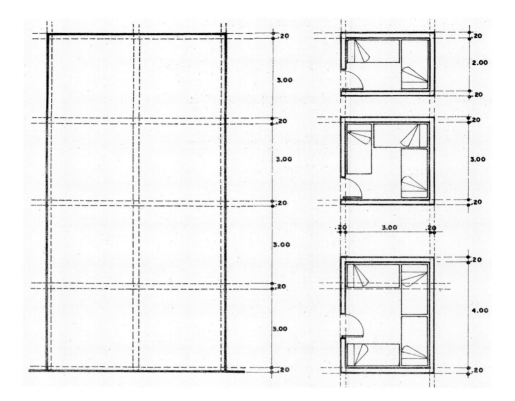

Figure 6.20. Federico Mevius, PREVI PP3, 1971–1972. Basic grid of the lot dimensional system as determined by the *módulo cama* (bed module); three bedroom types generated by the módulo cama. *Source*: MV and ININVI, *Publicación PREVI*, vol. 26, *PREVI PP3: Proyecto de lotes y servicios* (Lima: MV and ININVI, 1979).

and urban services), housing, construction, administrative systems, social work, and financing. Changes made in the implementation phase meant that few of these innovations were tested, but they nonetheless explored valuable alternative approaches to aided self-help housing.

Mevius argued that the proposals in the areas of site selection and urbanización were of particular importance, together constituting "the first truly realistic step for the control of spontaneous urban development." The approach to site selection recalled a position that Mevius had articulated in the expropriations plan for Lima he prepared for the Junta Nacional de la Vivienda in 1963: rather than being relegated to the urban margins, well-situated sites were crucial for the lowest-income residents, since any earnings spent on transport to a distant workplace would undermine

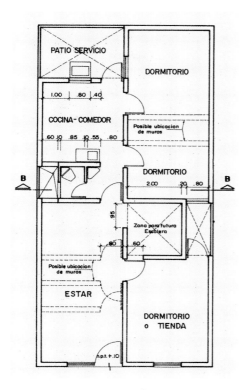

Figure 6.21. Federico Mevius, PREVI PP3, 1971–1972. One iteration of the rectangular house, incorporating an example of each of the bedroom types. *Source*: MV and ININVI, *Publicación PREVI*, vol. 26, *PREVI PP3: Proyecto de lotes y servicios* (Lima: MV and ININVI, 1979).

their ability to invest in their houses, and thus delay consolidation of the settlement. At PREVI PP3, this principle led to the rejection of a site on Lima's southern fringes in favor of one more centrally located (in Callao, adjacent to Urbanización Condevilla Señor), and its successful acquisition via forced expropriation for a much lower cost than the original proposed site. The proposals relating to urbanización included a new approach to site development, reorganizing the sequence of installing urban services so that the work of constructing houses could begin before all the infrastructure was finished; Mevius argued that this was essential to address the urgent demand for housing, and thereby deter invasions. In terms of urban planning, the layout emphasized green space (sorely lacking in the barriadas), arranged "in small nuclei, facing onto the largest number of dwellings"; this measure—inspired by "the local tradition of converting public spaces adjacent to the dwelling into gardens"—aimed to promote a sense of ownership over these small parks and thus ensure their ongoing maintenance by local residents.[53]

The urban scheme created a high level of density, reducing the average lot size to 92 square meters in order to accommodate more families in need. The dimensions of the lot (and of the dwelling itself) were derived by working from the inside outward, using a "módulo cama" (bed module) of 1 by 2 meters (fig. 6.20). The stated aim was "to shelter the greatest number of users" via the head-to-toe arrangement of beds, allowing more beds per room, and thereby (potentially) lowering the number of people per bed—an urgent need, since a recent study of barriadas had found that on average there were "more than two people" in each bed. (Another of the un-realized proposals was "indirect financing [to address] the deficit of beds by a reduction of the initial payment" for the house.)[54] The módulo cama generated a basic dimensional grid of 3 by 3 meters, which could be converted into two types of housing lots—square (three-by-three grid) or rectangular (two-by-four grid)—each of which could be laid out in a variety of ways (fig. 6.21). Mevius argued that allowing individual families to determine the essential outline of the house could be carried out quickly—in Arequipa, families had taken "no more than half an hour to select the definitive design of the dwelling along with the architect"—and could be easily imple-mented in the construction phase since it only involved shifting a few structural elements. Furthermore, allowing greater choice ini-tially would lessen the need for subsequent modifications, resulting in savings for each family. Other innovations in the design of the house included "patios enclosed by neighboring houses, without *cercos*" (thereby saving the expense of building a perimeter wall for each house), and situating the first stage of the dwelling at the front of the lot (thereby creating "from the outset definitive urban spaces" to give the neighborhood a sense of coherence).[55] Finally, improved construction materials were developed for self-building: a redesigned system of concrete components would facilitate the autofabricación not only of bricks but also more complex elements such as roofing beams and stairway components. In addition, fire-resistant esteras treated with a mixture of gypsum, lime, and fine sand would improve the safety performance of provisional dwellings while the permanent housing was under construction.

On the administrative level, the proposal endeavored to encour-age greater user control by individual participants. Rather than being assigned from above, neighborhood groups would self-select their members—a process labeled "autoformación" (self-formation) —and choose a location for their houses within the site. This ap-proach would both reinforce a sense of neighborhood cohesion and relieve project planners of the often difficult and time-consuming work of social organization. For financing, Mevius advocated using supervised credit, arguing that it represented the most successful approach to aided self-help that had been implemented in Peru. This gave the resident more control over the construction process: beyond providing labor, the resident effectively acted as "contractor of his own dwelling" by taking responsibility for purchasing materials and hiring laborers, as needed. This also substantially reduced the number of professional staff required: Mevius estimated that staffing for the proposed program of one thousand houses would be "minimal"—"an architect, five building contractors, two inspectors, two social assistants, very limited accounting personnel"—thereby offering a "debureaucratized solution" to the provision of aided self-help. Finally, Mevius proposed to combine three initiatives that had been successfully implemented in previous supervised credit programs: credit disbursed in stages (applied at Huascarán); inspectors to review daily progress (Arequipa); and the review and approval of specialized building contractors available to self-builders (San Martín de Porres). In this way, PREVI PP3 aimed "to try to improve upon the most advantageous known solution" already applied, thereby maximizing the project's effectiveness as a venue for experimentation.[56]

In early 1973, work began at the PREVI PP3 site (now Urbanización Previ Bocanegra, Callao), preparing 1,007 lots, and installing water and sewerage lines. However, it was soon decided to abandon the aided self-help approach in favor of building a total of 286 "basic, incomplete dwellings" utilizing mass construction (fig. 6.22). These units were finished in January 1975; by the time Mevius undertook a postoccupancy study in 1979, no additional units had been built, while a majority of the original houses had been extended using unaided self-help. Since only a handful of the proposed innovations—limited to site selection and urbanización—were actually implemented, Mevius advocated a followup trial to test the unexecuted proposals. In view of the country's deteriorating economic situation, Mevius reframed the project in line with available resources, acknowledging that it would have to be realized "within much lower standards" than the original scheme: that is, based on *lotes tizados* (surveyed lots outlined with chalk) and the staged installation of infrastructure, creating, initially, an urban grid of sites-without-services. The residents' work of constructing a neighborhood upon these foundations would be supported via a program of supervised credit. For Mevius, an architect with sub-

Figure 6.22. PREVI PP3 (now Urbanización Previ Bocanegra), Lima, 1973–1975. Aerial view of part of the PP3 site (outlined); the fully developed section is in the lower left corner. *Source*: MV and ININVI, *Publicación PREVI*, vol. 26, *PREVI PP3: Proyecto de lotes y servicios* (Lima: MV and ININVI, 1979).

stantial experience in aided self-help housing, the key to the revised "experimental housing project" was not the dwelling, or even basic services, but a lot paired with carefully administered financing. In the end, however, no additional trial was implemented, and PREVI PP3 would remain (in essence) unrealized.

In his conclusion to the PREVI PP3 evaluation, Mevius called for the creation of an Office of Evaluation and Experimentation in housing, which would also be responsible for studying the process of barriada formation, in order to design policies "with realistic bases for the interventions that are attempted into said process." It was essential "to rationalize *from the outset*" the evolving shape of spontaneous settlements, because once consolidation was underway, modifications were more difficult and more expensive to undertake. Furthermore, because any planned intervention would be constrained by existing construction, "said settlement cannot achieve its optimum expression."[57] For Mevius, at this point there was little distance between housing policy and barriada policy: his highly pragmatic exploration of the real possibilities of aided self-help housing, or technical assistance to self-builders, had reached its absolute limit in managed credit for sites-without-services. Beyond that was the barriada itself, where the focus shifted to the design of tactical interventions to optimize unfolding urban development, providing the basic outlines for a semi-improvised city.

Across the pilot projects, the modes of formal-informal collaboration explored by PREVI ranged from avant-gardist invention to chalk-drawn lot. At the upper end of the economic spectrum served by the project, PREVI PP1 offered new approaches to the design of the "growing house" and innovative construction systems, without providing compelling evidence that this would translate into significant savings. At the other extreme, PREVI PP3 demonstrated the real challenges of designing housing for very limited budgets, and with it the shrinking opportunities for architecture to make a contribution. While PREVI had not discovered a definitive solution to the provision of low-cost housing, the efforts of Mevius, among others, to continually recalibrate the design response suggested that there was still space for exploring alternative approaches, better matched to residents' resources and the state's capacity to provide meaningful support.

7

REVOLUTIONS
IN SELF-HELP,
1968–1980

In a speech delivered in Vancouver in June 1976 to delegates from 132 countries and various intergovernmental organizations, British economist Barbara Ward began with the observation: "One of the most hopeful developments of the seventies is the degree to which world society has begun to examine, seriously and together, what one might call the basic facts of 'planetary housekeeping.'" This examination had been initiated with the UN Conference on the Human Environment (Stockholm, 1972), and continued via a series of meetings on issues of global concern: the World Population Conference (Bucharest, 1974), the World Food Conference (Rome, 1974), the World Conference on Women (Mexico City, 1975), and now Habitat: UN Conference on Human Settlements (Vancouver, 1976). Reflecting on the unprecedented and intertwined crises now emerging—escalating rates of population growth, food shortages, rising energy costs, and massive urban agglomerations caused by "the lemming-like surges of peasant to city which threaten to overwhelm even the bravest urban plans"—Ward called for a radical rethinking of social responsibility at the global level, linking "planetary housekeeping" to the task of developing "a 'new international economic order' aiming at justice and cooperation." In this vision, "the old blind dependence upon market forces" would diminish as the pull of social factors increasingly influenced calculations of economic and political interest, resulting in policies shaped by "some concept of the general welfare."[1] Ward envisaged broad support for initiatives to implement basic urban infrastructure, public housing, and education programs in the cities of the developing world. Most immediately, she endorsed a World Bank proposal promoting sites-and-services and self-help housing projects, along with initiatives in transport, health, and clean water; costing $30 billion a year, this could be funded by redirecting just 10 percent of the $300 billion spent annually on arms. Such measures, it seemed, would be entirely within the means of an emergent imagined international community.

While Ward's proposal to channel funding from arms to aid was not to be embraced, the Habitat conference did become a catalyst for significant changes on the policy level. The new conceptual category of "human settlements" promoted by Habitat facilitated a more nuanced understanding of the complex dynamics of unplanned urban development, and opened the way for the widespread adoption of sites-and-services and self-help housing schemes by national governments and international development agencies alike. The broader project of a "new international economic order"—which had initially been proposed by Third World nations as an impetus for global redistributive policies—was to be short-lived.[2] As the immediate challenges to global well-being subsided, the urgency for radical change faded to a historical footnote. Soon enough, the fall of communism confirmed the (apparently) inevitable collapse of any alternative to the capitalist model, setting the stage for the inexorable rise of neoliberalism and its own concomitant new global economic order.

Against the background of these larger shifts, this chapter examines the fortunes of aided self-help housing in Peru during a period of profound political and cultural change. The perspective moves between the national and international spheres, between the practical and the theoretical, discussing programs designed and executed in Peru, along with key texts by anthropologist Carlos Delgado, architect Diego Robles, and John F. C. Turner, the latter contributing to a reframing of housing policy at the World Bank and the UN.

The Revolution Will Be Organized

> If our Revolution aspires to recreate the whole universe of our
> nation, to reshape its history and to forge in Peru a new society for
> a new man, we have no other recourse than ... to stand up to the
> great problem of reappraising utopias, of creatively reconstituting
> idealisms, of erecting our action on the foundation of an imagina-
> tive creative capacity for whose adventures of thought there are no
> more taboos, nor impassable barriers.
>
> — **President Juan Velasco Alvarado**, at the Centro de Altos
> Estudios Militares, Lima, December 1972[3]

The Peruvian Revolution began in the early hours of October 3,
1968, as leftist radicals within the military detained President
Fernando Belaúnde Terry and then sent him into exile in Argentina. The self-styled Gobierno Revolucionario de la Fuerza Armada
(Revolutionary Government of the Armed Forces) that assumed
control explained its actions in a manifesto: the Belaúnde government had come to power with promises of comprehensive reform,
but had betrayed the hopes placed in it—incompetent, corrupt, and
subservient to foreign interests, it was no longer fit to govern. As
for its own vision of the future: "The Revolutionary Government,
fully identified with the aspirations of the Peruvian people, calls
upon them—together with the Armed Forces—to fight to achieve an
authentic social justice, a dynamic national development, and the
reestablishment of moral values that will affirm our homeland in
the achievement of its higher destiny."[4]

Rhetoric aside, it was true that much of Belaúnde's legislative
agenda had been stymied by a powerful opposition coalition in the
parliament. In addition, Belaúnde's developmentalist vision had
entailed large expenditures on projects such as housing construction and infrastructure, particularly the Forest-Edge Highway,
which dramatically increased foreign debt. These fiscal difficulties
were compounded by the US decision to withhold financial aid to
Peru in an effort to influence the government's position in renego-
tiating its contract with IPC (International Petroleum Company, a
subsidiary of Standard Oil of New Jersey). In the end, Belaúnde's
anxiety to resolve the IPC dispute led to the signing of a contract
whose overly favorable terms were widely perceived as a national
disgrace. This provided the immediate trigger for the coup, and the
new Revolutionary Government settled the issue by nationalizing

the company, arguing that it was "fulfilling its constitutional duty, . . . defending one of [Peru's] natural sources of wealth, which being Peruvian, should be for Peruvians." Filtered through the language of contemporaneous debates around dependency, Belaúnde's proposed deal was framed as increasing the country's "dependence on economic powers" (specifically, the United States) and postponing efforts to "overcome our current state of underdevelopment."[5] Conversely, reasserting national sovereignty and geopolitical autonomy was a prerequisite for realizing transformative economic development, as Peru would draw on its human and natural resources in order to achieve greater self-sufficiency.

In these and other initiatives—agrarian reform, improving administrative processes, extending the franchise to the illiterate (over 38 percent of the population in 1961)—the Revolutionary Government was enacting policies that had been proposed by a number of reform-minded parties, including the Movimiento Social Progresista (MSP), Alianza Popular Revolucionaria Americana (APRA), Partido Demócrata Cristiano, and Belaúnde's own Acción Popular. As Abraham F. Lowenthal observed: "What distinguished Peru's military rulers was not the originality of their program, but their capacity to put familiar ideas into effect."[6] Among the factors that contributed to the radicalization of this generation of Peruvian officers, two are particularly notable. First, the program of study at the Centro de Altos Estudios Militares (Center for Higher Military Studies), which emphasized issues of economic development and social reform, and brought officers into contact with progressive intellectuals such as those associated with the MSP, including José Matos Mar. Second, the experience of suppressing a large-scale rural insurgency in 1965–1966, ordered by Belaúnde, which resulted in an estimated eight thousand dead and ultimately left many in the military with greater sympathy for the underlying grievances that had led to the protests. In 1968 Peru was rated poorly in terms of income, literacy, and the overall standard of living, and the distribution of wealth and property was highly unequal. The prevailing oligarchy had clearly failed a majority of the population, and for military leaders, aside from issues of social justice, a fundamental reshaping of society was seen as a national security issue.

Freed from the complications of electoral politics and parliamentary negotiations, the Revolutionary Government envisaged itself guiding the country's development for one or two decades in order to implement a comprehensive program of structural reforms, after which it would reintroduce democratic government. (At this period in Peru's history, military rule functioned as a normative means of resolving political deadlocks, as had been evidenced only a few years earlier with the 1962 coup that effectively opened the way for Belaúnde's victory in the 1963 presidential election.) After twelve years of military government—led first by General Juan Velasco Alvarado (1968–1975), then General Francisco Morales Bermúdez (1975–1980)—Belaúnde reemerged as president in the 1980 elections that returned Peru to democracy. This passage "from Belaúnde to Belaúnde"—as one writer has termed it—reinforces the sense that the revolutionary decade was a mirage, nothing more than a misstep en route to the neoliberal reform initiatives of the 1980s and 1990s.[7] However, the very unlikelihood of this late flowering of revolutionary utopianism heightens the impact of its actions and its rhetorical imagination. This deviation from the apparently straight line of historical inevitablility recalls (and perhaps projects) a moment of other possibilities—an alternative future contemporaneous with the promise of Ward's incipient "world society."

Neither capitalist nor communist, but combining elements of both socialist and Christian thought, Peru's "humanist revolution" envisioned building "a social democracy of full participation" in place of the existing oligarchy. The key figure in articulating the revolution's theoretical and ideological framework was Carlos Delgado, an anthropologist/sociologist who was recruited shortly after the coup by Velasco to act as his advisor and speechwriter (he likely wrote the address quoted above).

In a timely essay first published in January 1969, Delgado dissected the concept of development, arguing that sociology needed to refine its own understanding of the subject by outlining a clear definition of social as opposed to economic development. For Delgado, interventions to improve standards of literacy, nutrition, sanitation, and so on did not constitute social development but were simply the solutions of discrete social issues using an "isolated and static" approach. Rather, genuine social development described a *"dynamic of collective action"* that would entail a radical reconstitution of the social structure, via "a process of transformation oriented toward the creation of a new social order." In the case of "underdeveloped societies" such as Peru, this transformational process needed to operate with a dual focus: internally, via "a substantive alteration of the structures of political, economic, and social power"; and externally, via "a radical suspension of the dependency that binds these societies to the designs of imperial powers"—both capitalist and communist, Western and Eastern blocs. In this context, the Revolutionary Government's nationalization of extractive industries formerly under the control of foreign-owned companies—this included the mining and fishing industries, as well as IPC—and its new alliance with the nonaligned nations, were primary gestures toward the achievement of a "new social order" internationally. Domestically, while raising living standards in line with developed nations was a worthwhile goal, social development meant more than achieving material progress—its political dimension resided in "the *meaning* of such achievements in terms of the type of society that they obtain." For Delgado, this would be a society founded on a politics of engagement, establishing "a social environment that is optimistic, creative, dynamic, affirmative." It would also be a society defined by a sense of collective purpose: thus, social development entailed an ongoing effort to attain "an ever greater participation of its members" in decision-making processes, along with "growing accessibility to the mechanisms of power."[8] In short, it would engender a social democracy of full participation.

It was in this context that the cooperative ethos of squatter settlements, evident in the shared labor of communal construction projects, became a privileged image, symbolizing the revolutionary collective working as one for the common good (fig. 7.1). No longer considered marginal, the self-built community represented an alternative model of development, based on the values of self-help and mutual support; it heralded both the emergence of a new revolutionary polity and the revival of a social solidarity that was framed as essentially Peruvian, rooted in a tradition leading back to the Incas, which had been damaged but not destroyed by capitalism, colonialism, and neocolonial exploitation. Updating inherited creole mythologies of an idealized precolonial past, according to one educational pamphlet, in the foreseeable revolutionary future, "like our Inca forebears" the Peruvian people would "not lie, nor steal, nor live from alienated labor."[9] This ethos was embodied by the figure of Túpac Amaru II, an eighteenth-century anticolonial revolutionary of indigenous ancestry, who had anticipated a modern state founded on Inca principles of governance, and whose stern but noble demeanor became central to the iconography of the revolution.

A key aim of the Revolutionary Government was to foster economic development via coordinated national planning, thereby remedying the disequilibrium caused by relations of dependency (an initia-

Figure 7.1. The collective, revolutionary self-help home builder: "Popular revolutionary work; Popular participation is revolution." *Source*: SINAMOS, *Guia para la organización de los pueblos jóvenes* (Lima: SINAMOS, ca. 1972), CDI-MVCS.

tive that came to be packaged under the suitably nativist rubric "Plan Inca"). In the short term this would be directed by competent agencies within the (military, revolutionary) state, but in the longer term control would pass to everyday representatives of the new nation. To this end, the Revolutionary Government created two agencies to organize and train its citizens: the Oficina Nacional de Desarrollo de Pueblos Jóvenes (ONDEPJOV, National Office for the Development of Young Towns), which was essentially a community development program focused on squatter settlements, and the Sistema Nacional de Apoyo a la Movilización Social (SINAMOS, National System of Support for Social Mobilization), whose mission was to promote the ideals of participation and grassroots organization.

ONDEPJOV was established in December 1968, in the first months of the revolution, with the personal input of Velasco. As a sign of the Revolutionary Government's new outlook, the term *barriada* was condemned as derogatory, and was replaced in all official communications, including the title of the new agency, by "pueblo joven" (young town, or young community). According to ONDEPJOV, the denomination "ha[d] been proposed by the residents themselves as an expression of their recent formation, the predominance of youth in their population, and the will for advancement that they embody."[10]

While the general coordinator of ONDEPJOV and the directors of all the regional and sector offices were from the military, it had as its civilian head Diego Robles, an architect who had worked on aided self-help housing programs in Paramonga and Chimbote. Robles recalled that ONDEPJOV's broad mandate engaged experts from various disciplines (sociology, anthropology, economics) along with architects and engineers. It also coordinated with a range of government ministries to implement directives in different sectors: education (promoting literacy), health (improving access to preventative care), and agriculture (supplying affordable produce to markets in the pueblos jóvenes). Supplementing these contributions were ONDEPJOV staff with a military background, with deep knowledge "about the [national] territory, about underlying conflicts"; for Robles, this civil-military collaboration created a "symbiosis" that at its best was highly productive, despite being short-lived.[11]

While working in Chimbote, Robles had begun to consider the relationship between self-help housing projects and urban development, noting, for example, that a poorly located site could jeopardize a project's success. Studying with Otto Koenigsberger at the Architectural Association's School of Tropical Architecture in 1965 allowed him to further explore these issues, and upon returning to Peru, he shifted his professional focus toward the urban scale. This led to an assignment as a researcher with the Plan de Desarrollo Metropolitano Lima-Callao (PLANDEMET, Metropolitan Development Plan for Lima-Callao), established under the Belaúnde government in 1967. In contrast to the 1949 Plan Piloto for Lima, which had ignored barriadas altogether, PLANDEMET in essence reiterated the principles of Law 13517: existing barriadas would be upgraded, and the formation of new ones prohibited, while those in need of low-cost housing would be accommodated in *urbanizaciones populares* executed by state housing agencies. To this end, PLANDEMET identified key "corridors" of expansion along major roadways, in order to earmark suitable sites for the establishment of such settlements within the city's overall land-use planning. Over time, the goal was to accomplish the "gradual replacement of the barriadas with *urbanizaciones populares.*"[12]

However, some within PLANDEMET, including Robles, were less sanguine about the prospects of eliminating the barriadas, instead viewing them as an integral part of Lima's existing urban fabric and its foreseeable future growth. In late 1968 Delgado, then working alongside Robles as a researcher at PLANDEMET, wrote a key text articulating this emerging viewpoint. (Incidentally, two years before, Delgado had undertaken an anthropological study of two early Corporación Nacional de la Vivienda projects, exploring possible refinements "of the *unidad vecinal* concepts conditioning the community structure."[13] Although he questioned the applicability of the term *community* in a modern urban context, he nonetheless concluded that the unidad vecinal did offer an effective planning tool, with its focus on plazas, parks, and walkways as spaces of social interaction.) Delgado's 1968 article began by arguing, "If the process of urbanization cannot be arrested, and if the migrations cannot be curbed, the 'barriadas' cannot be eradicated. Day by day their existence is encircled by conditions of virtual inexorability." Furthermore, over the previous two decades the *pobladores* had contributed more to solving Lima's housing crisis than all the efforts of the various state agencies combined, being responsible for 100,000 dwellings in the capital, housing a quarter of the population. By contrast, the state had constructed around 31,000 units, 1,609 of them provisional or emergency shelters. For this reason, the settlements should be seen as "a positive factor of the urbanization process" and urban planners should recognize that "they possess an appreciable potential for development not yet utilized but crucially necessary" in meeting the challenges of rapid urban growth. Delgado understood these settlements to be highly heterogeneous in their character and prognosis, whether tending toward "tugurización" (slum formation) via overcrowding and physical deterioration, or emerging as neighborhoods "of great dynamism and high potential for *autogestión* [self-management]"— that is, in addition to contributing their self-help dwellings to the city, in certain cases the pobladores had the capacity to collectively self-manage the development of their community.[14]

Using three key factors—population density, location (whether central or peripheral), and level of consolidation—Delgado devised an "operational typology" of barriada development, and proposed that urban planners deploy this insight to sharpen their interventions, reorienting each settlement for the greatest chance of successful evolution. Significantly, Delgado measured their success or failure in relation to other barriadas that had thrived or stagnated—not in terms of whether they met specific standards of physical improvement that would bring them in line with conventional urban settlements, as Law 13517 had proposed. Rather than aspiring toward a platonic ideal of urban form that Delgado clearly regarded as unattainable, he suggested that planners establish new benchmarks based on a realistic view of the situation at hand; rather than continuing Law 13517's efforts to eliminate the barriadas, he advocated fostering their innate "potential for development" via strategic interventions.

As for the government's own housing efforts, Delgado observed that it could not possibly build the five hundred thousand units needed in the capital over the next twelve years. Instead, it should adopt as its overarching principle the "abandonment of the paternalistic notion that the *pobladores* of underdeveloped and developing settlements lack the capacity to solve . . . their housing problems."[15] Residents should have a larger role in determining how resources were deployed, and in devising new housing standards more closely attuned to their needs and preferences. For its part, the government's contribution should be focused on providing suitable sites with legal ownership, and technical assistance in construction. In sum, Delgado was advocating for basic sites-and-services projects that better reflected residents' actual needs and financial resources. This approach would have very little appeal to Belaúnde, PLANDEMET's initial sponsor, but was absolutely in keeping with the Revolutionary Government's ambition to use agencies such as ONDEPJOV to construct a new dynamic between the state and its citizens, with participation and grassroots democracy at its foundation.

ONDEPJOV had two precedents of sorts: the residents' own associations, in particular the Pro-Obras de Bienestar Social (Support for Projects of Social Well-Being), a federation that by September 1968 included over six hundred local groups representing one hundred thousand people in Lima; and the organizing work of the Catholic church, beginning around 1963 under the leadership of Monsignor Luis Bambarén, auxiliary bishop of Lima. ONDEPJOV was intended to surpass these efforts—as well as previous state-run programs—by linking ground-up self-help community development with plans for national economic growth, since better incomes and employment opportunities were essential for sustainable improvement in the lives of the pobladores. To this end, ONDEPJOV would coordinate the contributions of the public sector and the private (primarily the church), with those of the residents themselves. At the grassroots level, the aim was to supplant the old approach to barriadas, mired in paternalistic political patronage, by empowering the "pueblos jóvenes"—the young communities—to unlock their latent potential to enact collective self-improvement. The focus of self-help action would not be on housing per se but rather on fostering civic engagement as a basis for enacting communal projects, such as infrastructure and public facilities. In an effort to increase participation, ONDEPJOV produced a wide range of promotional materials, including handbooks with clear illustrations and limited text to convey the values of a revolutionary democracy to semiliterate citizens—an approach that in itself marked a further concrete step toward genuine social inclusion (fig. 7.2).

To organize its work, ONDEPJOV established twenty-one regional offices throughout the country; in addition, four sector offices covered Lima's peripheral pueblos jóvenes. Within this structure, the settlements were to be integrated into a clear hierarchical system: each block of thirty or so households would elect its own three-person neighborhood committee; these representatives attended the zone-wide advancement and development committee, which elected a central board of directors; finally, the board's secretary general joined the coordination committee for the regional or sector office, which provided liaison with ONDEPJOV officials and professional staff. This machinery was intended to systematize the political interactions—from grassroots to government—of a significant proportion of the population. In 1970 ONDEPJOV identified 610 pueblos jóvenes across Peru, with 273 in greater Lima alone; 760,000 people, a quarter of the capital's population, lived in such

Figure 7.2. A new ethics of community development: 4. "What needs to be done in our *pueblo joven*? We arrived in the barrio . . . without knowing each other. But . . . communal needs became evident to us." 5. "With this unity we did various projects. Then . . . little by little and without us realizing it, enthusiasm and unification were lost." *Source*: ONDEPJOV, *Folleto de Divulgación No. 1: Guia para la organización de los pueblos jóvenes* (Lima: ONDEPJOV, ca. 1970), CDI-MVCS.

settlements. Absorbing this population into ONDEPJOV while maintaining the granularity proposed by the organizational model would generate a substantial administrative infrastructure: by mid-1972 there were 4,875 neighborhood committees throughout Lima; by August 1974 there were over 8,000, covering 95 percent of residents.[16] Through this process, ONDEPJOV incorporated into its membership structure the earlier resident-run and church-affiliated groups, effectively neutralizing any independent organizations. In theory, ONDEPJOV's multitiered system of representation embodied "a social democracy of full participation"—the new Peru in microcosm. In practice, actual citizen involvement often failed to meet the regime's aspirations: reporting in late 1971, one observer noted that "in many provincial cities [the committees] were simply designated by military officers assigned to create them."[17]

Initially ONDEPJOV was largely focused on upgrading and remodeling projects, which would previously have been the responsibility of the Junta Nacional de la Vivienda. However, it soon began to design new programs in line with its mission of fostering integrated development. These ranged from training local organizers in methods of community development to initiatives encouraging savings and loan cooperatives, and a proposal to bolster technical education in order to provide Peru with the "specialized blue-collar workers" that it required as a developing nation. This ambitious scheme had an urban as well as an economic dimension, since its ultimate aim was to create small-scale industrial enterprises within the pueblos jóvenes, decentralizing productive activities and job opportunities, "so that the *pueblos jóvenes* are not heaped with marginalized people or a mass that is only scattered across the city to find scraps of work, but are organic entities that within a short time will be converted into developing zones of Greater Lima."[18] This proposal contained the seeds of ONDEPJOV's larger vision of development, which Robles would play a key role in advancing.

Robles was a close observer of the dynamics of squatter settlement formation and consolidation. Writing shortly before the revolution, in August 1968, he emphasized as a positive the fact that barriadas allowed pobladores to be proactive in solving their housing problems by making full use of their nonmonetary resources: "community organization, free time, inventive capacity, practical ability, etc." However, residents' organizations tended to fragment once they had met their immediate needs for basic services and secure tenure, achieved via the traditional mechanisms of clientelistic politics. Thus, ultimately, "even if this form of collective action solves specific problems for the families, it does not represent a radical change in respect to formal established society." In fact it tended toward a certain conservatism, because once residents had managed to make gains by working through clientelism, they were invested in maintaining the system from which they had benefited. In a subsequent article, "Development Alternatives for the Peruvian Barriada" (1972), Robles employed a Marxist framework inflected with the language of dependency to further his analysis. Barriadas "typify the process of urban domination and rapid dependent urbanization"; they were a symptom of uneven economic development within Peru, which was in turn a symptom of uneven economic relations between Peru and foreign powers. In contrast to Turner's anarcho-Geddesian vision of the liberatory possibilities of user-controlled self-help building in the barriada, Robles argued that within the capitalist system, this limited domain of self-help action had not allowed the pobladores to improve their socioeconomic situation, but had only reinforced prevailing structural inequalities. Further, self-help programs retarded social change because "mutual aid in the barriada is restricted to immediate action and is not oriented toward the *poblador*'s basic interests, such as increase in income levels, opportunity for stable occupation, and active participation in the urban production structure."[19] Therefore, like Adolfo Córdova in 1958, Robles identified economic development, not housing, as the key issue to be addressed.

In November 1969 Robles represented ONDEPJOV as part of the Peruvian delegation attending a meeting on squatter settlements organized by USAID in Washington, DC. The Peruvian presentation included an outline of ONDEPJOV's Plan Nacional de Desarrollo del Sector Popular (National Plan for the Development of the Popular Sector), which aimed to undo Peru's structural inequality—"its hierarchy of social classes within the system of internal domination and exterior dependency"—by increasing wages and stable employment in the short term, while planning for a fundamental redistribution of political power and economic resources in the long term. Land, housing, finance capital, consumer goods—all these "must be redistributed in function of the new interests of the popular sector. [Likewise t]he use of productive assets via *autogestión*, popular participation in the benefits of economic activity, not only in the field of labor, but also other fields." Extending Delgado's call for autogestión as self-managed urban development, here ONDEPJOV advocated for the popular sector's self-management of economic assets in order to catalyze broad-based development. One concrete example would be a reformed urban land market, with sites reserved for new pueblos jóvenes "in order to avoid speculation."[20] Unsurprisingly, support for such radical proposals within the Revolutionary Government was uneven, and efforts to implement initiatives along these lines fell short of ONDEPJOV's highest ambitions.

In mid-1971 the Revolutionary Government turned its attention to the question of how to institutionalize its vision of Peruvian society, an issue made more urgent by the appearance of spontaneously organized "Committees for the Defense of the Revolution" across the country that needed to be brought within an official framework. This led to the establishment of a new agency, SINAMOS, with Delgado appointed as its highest civilian official and intellectual architect. The founding legislation identified its objectives as "the training, guidance, and organization of the national population" while establishing a framework for dialogue between the government and the people. This would be achieved through the twin pillars of participation and social mobilization. In a sense this was a mutual-aid self-help community development project extrapolated to the national scale, counting among its tasks "fostering the creative capacity of the population so that it unfolds its energies and potentials in actions for its own development, with the support of the Government."[21] In addition to two thousand new staff members, SINAMOS absorbed five thousand staff and other resources from eight existing government agencies, including ONDEPJOV. Eventually SINAMOS would reach out to mobilize the entire nation, but initially its mission was to focus on six prioritized areas: rural organizations, youth, unions, cultural and professional associations, new workplace cooperatives, and pueblos jóvenes and "áreas de sub-desarrollo urbano interno" (underdeveloped inner-city areas; the term reflected the influence of dependency theory, and was intended to replace *tugurio*). In each case SINAMOS sought to build on existing organizational structures; for example, it retained the neighborhood committee system already established under ONDEPJOV.

SINAMOS contained an inherent contradiction: in addition to being the agency's acronym, "sin amos" means "without masters"—yet the agency was founded on the understanding that the correct orientation of collective action could only be ensured with concerted guidance from above. The claim of inclusiveness and popular empowerment was confounded by an organizational model based on a four-tiered structure—of national, regional, zonal, and local leadership—making very clear each operative's position and function. SINAMOS operated at the blurred edge between the utopian and the sinister, where concerned guidance slipped into control. This tension was already latent within ONDEPJOV, but now intensified as efforts moved from concrete development projects toward the work of ideological instruction. On the one hand, the sheer volume of the educational and exhortatory materials produced to promote the engagement of the masses demonstrated the Revolutionary Government's commitment to social mobilization and the capacity for human improvement: the *SINAMOS Informa* (SINAMOS Reports) bimonthly magazine; booklets on the characteristics, achievements, and uniqueness of the Peruvian Revolution; educational materials on subjects ranging from rural training in Chile and study groups in China to planning for social change. But on the other hand, SINAMOS was wielded by some within the government as a tool to carry out surveillance of nonsanctioned political organizations, particularly within the pueblos jóvenes. A sociologist involved with SINAMOS recalled: "Most of all I remember the detailed info on the opposition. . . . After a while it seemed as if I was working in a police station, reading detective reports."[22]

The contradictory impulses within the Revolutionary Government were particularly evident in its policies toward property title within the pueblos jóvenes. Theoretically, it espoused a new ethics of property. An educational pamphlet produced by SINAMOS, *¿Qué son los títulos de propiedad?* (What are Property Titles?), reiterated the principles established by Law 13517 some years earlier, underscoring the fact that the law restricted the sale of land designated for housing, whether planned sites in Urbanización Popular de Interés Social (UPIS) projects or squatted sites in recognized *barrios marginales*: "The lot is for those who need it" and selling one "threatens the interests of the people."[23] Previously, restrictions on such sales had been couched as protecting residents from real estate speculation; now the strategy was to present the case for the collective good, which prioritized the use value of the land over its exchange value.

A similar argument was made for the redistribution of rural land through agrarian reform, and indeed the language of the SINAMOS pamphlet echoed a well-known televised address given by Velasco in June 1969 to announce those reforms, in which he articulated the regime's wish that "land serves its social function in a new system of justice."[24] This foreshadowed a revolution in the entire category of property ownership as it had been framed under liberalism. Significantly, the agrarian reform law also included provisions intended to halt speculation in urban land, by requiring that landowners in designated "expansion areas" prepare these sites for urban development by 1974, or have them revert to state ownership. Against this threat, some landowners resorted to selling their land illegally, making contact through clandestine channels with informal brokers who arranged a deal with prospective pobladores. After the transaction was finalized, the occupation of the land typically took place via mass invasion, which the supposed legal—but de facto former—landowner declined to contest, leaving the site in the purchasers' hands. In this way, land sales that contravened the regime's ethics of property were concealed under the performance of an invasion—an extralegal, but commonly sanctioned, means of acquiring land—that in this instance masked an underlying illegal—but consensual—transaction.

However, ethics aside, the Revolutionary Government oversaw a massive increase in property titling in the pueblos jóvenes. Only 3,000 titles were granted in the seven years from the passage of Law 13517 in early 1961 to October 1968; following the introduction of a simplified titling process at the end of the Belaúnde administration, over 10,000 titles were granted between October 1968 and October 1972, and another 6,500 by the end of August 1974. This was not an unconsidered or passive continuation of the previous policy. As one observer noted, the Revolutionary Government generally granted title only after the entire settlement had completed "all phases of the organizational training and election processes" required for the SINAMOS neighborhood committees, making the aspiration to gain title "a major incentive for cooperation" with the agency. In the words of one SINAMOS official: "We want participation but it should be organized participation. We want to make as many people as possible homeowners, then they will act responsibly toward their community and have a stake in it."[25] Under this logic, property title was intended to instill in beneficiaries a more concrete sense of having something to gain from the new Peru, and therefore something to lose by failing to "participate" in the state's programs—a policy that played on the tendency toward conservatism engendered by property ownership earlier identified by Robles.

While the more radical proposals outlined by ONDEPJOV and SINAMOS under Velasco were beyond the real abilities of the Revolutionary Government to enact, on occasion it did find opportunities to explore innovative responses to the pueblos jóvenes. The most important of these projects, implemented with varying effectiveness, was Villa El Salvador, in Lima.

A Social Laboratory

In the early morning of April 29, 1971, two hundred families invaded a site at Pamplona Alta to the south of Lima, seizing state-owned land where several dozen as yet unserviced sites had been laid out to house low-level government employees. Within days the invasion had swelled to around nine thousand families. The action was carefully timed: Lima was due to host a meeting of the Inter-American Development Bank (IDB) beginning on May 10, and the invasion organizers hoped that some embarrassment to the government would hasten a decision in their favor (fig. 7.3). Instead,

Figure 7.3. Pamplona Alta, Lima, 1971. The banner reads: "Long live the Revolution. Support us, General Velasco!" *Source*: Nicholas G. d'A Houghton, "The Barriadas of Lima" (thesis, Architectural Association, London, 1972), John F. C. Turner Archive.

the government launched a public relations assault, labeling the invasion anti-Peruvian, an effort to discredit the revolution, and the work of agitators. However, once it became clear that this strategy would not work—the invasion having grown too large to suppress by force, and having won too much popular support to defeat with a smear campaign—Velasco and other officials made well-publicized visits to the pobladores to express solidarity with their plight and to propose a coordinated plan to resolve the crisis.

Planning officials quickly identified a relocation site further south at Tablada de Lurín—more than 25 kilometers from the center of Lima—on desert terrain that had previously been identified by PLANDEMET as a suitable zone for urban expansion, although no feasibility study had been carried out for the provision of water, sewerage, and electricity. They produced a rapid-response conceptual urban plan, and on May 11 the mass transfer of families began, assisted by the military. Scenes of soldiers assisting with construction work in the new pueblo joven appeared in sympathetic newspaper accounts, reversing the previously antagonistic relationship between squatter settlers and the armed forces—former defenders

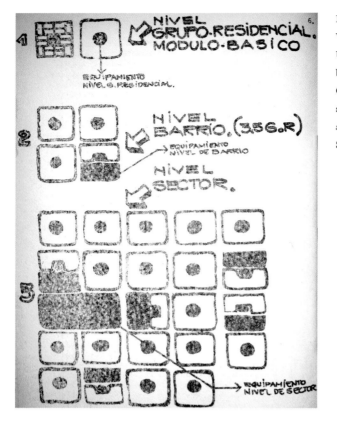

Figure 7.4. Ministerio de Vivienda, Villa El Salvador, Lima, 1971. Urban modules—residential group, barrio, sector. *Source*: SINAMOS, ORAMS X, and Comisión Especial sobre Villa El Salvador, *Informe sobre Villa El Salvador* (Lima: SINAMOS; ORAMS X, 1974).

of the status quo, deployed to protect existing property regimes. This revolutionary collaboration was less implausible than it first appears, since many members of the armed forces, as well as the police, lived in pueblos jóvenes. By mid-May seven thousand families from the Pamplona Alta invasion had arrived at the relocation site, renamed Villa El Salvador. The remaining two thousand Pamplona Alta families returned to their places of residence, apparently discouraged by the remoteness of the new site. However, they were soon replaced by would-be residents from other parts of the city, and even further afield, including some who had lost their homes in the May 1970 earthquake in Ancash. Within a few weeks, the new settlement had a population of around thirty-three thousand people, who now began to establish provisional dwellings on their allocated lots. Although Villa El Salvador was born under contentious circumstances, it would quickly become a showpiece of the regime's radically different approach to the urban housing crisis.

The design of Villa El Salvador was based on the progressive ag-

Figure 7.5. Villa El Salvador, Lima, ca. 1971. *Source*: Unknown photographer, John F. C. Turner Archive.

gregation of social units, constructing what SINAMOS would later describe as a "clear urban ordering in its distinct levels" that it believed was a key factor in the impressive "level of development of the revolutionary process" demonstrated by residents.[26] The basic "urban module" was the *grupo residencial* (residential group) housing two thousand people, comprising sixteen *manzanas* (blocks) of twenty-four lots each (fig. 7.4). The square form of the grupo residencial was easily aggregated into a grid structure, facilitating the fast and efficient layout of the site. Three and a half grupo residencial modules formed a *barrio* (neighborhood), housing 7,500, with the remaining half module dedicated to public facilities; twelve to twenty grupos residenciales formed a *sector*, housing thirty to forty-six thousand. Overall, the site was divided into seven sectors (with one reserved for communal agriculture), projected to house an eventual population of 250,000. Open space at the center of each grupo residencial would be used for communal services—such as parks, kindergartens, or meeting rooms—which were to be organized and maintained by the local residents; at the level of the barrio and the sector larger spaces would be reserved for additional facilities (fig. 7.5). The initial master plan also included zones for commerce, multifamily housing, and industry, recalling the earlier concept of the self-sufficient satellite city, just as the invasion drama replayed the Ciudad de Dios scenario.

The regime's decisive action in establishing Villa El Salvador was quickly followed by a series of commitments to provide it with comprehensive services. Within weeks of its foundation, an electricity-generating substation was installed, providing street lighting to the first few blocks of Sector I, closest to the established city. As evidence of the new settlement's favored status, the infrastructure required to provide this service had to cover a considerable distance, in the process bypassing a number of existing pueblos jóvenes that had yet to receive electricity. In November 1971 the government announced that water and sewerage infrastructure would be installed within a few months; in July 1972 officials committed to beginning work on domestic electricity connections by the end of the year. In practice, the provision of services lagged far behind the initial schedule, in part because of the settlement's distant location, and in part because of residents' inability to cover the installation costs. As a consequence, by April 1976 most Villa El Salvador residents had street lighting, but only half had domestic electricity; water was provided via communal standpipes, but the installation of domestic water and sewerage connections had only recently begun, and would not be completed until 1979. Making the most of this partial urbanism, the residents of necessity provided a city for themselves (fig. 7.6).

The regime's efforts to organize the community met with greater success, at least initially. Already in June 1971 Villa El Salvador residents had mobilized themselves to provide educational facilities for their children, since travel to the closest schools in the established city was long and difficult. Residents formed local committees that erected provisional classrooms out of *esteras*, and arranged for them to be staffed by volunteer teachers. In January 1972 ONDEPJOV began to formally organize residents, employing its standard block-by-block representative structure; some months later this work was taken over by SINAMOS, as ONDEPJOV's activities were folded into the new agency.

According to Gustavo Riofrío's detailed account, ideological conflicts within SINAMOS—and within the Revolutionary Government more broadly—played out in competing proposals for Villa El Salvador's development. SINAMOS was divided into regions that mirrored the Peruvian army's organizational structure, with the Departamento de Lima (comprising the area surrounding the capital) belonging to Region IV, while the city of Lima itself, along with its pueblos jóvenes, was part of Region X. Region IV, which had

Figure 7.6. Villa El Salvador, Lima, ca. 1974. *Source*: Servicio Aerofotográfico Nacional, Perú.

influence in Sector I of Villa El Salvador, was dominated by conservative factions within the regime, who promoted aided self-help housing programs, granting individual property title, and the legal constitution of Villa El Salvador as a cooperative—a structure that was generally used to promote homeownership through *mutuales*. By contrast, Region X, which held sway over the other sectors, was aligned with radicals, who favored communal title, and rejected the framing of Villa El Salvador "as a simple housing program" in favor of establishing the settlement as an "empresa comunal" (communal enterprise). This was connected to the Revolutionary Government's promotion of "propiedad social" (social property), or worker-owned businesses, as a new category of property within the reimagined Peruvian economy. For this faction of SINAMOS, Villa El Salvador offered a "pilot project . . . that contained elements allied to state corporatism on one hand, and to models of [nineteenth-century] utopian socialism on the other."[27] It was paradigmatic of the participatory self-help ethos of the Peruvian Revolution, and an ideal vision of the regime's engagement with the pueblos jóvenes.

The influence of the Region X position can be seen in the resident-led repudiation of government programs focused on housing construction—"even by *autoconstrucción*"—which they condemned (according to the account of SINAMOS Region X) as diverting resources away from "productive investments" (such as starting local businesses to increase job opportunities), while generating "privileged elites who, once they have attained their housing objective, are not interested in community participation." Consequently, a number of housing initiatives withered due to lack of resident support. For example, planning officials' initial proposals for Villa El Salvador had included a project "to encourage the construction of low-cost dwellings made with rustic materials (*esteras*, cement, lime, sand, and stones)" using an experimental building system.[28] Two model houses along these lines were installed by the Dirección de Promoción Comunal Urbana (Department of Urban Community Advancement), the division responsible for pueblos jóvenes within the new Ministerio de Vivienda (Ministry of Housing). However, the "sizeable market" officials anticipated for these dwellings, and the associated technical assistance required to build them, failed to materialize. Similarly, a pilot program of "self-help group construction of prefabricated dwellings" initiated by an architect connected to SINAMOS resulted in only sixty-nine houses. Finally, 630 low-cost houses built by the state-owned Empresa de Administración de Inmuebles del Perú (EMADI, Real Estate Administration Enterprise) were so unpopular that "some units remained unsold as late as 1976, more than three years after they had been built."[29]

At the same time, residents began to articulate their own priorities for their young community, culminating in two initiatives in mid-1973: a self-census, intended to inform the design of a community-led development program, held on July 22; and the First Convention of Leaders of Villa El Salvador, held on July 28–29. This meeting, attended by over seven hundred delegates representing a population that now surpassed one hundred thousand, issued a communiqué outlining the residents' vision of the new model of "communal urban organization" that they aimed to realize. In November 1973 this was formalized via the constitution of the Comunidad Urbana Autogestionaria de Villa El Salvador (CUAVES, Self-Managing Urban Community of Villa El Salvador). The First Convention's communiqué, likely written in collaboration with sympathetic SINAMOS officials, and running over twenty-six pages in *Informe sobre Villa El Salvador* (1974), a sixty-page report produced by SINAMOS Region X, opened with the statement: "After two years of living in these *arenales* [stretches of sand], we affirm that we came here precisely because we are victims of the capitalist system that exploits us." They would never find a solution to their problems in "constructing pretty houses, nor having all the services, which at the end of the day, we have to pay for"—this would only increase their "dependency on the exploiters" as they surrendered their hard-won capital for the consumption of these goods. The only way "to break this cycle of dependency, of poverty" was a revolutionary mode of economic and social development: "Before houses, Factories! This concise cry . . . synthesizes the conviction that only to the extent that our organized Community has the means of production and of services in its hands, only in this way will we make it possible for our children—within 10 or 15 years—not to invade other *arenales* in search of a piece of land so that they can live as primitive beings, with homes that they can fashion however arduously."[30] Beyond the autoconstrucción of houses for the benefit of individual families, the residents imagined the collective self-help construction of Villa El Salvador via autogestión—the self-management of its shared resources, supplemented by whatever aid the revolution could provide.

In order to build this community, the First Convention proposed a new approach to neighborhood organization, since SINAMOS's standard organizational model belonged to "a stage already surpassed by our revolution in Villa El Salvador." Under the revised system, each of the sixty-six existing grupos residenciales would elect delegates to five new *consejos* (councils) focused on the economic and social functioning of the self-managing urban community. These included a number of standard portfolios for a local government authority, albeit with a progressive slant: services (managing sanitation, street lighting, parks, public transport, urban planning, and so on); education (comprising the political education of the residents as well as childhood education); and health (offering community-based preventative medicine).[31]

More radically, the *consejo de comercialización* (trading council) framed Villa El Salvador as an urban cooperative, which it would serve by "rationalizing the purchase of provisions directly from centers of production . . . providing us with foods of good quality and low prices, furthermore seeing that we pay a fair price to our peasant brother producers." The *consejo de producción* (production council) would be responsible for overseeing "empresas de propiedad social-comunal" (enterprises organized as communal-social property): beyond the "propiedad social" model proposed by the Revolutionary Government, the residents envisaged enterprises whose profits, rather than being distributed to the worker-owners of each business, would be invested for the benefit of the community as a whole, funding essential services. These new enterprises would provide a source of income for residents while satisfying the local demand for priority commodities, such as low-cost building materials. The ultimate goal was to export these products, and the enterprises themselves, to the rest of Peru, where they would function as "schools of permanent learning and fraternal coexistence, without egoism of group or place." Operating independently of both the failing capitalist system and the new state-run enterprises, CUAVES envisaged a model of self-managed, coordinated "economic pluralism" that encompassed medium-scale industrial or agricultural concerns, as well as group- or home-based workshops: "All are free to produce economically, but in a rational and planned manner, in order that we obtain a better result."[32] As one example, the consejo de producción would coordinate with the consejo de servicios, responsible for electricity provision, to ensure that any machinery required for local workshops was supported by the necessary infrastructure.

SINAMOS Region X's *Informe sobre Villa El Salvador* hailed the incipient CUAVES as a "social laboratory where the praxis of the societal model planned for Peru will be developed on a small scale." Such laudatory descriptions should perhaps be read as a sortie aimed to win a battle within the regime over the legitimacy of this approach to community development. To this end, CUAVES's proposal for participatory planning via the consejos, and its vision of development as transcending economic growth to catalyze social change via the communal-social enterprises, were framed by SINAMOS as materializing out of "a truly responsible and conscious militant attitude . . . foreign to all paternalism and manipulation" that was essential to consolidating the revolutionary process. These initiatives would be trialed and refined in the "social laboratory" of CUAVES, in preparation for implementation across Peru.[33]

Moreover, CUAVES offered "a new pattern of urban development" to address the core needs of low-income urban populations:

it was a model for integrated "Urban-Industrial Self-Managing Settlements" with local job opportunities and ample public facilities. In Lima, three such settlements could be planned for one hundred thousand to three hundred thousand residents each, located on strategically selected sites on the city's expansion "corridors" to the south, east, and northwest. These would be large enough to act as "reception areas" for migrants from rural areas as well as for "la población potencialmente excedente" (the potentially surplus population) of pueblos jóvenes facing overcrowding, in the process reducing the likelihood of land invasions.[34] (The concept of "excedentes de barriadas"—or simply "excedentes"—derives from the principle that "each family unit has the right to be awarded a lot"; beginning in the 1960s, barriada residents' organizations in Lima began to compile registers of excedentes within their settlements, and to support them in their claims for a lot of their own.)[35] Constructed upon the firm foundation of "productive units of a self-managing character"—that is, resident-run communal-social enterprises—these settlements would from the outset be equipped with the tools to eliminate their residents' "economic marginality" while simultaneously boosting their "social cohesion" through their strong participatory governance structure.

The first concrete step toward realizing CUAVES's vision was the establishment of a *caja comunal* (community savings bank) in August 1974, to manage residents' savings as well as the community-mandated levies that funded essential services such as garbage collection and building schools. By the end of 1975 the caja comunal had helped to fund the installation of electricity infrastructure, the construction of 160 schoolrooms (primarily built with communal labor), and the launching of a clothing workshop run as a communal-social enterprise. By early 1976 the CUAVES consejo de comercialización had installed a number of community-owned kerosene pumps, providing low-cost fuel to households without electricity, as well as a community-owned construction materials depot, distributing thousands of bags of cement a day at the affordable "official" price. The CUAVES consejo de producción tried to foster a number of business initiatives—with the assistance of financing from international organizations intrigued by the CUAVES model—ranging from a poultry farm to workshops for wood and metal fabrication, as well as factories producing glass and cement blocks. (The latter recalled the pobladores' vision of Ciudad de Dios as a self-sufficient city, producing the building materials needed for its own fabrication, as well as the *dependista* strategy of economic development via import substitution initiatives. In this context, autogestión represented economic self-sufficiency writ small, writ local.) In all, CUAVES made feasibility studies for more than thirty-five projects, which would have generated 6,900 jobs, but required funding far beyond the community's means.

This burst of entrepreneurial energy was to be short-lived, as many of the enterprises failed to become competitive: the glass factory used artisanal methods that left it lagging behind more technologically advanced manufacturers; the cement block factory couldn't make its products cheap enough to compete with bricks; the kerosene pumps had insufficient turnover to be profitable and were soon handed over to private concessionaires. While the residents' plea for "factories before houses" was embraced rhetorically, CUAVES was not provided with the resources it needed to flourish, to become self-sufficient. Perhaps with more time and more organizational support from the regime the enterprises could have survived, but by the end of 1976 Peru was facing an increasingly difficult economic crisis, leading to the collapse of the caja comunal, with many families losing their savings. Without the caja comunal, the economic framework of autogestión was deeply compromised. Already in August 1975, after the Second Convention of CUAVES had elected a new slate of leaders who broke with the Velasco government, the regime's support had begun to dissolve. Since neither CUAVES nor the caja comunal had been granted full legal status by the regime, they were highly dependent on the state for support, and had no viable options for an alternative patron.

On the urban level, the collapse of autogestión was evident in a rash of invasions of areas reserved for public use that took place toward the end of the 1970s. In particular, the large open spaces in the center of the first grupos residenciales, which had never been filled with the anticipated communal facilities, were far more attractive to aspiring pobladores than the designated expansion zones, which were further away from central Lima, and from the ad hoc commercial center that had arisen around public transport nodes in the more established sectors of Villa El Salvador. Similarly, since the industrial zone was slow to develop, organized invasions occupied a significant portion of that sector, taking advantage of the infrastructure that had been installed. Beginning in 1985, these squatter settlements within the still-developing pueblo joven were legally recognized. Building upon the slender assistance of the regime, over subsequent years Villa El Salvador was gradually consolidated through individual efforts to construct housing, and collective efforts to provide public facilities. Beginning with a population of 33,000 in mid-1971, by 2014 it had grown to over 454,000.[36]

In the years immediately following the establishment of Villa El Salvador, there were few invasions of entirely new sites, but there were a number of cases where excedentes illegally occupied land around the perimeter of their settlements, with the support of their neighbors, although these areas had been officially declared unfit for urban development (due to the steepness of the terrain, for example). The regime refused to recognize these improvised extensions, leaving Villa El Salvador as the only legally sanctioned alternative for these households, but its distance from the city (and thus work opportunities) made it unattractive for many.

On January 19, 1976, the years-long truce was broken, as 220 families of excedentes from UPIS Caja de Agua, constructed in the early 1960s, invaded an empty—and high-profile—site near Puente Huáscar in central Lima, only a few minutes' walk from the Plaza de Armas. Within two weeks, almost five thousand people had assembled on the site. One observer noted that the pobladores aimed not to secure this site but to use their occupation to pressure the regime into offering them a relocation site, following the pattern set at Pamplona. This act of political theater worked: the pobladores were given a choice between lots at Villa El Salvador—distant from central Lima but reasonably well established—or at a new site in the Pampas de Canto Grande—closer to the center, but isolated at the end of a ravine, and furnished with only the promise of services. A majority chose the new site, and on February 23 the transfer began.

Canto Grande was already home to some thirteen pueblos jóvenes and a large number of privately developed, middle-income subdivisions. The Ministerio de Vivienda devised a project for the "integrated development" of the entire area, encompassing the provision of basic services and roadways for the existing populations, as well as the outlines of a new settlement, given the name UPIS Puente Huáscar, signaling an ambition to revive the earlier UPIS model, and with it to reassert control over urban development. The scheme envisaged 81,000 lots, bringing the total population to 550,000, and reached beyond the UPIS model to incorporate some elements reminiscent of CUAVES: the "integrated development" would include not just infrastructure and urban facilities but also economic development via "promotion and technical assistance for this population's productive activities." In order to ensure that the plan's proposed amenities would suit the "socioeconomic reality" of the various resident groups, it aimed to foster "new forms of invest-ment-work such as *autoconstrucción, ayuda mutua*, and similar."[37] Some residents even spoke of UPIS Puente Huáscar becoming a "ciudad autogestionaria" that within two years would surpass what Villa El Salvador had achieved. There was initially a high level of enthusiasm in the volunteer work brigades, but this energy and cohesion dissipated within months, as the Ministerio de Vivienda's project stalled, leaving UPIS Puente Huáscar a sparse landscape of unserviced sites, gradually consolidated via unaided self-help.

Two years later, a group of families proclaiming their allegiance to the Peruvian Revolution invaded a site in Callao. Once again the invasion quickly swelled into the thousands, and once again the re-gime provided a relocation site, given the name Pueblo Joven Fundo Márquez. This time officials announced no grand scheme—simply the coordinated transfer of some two thousand families who were allocated unserviced lots.

In each case—Villa El Salvador (1971), UPIS Puente Huáscar (1976), and Fundo Márquez (1978)—although all the relocations were to sites previously identified by PLANDEMET as appropriate for urbanizaciones populares, being located on the city's key ex-pansion "corridors" respectively to the south, east, and northwest, the state was always carrying out its plans in a reactive mode, rath-er than implementing orderly urban development. This sequence of three invasion-relocation dramas also illustrates the contin-uously lowered ambitions of official plans, reflecting the overall trajectory of the revolutionary era. After suffering a serious illness in early 1973, Velasco had become increasingly isolated from his cabinet, and in August 1975 he was replaced in a palace coup by General Francisco Morales Bermúdez. Despite an initial promise to strengthen the regime's socialist credentials—announcing that the revolution was now moving into its "second phase"—Morales Bermúdez oversaw an unwinding of revolutionary rhetoric and a move to the right, and by the end of 1976 all remaining Velasco sympathizers had been removed from positions of power. In this new climate, the pueblos jóvenes no longer held much interest for the regime; likewise, SINAMOS was weakened and then disman-tled outright in 1978.

The revolutionary era had achieved some successes in strength-ening state administration and shifting Peru toward a more inclusive democracy, but efforts to promote economic development failed, and overall the regime's policies worsened the situation of the lowest-income citizens. The dissolution of the Revolutionary Government itself was set in motion by a series of general strikes beginning in July 1977, organized to protest against austerity measures introduced in an effort to refinance foreign debt, and to call for an end to military rule. In a sense, the International Monetary Fund, the World Bank, and US president Jimmy Carter shared joint responsibility for definitively ending the revolutionary experiment, since the loans that they provided to address Peru's ever-growing economic crisis came with the requirements to enact structural adjustment policies and to return the country to representative democracy. Accordingly, a general election was set for 1980.

Finding himself at odds with the Morales Bermúdez regime, Robles felt compelled to leave the country, and in 1976 he began working for the UN as an expert on housing and urban development, first in Guatemala, then Mozambique, Cape Verde, and Central America, returning to Peru only in 1997.[38] Robles's experience of the rise and fall of a revolutionary commitment to the pueblos jóvenes corresponded to a similarly fertile period in Turner's career, as his move from Peru to the United States and from housing official to academic prompted him to entirely reformulate his own position on self-help housing.

An Architecture that Works

In September 1965 Turner arrived at the Harvard-MIT Joint Center on Urban Studies, where he worked as a research associate for two years, and then continued in a teaching position at MIT for another six years. In June 1973 he returned to England, teaching at the Architectural Association's School of Tropical Architecture under Koenigsberger, and then at the Development Planning Unit, University College London, until 1983. Turner's long-term focus as he moved into this new role as an academic and a writer was to systematize his ideas on housing into a larger work, which would become *Housing by People: Towards Autonomy in Building Environments* (1976).

In an influential paper "Uncontrolled Urban Settlement" (first presented 1966, published 1968), Turner had endorsed the role of the architect in providing expertise to improve outcomes in the framing of urban plans and in the design and construction of housing in squatter settlements. He also considered the role of the state in supporting this work, pointing to infrastructure, legislation, and technical assistance as some key areas where governments could intervene to facilitate the actions of individual residents or local communities. Most crucially, Turner emphasized that the state should not act unilaterally "as a provider"—handing out assistance according to its own priorities and interests, but "as the servant—providing tools."[39] In this model, the relationship between state and citizen was to be a collaborative "working with" that responded to the input of residents. In his subsequent writings, the emphasis of "control" gradually shifted away from the professional's imperative to control and direct urban development, and toward the end user's right to control their own housing decisions. In these later writings, self-help housing was less important for its particular techniques than for what it represented of the possibility of user control, increasingly articulated as the "freedom" or autonomy to guide and shape one's own living environment.

This discussion was informed by the development of a second major theme in Turner's work: the very definition of housing—or the value of housing for its users. In "A New View of the Housing Deficit" (first presented 1966, published in English 1971), Turner argued that while state housing agencies tended to focus on the provision of "modern standard dwellings" whatever the context and the situation of prospective residents, this was not an immediate priority for many families, and was in fact often beyond their means. As the basis for an alternative—and more realistic—approach to the problem, it was necessary to move away from considering housing exclusively on the basis of its material qualities or "appearance" (its standards of "modernity"), and instead evaluate it in terms of three core attributes—defined by Turner as "shelter" (protection from the elements), "security" (guaranteed tenure), and "location" (access to employment, transport, urban facilities).[40] Ideally, housing would fulfill each of these requirements, but in practice residents would weigh the relative importance of each attribute in their own particular circumstances, as well as their costs and benefits, and make decisions accordingly. Turner argued that for recent migrants to the city, a central location is the main priority because this facilitates access to employment opportunities, allowing the family to build up its economic resources. The quality of the shelter and long-term security are far less important, so renting substandard housing in the central city may be the best available (or only affordable) option in this circumstance. When families are more financially stable, priorities shift to establishing long-term security and gradually improving the quality of the dwelling, both of which can be achieved through homeownership in a squatter settlement; these advantages are usually offset by a peripheral location, but the money and time that must be devoted to a longer commute are considered an acceptable sacrifice.

Significantly, Turner did not argue that self-built squatter settlement housing was the best option in all circumstances, any more than the "modern standard dwelling" could be a universal solution. With this understanding, housing providers should develop greater flexibility in devising specific solutions, which must always be informed by the available resources. Most importantly, as Turner argued in "Housing Issues and the Standards Problem" (1972), households must have the ability to determine their own priorities in housing—not to have their needs defined, assessed, and resolved by an expert or government agency: "The best results are obtained by the user who is in full control of the design, construction, and management of his own home. Whether or not he builds it with his own hands is of secondary importance—unless he is very poor." In this reading, scarce public resources should be deployed to "support local action" and "help the mass of the people make the best use of their own resources and in their own ways." There was still a clear imperative "to avoid the disorder and diseconomies of unplanned direct action"—but governments could not expect to control the entire process of housing provision, only to make strategic interventions. Instead of constructing "conventional and now discredited closed housing projects" they must focus their energies on "the development of open housing service systems."[41]

Turner further developed this concept of "closed" or "open" interventions into housing provision in a memo to Robert Sadove of the International Bank for Reconstruction and Development (IBRD, an agency of the World Bank) in November 1971. Following Robert McNamara's appointment as president of the World Bank in 1968, the organization had shifted its focus to include issues of housing and urbanization. In June 1972 it would release its first detailed report on the topic, determining that for its own projects, "direct lending for house construction appears of lower priority than for site and services type projects which can mobilize self-help, reach the poorer levels of population, and stimulate savings and employment."[42] Turner's memo argued that there were three "levels of housing action" available to state agencies: "packages" (the complete housing project), "components" ("a discrete part with a discrete function"—such as a street, water supply infrastructure, school, or individual dwelling), and "elements" (the basic building blocks of housing—land, materials, tools, labor, financing). The "package" required a large investment from the public sector, and offered little space for the prospective resident to contribute their own resources to improving their housing; "component"-based projects were less costly on a per capita basis, so could benefit a larger population, and presented the opportunity for greater "private sector response to public action"; finally, "elements" were the most cost-effective, and "open-ended" in encouraging individual action.[43]

Translating this theory into practice, Turner argued that "the measure of effectiveness for any public policy on housing . . . is the ratio between public expenditure and consequent private investment": it was therefore clear that intervention at the level of "elements" was the preferred solution. For example, "a government can precipitate immense housing investments through relatively simple legislative actions of low cost and risk to the public"; a key example was the mortgage guarantee system backed by the US Federal Housing Administration. Other element-level interventions could include the revision of minimum housing standards, legalization of tenure in squatter settlements, expanding access to low-cost credit, or exercising controls on land markets. However, as Turner advised Sadove, the overarching challenge was to achieve a kind of structural transformation of the housing sphere, making "the necessary change-over from packaged products to open component service programs." In this context, the significance of sites-and-services programs was that they operated midway between the "package" and the "component" level—consequently, they provided more "freedom of action for the users" and could be deployed as "the thin end of a wedge" to further open up systems of housing support. Turner emphasized to Sadove that the sites-and-services approach should be employed only as a "temporary strategy"—as a transitional device—because it still functioned at "the high-risk/low-payoff end of the spectrum" and was predicated on "certain assumptions about the nature of financing and the building materials submarkets that might be more effectively dealt with if addressed directly." In his accompanying letter to Sadove, Turner underscored his reservations, expressing concern that his backing for the method should be understood as limited in scope, and far from an outright endorsement.[44]

In effect, Turner was advocating that the World Bank support significant state intervention to restructure markets in "elements" in order to create the conditions of possibility for effective local action. As Turner reemphasized in the introduction to the US edition of *Housing by People* (1977)—in an effort to correct misunderstandings concerning his position on the role of the state—government should "concentrate on what it has the authority to do: to ensure equitable access to resources which local communities and people cannot provide for themselves." The state had a responsibility to rebalance the distribution of resources in favor of low-income citizens, and thus to provide them with the means to undertake self-determined and empowered initiatives to house themselves. This vision of a powerful activist state would seem to be at odds with Turner's anarchist beliefs, but it had already been foreshadowed in his UN-commissioned report on the Arequipa projects, which argued for the importance of connecting "the complementary forces of coordinated government planning and mobilized local action."[45] In response to a Marxist critique of his approach—questioning his apparent assumption "that the interests of industrial, finance, landed, and property capital are going to legislate against themselves"—Turner underscored his position: "only radical anarchists will argue that modern society is possible without any central controls or government; conservative anarchists like myself accept the necessity of central planning." Turner added that his own philosophy was best expressed by Patrick Geddes's anarchist-like vision of an organic withering away of the state: "For fulfilment there must be a resorbtion of government into the body of the community. How? By cultivating the habit of direct action instead of waiting upon representative agencies."[46]

Turner was paradoxically a pro-state anarchist, but he envisioned a version of the state that does not exist, reflecting a scientistic understanding of government as a rational actor distributing resources according to clearly established and agreed-upon technical requirements; framed in relation to an abstracted world, it appeared to be unaffected by the forces of political or economic power. Symptomatically, his observations concerning the viability of self-help housing in the United States identified a huge set of preconditions that would be necessary to allow individuals and local groups to "maximize the use of their own resources"—but which he nonetheless believed were achievable with the correct action from above: "As long as building plots or vacant buildings were available at reasonable prices and not inflated by speculation or monopolistic aggregation; as long as there was a plentiful supply of appropriate tools and materials through local distributors who did not discriminate against small or non-professional purchasers; and as long as local banks gave credit and were not absorbed into impersonally administered national corporations: then individual households and small groups could maximize the use of their own resources."[47] As long as the prospective self-builders existed outside of capitalism—Turner seemed to argue—they were free to determine and direct their own housing.

In the August 1968 issue of *Architectural Design* (on the theme of the "Architecture of Democracy"), Turner returned to the topic of the squatter settlements that he had introduced to the magazine's readers five years earlier—now less concerned with the government-run aided self-help housing programs that had been intended to improve the settlements than with their innate, unimproved qualities. For Turner, this was "an architecture that works": developed by residents with their own hands, in accordance with their own desires, it was the epitome of "freedom to build" or self-determined action. It "worked" both in pragmatic terms, reflecting the capacities of a developing economy, and in human and ethical terms, facilitating the empowerment of individuals and their communities. In contrast to the lives of "the urban poor in wealthy and highly institutionalized mass-consumption society" in the West, the squatter self-builder "finds in the responsibilities and activities of home-building and local improvement the creative dialogue essential for self-discovery and growth."[48] The "existential value" of this mode of living emerged from three essential "freedoms" available to the squatter self-builder: freedom to form self-selected community groupings, freedom to budget and organize the resources at hand, and freedom to shape the immediate environment.

The question of how to transfer these "freedoms" into the context of Western consumer society would become a major theme in Turner's work, as he sought to derive universal principles from the squatter settlement; practices such as urban homesteading, sweat equity, and squatting cooperatives that emerged in some US cities in the early 1970s appeared to replicate some of these existential values. Nonetheless there was (at least on occasion) an acknowledgment of the harsh realities framing the "freedoms" of squatter settlement residents. While Turner viewed the urban poor in the United States as being "helped" into dependency (taking cues from

Oscar Lewis's concept of the "culture of poverty"), in Peru "people are almost forced into helping themselves": "Autonomy is born of desperation and the resulting initiative of the squatters has its own reward in increased self-esteem, high morale, and the achievement of creating a community."[49] If Turner's position is often vulnerable to charges of romanticization, here this alternates with a brutal realism in its assessment of the conditions facing squatter settlers, celebrating the imposition of "self-help" (the only remaining option) as the ends justifying the means. Ultimately the question of how much "freedom" they could really expect to exercise without having real (economic, political) power is never addressed.

In *Housing by People* the issue of the user's freedom to act, to control their decisions concerning housing, was once again central. However, the discussion was often abstract, as Turner searched for a means to systematize solutions to facilitate local action. Under the influence of anarchist thought, the modes of housing provision were defined in terms of how much control individuals or local groups were able to exert, based on the polarity of "autonomous" (self-determined) and "heteronomous" (other-determined) construction. Translated into the terms of mainstream Western architectural production, this dichotomy explained the failure of Pruitt-Igoe (developed heteronomously and hierarchically, with insufficient user input), and the success of the English village (the outcome of autonomous organization and network planning). Turner's supplementary example of "heteronomous" housing, the Fergusleigh Park public housing estate in Scotland, was "traditional" in form, clarifying that for Turner the core failure was not due to modernism—as Charles Jencks argued in *The Language of Postmodern Architecture* (1977)—but the underlying mode of social organization guiding the development of the project (fig. 7.7). Although Turner's focus was far from mainstream architectural culture, on the question of user control there are clear resonances with contemporaneous debates concerning architecture as an open system, as seen in Herman Hertzberger's Diagoon Housing, Delft (1967–1972), and Ralph Erskine's Byker Housing Estate, Newcastle-upon-Tyne (1968–1981).

In another direction, Turner's writings marked a connection between architectural culture, the academy, and the international development sphere, engaging with both the UN and the World Bank, although in the latter case the institutionalization of sites-and-services tended to erase much of the nuance of Turner's ideas.

Fig. 12. Pruitt-Igoe, an architectural-award-winning public housing project built in St. Louis, Missouri, was partly demolished twenty years later as a result of its unpopularity and vandalization. (Photo by UPI.)

Fig. 13. Fergusleigh Park, Paisley, Scotland: abandoned houses destroyed by 'vandals' forty years after this once popular model public housing estate was built.

32

Figure 7.7. "Pruitt-Igoe, an architectural award-winning public housing project . . . was partly demolished twenty years later as a result of its unpopularity and vandalization." "Fergusleigh Park, Paisley, Scotland: abandoned houses destroyed by 'vandals' forty years after this once popular model public housing estate was built." *Source*: John F. C. Turner, *Housing by People: Towards Autonomy in Building Environments* (London: Marion Boyars, 1976).

Within the UN, the Housing and Town and Country Planning Program—later the UN Centre for Housing, Building and Planning (UN-CHBP)—had been operative since 1949, but the Habitat conference in 1976 represented a significant elevation of the profile of housing and urbanization as issues of global concern within the organization.

The "ideological framework" for the conference was established via discussions at a four-day meeting held in Dubrovnik in May 1975, chaired by Koenigsberger. The thirty-one participating experts included development-focused economists such as Fernando Cardoso and Albert Hirschman, along with architects claiming a specialization in this field: Turner, Panayotis Psomopoulos (representing the Athens Centre of Ekistics, since Constantinos A. Doxiadis's failing health prevented him from attending), Charles Correa, Yona Friedman, Eduardo Neira (then working for the Economic Commission for Latin America), Nuno Portas (architect and director of the Portuguese participatory housing program SAAL, Serviço Ambulatório de Apoio Local, or Local Ambulatory Support Service), and Ernest Weissmann (director of UNCHBP, 1951–1965). The report emerging from Dubrovnik drew on the language of dependency to diagnose the cause of the problems facing the developing world: "underdevelopment" (as manifested in the uncontrolled urbanization of "human settlements") was ultimately due to the "unequal economic and political relations between nations"; the remedy for these global structural inequalities was "a new international economic order" based on principles of social justice (as endorsed by Barbara Ward). Within nations, the report called for more equitable access to land, and furthermore, for any benefits from the improvement to land to belong to the local community: "As a capital asset ... any increase in its value is [due] not only to individual effort but also to the decisions and investments of society as a whole and of the local community. Consequently, it belongs to them." In terms of housing, the report definitively rejected direct construction by governments as a viable solution, in favor of providing support to the initiatives of local communities: "It should be noted in particular that in vast areas of the Third World self-help construction and improvement of housing on the basis of investments of human resources seem to offer the only realistic way of meeting the needs of the majority."[50]

In Vancouver, at the Habitat conference itself, these discussions around "human settlements" made the awkward transition from the technical to the diplomatic sphere. Representatives from 132 countries attended, along with observers from various UN bodies, and high-profile intergovernmental organizations such as the IDB and the Organization of American States. The resulting Vancouver Declaration on Human Settlements—nineteen general principles, twenty-four guidelines for action, and eighty pages of recommendations subdivided into six categories—was intended to outline the way forward for both governments and the UN itself. Meanwhile, the Habitat Forum, a meeting of nongovernmental organizations, was held in parallel with the main conference, with over five thousand participants from ninety countries. Topics for discussion ranged from self-help housing to rural development, appropriate technology, and nuclear energy. Turner helped to coordinate the Self-Help and Low-Cost Housing Symposium and gave a keynote speech (including a pointed critique of his own position as expert, protesting the fact that he had been selected to speak, rather than a representative of "the people whose problems we have met here to discuss").[51] In the end, this conjunction of professional and political connections was pivotal in transforming conceptions of the "uncontrolled urban settlement" (as Turner had denominated it a decade earlier). The new discourse of human settlements reframed improvised urbanism as a manifestation of inequality rather than an aberrant outgrowth, echoing the logic deployed by the Revolutionary Government to destigmatize the pueblos jóvenes. This rhetorical shift was fundamental in allowing governments, planners, and housing officials to reconsider the issue in all its complexities, and to recalibrate their responses accordingly.

Specifically, the Vancouver Declaration argued for the importance of defining "progressive minimum standards for an acceptable quality of life"—an acknowledgment that previous benchmarks could not be met for the majority, but nonetheless some sense of a "minimum" dwelling should be preserved as an eventual goal. On a practical level, the document advocated both the "reorganization of spontaneous urban settlements" in a manner that engaged the participation of local communities (as opposed to a top-down "slum clearance" approach), as well as a strong emphasis on aided self-help. Here, government support could take the form of sites-and-services schemes, or promoting initiatives that Turner would have defined as element-level interventions: regularizing tenure, simplifying procedures for acquiring land for low-cost housing, and facilitating building permits and financing options.[52]

However, any sense of a developing consensus around the new approach was to be short-lived. Already in June 1976, in a journal issue coinciding with the Habitat conference, one expert raised questions about the effectiveness of sites-and-services in practice, expressing concern that the "considerable savings" anticipated had not materialized. Furthermore, many projects had delivered poor outcomes in terms of housing quality—an issue that was exacerbated by the selection of remote urban sites, which had the advantage of being inexpensive, but isolated low-income citizens from employment and urban facilities, and ultimately reflected the low priority placed on their well-being by their governments. In sum, these experiences had shown that despite the promise of self-sufficiency offered by this bare-bones method of housing provision, in actuality, "providing shelter for the urban poor requires subsidy"—a realization that would undercut the appeal of such programs among potential sponsors.[53]

On another front, theoretical and ideological critiques of aided self-help housing were starting to accumulate. In April 1976 *Architectural Design* published a summary of Robles's "Development Alternatives for the Peruvian Barriada" as a response to the last of a series of eight articles by Turner that the magazine had presented over successive months under the title "Housing by People: From the Bottom Up or From the Top Down?" It had included this text by Robles, who was still working closely with pueblos jóvenes a decade after Turner had left Peru, to signal that "by ignoring the issues of urban domination [underlying barriada formation], the reality of the barriada has been distorted." The previous year, Robles had published another text (referenced in the introduction to this book) that was highly critical of "officialized *ayuda mutua*" as working against the actions of squatter settlers, who had "discovered their own forms of participation" and unaided self-help that were potentially transformative.[54] In this reading, institutionally organized mutual aid directed toward housing provision was a palliative, while self-managed mutual aid deployed for collective mobilization had the capacity to remake the social order, and with it to redefine the very conditions of housing production.

Also in 1976 Emilio Pradilla—who would become a prominent critic within Latin America of autoconstrucción and of Turner's role in providing it with theoretical support—published a key text outlining his critique. By evading questions of class relations, Turner had failed to perceive that substandard housing was a by-product of the poverty consequent to social inequality. Further, the perpetual "housing crisis" played a particular role in class domination, and governments' apparent inability to solve it was in reality deliberate inaction, since established power structures were invested in maintaining the status quo. The evasion of class also allowed Turner to ignore the fact that autoconstrucción served to bolster the existing social order: by "reproducing the ideology of private property" among pobladores, it had the effect of "justifying the social regime that rests upon it." Moreover, to lionize the barriada was to normalize substandard living conditions, while to promote sites-and-services was to erase the barriada's key advantage—its affordability, which was dependent upon its illegality ("invasion of sites, absence of expenses for services, nonpayment of taxes, etc."). In fact, none of these options was the solution that Turner and others claimed. For Pradilla, improved socioeconomic conditions for the majority—and with it, improved housing—would never materialize without "the revolutionary transformation of society."[55] In the Latin America of 1976, Cuba provided one example of such a transformation, as did Peru, although tentatively, and as had Chile, incipiently, until very recently. If it was architecture (under the prevailing conditions of extreme social inequality) or revolution, for critics such as Pradilla the latter seemed the more compelling alternative.

As these debates make clear, despite its rising fortunes within the international development sphere, the politics of aided self-help housing—as well as the effectiveness of its practices—were still very much open to question.

8

OTHER
PATHS,
1980–1986

On May 18, 1980, Fernando Belaúnde Terry was elected in a landslide to his second term as president (1980–1985). With his Acción Popular party holding the largest number of seats in both houses of congress, he was poised to realize his campaign promises of visionary construction projects and a million new jobs—in essence, reviving a developmentalist agenda that had been cut short by his ouster in 1968. The previous day, militants from the Sendero Luminoso (Shining Path) Maoist guerrilla movement had seized and then burned the ballots being stored in a town hall in the Ayacucho region of the central highlands. This minor act of political protest had few immediate consequences, as the ballots were replaced the next day, and the election proceeded peacefully. Neither event was an accurate indicator of how the coming decade would unfold. Belaúnde's term ended in economic crisis, only to be followed by hyperinflation under his successor, Alan García (1985–1990), reaching 1,722 percent in 1988, and 2,775 percent in 1989. Meanwhile, Shining Path's ongoing campaign of insurrection led Belaúnde to launch a military campaign against the guerrillas in late 1982, fueling an escalating cycle of insurgent violence and state repression that by 1990 had forced two hundred thousand displaced persons to the capital, and would subside only after the capture of Shining Path leader Abimael Guzmán in September 1992.

The return to democracy in 1980 brought with it an opening up of democratic processes via the expansion of the franchise: with the literacy requirement removed and the voting age lowered to eighteen, in the 1978 election for a Constituent Assembly charged with writing a new constitution (the first national election held since 1963), 60 percent of the electorate was casting their first ballot. Further, reforms to governance that devolved responsibilities to local municipalities entailed both a decentralization of the power of the national government and a democratization of decision making on issues affecting the everyday life of local communities. In some cases, these new municipal governments were far more responsive to the grassroots, making a concerted effort to empower a growing constituency of low-income citizens who had systematically been denied their right to the city. At the same time, challenges to democracy emerged via calls for revolutionary violence in order to achieve long-standing demands for social reform—most prominently from Shining Path, but also the Movimiento Revolucionario Túpac Amaru (MRTA, Túpac Amaru Revolutionary Movement). These appeals resonated as the Belaúnde administration enacted structural adjustment policies that initiated a protracted and often painful period of transition, with increasing economic and social instability. With this explosion of viewpoints and visions for the country's future, one analyst has characterized Peru in this period as "present[ing] an extreme case of historical coexistence and compression where populists, developmentalists, revolutionaries, 'dirty war' leaders, neoliberals, and unknowns could all build a formidable political presence for a time" and then just as quickly disappear.[1]

The housing field experienced a similar volatility of viewpoints, with the close coexistence of sharply competing policies and proposals. The developmentalist position, embodied by Belaúnde, advocated for the return of conventional housing projects, in the hope of realizing his deferred dream of an Andean welfare state. The populists comprised on the one hand the transactional populism of Alan García's Alianza Popular Revolucionaria Americana (APRA), imbuing every housing initiative with calculations of clientelism, and on the other hand a new coalition of progressive parties, Izquierda Unida (IU, United Left), promoting a genuinely inclusive and prodemocratic populism. IU emerged as a force in the

1983 municipal elections, and undertook innovative low-cost housing projects in Lima based on grassroots participation, community
building, and aided self-help. The revolutionaries of Shining Path
interpreted any efforts at popular participation or *autogestión* as
had first been explored at Villa El Salvador as counterrevolution-
ary, and instructed its militants to obstruct or derail them. Finally,
the neoliberals were represented by Hernando de Soto, who viewed
"informal" self-help housing as the ultimate validation of private
enterprise and private property, and proposed leveraging the self-
built *barriada* as an engine of economic growth.

The chapter begins with a brief overview of housing policies enacted by the Belaúnde and García governments, before turning to
its primary focus: two projects implemented by IU in Lima between
1984 and 1986, Huaycán and Laderas de Chillón; and the impact of
Hernando de Soto's *El otro sendero: La revolución informal* (1986) on
housing and urban development policies within Peru and beyond.
Overall, the discussion traces the shifting weight of responsibilities
in the provision of low-cost housing between the national government, municipality, local community, individual, and market.

Belaúnde's housing policy was summarized by the slogan "Make
the dispossessed into small property owners."[2] This signaled a
return to the state construction of conventional housing projects,
with units purchased by beneficiaries with enough economic security to access subsidized loans. In theory, state housing agencies
aimed to provide a variety of housing options for a wide range of
incomes; in practice, the primary focus was on apartment buildings for middle-income households that harked back to the prestige
projects of the 1960s. When state housing agencies did make an
effort to grapple with the needs of low-income applicants, the approach was to reduce costs by selecting peripheral sites, providing
the minimum public facilities, building *núcleo básico* dwellings
intended for gradual extension, and relying on economies of scale.
This led to the creation of sparse, oversized satellite settlements or-
biting around the edge of the established city, which were slow to be
populated and consolidate themselves as viable neighborhoods (fig.
8.1). As a final measure to lower costs, the Belaúnde government established some sites-and-services projects, without any provisions
for technical assistance in the self-help construction of dwellings.
However, the seventeen thousand serviced sites it provided in Lima

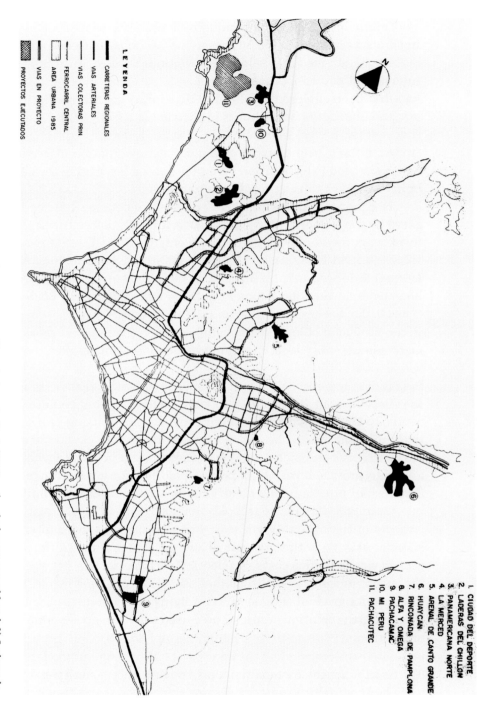

Figure 8.1. Projects built with government support in Lima, 1984–1990. Of particular note: Ciudad Mi Peru (marked no. 10, *second from left*), Laderas de Chillón (no. 2, *fourth from left*), Huaycán (no. 6, *top center*, adjacent to the Carretera Central), Pachacámac (no. 9, *far right*, on the southern edge of Villa El Salvador and near the Panamericana Sur). *Source:* INADUR, *Estudio de evaluación integral de los programas de vivienda ejecutados y/o promovidos por el Estado*, vol. 3, *Informe período 1985–1990* (Lima: INADUR, 1991), CDI-MVCS.

LEYENDA

═══ CARRETERAS REGIONALES

─── VIAS ARTERIALES

─── VIAS COLECTORAS PRIN

┅┅┅ FERROCARRIL CENTRAL

☐ AREA URBANA 1985

░ PROYECTOS EJECUTADOS

─── VIAS EN PROYECTO

▓ PROYECTOS EJECUTADOS

1. CIUDAD DEL DEPORTE
2. LADERAS DEL CHILLON
3. PANAMERICANA NORTE
4. LA MERCED
5. ARENAL DE CANTO GRANDE
6. HUAYCAN
7. RINCONADA DE PAMPLONA
8. ALFA Y OMEGA
9. PACHACAMAC
10. MI PERU
11. PACHACUTEC

Figure 8.2. Agrupación Pachacámac, Villa El Salvador, Lima, 1980–1985. View of núcleo básico units, most of which are yet to be roofed by residents. *Source*: ENACE, *Revolución habitacional en democracia* (Lima: ENACE, 1985).

fell far behind the seventy thousand lots created via land invasions over the same period. Among the largest of the Belaúnde-era projects was Agrupación Pachacámac, built on land appropriated from the southern edge of the Villa El Salvador site, in part using space that had been set aside for its industrial zone. The site was not only distant from central Lima but also disconnected from the more established core of Villa El Salvador. Planned for more than 14,000 lots in total, the first stage (1980–1985) comprised 3,953 sites-and-services lots, as well as 3,116 núcleos básicos—in this case, unroofed, single-room dwellings, with an adjacent bathroom (fig. 8.2). This project was apparently intended for low-level public sector workers, but many of the housing units and the lots remained vacant—a measure of their lack of appeal to prospective residents—and were eventually occupied by squatter households.

In July 1985 the long-outlawed APRA assumed power for the first time, with Alan García elected president. In Lima this resulted in mass land invasions at Fundo Bocanegra and Fundo Garagay: in contrast to earlier patterns, these occupied vacant private land that was close to the urban core, and therefore valuable. The initial

Figures 8.3 (*top*) and 8.4 (*bottom*). Ministerio de Vivienda, Ciudad Mi Perú, Ventanilla, Lima, 1986. *Lotes tizados* and public standpipes, two of the basic services provided. *Source*: "Reubicación y adjudicación de lotes básicos a las familias desalojadas del ex-Fundo Bocanegra en Ciudad Mi Perú, Ventanilla," 1986, CDI-MVCS.

invaders were connected to APRA, and had anticipated negotiating with the government and the landowners for a relocation site, but instead faced violent efforts to evict them. Eventually, the government granted amnesty to some of the invaders, and began negotiations for them to purchase the land. In addition, twenty-two of the families were relocated to Ciudad Mi Perú in Ventanilla, a peripheral settlement far to the north of the city, where they were provided with little more than secure tenure on a grid in the sand, with *lotes tizados* and very basic communal services (latrines, water pipes, graded but unpaved roads) (figs. 8.3–8.4). Otherwise, the García government put few resources into housing, apart from implementing a small number of núcleo básico and sites-and-services projects in cities outside the capital (Trujillo, Arequipa, Chimbote, and Cuzco), and executing extensions to Pachacámac. In any case, by 1988 the Peruvian economy was suffering from hyperinflation and on the verge of collapse, making state investment in housing or urban development projects impossible. Meanwhile, an increasing number of low-income families strained to even purchase sufficient food, leaving nothing to dedicate to housing.

Aside from constructing housing projects, the Belaúnde government fostered some institutional support for self-help housing, via the Banco de Materiales (Banmat, Materials Bank). Created in September 1980, Banmat aimed to facilitate the self-build construction of barriada housing as well as public facilities such as schools, with modest loans of up to $3,000 for construction materials. (A similar idea had been implemented via small-scale trials in the early 1960s.) In its first six years, Banmat granted fifteen thousand loans, totaling $13.5 million (or $900 on average), with 23 percent going to barriada residents and 43 percent to housing cooperatives, whose members were in the upper tier of the low-income bracket. Under García, Banmat incorporated a supervised credit program, which offered technical advice to *pobladores*, and made funds available in stages as construction advanced to satisfactory standards. By the early 1990s Banmat was making thirteen thousand loans annually. Nonetheless, the majority of barriada residents continued to build using their own resources.

In parallel to these initiatives at the national level, reforms to municipal governance initiated by Belaúnde had given local municipalities greater control over urban development, opening up the possibility of alternative approaches to the housing problem.

Making Lima a City for All

Beginning in 1980, the task of managing requests to utilize parcels of state land within greater Lima for housing was transferred from the national government to the Municipalidad de Lima Metropolitana (MLM, Municipality of Metropolitan Lima). Early in 1982 the MLM was given the additional responsibility of administering legal recognition to *asentamientos humanos* (human settlements) within its jurisdiction, and of granting property title to their residents. In the first eighteen months the MLM recognized 81 asentamientos humanos, approved 83 urban plans totaling 71,814 lots, and processed 55,915 individual property titles—2.7 times more than had been granted in the first two decades following the passage of Law 13517.[3]

In late 1983 municipal elections across Peru resulted in sweeping victories for parties of the left: of the twenty-four departmental capitals, APRA won thirteen and IU won nine. In Lima the mayoralty was won by Alfonso Barrantes, representing IU, under the campaign slogan "Making Lima a City for All." Observing the political dynamic between squatters and their governments, Manuel Castells argued in *The City and the Grassroots* (1983) that "urban populism always walks on the thin edge between clientelism and the triggering of urban social movements"; if APRA embodied the first tendency, then IU was aligned with the second. According to Castells, traditional clientelistic politics, as practiced by APRA (following Manuel Odría, among others), perpetuated relations of dependency between squatters and the state, limiting political engagement to negotiations over trading goods for votes: as this system of patronage displaced the autonomous exercise of rights, clientelism generated a "dependent city . . . a city without citizens."[4] By contrast, IU aimed to foster broad-based urban citizenship, building channels for grassroots participation and increasing input into decision making, in order to establish democratic practices as a bulwark against clientelism. Over the previous decade, the Revolutionary Government had endeavored to replace Peru's entrenched oligarchy with a social democracy of full participation, with the caveat that it operate under the guidelines set by state-directed organizations. Now IU aspired to forge a freestanding democracy that encompassed all sectors of society, and that would only be fortified by the emergence of urban social movements—or more precisely, of engaged urban political communities.

Upon taking office in January 1984, Barrantes immediately instituted an "emergency program" addressing the needs of residents living in extreme poverty, including preventative health, sanitation, and nutrition. The latter comprised two initiatives coordinated by a large network of women's organizations that had been promoted by Barrantes, consistent with a core IU policy of fostering democratization via grassroots participation: first, the Vaso de Leche (Glass of Milk) program, which by the end of 1984 was distributing more than seven hundred thousand servings of milk per day to children, pregnant women, and nursing mothers; second, the establishment of over three hundred *comedores populares* (community-run dining halls). The latter had begun to appear in Villa El Salvador in 1979 as the country's economic situation worsened, organized by local women pooling their resources to buy ingredients in bulk (sometimes supplemented by donations from church groups or NGOs), saving households time and money by preparing meals at very low cost; they were especially crucial for families who had yet to establish cooking facilities at home.

Shortly after Barrantes took office, additional reforms to municipal governance were instituted, giving municipalities greater control over the management of urban land, including the preparation of development plans and setting land-use guidelines. Barrantes was now in a position to implement a progressive agenda for Lima's urban development, articulating as key principles a more "rational" approach to zoning (preserving certain areas for agriculture, for example), and enacting a "democratization" of access to land by refusing to relegate low-income settlements to the urban periphery.

Already in the early 1980s the MLM had begun to receive a large number of requests from self-organized housing associations seeking permission to establish settlements on land in the Huaycán gorge, located in the Ate-Vitarte District Municipality, in the city's eastern zone. Huaycán had been reserved as an archaeological site by a state agency, but subsequent studies determined that only one section of the area had historical value. By 1984 the MLM and the Ate-Vitarte municipality were facing increasing pressure to release the land, but given the number of overlapping claims, officials decided that it would be preferable to institute their own housing project.

On May 3, 1984, the MLM created the Programa Especial de Habilitación Urbana de Huaycán (Special Program for the Urban Development of Huaycán), in order to coordinate the planning of a new settlement between the MLM, Ate-Vitarte, and the various organizations of prospective residents—of which there were twenty-three in all. These would-be pobladores belonged to two distinct social groups. First, several upper-tier low-income housing associations (representing teachers, white-collar workers, and employees of both the MLM and the Ate-Vitarte municipality, among others) had made their applications to the previous MLM mayor, a member of Belaúnde's Acción Popular party. Second, after the election of Barrantes, they were joined by organizations of *excedentes de barriadas*, generally the children of pobladores who had established settlements in the early 1960s and who were now facing overcrowded living conditions as they started their own families. Since Barrantes had been elected with their support, they believed he would be sympathetic to their interests. These two groups had conflicting expectations and needs concerning the new settlement. The first group had systematically been making their plans and setting aside their savings, "looking for a piece of land to realize an *urbanización* within the reach of their wallets"; the excedentes had signed up en masse at the prospect of being selected for a housing program, and sought to assert their claims through force of numbers. Furthermore, while the excedentes had the most urgent need for housing—and "in a moment of desperation would be capable of invading any site"—the more established, and somewhat more affluent, housing associations had the potential "to invigorate the life of the neighborhood" due to their more stable economic situation.[5] In the end, despite their differences, project planners judged that the two groups could coexist productively at Huaycán, given adequate guidance.

The Huaycán program envisaged an eventual population of around 130,000, with 12,000 families (or 66,000 residents) accommodated in stage one. The first task was to register the approved participants, with each household paying a small fee (approximately $10) that would be used to finance preliminary site studies. For its part, the MLM initially allocated the program no budget and few staff: in the first six months, its personnel consisted of two architects, a field assistant, and a secretary. This reflected the fact that while the national government had transferred responsibility for urban development to the municipalities, it had not provided them with the necessary resources to effectively manage it. As a consequence, the preparatory work progressed too slowly for many of the more restive pobladores, prompting municipal officials to decide that "the only way of confronting the threats of invasion by some of these groups" was to organize its own invasion first.[6] Accordingly, on July 15, 1984, two thousand of the twelve thousand registered families established the Asentamiento Humano de Huaycán under municipal supervision by occupying a strip of land that effectively controlled access to the entire Huaycán gorge—even though neither the site preparation nor the urban plan had been completed, and the legal status of the land was still unresolved. By August four thousand families had established themselves on the site, those with the lowest incomes and fewest alternatives—the excedentes—living there full time, and the others setting a symbolic stake in the ground.

An MLM information bulletin characterized Huaycán as "an alternative experiment in democratic management and technological innovation" that would provide "minimum essential services" to twelve thousand families within two years, at a fraction of the cost of state housing projects. This would be achieved in part because the site offered more favorable conditions for the provision of services than the compromised sites typically allocated for low-cost housing, located in peripheral areas or on steep hillsides. Although Huaycán was 17 kilometers from central Lima, it was only a short distance from the Carretera Central, a major highway providing direct access into the city. Further, existing electricity lines in the vicinity could easily be extended to Huaycán, and a nearby river offered a potential water source. The project would also reduce costs by mobilizing "the participation of the population" to provide much of the labor, and by avoiding the expensive and ill-advised practices—"bureaucratic management, . . . unrealistic or obsolete norms, . . . inappropriate technology, . . . onerous bidding procedures"—that left state housing projects dependent upon unsustainable government subsidies.[7]

The sociospatial foundation of Huaycán's "experiment in democratic management" would be the Unidad Comunal de Vivienda (UCV, Communal Dwelling Unit): roughly a hectare in size, they were described as "residential groupings of sixty families that occupy a lot held as common property and in practice act like small cooperatives."[8] The UCV's scale was judged to be both small enough "to ensure its consolidation as the nucleus of neighborhood identity" and large enough to take advantage of economies of scale to access credit and undertake communal projects.[9] The final design of each UCV would be determined by the residents as a group, developed through a series of meetings with project planners.

In early October, a management committee was established including officials and *técnicos* from the MLM and Ate-Vitarte municipality, as well as representatives of the various resident groups.

In contrast to the paternalistic approach of earlier projects, this model of *cogestión* (comanagement) acknowledged the agency of the pobladores as collaborators rather than "managed" participants, in an effort to create a more democratic or "horizontal" relationship with project planners, consistent with IU's goal of fostering grassroots participation. The MLM's information bulletin on Huaycán observed that "insecure settlement [*asentamiento precario*] is currently the most dynamic and extensive form of urban development" in Peru; however, such settlements were often marred by "a conflictual character that cancels out much of the positive manifestations of community participation."[10] At Huaycán, the strategy of cogestión aimed to harness this dynamism while mitigating any conflicts: it would provide a forum to iron out intracommunal disagreements, while laying the groundwork for a meaningful partnership between residents, officials, and técnicos to guide the project's development. On a practical level, the committee's first responsibilities included managing the project's funds (deriving from the residents' registration fees), approving the outlines of the urban plan, and assisting in organizing the "cooperatives" of sixty families that would form each UCV.

Whether in full-time residence or not, each cooperative was required to contribute twenty-four work-hours per week to Sunday sessions constructing roads, schools, and other amenities serving the entire settlement. Disputes quickly emerged between the disparate resident organizations over who would be allocated the most favorable locations within the site, particularly the first two sectors to be prepared, which had the advantages of possessing the most level terrain and being closest to the highway. In the end, these first sites were granted to groups of excedentes: their constant presence at Huaycán worked to their benefit, demonstrating that they were ready to establish their homes to the best of their ability as soon as they were allocated space. In November 1984 the various residential cooperatives were finally able to occupy their designated locations.

The site was organized into several *supermanzanas* (superblocks) outlined by the crisscrossing roadways that had been laid out in response to the irregular topography (fig. 8.5). Within each supermanzana were one dozen to two dozen UCVs. The UCV was defined not by a set shape (in practice they varied from rectangle to irregular polygon) but rather set principles that governed the placement of the key elements. In order to promote social cohesion,

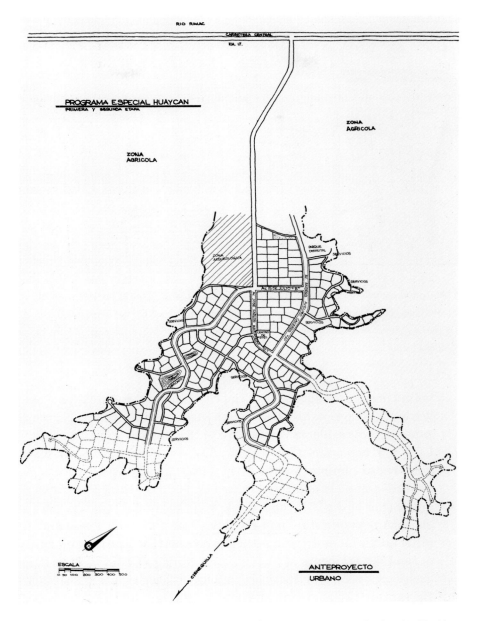

Figure 8.5. MML (architect: Eduardo Figari), Huaycán, Lima, 1984. Stage 1 (outlined in black) and stage 2 (dotted line). Roadways divide the site into *supermanzanas* (superblocks). *Source*: Eduardo Figari, "Huaycán: Una experiencia de urbanismo popular," *HUACA* 1 (July 1987).

a strongly articulated boundary was demarcated by a line of dwellings facing onto an open community space, with their backs adjoining the backs of dwellings in the neighboring UCV (fig. 8.6). Access

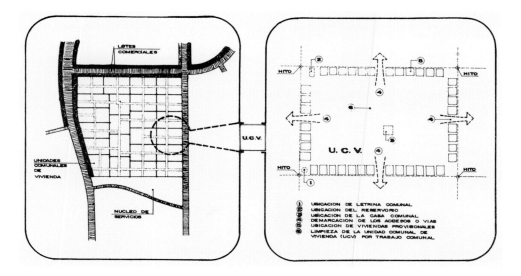

Figure 8.6. MML (architect: Eduardo Figari), Huaycán, Lima, 1984. Layout of the interior streets within a *supermanzana* (superblock) (*left*). Organization of the UCV (*right*): provisional dwellings line the perimeter of the UCV; the *casa comunal* (community center) is in the middle. *Source*: MLM, *Programa Especial Huaycán* (Lima: MLM, ca. 1985).

points perforated each side of the UCV, in order to establish a network of predominantly pedestrian streets within the supermanzana, so that residents would have to cross no more than one other UCV to reach a main road. Each UCV would have a central plaza with a *casa comunal* (community center) nearby, easily accessible from all points. In addition, communal latrines would be located in one corner of the UCV, and a reservoir for potable water in another, serving public standpipes and the casa comunal. These and all other public amenities would be the property and the responsibility of the UCV residents as a group. According to Eduardo Figari, the architect overseeing Huaycán and an advisor to the MLM under Barrantes, the casa comunal could offer a range of shared services, effectively supplementing the limited space of the house and thereby "alleviating the pressures on the family unit."[11] Depending on residents' needs, these could include a community-run kitchen, an open-air laundry, a phone, hot water and refrigeration facilities, or a children's play area.

In the first stage of occupation, the outlines of the UCV were indicated by an *hito* (boundary marker) in each corner. Small provisional dwellings—of *esteras*, as was usual—would be positioned

Figure 8.7. MML, Final design of UCV Modelo No. 69, Huaycán, Lima, ca. 1985. Outward-facing commercial lots line the main road on the right edge of the UCV. The *casa comunal* (community center) is located on the top edge, facing onto a small plaza and adjacent to one of the access points into the UCV. *Source*: PEHU Huaycán.

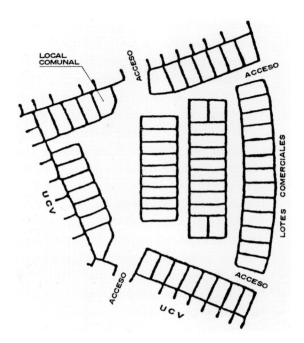

around the perimeter of the UCV, facing onto the common space, which would then be cleared and prepared for permanent construction by the residents. Since Huaycán residents were members of self-organized groups, it was anticipated that there would be some degree of social cohesion among them prior to occupation. In the definitive UCV plan, determined through extensive consultation, each household was to be allocated a 90-square-meter lot (fig. 8.7). Slightly larger lots for commerce or small industry were set aside on the main roads; the sale of these lots would contribute to financing communal construction projects.

In an effort to make the project economically sustainable, Huaycán promised technological innovations in the provision of basic services via two strategies: progressive development and resident participation in the construction and ongoing maintenance of key infrastructure. In the first instance, Figari noted that in typical low-cost housing projects, "the quality of housing is degraded toward intolerable limits" as architects continually shrink the lots and reduce urban services; when the concept of progressive development is invoked in this context, "the progressive is understood as how to make less of the same: conventional designs are subdivided into more stages, each time the first stage being more meager."[12] Valdiviezo, Caja de Agua, and the more recent Agrupación Pachacámac were all examples of this strategy, offering very basic core units and limited services, leaving residents to mobilize themselves to complete them at a later date. By contrast, Huaycán proposed to utilize progressive development for the incremental upgrading of services, organized so that no investment would be made in temporary measures, with every installation providing the foundation for the next.

In the case of water provision, in stage one, each UCV's communal reservoir would be filled by tanker truck; in stage two, these reservoirs would be connected to a settlement-wide reservoir; in stage three, domestic water service would be installed via connections from the local UCV reservoir, on a timeframe determined by the residents. In parallel, and to minimize the demands on potable water, untreated water from the Río Rímac would be utilized for irrigation. Similarly, sewage disposal would be progressively upgraded, starting in stage one with communal ventilated dry pit latrines. In stage two, single-family sanitary facilities would be installed, with each household provided with two absorbent pits functioning as simple sedimentation tanks, used alternately on a three-year cycle to allow for the breakdown of the waste; the wastewater could be safely discharged into the surrounding earth, since there were no nearby subterranean water sources at risk of contamination. In the final stage, a piped system would carry the wastewater to irrigate green spaces within the settlement—to this end, the overall site plan envisaged planting trees that would be sustained via this integrated sanitation system. Finally, electricity would initially be supplied to each UCV via a single, medium-voltage connection, powering public buildings (schools, health posts) and street lighting; transformers for residential electricity would be installed later. Delivering shared services in this manner would greatly reduce the investment required for the initial infrastructure: serving twelve thousand families (or two hundred UCVs, with sixty families each) would entail one-sixtieth of the connections required for individual domestic service, at a cost of approximately $200 per household. By contrast, the Huaycán project planners claimed that the average cost of a lot in a government sites-and-services project in Lima was $1,500, and a modest single-family house was roughly $20,000, or "the totality of the minimum living wage earned by a worker over sixty years."[13]

To promote resident participation, Huaycán aimed to provide ongoing technical assistance to self-builders, with specialized training in the techniques of *autoconstrucción*, and the creation of a team responsible for maintaining construction equipment and machinery, as well as the on-site fabrication of building materials. In the first year of occupation alone, more than six thousand families contributed thirty thousand work-hours to build education, health, and market facilities, as well as communal kitchens. By 1987 Figari reported that more than a dozen local workshops were in operation, producing concrete blocks, prefabricated roofing elements, and blocks shaped from local stone, which were employed as a paving material to construct Huaycán's roads, and for the walls of some public buildings.

Reynaldo Ledgard, an architect who worked on Huaycán under Figari, noted that Figari had been developing the UCV concept for some time. Connecting it to Figari's background as a student leader in the 1960s and a prominent member of the radical left in the 1970s, Ledgard interpreted the UCV as "a model of social life as much as an architectonic and urban form" that offered "the nucleus of a proposal to construct a new urban reality, and even a new society."[14]

In his own discussion of the conceptual underpinnings of Huaycán, Figari indicated that he had framed the project in response to detailed observations of the processes of barriada settlement and consolidation, devising selective interventions into those processes in order to propose this "new urban reality." Figari expressed admiration for the collaborative ethos of the initial stages of barriada settlement, which was all too soon atomized by a focus on gaining title for the single-family house. Accordingly, the UCV endeavored to replicate and further sustain the barriada's foundational collective dimension, primarily by foregrounding the importance of shared space in the urban plan. In this way, the UCV represented an inversion of the typical urban grid employed in Peru, where the streets framing the perimeter of the blocks act as "frontiers that separate each group"; housing lots facing these streets effectively open onto a no-man's-land. By contrast, the UCV was organized around "the intersection of the streets crossing it, streets that form part of the communal domain" that was jointly owned and self-managed by the cooperative of UCV residents. These streets offered connections rather than mandating separations, with housing lots that opened onto small plazas or faced their neighbors directly across intimate passageways (fig. 8.8). The collaborative ethos was further reinforced by the nature of the UCV design process, whereby each group shaped its own living space through negotiation, so that "a firm identification has been achieved between the *pobladores'* social organization and the organization of urban space."[15]

Figure 8.8. MML (architect: Eduardo Figari), Huaycán, Lima, 1984. View of a UCV in the process of consolidation. According to the caption, incorporating the public road into the UCV gives "the barrio the responsibility for its maintenance and improvement, and relates the private dwelling to the collectivity." *Source*: MLM, *Programa Especial Huaycán* (Lima: MLM, ca. 1985).

Further, the design not only of the "multifamily" areas but of the dwellings themselves aimed to foster the collective dimension, to forestall the "process of progressive closure and isolation of single-

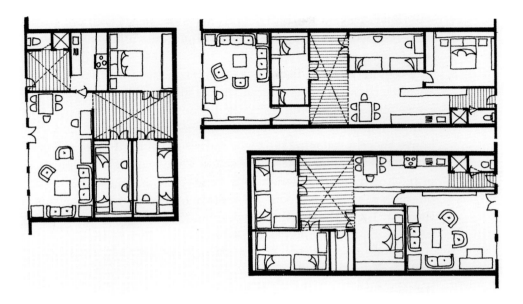

Figure 8.9. MML (architect: Eduardo Figari), Huaycán, Lima, 1984. Three housing types. *Source*: Eduardo Figari, "Huaycán: Una experiencia de urbanismo popular," *HUACA* 1 (July 1987).

family dwellings" that characterized barriada consolidation. Model house designs reflecting this ambition were made available to residents, for roughly 90-square-meter lots ranging in footprint from square to elongated rectangle (fig. 8.9). More importantly for Figari, the key "patterns" that were employed in the model designs were to be communicated directly to the residents, "so that each *poblador* applies them according to his desires and needs." These patterns included the principle of progressive development, which would see the dwelling extend vertically up to three stories: the fact that Huaycán employed smaller lots than was usual in state housing projects would promote this upward growth and with it densification, creating the character of a multifamily development of low-rise apartments. Similarly, the pattern allowing for an exterior staircase to access an independent upper-level dwelling would not only provide the primary household with much-needed rental income but also work against the "closure and isolation" inherent to single-family housing. For the layout of the house, the pattern of a "transitional space between the interior and exterior, of the 'porch' type" would undercut the usual sense of isolation from the life of the street.[16] In the model house plans, this feature is suggested by the permeable exterior wall fronting the *sala*, depicted as a series of

347

wide apertures rather than a solid enclosure. In a sketch imagining daily life in the UCV, a porchlike awning fronts many of the dwellings (see fig. 8.8).

Other patterns addressed the social functioning of the dwelling within a constrained footprint. Due to the small lot size, the model house plans eschewed a rear patio in favor of an interior patio that functioned as a point of connection between the various zones of the house, thereby reducing the space dedicated to circulation, and maximizing the amount of habitable space. There was a clear separation of public and private zones: following Peruvian tradition, the sala offered a social space open to visitors, while an intimate "nucleus of the daily life of the dwelling" was created by the grouping of dining room, kitchen, and interior patio, which together formed a private social zone reserved for the use of the household.[17] In addition, the pattern of placing the bedrooms with a direct opening onto the patio would improve ventilation, and with it enhance a sense of spaciousness. On a more functional level, in order to facilitate the progressive installation of water and sanitation services, one pattern suggested locating the bathroom on a side of the dwelling accessible to the street; in each of the model plans, it was sited adjacent to the service entry, with the kitchen immediately behind it. With this layout, the gradual upgrading of domestic services could be executed with minimal expense and disruption to the fabric of the dwelling.

Writing in 1987, Figari concluded that although the UCV had no direct precedent in Peruvian urbanism, it had nonetheless successfully established itself as the "foundation" of Huaycán. He interpreted its acceptance by the residents as a reflection of the fact that "it inscribes itself in popular traditions that the modern city subordinates, but that can be recuperated."[18] In short, Figari believed that the UCV had proved itself capable of reviving the collective character of the barriada, and that this would in turn support the development of Huaycán as a community.

Ledgard concurred, arguing that based on his experience of designing several UCVs, the concept had been "appropriated and utilized creatively" by the pobladores, who had shown "in people living in conditions of extreme harshness, an admirable capacity to discuss alternatives and to imagine the future." For Ledgard, the key to the UCV's success was its "design of participation": the collaborative process began with the architect explaining any factors constraining the design of the UCV, such as topography and neighboring construction. The next task was to determine the overall lot plan. Making a virtue out of the necessity of the initial provisional dwellings, the lots were not definitively assigned at this stage, ensuring that the discussion remained focused on the placement of the streets and shared spaces, establishing optimum conditions for the UCV as a whole, because "only the democratic distribution of collective benefit, achieved via a global design, would permit subsequent individual benefit." Ledgard noted that the urban forms that emerged from this process were highly variable: some groups preferred open access to neighboring UCVs, and others greater control; some groups selected "wide and straight streets, so that each lot opens onto a generous space; in other cases, the inclination is toward a large open space, even sacrificing the dimensions of the streets and the secondary spaces; . . . [or] small-scale open spaces, distributed equitably throughout the site and connected by passageways." For Ledgard, a key factor in facilitating the pobladores' meaningful participation in the design process was the fact that they were already living on the site, and understood its contours and character from everyday experience. This allowed them to "interiorize the relationship between the potential but abstract order of a plan and the physical reality in which they found themselves" so that their decisions in shaping the design were well informed.[19]

In some instances there was a more political—or rather micropolitical—inflection to the connections drawn by the pobladores between social structure and spatial form. Ledgard observed that although the Huaycán program specified a 90-square-meter lot, in some UCVs the pobladores decided to create lots of different sizes, utilizing this variance "to assign the better lots to those members who most support the communal work and who participate in the most positive way in the diverse activities of the UCV."[20] With only sixty families per UCV, the residents came to know their neighbors well through their labor. They evaluated their contributions, and then asserted social distinctions that reflected the degree to which each household was considered to belong to the whole: those members who had signed up for lots but lived elsewhere and only rarely participated were known as "tourists"; those who did not participate at all were eventually ejected from their UCV, their lots reassigned to new pobladores. Ledgard viewed this social dynamic of residents establishing and enforcing their own codes of behavior as part of a larger "process of democratization" that made Huaycán quite distinct from the barriada. In a barriada with hundreds of households, the leader of the residents' association could set himself apart from the rank-and-file membership, acting as director and decision maker, as chief negotiator with the authorities over matters of tenure or service provision. At Huaycán, the smaller domain of the UCV made the "leader" equal to his neighbors, required to contribute his labor on exactly the same terms.

Finally, Ledgard traced the roots of the strong collective identity of the UCV to the temporal dimension of its establishment—"this process of the gradual shaping of the urban form." Ledgard observed that in barriadas created through mass invasion, the sense of community quickly begins to dissipate, because upon seizing the site, each poblador is transformed at a stroke "from a member of an undifferentiated mass into an isolated individual" focused on securing a lot.[21] At Huaycán, the time taken to negotiate the UCV's form allowed for the moment of establishing private property to be delayed, as the definitive location of each lot would be decided upon only once the UCV's dynamic had begun to solidify through the physical labor of preparing the site, and the social labor of building relationships. By foregrounding the participatory element of the design process, Huaycán's planners also hoped to promote community cohesion and thereby a commitment to building and maintaining the collectively owned spaces, in turn fostering the rapid consolidation of individual dwellings.

The second major housing project initiated by the MLM under Barrantes was Laderas de Chillón, in the city's northern zone, which was specifically intended to house excedentes from barriadas in the five local district municipalities in this area of Lima. Once again, the selected site had the advantages of easy road access and viable options for providing water and other basic services, reflecting IU's policy of democratizing access to urban land. The project descriptions echoed the core IU principles of promoting popular participation and building grassroots democracy, but lacked Huaycán's ambition to make resident participation integral to the design process in order to achieve these social goals. Further, the Barrantes administration's decision to let local district municipalities prepare the lists of prospective residents allowed clientelism to enter the selection process, undermining IU's efforts to foster democratic cogestión of the project's development.

Prior to the MLM securing responsibility for the Laderas de Chillón site, a state agency had granted exploration rights to five mining companies. The MLM immediately sought to end these mining concessions in order to utilize the site for housing, but ad-

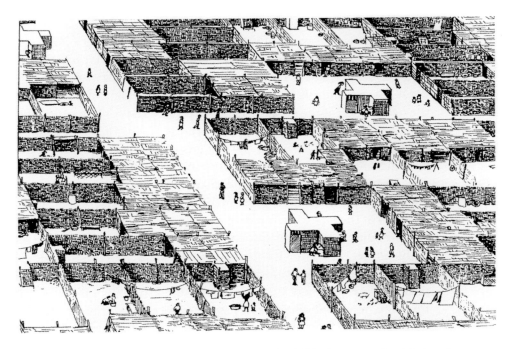

Figure 8.10. MML (architect: Miguel Alvariño), Laderas de Chillón, Lima, 1985. Partial view of a *macromanzana* (macroblock) including two *plazoletas* (small squares), with their shared sanitary facilities housed in pinwheel-shaped structures. Source: Wiley Ludeña Urquizo, *Lima: Historia y urbanismo en cifras, 1821–1970* (Lima: MVCS, 2004).

ministrative delays by the agency purposefully slowed the process of transferring the land. In the meantime, the mining companies continued their explorations, and municipal officials were unable to gain access to the site due to the obstruction of a neighboring landowner. As a result, planners were left to rely on aerial photographs in drawing up the urban plan. The site consisted of three adjacent *explanadas* (leveled areas) in between foothills, which planners judged would be able to accommodate 2,500 6-by-18-meter residential lots. The basic unit of the urban design was the *macromanzana* (macroblock), consisting of eighty-eight residential lots. Each macromanzana was subdivided into four sectors by two roadways crossing it at right angles; each sector of twenty-two lots featured a *plazoleta* (small square), which in stage one would include a *núcleo sanitario básico* (basic sanitary nucleus) with shared showers, laundry facilities, and water taps (fig. 8.10). The design of the macromanzana was primarily driven by the need to maximize the number of lots via the most efficient use of land, but also aimed to promote the social life of the neighborbood via the small-scale public space of the plazoleta.

While waiting to gain access to the site, project planners finalized the urban plan and allocated the lots to the registered pobladores. By completing these preparations in advance of overseeing the occupation of the site, they hoped to avoid the conflicts that had emerged between groups of pobladores at Huaycán. By mid-June 1985 planners had assigned the 913 lots of the first and largest explanada and were ready to manage the orderly occupation of the site. However, as soon as the técnicos and pobladores arrived, it became clear that the proposed urban plan was unworkable: some sections of the site were far steeper than anticipated, and in others mining company excavations had left deep holes, making hundreds of the already allocated lots unusable. The MLM officials and técnicos immediately lost the trust of the pobladores, and the initial project team resigned. With less viable land than the planners had foreseen, many who had been promised lots faced the prospect of being excluded from the project. Some simply left, some tried to occupy their compromised lots, and others threatened to invade the areas set aside for communal facilities.

After months of contentious negotiations, in December a new planning team assessed the conditions on the ground, and began the process of drawing up a revised urban plan, developed via extensive consultations with residents. Given the fragmented and irregular nature of the site, the planners were forced to abandon the macromanzana concept, although they did retain the plazoletas. Finally, after almost a year, the new urban plan was completed, and the lots were reallocated. According to one assessment, Laderas de Chillón was little more than an "ordered barriada"; nonetheless, and despite the difficulties of its realization, residents still viewed it as preferable to a "conventional barriada" because the land had been provided for free, and property titles had been granted within a year of settlement.[22] Laderas de Chillón was better than the alternatives available to low-income residents—but it fell far short of the IU administration's initial ambitions to establish a new mode of urban settlement.

Meanwhile, after the initial optimism expressed by Figari and Ledgard at Huaycán, an independent evaluation published in 1989 revealed some challenges. Each UCV had built its casa comunal, with active participation from the residents, and they were well used, playing a key role in the social life of each neighborhood.

However, most of the technological innovations underpinning the proposed progressive infrastructure went unrealized, in large part due to resistance from the state agencies responsible for providing these services. Ultimately, the Barrantes administration had no influence over these agencies, and without their cooperation in pursuing the proposed innovations, it had no means of executing them. In cases where experimental technologies were installed, there was insufficient education for residents concerning their proper maintenance. This proved to be a particular issue with the sedimentation tanks for the domestic sanitation system, which were completely unfamiliar to residents. Other approaches to service provision were all too familiar, and were rejected because of their undesirable connotations: the communal standpipes and latrines were unacceptable to pobladores because of their strong associations with *callejón* housing. This traditional form of low-income rental housing in Lima, characterized by rows of small dwellings tightly packed along a central alleyway, with several families sharing water and sanitation services, represented precisely the kind of living conditions that the pobladores sought to leave behind by establishing themselves at Huaycán.

The small size of the lot was another point of contention. The técnicos argued that in a middle-class settlement, "a lot of 160 square meters normally has a built area of 60, 70, or 80 square meters per floor"; therefore, Huaycán's 90-square-meter lots should be perfectly adequate to accommodate any house the pobladores aspired to build.[23] However, this explanation failed to convince the pobladores, since the real issue was not the amount of built space per se but rather the cultural expectation of being able to realize the dream of a "chalet"—a single-family home with a backyard. For some observers, this indicated that the pobladores had regrettably internalized a bourgeois vision of domesticity; an alternative interpretation suggested that the small size of the residential lots raised legitimate concerns, since they would be difficult to adapt for workshop or commercial purposes—a vital supplementary source of income for many households. Meanwhile, technical assistance for autoconstrucción or training in the use of the proposed experimental materials was nonexistent, despite the project planners' ambitions. Since the assigned architects were unable to assist self-help home builders on an individual basis, a number of small-scale entrepreneurs stepped into the breach, such as contractors who established on-site "offices for the elaboration of plans" for the pobladores.[24]

IU's larger goals—the planning project of promoting cogestión as a more inclusive approach to designing and managing urban settlements, and the social project of curtailing clientelism by fostering grassroots democracy and urban citizenship—faced serious challenges. In the first instance, in the view of one técnico assigned to Laderas de Chillón, the question of whether it was possible to achieve an equitable or "horizontal relationship" between técnicos and pobladores via cogestión was complicated by the underlying power dynamic, which was both uneven and unstable. The power of the técnicos came from their institutional connections and their professional experience; the power of the pobladores came from their willingness (or not) to provide the labor that was indispensable to realizing any initiatives proposed by the técnicos: "So on one hand there is the power of knowledge and resources, and on the other hand is the power of organization and the power of implementation.... [and] in specific moments the power of the one or the other can shift."[25] Despite the best intentions of the técnicos, this was not a matter they could resolve in the abstract by determining a perfect point of equilibrium between the two parties; rather, it would require an ongoing process of negotiation, dependent on the good faith of both sides. Though not impossible to achieve, this would be greatly complicated by factors such as the poor advance planning at Laderas de Chillón, which strained relations from the outset.

In the second instance, Huaycán's social project proved to be highly dependent on the goodwill and overall outlook of the prevailing municipal administration as well as its national counterpart. In 1985 Alan García won the presidential election; theoretically, this could have resulted in increased support for housing projects initiated by the IU municipal administration, since APRA was closer in political outlook to IU than Belaúnde's Acción Popular. Indeed, at the official level, the Barrantes and García administrations worked together well. However, at the grassroots level in Huaycán there were political struggles between representatives of the two parties, precisely because they were both competing for voters on the left. Once APRA was in power nationally, there was a surge in support for its candidates in local elections at Huaycán—less the result of an ideological conversion than a strategic alliance, with the pobladores judging that APRA representatives would be better positioned to secure commitments from the government for basic services and community facilities. In other words, the ethos of grassroots democracy and urban citizenship that IU had tried to foster at Huaycán was not strong enough to withstand the siren call of clientelism from APRA, representing as it did the customary means for pobladores to advance their demands for their settlements.

APRA's victory in the presidential election was followed by success in the next MLM election, with its candidate Jorge del Castillo elected mayor (1987–1989). The del Castillo administration discontinued IU's core policy of democratizing access to urban land, making no effort to reserve sites for future low-income settlements, let alone initiating new housing projects. Furthermore, it undermined the progress of existing settlements in its portfolio—Huaycán and Laderas de Chillón—through neglect. There was a high turnover of the teams implementing both projects, with many of the incoming técnicos far less committed to the underlying social goals than the initial teams had been. Residents' frustration with the slowed rate of progress led to a series of confrontations with officials; this was particularly an issue at Huaycán, where the vehemence of opposition to some initiatives led certain officials to "consider Huaycán to be a 'refuge of terrorists.'"[26]

In fact, this prejudice was not entirely unfounded. The ongoing power struggle between IU and APRA created internal divisions that had left Huaycán vulnerable to infiltration by Shining Path. Already in July 1985, at a public meeting convened to discuss issues of community management, its militants had emerged as a force in local politics. According to the account of a community leader affiliated with IU, Shining Path "used the opportunity to deploy a large military operation with 100 armed men" and hijacked the meeting for several hours, delivering "revolutionary harangues and ask[ing] for 'voluntary' contributions." Subsequently, those sectors of Huaycán where Shining Path was active mobilized to reject the installation of services, condemning them as "palliative measures" that undermined the revolutionary project.[27]

In the first years of its insurgency, Shining Path had maintained a low profile in Lima, while rural areas bore the brunt of the violence between the militants and government forces, leading thousands to flee for the relative safety of the capital. The first refugee squatter settlement was established at Huanta I in northeast Lima in 1984, and other similar settlements soon followed.

Shining Path took advantage of these movements of internally displaced persons to redeploy some of its militants to the capital, concentrating them in Huaycán. It shrewdly exploited the divergent interests of the various constituencies that made up Huaycán,

in particular recruiting recently arrived pobladores who struggled to establish themselves on the uneven ground of the slopes
surrounding the core of the settlement. Shining Path stoked their
resentment toward project participants who were marginally more
economically secure and were not yet living permanently at the site;
in the words of one observer: "Their battle cry was 'land for those
who live in Huaycán' and against the 'weekend tourists.'" Shining
Path also used these peripheral, newly settled areas for "midnight
marches and guerrilla unit training sessions" that often involved
recruits from other parts of Lima, and they organized armed pa-
trols throughout the settlement with the dual purpose of deterring
crime and underscoring their presence. These activities led the
police and the army to target Huaycán as a "'red zone'—making
it "subject to continuous surveillance, searches, and roundups of
residents and community leaders."[28] This policing was especially
intense in the extended period when Lima was under curfew, from
February 1986 to July 1988.

The primary reason for Shining Path's attraction to Huaycán
was its location near the Carretera Central, the main highway
connecting Lima to the central Andes, where essential foodstuffs
and valuable commodities (chiefly minerals and metals) were produced. The Ate-Vitarte district was also a key node controlling
Lima's water and electricity networks: 60 percent of the capital's
electricity was generated by plants located in the district, and the
remainder of the supply was produced in the central Andes and
conveyed to the capital via transmission lines that ran through the
area. Early in the presidency of Alberto Fujimori (1990–2000), as
his "Fujishock" economic stabilization program plunged almost
half of the country's population into conditions of extreme poverty, Shining Path moved to escalate its revolutionary campaign. In
May 1991, Shining Path leader Abimael Guzmán announced that it
would launch more aggressive assaults on all fronts, particularly
in Lima's strategic barriadas—not only Huaycán but also Villa El
Salvador, which, Guzmán argued, when connected to other barriadas around Lima's periphery, would form an "iron belt of misery"
encircling the capital and holding it captive.[29] Just as Huaycán had
strategic value due to its location on the Carretera Central, Villa
El Salvador's position close to the Panamericana Sur, the highway
linking Lima to southern Peru, made it very attractive in military
terms (see fig. 8.1). In theory, if Shining Path had been able to gain
control of both of these settlements, and from there limit move-

ment on the nearby highways, it could have effectively blockaded the capital.

Villa El Salvador held an additional attraction for Shining Path. Following numerous early setbacks, in 1983 it had become an independent municipal district, and its first mayor, Michel Azcueta, elected on an IU ticket, had revived the project of transforming the settlement into the Comunidad Urbana Autogestionaria de Villa El Salvador (CUAVES). Azcueta resurrected the dormant industrial park, and by 1990 there were nearly two hundred small businesses in operation, established with funding from the national government and international agencies. Villa El Salvador had come to embody the values of autogestión, grassroots democracy, and popular participation that were advocated by the mainstream left—or as Shining Path dubbed it, the "revisionist left"—and as such it represented an impediment on the route to revolution. In late 1987 community leaders in Huaycán affiliated with IU voted for the settlement to follow the lead of Villa El Salvador and declare itself the Comunidad Urbana Autogestionaria de Huaycán; following the vote, an armed group of Shining Path militants interrupted the meeting and burned the minutes. Nonetheless, the community ultimately ratified the decision.

Beginning in 1989, Shining Path's newspaper *El Diario* published frequent and vehement criticisms of Villa El Salvador's autogestión model, of community leaders including Azcueta, and of the vice-mayor María Elena Moyano, who was a leading figure in local women's organizations, whose activities were likewise targets of Shining Path denunciations: "The objective of the so-called 'self-management' model is to ensure that the masses do not combat this bureaucratic, oligarchic state, and that they content themselves with palliatives within the system so that they can ostensibly resolve their problems. . . . The same thing happens with the soup kitchens and the milk committees, that is, making the masses, with their unpaid labor, conform themselves with receiving charity from the NGOs, so they won't fight for their rights."[30] By late 1991 the Shining Path attacks were no longer limited to print. In August Juana López, the organizer of a soup kitchen in the port district of Callao, was assassinated. In September a bomb destroyed a warehouse in Villa El Salvador used for storing supplies for the comedores populares. This was followed by unsuccessful attempts against Azcueta, and in February 1992, the assassination of Moyano. In April 1992, days after Fujimori's *autogolpe* (self-coup) dissolved the national congress and suspended the constitution, Shining Path initiated an all-out assault in Lima, including a bus bomb in Villa El Salvador that shattered part of the municipal building, the police station, an NGO promoting education, and a number of houses. According to one estimate, more than a hundred community leaders and activists involved in programs such as Vaso de Leche were killed by Shining Path in Lima.[31]

In sum, while the decade had begun with Belaúnde's optimistic visions of a Peru transformed by the twin pillars of development and democracy, both had proved illusory—the one vulnerable to the realities of Peru's profound economic challenges, and the other fragile in the face of an entrenched culture of clientelism. The mainstream left's proposals for grassroots democracy and self-managing communities had been implemented only fitfully and partially at Huaycán, and not at all at Laderas de Chillón. Meanwhile the revolutionary left of Shining Path offered the promise of a luminous future, at the immense expense of crippling and inescapable violence in the present. Against this background, Hernando de Soto and his think tank, the Instituto Libertad y Democracia (ILD, Institute for Liberty and Democracy), announced an alternative way forward.

Freedom to Borrow

The publication of de Soto's *El otro sendero: La revolución informal* (1986, published in English in 1989 as *The Other Path: The Invisible Revolution in the Third World*) declared that an "informal revolution" was under way in Peru, nurtured within the grey zone of the extralegal economy. As opposed to the Maoist road map to a new revolutionary society, de Soto and the ILD argued that "we Peruvians" should be able to determine "a deliberate path which will enable us to escape from backwardness and advance toward a modern society" that would be built on the entrepreneurship evidenced in "informal" markets. According to novelist Mario Vargas Llosa—who provided a preface to the book, introduced its ideas to a US audience via an article in the *New York Times*, and would later adopt it as a virtual manifesto for his 1990 presidential campaign—the state was incapable of solving Peru's chronic underdevelopment because it was itself part of the problem: "The informal market is actually the solution . . . the spontaneous and creative response of the impoverished masses to the state's inability to satisfy their basic needs."[32]

De Soto focused on informal economic activity in three sectors—housing, trade, and transport—described as having emerged spontaneously in response to social needs. Scorned as criminal by mainstream society, for de Soto these markets were essential to the development of the broader economy, and operated perfectly well as self-regulating systems until encountering interference from official bureaucracies. Rather than attempting to impose regulation on informal markets, the state should recognize that promoting the "incipient market economy generated by the popular classes in Peru"[33] was the only real path to economic takeoff. The state should concern itself with how to facilitate these mechanisms of private entrepreneurship, via deregulation and the removal of any obstacles to the growth of informal markets.

The market in informal housing was central to de Soto's argument. His narration of the process of squatter settlement formation emphasized not community-organized action (valorized by the Revolutionary Government and John F. C. Turner alike) but the role of small-scale spontaneous entrepreneurs—such as professional invasion organizers, operators of ad hoc bus routes, or the on-site sellers of water, fuel, or building materials—who found business opportunities in the niche markets serving these emerging settlements. For de Soto, these *asentamientos informales* (informal settlements) were primarily "an expression of the people's desire to own property"; furthermore, the ultimate aim of any "communal activity" by settlement residents—lobbying for secure tenure or urban services, for example—was to accrue benefits to their private property (fig. 8.11). This vision of a neoliberalized "self"-help housing was contrasted to what would have occurred if these households had elected to remain as renters in *tugurios*, thereby contributing to overcrowding and turning Lima into "one vast slum."[34]

Another key aspect of de Soto's argument was the claimed monetary value of informal housing, estimated in terms of its "replacement cost" in mid-1984: "the average value of an informal dwelling was $22,038 and the total value of the building located in Lima's informal settlements came to $8,319.8 million, an amount equivalent to 69 percent of Peru's total long-term external debt in that same year." By comparison, the state's investment in housing for lower-income residents from 1960 to 1984 was $173.6 million, "a mere

Calles privadas. Las pistas sólo pasan delante de las casas de quienes contribuyen a su construcción. "La Balanza" — Comas, 1986.

Defendiendo la propiedad invadida. Piquetes en el asentamiento "Huaycán", 1984.

Figure 8.11. The self-help home builder as principled defender of private property. Above: "Private streets. The paving only goes in front of the houses of those who contribute to its construction, La Balanza, Comas, 1986." Below: "Defending the invaded property. Pickets in the Huaycán settlement, 1984." *Source*: Hernando de Soto, *El otro sendero* (Lima: Instituto Libertad y Democracia, 1986).

2.1 percent of the informal investment."[35] By this method of calculation Peru possessed an immense treasury of dormant wealth awaiting realization. However, government bureaucracy had been stifling this economic potential by imposing unnecessarily burdensome requirements on pobladores aiming to acquire legal title to their lots, stymieing their efforts to transform the equity in their self-built housing into capital for entrepreneurial initiatives.

The primary legislation in this area (Law 13517 passed in 1961) had sought to establish secure tenure for residents of squatter settlements, but did not grant full transferrable legal title until the household had completed seven years of residence. This measure was intended to promote the consolidation of the settlement: assuring residents that they would not be evicted would encourage them to invest their resources in their housing; requiring owner-occupancy would counteract land speculation and foster an active community eager to engage in improvement projects. In essence, Law 13517 sought to improve the housing opportunities of residents of squatter settlements, but did not grant them the right to profit from the real estate that they had claimed. According to de Soto, these antispeculation measures were "discriminatory"—creating a second-class system of ownership, "a kind of legal apartheid"—and prevented capital accumulation via the real property of the self-built dwelling (even if it had originated with the extralegal occupation of land), and was thus an infringement of personal liberty.[36] The larger public interest of antispeculation measures was not a concern for de Soto; in fact, generating a land market should be encouraged, without any limits or constraints.

Throughout, de Soto's rejection of the state was complemented by a renewed mystification of the supposed unassailable logic of the self-regulating (read: unregulated) market. He viewed the interactions of the individual and the state as a struggle between competing, irreconcilable interests. In his account, the "defeat" of the state by the "informals"—that is, the failure of Peruvian officialdom to control informal economic activity—was a moral victory, proving the survival of the fittest in the marketplace, rather than being the predictable outcome when an ineffective, immature bureaucracy tries to take on a problem of this scale with few resources.

In the background of de Soto's narrative was a different kind of struggle—that of class and culture. The 1950s language of barriada "invasion" expressed the fears of coastal elites faced with new migrants from rural areas, who flouted the law with no consequences.

According to de Soto, these illegalities actually formed their own system in a self-regulating "informal" economy, representing at heart an insurgent capitalism, which might have an unfamiliar face but ultimately operated within a reassuringly familiar market mechanism. Rather than lawless and uncultured peasant invaders (a specter reappearing in the very concrete form of Shining Path), de Soto saw a petite bourgeoisie in waiting.

Despite Mike Davis's characterization of de Soto as "a John Turner for the 1990s" in a critique that favors polemic over analysis, the real points of convergence and difference between the two figures are more complex. Turner's own view was that de Soto's work replicated his earlier findings concerning the long-term investment that the consolidated squatter house represents, providing proof that a standard middle-class house could be achieved over time by the self-help method.[37] However, on this point both writers minimized the time, effort, and difficulties of the consolidation process while overemphasizing the efficacy of the self-built house as a means of securing socioeconomic advancement. A number of studies have provided convincing evidence that by and large squatter households are not able to build their way out of poverty, one of the earliest being Peter M. Ward's research on Mexico City, which found that "squatting, by itself, does not provide a vehicle for socioeconomic mobility for low-income households." Ward demonstrated that when individual households or settlements manage to consolidate, this is largely due to the health of the overall economy; conversely, in a weak economy "low-income groups might be able to *survive* through opting for squatter settlement residence, but would not be able to achieve anything but very modest improvements through self-help."[38]

Both Turner and de Soto emphasized the importance of people doing things for themselves, but for Turner this was an exercise in community building, not profit-focused entrepreneurship or wealth generation or single-minded "self"-determined initiative. Turner explicitly distinguished his vision of self-help from that of Samuel Smiles, the Victorian apostle of self-improvement who first popularized the term: Turner's was not a "capitalistic version of self-help" or "individual self-sufficiency"—it was grounded in the "mutual aid" ethos advocated by Kropotkin.[39] The CUAVES model of collective, self-managed entrepreneurship from below—completely sidestepped by de Soto—could serve as one example. Their views of the state also contrasted sharply: de Soto would limit government's role to facilitating titling as a stimulant to entrepreneurship, while Turner envisaged a substantial intervention in promoting equitable access to resources. Turner believed that the state had the responsibility to actively reshape markets in order to facilitate individual and community initiative, while de Soto's faith in the free market was absolute.

Fundamentally, the two parted ways on the question of the value of housing: of use value versus exchange value, of housing as an end in itself versus housing as equity. For Turner, the emphasis was always on the "freedom to build" (not only building shelter, but always also building community), while de Soto's focus was on establishing the foundations for a freedom to borrow—to undertake credit obligations as the basis for small-scale entrepreneurial initiatives. For Turner, the barriada was "an architecture that works" because it facilitated the empowerment of individuals and their communities, while for de Soto, the architecture of the informal settlement "works" by literally acting as a generator of capital and an engine of economic growth.[40] However, both writers failed to address the extent to which self-built shelter "works" at the expense of the resident-builders themselves, while the cost to the state is minimized.

On this point, sociologist Gustavo Riofrío's *Producir la ciudad (popular) de los '90: Entre el mercado y el Estado* (1991), his response to *El otro sendero*, offered a very different vision of the respective roles of the market and the state in facilitating access to very low-cost housing. Riofrío's analysis encompassed a critique of de Soto's interpretation, methodology, and data (which for both the Spanish and English editions was not included in the book itself—on the grounds that this might have "discouraged readers"—but was only available as a separate publication, which could be obtained by writing to the ILD offices). In Riofrío's description, from the perspective of a committed leftist, housing in squatter settlements existed in a highly particularized market: "A market that is protected so that it only allows access to those who are going to build their houses there, which they will occupy permanently. . . . This market, called 'informal' by de Soto, only gives access to those who are willing to self-urbanize [*autourbanizar*] and self-build [*autoedificar*]." In the barriada (Riofrío refused de Soto's coinage of *asentamiento informal*, returning to the earlier designation), even if part of the dwelling is used to generate rental income, it always "fundamentally has a use value, not an exchange value"; the logic of the restrictions on resale and on taking out mortgages is that this protects the "social interest" of residents as a collective. Riofrío argued that this very specific kind

363

of market—governed by its own ethos, which is not reducible to pure exchange—should be allowed to continue functioning according to its own rules, rather than "destroying the existing markets and replacing them with a single free market *al estilo norteamericano*"— that is, an imported model of US capitalism entirely foreign to Peru.[41]

Riofrío also took issue with de Soto's account of construction processes in the barriada, which did not distinguish between the construction of urban improvements and of housing per se. While de Soto suggested that residents were primarily concerned with building the individual house, Riofrío clarified that in fact, the usual pattern was that "the community will immediately begin to make large investments in order to provide electricity and water—as well as other services and communal facilities—to the settlement. The construction of the family dwelling is not the first 'large' investment of families, and happens . . . when there are minimum services in the neighborhood."[42] Further, Riofrío argued that de Soto exaggerated the importance of legal title in encouraging investment and consolidation, pointing out that generally security of tenure alone was sufficient for residents to commit to building. This could be established by the state formally granting right of residence, or more concretely by investing its own capital in the neighborhood via installing services.

Importantly, Riofrío closely scrutinized de Soto's claim concerning the monetary value of extralegal housing, pointing out that de Soto's estimated valuation of $22,038 per dwelling (which appeared to be loosely based on the valuations used to calculate property tax) assumed that the average house was in much better condition than would actually be the case. Specifically, it assumed that: all the construction would be "in a good or very good state of conservation"; more than half of the dwellings "would be less than five years old"; only 4 percent would lack electricity, water, and sewerage connections; and 45 percent would have tiled bathrooms. This was clearly disproved by a detailed study of the progressive development of self-built settlements in Lima by Riofrío and Jean-Claude Driant, published as *¿Qué vivienda han construido? Nuevos problemas en viejas barriadas* (1987). Riofrío noted that this survey, which focused on well-consolidated zones and thus above-average housing, found that less than half of the dwellings had finished floors, windows, doors, and surfaced walls; 16 percent of homeowners "did not have a separate room to cook"; almost all had bathrooms but 27 percent had to share them with tenants or lodgers. Riofrío concluded that de Soto's data had been shaped "in order to exaggerate the value of what is built by the popular sectors"; the total investment of $8,319.8 million claimed by de Soto was thus essentially an empty figure, a fiction.[43]

Finally, presenting his own vision of the path forward, Riofrío argued that the market alone could not provide an adequate solution to the problem of low-cost housing. Riofrío conceded that de Soto and the ILD had achieved some success in lobbying to simplify and speed up administrative processes in relation to housing, thereby correcting some of the inefficiencies of the state. However, the state's further withdrawal of responsibility, let alone the complete deregulation of the housing sector, was not advisable: "The state has to fulfill the obligation to supervise the quality of habitat." In particular, the state should provide technical assistance in construction and better access to credit (that is, credit to build dwellings, not to borrow against them). It should act in a supporting role to improve existing low-cost housing construction; the "self-build tradition" should be the starting point for the large-scale production of low-cost housing under the guidance of the state—an approach that Riofrío estimated could produce at least twenty thousand dwellings per year.[44]

Notwithstanding the acuity of Riofrío's critique, de Soto's vision of neoliberalized self-help in *El otro sendero* gained a wide and enthusiastic readership, and the authority granted by the book ensured the success of de Soto's follow-up, *The Mystery of Credit* (2000). The appeal of de Soto—characterized by one commentator as "a highly effective transnational policy entrepreneur"[45]—largely stemmed from his position as a "Third World" intellectual espousing neoliberalism, reinforcing familiar arguments from an unexpected geographical position.

Within international development agencies, the neoliberal turn represented a dramatic shift in policy concerns and funding priorities. A decade after Habitat in Vancouver, in 1986 the UN Centre for Human Settlements prepared its first *Global Report on Human Settlements*, signaling a revised approach to the provision of low-cost housing. The language of dependency and structural inequality was superseded by "integrated management" and economic efficiency. Housing was not a "social welfare concern" but a question of "industrial output and marketing"; instead of a "narrow focus on sites-and-services and squatter-settlement upgrading schemes" the key was to "scale up" housing production, suggesting a return to the economies of scale promised by mass housing. Rather than

undertaking housing projects themselves, governments now needed to focus on "enabling strategies" to foster the contributions of
the private sector: "Governmental measures will be concentrated
mainly on improving institutional structures and mobilizing the
resources needed to support action by others." However, the report
did acknowledge that this approach could not offer a universal solution: "those who live in destitution"—as opposed to the "poor" and
"very poor"—"will need to be assisted directly through programs
shaped by principles other than those of affordability and cost-
recovery."[46] Here the report recognized the limitations of market
efficiency under certain economic conditions, while remaining
vague about exactly where the line between a workable level of
poverty and irremediable destitution could be drawn.

At the World Bank, neoliberal ideas spurred a transfer of interest and funding from "housing" as physical object and associated
infrastructure, toward the granting of property title. In 1993 the
World Bank announced a revision of its policies in *Housing: Enabling Markets to Work* (a report cowritten by Shlomo Angel, formerly of the Center for Environmental Structure and one of the
architects involved with its PREVI proposal): "The Bank now ex-
pects the housing sector, both formal and informal, to contribute to
economic growth and public revenues, rather than to be a drain on
limited public resources." Accordingly, the World Bank proposed to
focus on "property rights development" via programs of "land tenure regularization in squatter settlements" (that is, granting formal property title) as well as privatizing "public housing stock,
particularly in formerly centrally planned economies." As far as
the World Bank was concerned, the effectiveness of the tenure
regularization approach had been proven by the example of Lima,
where "the average squatter dwelling had a replacement value of
US$22,000, and the total squatter housing stock had a replacement
value of US$8.3 billion."[47] The appeal of de Soto's message had tran-
scended the veracity (or lack thereof) of his supporting data.

In 1996 President Alberto Fujimori established the Comisión de
Formalización de la Propiedad Informal (COFOPRI, or Commission for the Official Registration of Informal Property) in order to
facilitate the granting of property titles—and not coincidentally, in
a classic clientelistic gesture, to build up a bank of goodwill among
beneficiaries in advance of his campaign for a third term. (Thus,
while de Soto's institute operated under the name of liberty and democracy, to the extent that the titling programs it promoted provid-

ed fuel for clientelism while undercutting the regulatory function of the state, they were in practice antidemocratic.) With COFOPRI, the long-standing limbo of tolerated illegality—where unauthorized urban development was neither policed nor penalized—was replaced by active campaigns to promote the "regularization" of "informal" settlements.

Beginning in 1999 the World Bank supported these initiatives through a loan of $36.12 million. This program was less concerned with improving the quality of housing than with stimulating economic development. Echoing de Soto: "The principal benefit . . . would be economic: more efficient use of the property, thanks to market mechanisms, as a result of the greater legal certainty . . . [which] could result in increased value of the properties, more numerous and frequent transactions in the real estate market, and use of property as a guarantee for obtaining credit." A report on the successes of the program noted that in five years it had registered 1.4 million title deeds, affecting some 5.7 million people, and that a large number of these properties had subsequently changed hands through the formal real estate market. However, the report regretted that the program's impact had been less than anticipated due to a generalized "ignorance of the benefits of credit"—both on the part of lenders apparently wary of former squatters and on the part of the residents themselves, most of whom were "not inclined to use their property to guarantee a loan."[48] For these low-income households, exercising their freedom to borrow brought substantial risks, since falling behind on repayments could mean losing both their home and (often) their only asset.

Furthermore, as a second report observed, the property titles that had been granted covered the land, but not the dwellings themselves. In fact, since "most of these structures are self-built, they do not meet building codes so cannot be registered"—nor could they be mortgaged until they had been "upgraded and regularized." Unable to arrange a mortgage on a substandard dwelling, or on the underlying land alone, "credit to these neighborhoods will be limited to shorter-term, unsecured credits mostly by microfinance institutions."[49] Thus the inability to access the mortgage credit promised by the World Bank program was not due to "ignorance" alone but was a direct consequence of the material reality of the residents' housing as housing—rather than as imagined equity.

Other critiques of titling in practice have pinpointed a further flaw in this approach: the limited value of property title in the absence of a market that would allow new residents to capitalize on their property (that is, a lack of effective demand, due to low residential mobility). Despite these shortcomings, the policy has managed to maintain active support.

On the ground, "regularization" was carried out with little regard for the potential adverse impacts on urban development. By the mid-2000s only the most physically or socially marginal settlements in Lima were yet to be formalized, because the challenges they faced—whether being difficult to access, subject to environmental risk, or impacted by violence—entailed higher administrative costs. Otherwise, with the removal of virtually all planning controls, pausing to assess the suitability of land for development, or the ability of residents to establish a viable community had become an unnecessary obstacle to legalizing—and thus capitalizing—the squatter city. Lima is now reaching the hard limits of urban expansion, and as a result the land invasions have moved further and further out, or onto difficult sites on hillsides or ravines, with steep gradients or poor soil composition. These newer squatter settlements are territorially isolated and, as a consequence, often socially fragmented. In the words of a recent critique: "These residents are not, as in previous decades, courageous pioneers heading off into the desert to *found* new cities. They are families who are *camping* in the city."[50]

The Cost of Unaided Self-Help

In his writings of the 1970s Turner had advocated for alternatives to state-sponsored housing projects via state support for the individual's "freedom to build"; by the mid-1980s the new "freedoms" promised by neoliberalism were in the ascendant, and fostering a free market was seen as paramount, with the promise that individuals granted titles to their self-built residences would be integrated into the market as property owners and credit consumers. However, already by the time of *El otro sendero*'s publication in 1986, some longer-term problems with the improvised, unaided construction of housing were becoming evident to researchers within Peru.

In particular, the survey conducted by Riofrío and Driant, *¿Qué vivienda han construido?*, suggested that the built outcomes of this "freedom" made the argument for a return to closer control, via a recalibration of the role of the state. Riofrío and Driant observed that self-built housing was extremely costly in financial terms in relation to comparable housing stock. Due to the piecemeal nature of construction, materials were purchased in small quantities and thus at greater expense, and inexpert builders were rarely able to devise the most efficient and cost-effective solutions. It was also costly in social terms, drawing the scarce resources of low-income families away from other core needs such as health and education. Further, the processes of consolidation within self-built settlements were protracted and burdensome on residents. Twenty-five years after the passage of Law 13517, they observed that while it was once assumed that difficult living conditions in self-built housing would be temporary, "today, badly equipped bathrooms, overcrowding in the few completed rooms, and the unfinished floors, windows, and doors" reveal that substandard housing had established itself as permanent.[51]

Many problems stemmed from the fact that a large number of dwellings that were conceived as single-family houses now accommodated more than one family—whether as renters (providing the owners with supplementary income), or more often as lodgers (generally members of the extended family, who were expected to cover certain household expenses or contribute their labor to running the house). Improvised modifications to accommodate these additional family groups, made out of immediate necessity without an overall conception of how they would affect the future growth of the house, led to a poor use of space, compromised ventilation and illumination, and little sense of privacy. It had become clear that there were "multiple and very serious limits" to what unaided self-built housing could achieve, and the situation would only worsen over time: "The deterioration of the living conditions in such a dwelling is foreseeable even before it has finished being built." A recent study confirms this prediction. One family, owners of a self-built dwelling established in the south of Lima in 1980, initially lived in two provisional shacks with a total area of 18 square meters. By 2013 the dwelling comprised 450 square meters, over four stories, housing nine people: the matriarch of the original household, four of her children, and two grandchildren. However, most of the dwelling was still unfinished, so despite the additional space, it had only two usable bedrooms, one bathroom, and one kitchen; the family hoped to complete additional bedrooms soon, and eventually subdivide

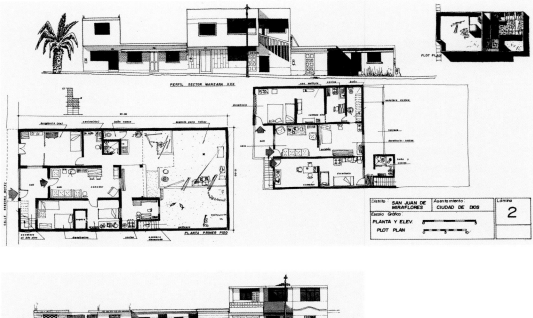

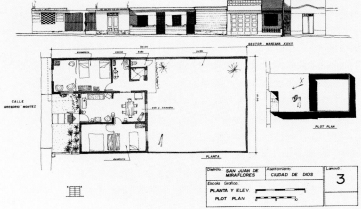

Figures 8.12 (*top*) and 8.13 (*bottom*). CNV, Ciudad de Dios, Lima, 1957. Improvised, self-built extensions to the "growing house" core. (*Top*) Thirteen people, nine of them lodgers, living in five bedrooms (one of them further subdivided by a closet), with space for a workshop and keeping chickens in the backyard. (*Bottom*) Five people living in three bedrooms; as with the house above, the kitchen-bathroom unit is in its original location, top-center on the plan. *Source*: Gustavo Riofrío Benavides and Jean-Claude Driant, *¿Qué vivienda han construido? Nuevos problemas en viejas barriadas* (Lima: CIDAP; IFEA; TAREA, 1987).

the house among the adult children. In another case, a family of twenty-four people—the parents and six adult children along with their families—shared seven bedrooms, with one bathroom and a communal kitchen.[52]

Riofrío and Driant's study primarily focused on examples from unauthorized settlements, but also included the *urbanización popular* Ciudad de Dios established by the Corporación Nacional de la Vivienda in the late 1950s. The authors observed that this planned settlement brought a couple of advantages: it had "developed with great speed in the early years due to the *núcleos básicos*" and the provision of basic services, although construction had subsequently stalled. The layout of the house, with three rooms facing the street (see fig. 2.7), as opposed to the usual barriada layout of two rooms separated by a corridor, resulted in more appropriately sized rooms and less wasted space, since one of the front rooms could "serve as a point of distribution" to the rest of the house in place of a corridor. However, the lack of any postoccupancy technical assistance meant that in the long run these dwellings were just as subject to overcrowding, substandard conditions, and structural problems (for example, one household had unwittingly removed structural elements in the course of executing extensions) (figs. 8.12–8.13).[53]

According to the authors, the general standard of self-help housing would be improved only by the state's commitment to providing meaningful technical assistance—not just for any new state-managed housing projects but also for existing incipient dwellings. Measures could include providing self-builders with construction materials at low cost, or reworking the system of granting construction licenses, utilizing this administrative process to supervise the work under way or to provide relevant skills training. In this way, tactical interventions into ad hoc building practices could begin "to convert the spontaneous into a 'system of *autoconstrucción*.'"[54]

At a moment of crisis in postwar urbanization, as planned processes of urban development were pushed to the point of collapse, aided self-help housing claimed to offer an efficient, effective, and economically viable solution to the provision of mass housing. Initially, architects drawn to this mode of practice were driven by a modernist commitment to housing reform and a concern for rational and orderly urban development; in material terms, the housing they envisaged adhered to minimum standards, or at least strived to achieve them at some point, as in the "growing house" model. For their part, residents focused on the struggle to improve their living conditions were often less concerned with architectural input into the design and construction of their houses than with secure tenure and infrastructure provision. Given this disjunction, Riofrío and Driant's prompt to rethink what aided self-help housing can offer is apposite because while it is clear that residents can benefit from technical assistance, it is equally clear that this assistance must be strategic in order to be effective and affordable.

Earlier iterations of aided self-help housing were often burdened with the high expectations of economic and social development—expectations that provided governments and international agencies with a clear justification to invest in them, but also damned them with unrealistic goals. In addition, projects of this era were predicated upon a paternalistic relationship between the técnico—policymaker, planner, architect—charged with directing the program, and the self-builder whose participation was being directed. Once unburdened from these aspirations and hierarchies, aided self-help housing could be recalibrated to focus more closely on the needs of the participant-builder-owner, with the architect repositioned in a supporting role. The targeted, tactical employment of architectural expertise may entail a shift away from a mode of practice focused on the realization of a preconceived design, and toward an advisory role, providing guidance on better alternatives for the shaping of space and the usage of materials, following the supervised credit model. At the urban level, a revised approach to sites and services may offer a tool to plan urban expansion, allocating land for the highest and best social purpose; in this way, the formal framework of urban development (essential services, roadways, transport) provides a clear structure for the neighborhood, even as its construction remains largely improvised.

The concept of aided self-help housing has been remarkably resilient, mutating to accommodate various ideological conditions: for Turner, it was informed by anarchism, mutual aid, and local action; for liberal policymakers, such as Pedro G. Beltrán and his supporters under the auspices of the Alliance for Progress, it signified the personal initiative and enterprise essential for the nation's economic development; for the Revolutionary Government, it embodied the principles of social mobilization, participation, and collectivity; for IU, if offered the potential to build grassroots democracy and urban citizenship; for the neoliberalism of de Soto, it was the seed of entrepreneurship heralding a spontaneously emerging capitalist economy.

These competing formulations of aided self-help differ fundamentally over which of the various actors involved should take primary responsibility for housing provision—the individual builder/ owner, the local community of an emerging self-built neighborhood, government (whether municipal or national), the global community as framed by international development agencies, or the market extolled by neoliberalism. Likewise, they disagree as to whether the "self" of aided self-help should be singular or plural. Many projects in the 1950s and 1960s had a strong community development component, drawing upon the ideas and practices of mutual aid; in the 1970s this was redeployed to promote revolutionary social mobilization, and after the end of military rule, to foster a revitalized democracy. By contrast, Beltrán and US aid agencies emphasized a decidedly individualistic (and anticommunist) self-builder, and more recently neoliberal self-help has assumed a singular, self-reliant actor—property owner, protocapitalist entrepreneur—primarily concerned with building the exchange value of the house. The current outcome seems to suggest that the vision of self-help as each to his own and "self"-improvement is to be validated, while any mutual aid or community-building aspirations offer little that is productive to capital. Yet these other paths have not been entirely foreclosed, and it is via their divergent trajectories that alternatives to the prevailing model can begin to be imagined.

EPILOGUE

> But keeping always in mind the necessity which created this
> first settlement, I seized a good opportunity, and without any
> disturbance or casualties the inhabitants were all moved near the
> town of San Simón de Villavista, a quarter of a league from Callao.
> There, with the streets and facilities that were given to them, they
> are building houses and *ranchos* [huts] where they can live more
> obedient and civilized lives.
>   — Manuel de Guirior

So wrote the viceroy of Peru in 1780, describing the relocation of a troublesome community to what was, in essence, a bare bones sites-and-services project. He had felt compelled to eradicate Pitipití, a settlement of two thousand people situated near the central plaza of the port city of Callao, near Lima, because its residents were believed to include all manner of criminals, and because its irregular residential fabric made it hard to police. While the trope of the con-quistador, the founder of new cities, was often invoked in narratives of barriada formation to naturalize the *poblador*'s seizure of land and self-built city-making as continuing a tradition of do-it-yourself urban development, this account brings to mind a more vexed tradi-tion—that of urban displacement, of problematic populations being relegated to the urban periphery and obliged to undertake a repeated resettling. Here the conquistador/poblador mythology dissolves, re-vealing less a noble pioneer than a land-hungry economic migrant.

Just visible on the margins of the viceroy's account is a contest over the right to the city in its rawest form; while the details of the incident are specific to this moment, the general outlines of the story would be replicated many times over, only escalating in scale and frequency with the pressures of postwar urbanization. According to the viceroy, the potential for any conflict—any "disturbance or casualties"—was resolved with the population's removal from the established city; once on the site of their new neighborhood, the work of constructing their homes presented a pacification technique in itself. Any disputes that may have occurred between the authorities and displaced residents over relocation, or among groups of residents following relocation, are erased. While it may be tempting to situate such conflicts outside of the realm of planning and designing low-cost housing, they must be seen as constitutive of it, and as integral to any history of these processes.

One of the objectives of this research has been to draw out the connections between the realm of the viceroy and his political descendants, the realm where decisions are made, and the streets of the improvised city, where the impacts of those decisions reverberate over time. The aided self-help housing projects discussed here—like other state-supported mass housing projects—operate at the point of contact between the articulation of political and ideological principles, the negotiation of housing and urban policies, the formation of design proposals, and the implementation of projects on the ground. Accordingly, the approach has been to read the historical material across these intersecting scales, employing a cross-sectional view.

At one end of the scale, high-level principles of politics and economics are debated through three decades of argument and counterargument, considering the rights of citizens to adequate housing and the responsibilities of the state to provide it, as well as the role of state support for housing within larger goals for economic and social development. These principles are seen to frame policies concerning housing and urban development that are devised by social theorists and design professionals at the national or international level, in the process either constraining or facilitating the possibilities for action. In turn, policies are translated into design proposals by experts in the field, setting up a testing ground for constructional, aesthetic, social, or spatial solutions. Finally, proposals are implemented as projects that manage participants' time and resources (financial as well as human) during the construction phase, and that ultimately seek to shape the spaces of their everyday lives, and the behaviors appropriate to the inhabitation of their new improved homes.

This outline of a cascading chain of effects from principles onward is, in practice, confounded by a messier reality. A cross-sectional view reveals the massive slippages from one scale to another, as the theoretical abstract is rendered as an actual object in space. As one instance, while a high-level view may suggest a straightforward political history of housing policy read in clear ideological polarities—Pedro G. Beltrán versus Fernando Belaúnde Terry, John F. C. Turner or Gustavo Riofrío versus Hernando de Soto—at a lower altitude, the narrative becomes more complicated and ambiguous. On the ground, politics operates in a more pragmatic mode, as pobladores negotiate within and around the narrow but real opportunities offered by clientelism, working now within, now against the guidelines set by the authorities for a particular program.

Ultimately, the value of an analysis that works across scales is to emphasize the diversity of actors involved in the production of aided self-help housing. This allows for an extended and more complex time line of architectural production, encompassing not only the policymaker's desk and the design office but also the building site and the gradual accretion of postoccupancy transformations. It also creates a more level playing field to examine the different modes of architectural practice that operate simultaneously here, taking as the starting point of analysis not the pedigree of the designer but the question of how each project functions as a housing solution.

Aided self-help has often been more powerful as an idea than as a practice: as much as it represented a challenge to conventional modernist architecture, it also appealed to its imagination, suggesting the opportunity for a more grounded practice via direct engagement with the work of the construction site, collaboration with the end user, and the promised mutuality of communal building projects. Yet as the necessary resources were rarely forthcoming from sponsoring agencies, low-income residents have been left to carry the burden: when the ratio of "aid" to "self-help" routinely falls short, somehow unlimited reservoirs of the latter are expected to compensate for deficits in the former. Nevertheless, in some cases this work of self-help can become activated as an instrument to foster self-determination. In theoretical terms, this appeared in Turner's advocacy for "autonomy in building environments"; more concretely, it was explored in the "self-management" model promoted by Diego Robles and Carlos Delgado and partially implemented at Villa El Salvador, as well as in Eduardo Figari's efforts at Huaycán to replicate the collaborative dimension of barriada settlement, using shared tenure arrangements as a hyper-local self-management strategy. While much of this narrative may suggest a catalogue of failures at every level—policy and project design, implementation and postoccupancy assistance—these cases demonstrate the value of continuing, creative efforts to rethink the possibilities of aided self-help housing.

GLOSSARY

alquiler-venta	rental-sale
autoconstrucción	self-building
autogestión	self-management
ayuda mutua	mutual aid
ayuda mutua dirigida	managed mutual aid
azotea	flat roof, often used as additional working or living space
barriada	shantytown; squatter settlement
barrio marginal	marginal neighborhood; squatter settlement
casa propia	home of one's own; a proper home
cerco	perimeter wall
empadronamiento	official registration of residents; official register of residents
empleado	white-collar worker
esfuerzo propio	one's own effort
estera	woven bamboo mat
excedentes de barriadas	surplus barriada residents
lotes tizados	surveyed lots outlined with chalk
minga (or mink'a)	collective labor to benefit the community
mutual	savings and loans association
núcleo básico	basic core unit
poblador	settler; resident of a squatter settlement
pueblo joven	young town, or young community; squatter settlement
sala	formal living room for entertaining guests; parlor
técnico	professional with specialized technical knowledge
tugurio	slum, generally degraded rental housing in the inner-urban area
unidad vecinal	neighborhood unit
urbanización popular	"popular" or low-income urban settlement

NOTES

Preface

1. Johan Lagae and Kim De Raedt, editorial, in "Global Experts 'Off Radar,'" special issue, *ABE Journal* 4 (2013): 1–17.

2. Kenny Cupers, *The Social Project: Housing Postwar France* (Minneapolis: University of Minnesota Press, 2014), xii, 135.

3. Janice Perlman, *Favela: Four Decades of Living on the Edge in Rio de Janeiro* (New York: Oxford University Press, 2010); Peter M. Ward, Edith R. Jiménez Huerta, and Mercedes Di Virgilio, eds., *Housing Policy in Latin American Cities: A New Generation of Strategies and Approaches for 2016 UN-Habitat III* (New York: Routledge, 2015); James Holston, "Housing Crises, Right to the City, and Citizenship," in *The Housing Question: Tensions, Continuities, and Contingencies in the Modern City*, ed. Edward Murphy and Najib B. Hourani (London: Routledge, 2013), 191, 193; see also Holston's *Insurgent Citizenship: Disjunctions of Democracy and Modernity in Brazil* (Princeton, NJ: Princeton University Press, 2008).

4. Edward Murphy, *For a Proper Home: Housing Rights in the Margins of Urban Chile, 1960–2010* (Pittsburgh, PA: University of Pittsburgh Press, 2015); Brodwyn Fischer, *A Poverty of Rights: Citizenship and Inequality in Twentieth-Century Rio de Janeiro* (Stanford, CA: Stanford University Press, 2008); Alejandro Velasco, *Barrio Rising: Urban Popular Politics and the Making of Modern Venezuela* (Oakland: University of California Press, 2015).

5. Philippe Boudon, *Lived-In Architecture: Le Corbusier's Pessac Revisited* (Cambridge, MA: MIT Press, 1972), 161; André Studer, qtd in Sascha Roesler, ed., *Habitat Marocain Documents: Dynamics between Formal and Informal Housing* (Zurich: Park, 2015), 26; Viviana d'Auria and Hannah le Roux, "Quand la vie prend le dessus: Les interactions entre l'utopie bâtie et l'habiter," in "Modernisme(s) Approprié(s)?" special issue, *CLARA Architecture/Recherche* 4 (2017): 17, 26.

Introduction

1. Julio Calderón Cockburn, *La ciudad ilegal: Lima en el siglo XX* (Lima: Universidad Nacional Mayor de San Marcos, Fondo Editorial de la Facultad de Ciencias Sociales, 2005), 42.

2. Luis Rivera Santos et al., *Manual para la organización de proyectos piloto de ayuda propia y ayuda mutua en vivienda* (Bogotá: Centro Interamericano de Vivienda, 1953), 17, 18.

3. Eduardo Neira Alva, "Anexo No. 4: El problema de las Urbanizaciones Populares en la ciudad de Arequipa," Feb. 27, 1954, 5, John Francis Charlewood Turner Collection, University of Westminster, London (hereafter JFCT-UW); Eduardo Neira Alva, "El problema de la vivienda en el Perú," *El Arquitecto Peruano* 20, no. 224–25 (Mar.–Apr. 1956): n.p.

4. John F. C. Turner, "The Housing and Planning Problems of Arequipa, Peru: A Case Study with Particular Reference to the Application of Self-Help Methods in Relation to the Squatter Settlements," n.d. [ca. 1959–1960], JFCT-UW; Instituto de la Vivienda (hereafter INVI), *Plan de Vivienda, 1962–1971* (Lima: INVI, 1961), 29, Centro de Documentación e Información, Ministerio de Vivienda, Construcción y Saneamiento, Lima (hereafter CDI-MVCS).

5. For an insightful discussion of this issue, see Alan Gilbert, "The Return of the Slum: Does Language Matter?" *International Journal of Urban and Regional Research* 31, no. 4 (Dec. 2007): 697–713.

6. Corporación Nacional de la Vivienda (hereafter CNV), *Planteamientos generales sobre el problema de la vivienda social* (Lima: CNV, Aug. 1956), 1.

7. For an informative and nuanced exploration of the topic see Ananya Roy and Nezar AlSayyad, eds., *Urban Informality: Transnational Perspectives from the Middle East, Latin America, and South Asia* (Lanham, MD: Lexington, 2004).

8. James Ferguson, "Decomposing Modernity: History and Hierarchy after Development," in *Postcolonial Studies and Beyond*, ed. Ania Loomba et al. (Durham, NC: Duke University Press, 2005), 168.

9. For an introduction to development theories, see H. W. Arndt, *Economic Development: The History of an Idea* (Chicago: University of Chicago Press, 1987); for a critique of their core assumptions, see Arturo Escobar, *Encountering Development: The Making and Unmaking of the Third World* (Princeton, NJ: Princeton University Press, 1995).

10. Francis Violich, "Urban Land Policies: Latin America," in *Urban Land Problems and Policies*, bulletin 7 of *Housing and Town and Country Planning* (1953): 91, 92, 95.

11. Violich, "Urban Land Policies," 94, 93.

12. Harley L. Browning, "Recent Trends in Latin American Urbanization," *Annals of the American Academy of Political and Social Science* 316 (Mar. 1958): 114, 117, 118.

13. José Medina Echavarría and Philip M. Hauser, "Rapporteurs' Report," in *Urbanization in Latin America*, ed. Hauser (New York: UNESCO, 1961), 25–26; "Conclusions of the Seminar," in Hauser, *Urbanization in Latin America*, 77.

14. Jennie Vásquez Solís, "De las barriadas a la selva," *La Prensa*, May 3, 1964; José Luis Leiva Estela, "La Morada, 50 años," *Aucayacu—Peru* (blog), Nov. 6, 2009, https://aucayacu.wordpress.com/2009/11/06/la-morada-50-anos/.

15. "Conclusions of the Seminar," 80, 82; Medina Echavarría and Hauser, "Rapporteurs' Report," 25.

16. José Matos Mar, "Migration and Urbanization: The Barriadas of Lima, an Example of Integration into Urban Life," in Hauser, *Urbanization in Latin America*, 174.

17. Janice E. Perlman, *The Myth of Marginality: Urban Poverty and Politics in Rio de Janeiro* (Berkeley: University of California Press, 1976), 91.

18. Matos Mar, "Migration and Urbanization," 177, 174, 176.

19. Medina Echavarría and Hauser, "Rapporteurs' Report," 60.

20. William Mangin, "Latin American Squatter Settlements: A Problem and a Solution," *Latin American Research Review* 2, no. 3 (Summer 1967): 79, 82, 67.

21. Aníbal Quijano, "Dependencia, cambio social y urbanización en Latinoamérica," *Revista Mexicana de Sociología* 30, no. 3 (July–Sept. 1968): 526.

22. Quijano, "Dependencia," 560.

23. Quijano, "Dependencia," 567.

24. Manuel Castells, "La urbanización dependiente en América Latina," in *Imperialismo y Urbanización en América Latina*, ed. Castells (Barcelona: Gustavo Gili, 1973), 26, 15, emphasis in original.

25. Manuel Castells, *The City and the Grassroots: A Cross-Cultural Theory of Urban Social Movements* (Berkeley: University of California Press, 1983), 178, 179.

26. Castells, *City and the Grassroots*, 190, 211, 212.

27. Ray Bromley, "Informality, de Soto Style: From Concept to Policy," in *Contrapunto: The Informal Sector Debate in Latin America*, ed. Cathy A. Rakowski (Albany: State University of New York Press, 1994), 132, 133.

28. Hernando de Soto with Instituto Libertad y Democracia, *The Other Path: The Invisible Revolution in the Third World*, trans. June Abbott (New York: Harper & Row, 1989), 18.

29. Richard Harris, "Slipping through the Cracks: The Origins of Aided Self-Help Housing, 1918–53," *Housing Studies* 14, no. 3 (1999): 281–309; Susan R. Henderson, "Self-Help Housing in the Weimar Republic: The Work of Ernst May," *Housing Studies* 14, no. 3 (1999): 311–28.

30. Patrick Geddes, *Town Planning towards City Development: A Report to the Durbar of Indore* (Indore: Holkar State Printing Press, 1918), 1:70–71, 2:113–14.

31. Richard Harris, "'A Burp in Church': Jacob L. Crane's Vision of Aided Self-Help Housing," *Planning History Studies* 11, no. 1 (1997): 4; Jacob L. Crane, "Workers' Housing in Puerto Rico," *International Labour Review* 49, no. 6 (June 1944): 628; Richard Harris, "The Silence of the Experts: Aided Self-Help Housing, 1939–1954," *Habitat International* 22, no. 2 (1998): 174 ; David Vega Christie, "Impresiones del Ingeniero Vega Christie a su retorno de los Estados Unidos," *El Arquitecto Peruano* 11, no. 119 (June 1947): n.p.

32. United Nations, Administrative Committee on Co-ordination, "Housing and Town and Country Planning," *Annals of Public and Cooperative Economics* 20, no. 3 (Sept. 1949): 339.

33. United Nations, Department of Social Affairs, *Survey of Problems of Low Cost Rural Housing in Tropical Areas: A Preliminary Report with Special Reference to the Caribbean Area* (New York: UN, Department of Social Affairs, 1950); UN Tropical Housing Mission, *Low Cost Housing in South and South East Asia* (New York: UN, Department of Social Affairs, 1951), 24.

34. "Housing in the Tropics," in *Housing in the Tropics*, bulletin 6 of *Housing and Town and Country Planning* (Jan. 1952): 2, 5; Charles Abrams, Vladimir Bodiansky, and Otto H. Koenigsberger, *Report on Housing in the Gold Coast* (1956); Abrams and Koenigsberger, *A Housing Program for Pakistan with Special Reference to Refugee Rehabilitation* (1957); Abrams and Koenigsberger, *A Housing Program for the Philippine Islands* (1959).

35. See M. Ijlal Muzaffar, "The Periphery Within: Modern Architecture and the Making of the Third World" (PhD diss., MIT, 2007).

36. Roger Maneville, "L'expérience 'Castor' aux Carrières Centrales de Casablanca," *Notes marocaines*, no. 7 (July 1956): 2; Rosemary Wakeman, "Reconstruction and the Self-Help Housing Movement: The French Experience," *Housing Studies* 14, no. 3 (May 1999): 355.

37. "Aleccionador ejemplo para nuestro problema," *La Prensa*, Aug. 7, 1954.

38. Sophie Hochhäusl, "From Vienna to Frankfurt Inside Core-House Type 7: A History of Scarcity through the Modern Kitchen," *Architectural Histories* 1, no. 1 (2013): 1–19.

39. Martin Wagner, *Neue Wege zum Kleinwohnungsbau: Ein Programm der Selbsthilfe* (Berlin: Vorwärts-Buchdruckerei, 1924), qtd in Wagner, *Das wachsende Haus: ein Beitrag zur Lösung der städtischen Wohnungsfrage* (Berlin: Bong, 1932), 4; Wagner, *Das wachsende Haus*, 5.

40. Viviana d'Auria, "In the Laboratory and in the Field: Hybrid Housing Design for the African City in Late-Colonial and Decolonising Ghana (1945–57)," *Journal of Architecture* 19, no. 3 (2014): 331; see also Eckhard Herrel, *Ernst May: Architekt und Stadtplaner in Afrika 1934–1953* (Frankfurt-am-Main: Deutsches Architekturmuseum, 2001), 123–24.

41. William Mangin and John F. C. Turner, "The Barriada Movement," *Progressive Architecture* 49 (May 1968): 154–62.

42. Javier Velarde, interview by Carlos Valladares and Eleodoro Ventocilla, "Para una concepción de la vivienda de interés social," (master's thesis, Universidad Nacional de Ingeniería, Lima, 1973), app. 7, 2:13.

43. Francisco Bullrich, *New Directions in Latin American Architecture* (London: Studio Vista, 1969), 11, 41, 44, 99–100; see also John F. C. Turner, ed., "Dwelling Resources in South America," special issue, *Architectural Design* 33, no. 8 (Aug. 1963).

44. Fernando Salinas, "La arquitectura revolucionaria del Tercer Mundo," *Tricontinental* no. 1 (July–Aug. 1967): 96.

45. Germán Samper, "Responsibilidad social del arquitecto," in *América Latina en su arquitectura*, ed. Roberto Segre (Mexico City: Siglo XXI, 1975), 214; Diego Robles Rivas, "La marginalidad urbana," in Segre, *América Latina*, 103.

46. Roberto Segre, "Comunicación y participación social," in Segre, *América Latina*, 297.

47. Jean-Claude Driant, *Las barriadas de Lima: Historia e interpretación* (Lima: IFEA, Instituto Francés de Estudios Andinos; DESCO, Centro de Estudios y Promoción del Desarrollo, 1991), 214.

1. The Challenge of the Affordable House, 1954–1958

1. Oficina Nacional de Planeamiento y Urbanismo (hereafter ONPU), *Lima: Plan Piloto* (Lima: ONPU, Apr. 1949), 16, Centro de Documentación e Información, Ministerio de Vivienda, Construcción y Saneamiento (hereafter CDI-MVCS); ONPU, *Lima Metropolitana: Algunos aspectos de su expediente urbano y soluciones parciales varias* (Lima: ONPU, 1954), 5, 8.

2. Luis Dorich, "Urbanization and Physical Planning in Peru," in *Urbanization in Latin America*, ed. Philip M. Hauser (New York: UNESCO, 1961), 290.

3. Wiley Ludeña Urquizo, *Tres buenos tigres: Vanguardia y urbanismo en el Perú del siglo XX* (Huancayo: Colegio de Arquitectos del Perú Regional Junín; Ur[b]es, 2004), 131; Fernando Belaúnde Terry, "El barrio unidad: Intento de decentralización urbana," *El Arquitecto Peruano* 8, no. 83 (June 1944): n.p.

4. ONPU, *Construcciones efectuadas por particulares y por entidades estatales en Lima Metropolitana, durante el período 1949–1956* (Lima: ONPU, Mar. 1957), CDI-MVCS; see also ONPU, *Construcciones efectuadas por particulares*

y por entidades estatales en Lima Metropolitana, durante el período 1949–1960 (Lima: ONPU, June 1961).

5. "Conclusiones aprobadas por el VI Congreso Panamericano de Arquitectos," *El Arquitecto Peruano* 11, no. 123 (Oct. 1947): n.p.; Fernando Belaúnde Terry, "El planeamiento en el antiguo y moderno Perú," *El Arquitecto Peruano* 18, no. 202 (May–June 1954): n.p.

6. Fernando Belaúnde Terry, "La incultura de las ciudades," *El Arquitecto Peruano* 17, no. 192–93 (Aug. 1953): n.p.; for Lewis Mumford, see in particular *The Culture of Cities* (New York: Harcourt, Brace and Company, 1938), 465–93. Thanks to Luis Castañeda for sharing his insights on this subject.

7. Belaúnde, "El barrio unidad," n.p.; "¿Qué es una unidad vecinal?" *El Arquitecto Peruano* 9, no. 98 (Sept. 1945): n.p.; Fernando Belaúnde Terry, "La ciudad risueña: Significado y misión de la Unidad Vecinal No. 3," *El Arquitecto Peruano* 13, no. 146 (Sept. 1949): n.p.; Corporación Nacional de la Vivienda (hereafter CNV), *Experiencias relativas de la vivienda de interés social en el Perú* (Lima: CNV, 1958), 22, CDI-MVCS.

8. Cecilia Mendez G., "Incas Sí, Indios No: Notes on Peruvian Creole Nationalism and Its Contemporary Crisis," *Journal of Latin American Studies* 28, no. 1 (Feb. 1996): 223, 222. For a discussion of Belaúnde's efforts to draft the Andean past in service of his political philosophy, see Luis Castañeda, "Pre-Columbian Skins, Developmentalist Souls: The Architect as Politician," in *Latin American Modern Architectures: Ambiguous Territories*, ed. Patricio del Real and Helen Gyger (London: Routledge, 2013), 93–114.

9. Arturo Salazar Larraín, "Introducción," in *Pedro G. Beltrán: Pensamiento y acción*, by Pedro Beltrán, ed. Salazar Larraín (Lima: Instituto de Economía de Libre Mercado, 1994), 7, 25.

10. According to José Matos Mar, Beltrán's afternoon tabloid, *Ultima Hora*, was also involved in promoting this campaign, but *La Prensa* seems to have led the charge. José Matos Mar, *Las barriadas de Lima, 1957* (Lima: Instituto de Estudios Peruanos, 1977), 16.

11. "Casa propia al alcance de todos y no solamente de unos cuantos," *La Prensa*, June 6, 1954.

12. "Casa propia," *La Prensa*, June 6, 1954.

13. Throughout the second half of 1954 the ANP's information bulletin appeared under its own masthead as a regular bimonthly supplement within the pages of *La Prensa*. *Boletín para todo el país de la Asociación Nacional de Propietarios* 1, no. 3, in *La Prensa*, June 12, 1954; *Boletín* 1, no. 6, *La Prensa*, July 11, 1954; *Boletín* 1, no. 10, *La Prensa*, Aug. 15, 1954; *Boletín* 1, no. 13, *La Prensa*, Sept. 5, 1954.

14. Pedro Felipe Cortázar, "San Cosme: Ciudad clandestina a las puertas de Lima," *La Prensa*, July 25, 1954.

15. "La casa propia puede dejar de ser en sueño," *La Prensa*, June 7, 1954; "Un nuevo sistema de construcción baja los costos," *La Prensa*, June 20, 1954; "Aleccionador ejemplo para nuestro problema," *La Prensa*, Aug. 7, 1954.

16. Fernando Belaúnde Terry, "Construyamos hoy para no tener que sanear mañana," *La Prensa*, June 13, 1954. The article was reprinted under a different title as part of *El Arquitecto Peruano*'s coverage of the competition: "Construyamos hoy para no tener que expropiar y demoler mañana," *El Arquitecto Peruano* 18, no. 204–5 (July–Aug. 1954): n.p.

17. "Comentando los proyectos premiados," *El Arquitecto Peruano* 18, no. 204–5 (July–Aug. 1954): n.p.

18. Santiago Agurto Calvo, interview with the author, Oct. 2008.

19. Victor Smirnoff, "25 años de vivienda en el Perú," *El Arquitecto Peruano*, no. 306–8 (Jan.–Mar. 1963): 44-80.

20. "Arq. Augurto expone su plan La casa que crece," *La Prensa*, Aug. 13, 1954; Santiago Agurto Calvo, "¿Por qué debe crecer la casa?" *La Prensa*, Oct. 24, 1954.

21. "Alegando ser dueños de los terrenos pobladores de Matute impiden iniciar construcción de casas de *La Prensa*," *La Prensa*, Oct. 26, 1954.

22. "Sólo tenía un cupón el nuevo propietario," *La Prensa*, Mar. 18, 1955; "Habla Ignacio Rajos Salazar," *La Prensa*, May 21, 1955; "Ganadora espera a su madre para acto de entrega," *La Prensa*, Dec. 26, 1955.

23. See José Matos Mar, "Informe preliminar sobre el estudio de la barriadas marginales," in *Informe sobre la vivienda en el Perú*, by Comisión para la Reforma Agraria y la Vivienda (hereafter CRAV) (Lima: CRAV, 1958), 334–38.

24. Stanley Baruch to Patrick Morris, memorandum, Oct. 2, 1956; Program—Housing FY 1957; General Subject Files, 1955–1959; International Cooperation Administration (hereafter ICA), US Operations Mission to Peru, Office of the Director, 6/30/1955–11/3/1961; Records of US Foreign Assistance Agencies, 1942–1963, Record Group 469; National Archives at College Park, College Park, MD (hereafter RG 469; NACP).

25. Stanley Baruch to Rollin S. Atwood, memorandum, Mar. 13, 1958; Program—Housing FY 1958; General Subject Files, 1955–1959; ICA, US Operations Mission to Peru, Office of the Director, 6/30/1955–11/3/1961; RG 469; NACP. The English translation was published as CRAV, *Report on Housing in Peru* (Mexico City: Regional Technical Aids Center, ICA, 1959).

26. Fernando Belaúnde Terry, *Peru's Own Conquest* (Lima: American Studies, 1965), 169, 97, 103. This publication is an expanded version of Belaúnde's *La conquista del Perú por los Peruanos* (Lima: Ediciones Tawantinsuyo, 1959).

27. Pedro G. Beltrán, "Oficio de remisión," in CRAV, *Informe*, 288, 289.

28. CRAV, *Informe*, 60.

29. "Decreto Supremo sobre las Oficinas de Asistencia Técnica," in CRAV, *Informe*, 331; CRAV, *Informe*, 61.

30. CRAV, *Informe*, 66; "Informe preliminar de la Comisión, Agosto de 1956," in CRAV, *Informe*, 298.

31. Adolfo Córdova Valdivia, *La vivienda en el Perú: Estado actual y evaluación de las necesidades* (Lima: CRAV, 1958), 144.

32. Córdova, *La vivienda*, 13, 148, 13.

33. ONPU, *Construcciones efectuadas por particulares y por entidades estatales en Lima Metropolitana, durante el período 1949–1956*, 5.

34. Centro Interamericano de Vivienda (hereafter CINVA), *Unidad Vecinal No. 3, Lima-Callao, de la Corporación Nacional de Vivienda del Perú* (Bogotá: CINVA, 1958), 104–5; Carlos Delgado, *La Unidad Vecinal No. 3 y Matute: Estudio social comparativo referido a problemas de planeamiento físico* (Lima: Oficina de Planificación Sectorial de Vivienda y Equipamiento Urbano, July 1966), 90.

2. The Barriada under the Microscope, 1955–1957

1. David Collier, *Squatters and Oligarchs: Authoritarian Rule and Policy Change in Peru* (Baltimore, MD: Johns Hopkins University Press, 1976); Eric Hobsbawm, "Peasant Land Occupations," *Past and Present* 62 (Feb. 1974): 121.

2. Brodwyn Fischer, *A Poverty of Rights: Citizenship and Inequality in Twentieth-Century Rio de Janeiro* (Stanford, CA: Stanford University Press, 2008), 9, 254.

3. Julio Calderón Cockburn, *La ciudad ilegal: Lima en el siglo XX* (Lima: Universidad Nacional Mayor de San Marcos, 2005), 97.

4. The following account has been assembled from articles published in *La Prensa* between December 28, 1954, and January 23, 1955.

5. "El Presidente de la República recibió a dirigentes de tres Asociaciones de Pobladores," *El Comercio*, Jan. 2, 1955, afternoon ed.

6. Fernando Belaúnde Terry, "Construyamos hoy para no tener que sanear mañana," *La Prensa*, June 13, 1954.

7. Carlos Iván Degregori and Pablo Sandoval, "Peru: From Otherness to a Shared Diversity," in *A Companion to Latin American Anthropology*, ed. Deborah Poole (Malden, MA: Blackwell, 2008), 156.

8. José Matos Mar, "Una experiencia de mejoramiento de comunidades indígenas en el Perú: El Proyecto Huarochirí," *Boletín Trimestral: Centro Regional de Educación Fundamental para la América Latina* 6, no. 3 (July 1954): 3, 12.

9. Sebastián Salazar Bondy, "Huarochirí: Ensayo actual de etnología aplicada," *La Prensa*, May 15, 1955.

10. See James Ferguson, "Anthropology and Its Evil Twin: 'Development' in the Constitution of a Discipline," in *International Development and the Social Sciences: Essays on the History and Politics of Knowledge*, ed. Frederick Cooper and Randall M. Packard (Berkeley: University of California Press, 1997), 150–75.

11. José Matos Mar, *Estudio de las barriadas limeñas: Informe presentado a Naciones Unidas en diciembre de 1955* (Lima: Instituto de Estudios Peruanos, 1966), 82. Matos Mar published much of this research in a revised form in 1977, with the addition of case histories and detailed maps of individual barriadas, as well as biographies of residents to complement the demographic data. The later publication does not include prescriptive recommendations for intervention in barriadas, and views them not as an aberrant phenomenon but as the all-but-inevitable expression of structural inequality in Peruvian society. It also attributes greater agency to residents themselves in improving their situation rather than insisting that the state must design and direct any solutions. See Matos Mar, *Las barriadas de Lima, 1957* (Lima: Instituto de Estudios Peruanos, 1977).

12. Matos Mar, *Estudio*, 15, 61, 62.

13. Matos Mar, *Estudio*, 49.

14. Matos Mar, *Estudio*, 63.

15. Luis Valcárcel, "Los ayllus," in *Tempestad en los Andes* (Lima: Populibros Peruanos, 1925), 37, qtd in Marisol de la Cadena, "Silent Racism and Intellectual Superiority in Peru," *Bulletin of Latin American Research* 17, no. 2 (1998): 149; Ángel Rama, *The Lettered City*, trans. John Charles Chasteen (Durham, NC: Duke University Press, 1996), 11.

16. Fondo Nacional de Salud y Bienestar Social (hereafter FNSBS), *La asistencia técnica a la vivienda y el problema de barriadas marginales* (Lima: FNSBS, 1958), 53; Víctor Andrés Belaúnde, *La realidad nacional* (Lima: Universitaria,

1964), 96, qtd in de la Cadena, "Silent Racism," 151; Baltazar Caravedo, Humberto Rotondo, and Javier Mariátegui, "Prefacio," in *Estudios de psiquiatría social en el Perú* (Lima: Ediciones del Sol, 1963), n.p.

17. "Reglamento de Urbanizaciones y Subdivisión de Tierras: Decreto Supremo No. 2," in Wiley Ludeña Urquizo, *Lima: Historia y urbanismo en cifras, 1821–1970* (Lima: Ministerio de Vivienda, Construcción y Saneamiento, 2004), 425, 428.

18. "Urbanización Popular será pronto realidad en la Ciudad de Dios," *La Prensa*, Jan. 9, 1955. Neira was head of the Departamento de Urbanismo at the Ministerio de Fomento y Obras Públicas, the agency that was given primary responsibility for dealing with the situation on the ground at Ciudad de Dios; the Ministerio de Fomento then asked ONPU to draw up an urban plan.

19. Matos Mar, *Estudio*, 47.

20. Corporación Nacional de la Vivienda (hereafter CNV), *Experiencias relativas de la vivienda de interés social en el Perú* (Lima: CNV, 1958), 76, Centro de Documentación e Información, Ministerio de Vivienda, Construcción y Saneamiento, Lima (hereafter CDI-MVCS); John F. C. Turner, "The Housing and Planning Problems of Arequipa, Peru: A Case Study with Particular Reference to the Application of Self-Help Methods in Relation to the Squatter Settlements," n.d. [ca. 1959–1960], 24, John Francis Charlewood Turner Collection, University of Westminster, London (hereafter JFCT-UW); "Construcción en masa ha permitido hacer 1,400 casas a un costo de 11 y 35 mil soles," *La Prensa*, Dec. 17, 1959.

21. Matos Mar, *Estudio*, 66; "No fueron desalojdos al cumplirse el plazo," *La Prensa*, Jan. 4, 1955.

22. Demetrio Túpac Yupanqui, "La Ciudad de Dios: Caldera del Diablo—Pobladores se niegan a pagar alquileres," *La Prensa*, Sept. 20, 1963.

23. Matos Mar, *Estudio*, 66; Matos Mar, *Las barriadas de Lima, 1957*, 16; Collier, *Squatters and Oligarchs*, 70.

24. Matos Mar, *Estudio*, 65, 66.

25. Typescripts of newspaper articles: "Habra reunión de urbanizadores en diario *El Deber* el proximo sabado 14," *El Deber*, Sept. 11, 1957; "Urbanizadores exigen labor a Oficina de Ayuda Técnica," *El Pueblo*, Sept. 9, 1957, JFCT-UW.

3. A Profession in Development, 1957–1960

1. John F. C. Turner, "Lima Barriadas Today," *Architectural Design* 33, no. 8 (Aug. 1963): 376.

2. John F. C. Turner, "The Scope of the Problem," *Architectural Design* 33, no. 8 (Aug. 1963): 363; John F. C. Turner, *Housing by People: Towards Autonomy in Building Environments*, 1st American ed. (New York: Pantheon, 1977), 3.

3. John F. C. Turner, interview with the author, June 2007, transcript, Oral History Research Office, Columbia University, New York.

4. See Peter Kropotkin, *Mutual Aid, A Factor of Evolution* (New York: McClure Phillips, 1903); Herbert Read, "The Paradox of Anarchism" (1941), in *A Coat of Many Colours: Essays* (London: Routledge & Paul, 1956), 63.

5. John F. C. Turner, and W. P. Keatinge-Clay, "The Geddes Diagrams: The Contribution of the Diagrams towards a Synthetic Form of Thought," in *Cities in Evolution*, by Patrick Geddes, 2nd ed., ed. Jaqueline Tyrwhitt (London: Williams & Norgate, 1949), app. 1, pt. 2, 200–5.

6. John F. C. Turner, "Architectural Education: The Intellectual for the Creative

Life," Mar. 1948, John Francis Charlewood Turner Collection, University of Westminster, London (hereafter JFCT-UW); Turner, "A Framework for Mapping Activity with a Faceted Index," Apr. 25, 2007, JFCT-UW. The 2007 manuscript continues Turner's interest in devising a workable adaptation of the Geddes diagram, developed in part through a resumed correspondence with AA colleague Bruce Martin.

7. John F. C. Turner, "The Work of Patrick Geddes," *Freedom: Anarchist Fortnightly*, Jan. 10, 1948.

8. "Architecture," *Plan* 6 (1949): 18, 27. *Plan* was the journal of the Architectural Students Association, a group affiliated with the National Union of Students, and was based at various architecture schools over the course of its life.

9. "Building," *Plan* 6 (1949): 19, 20, 21.

10. John F. C. Turner, "The Reeducation of a Professional," in *Freedom to Build: Dweller Control of the Housing Process*, ed. Turner and Robert Fichter (New York: Macmillan, 1972), 124; Turner, interview with the author, 2007.

11. See "Expresión de principios de la Agrupación Espacio," *El Arquitecto Peruano* 11, no. 119 (June 1947): n.p.

12. Eduardo Neira Alva, "Anexo No. 4: El problema de las Urbanizaciones Populares en la ciudad de Arequipa," Feb. 27, 1954, 3, JFCT-UW.

13. Neira, "Anexo No. 4," 5, JFCT-UW; Eduardo Neira Alva and José Dulanto Pinillos, "Informe acerca de las Urbanizaciones Populares de Arequipa," May 5, 1954, 7, JFCT-UW.

14. See Eduardo Neira Alva, *La transformación del habitat humano*, Colección Espacio y Forma 9 (Caracas: Facultad de Arquitectura y Urbanismo, Universidad Central de Venezuela, 1961), n.p., Centro de Documentación e Información, Ministerio de Vivienda, Construcción y Saneamiento, Lima (hereafter CDI-MVCS).

15. Eduardo Neira Alva, "El problema de la vivienda en el Perú," *El Arquitecto Peruano* 20, no. 224–225 (Mar. –Apr. 1956): n.p.; Eduardo Neira Alva, "Ahorro de Esfuerzo y Capital," typescript of article published in *La Prensa*, Apr. 7, 1957, JFCT-UW.

16. John F. C. Turner, "Materials & Elements: Systems & Results," n.d. [ca. 1957], JFCT-UW.

17. John F. C. Turner, "Inst[ituto] de Urb[anismo] lecture," May 29, 1957, JFCT-UW.

18. John F. C. Turner, "The Valley Section," n.d. [ca. 1957], JFCT-UW.

19. Neira and Dulanto Pinillos, "Informe acerca de las Urbanizaciones Populares de Arequipa," 7.

20. John F. C. Turner, "The Housing and Planning Problems of Arequipa, Peru: A Case Study with Particular Reference to the Application of Self-Help Methods in Relation to the Squatter Settlements," n.d. [ca. 1959–1960], 27, JFCT-UW.

21. "La Asociación de Urbanizaciones Populares de Arequipa (AUPA) Plantea sus necesidades," Sept. 17, 1956, JFCT-UW; "Informe preliminar de la Comisión, Agosto de 1956," in Comisión para la Reforma Agraria y la Vivienda (hereafter CRAV), *Informe sobre la vivienda en el Perú* (Lima: CRAV, 1958), 298.

22. Turner, "Housing and Planning Problems," 12.

23. Turner, "Housing and Planning Problems," 28.

24. John F. C. Turner, "Confidential Report on the technical assistance work of the Ministerio de Fomento, Departamento de Inspección de Urbanizaciones y Obras Públicas, Arequipa, from July to August 1957," n.d. [ca. Sept. 1957], 7, 3, JFCT-UW.

25. See Patrick Geddes, "Conservative Surgery," in *Patrick Geddes in India*, by Geddes, ed. Jaqueline Tyrwhitt (London: L. Humphries, 1947), 40–59.

26. Blanca Gálvez R. and Rosa Bustamante, "Un ensayo de trabajo experimental en la urbanización Mariano Melgar," Oct. 1957, JFCT-UW.

27. Turner, "Confidential Report," 11.

28. Turner, "Confidential Report," 7, 8.

29. John F. C. Turner, "Urbanización Miramar, Mollendo: Report on Revised Scheme," June 1957, JFCT-UW.

30. Typescript of articles, *El Deber*, Sept. 4 and Sept. 7, 1957, *El Pueblo*, Sept. 9, 1957, JFCT-UW; Turner, interview with the author, 2007.

31. Typescript of articles, *El Deber*, Sept. 16 and Sept. 18, 1957, JFCT-UW.

32. John F. C. Turner for OATA, "Las Urbanizaciones Populares de Arequipa: Estudio de los Origenes, Estado Actual y Propuestas para la solución del problema," Nov. 1957, JFCT-UW.

33. This quintessentially Geddesian term appears in one of the documents related to this program: John F. C. Turner, "Sumario de la Programa," n.d. [ca. 1957], JFCT-UW.

34. Luis Felipe Calle and John F. C. Turner, "Informe confidencial presentado por la Oficina de Asistencia Técnica de Arequipa relativo al problema de la urbanizaciones populares," Sept. 2, 1957, JFCT-UW; John F. C. Turner, "The Housing Problem in the City and Districts of Arequipa, Peru," n.d. [ca. July 1958], JFCT-UW.

35. John F. C. Turner to Eduardo Neira Alva, Sept. 7, 1957, JFCT-UW.

36. John F. C. Turner to Eduardo Neira Alva, Sept. 16, 1957, JFCT-UW.

37. Turner, "Housing and Planning Problems," 35, 39.

38. Crooke went on to manage a technical assistance program for self-build schools in the Peruvian highlands in 1959–1960. See Patrick Crooke and Carlo Doglio, "Scuole e comunità," *Comunità: Rivista mensile di cultura e informazione fondata da Adriano Olivetti* 14, no. 84 (1960): 28–57.

39. Turner, "Housing and Planning Problems," 38.

40. John F. C. Turner, "Memorandum on the Ciudad Mi Trabajo," n.d. [ca. Jan.–Feb. 1958], JFCT-UW; OATA, "Informe sobre Ciudad Mi Trabajo ubicada en Lara," June 26, 1958, JFCT-UW; Turner, "Housing Problem in the City and Districts of Arequipa."

41. "2,000 arequipeños abandonados," *El Pueblo*, Oct. 16, 1958; Raúl Becerra to John F. C. Turner, Oct. 1960, JFCT-UW.

42. "Aplicarán Plan de Mutual Mi Trabajo," *La Prensa*, July 9, 1961.

43. AmEmbassy/Lima to TOPEC-5, telegram, Sept. 29, 1961, and Frank Mankiewicz to William Killea, memorandum, Jan. 18, 1962; Central Subject Files, 1960–1962; USAID Mission to Peru, Executive Office, 11/4/1961–10/1/1979; Records of the Agency for International Development, 1948–2003, Record Group 286; National Archives at College Park, College Park, MD (hereafter RG 286; NACP).

44. Turner, "Housing and Planning Problems," 49.

45. Turner, "Housing and Planning Problems," 54.

46. "Vivienda por todos y para todos," *La Prensa*, Oct. 4, 1959, supplement; Turner, "Housing and Planning Problems," 43.

47. Turner, "Housing and Planning Problems," 42, 47; see also Luis Rivera Santos et al., *Manual para la organización de proyectos piloto de ayuda propia y ayuda mutua en vivienda* (Bogotá: Centro Interamericano de Vivienda, Servicio de Intercambio Científico, 1953).

48. Turner, *Housing by People*, 135; Turner, "Reeducation of a Professional," 138; Turner, "Housing and Planning Problems," 17–18.

49. Turner, "Housing and Planning Problems," 11–12, 57, 58.

50. Turner, "Housing and Planning Problems," 61, 62; Turner, interview with the author, June 2007; Ernest Weissmann to Manuel Prado, memorandum, Dec. 9, 1958, JFCT-UW.

51. Federico Mevius Andersen, letter to John F. C. Turner, n.d. [ca. June-July 1959], JFCT-UW; Junta de Rehabilitación y Desarrollo de Arequipa (hereafter JRDA), *Informe 10 años* (Arequipa: JRDA, Sept. 1968), 28, CDI-MVCS.

52. Corporación Nacional de la Vivienda (hereafter CNV), *Experiencias relativas de la vivienda de interés social en el Perú* (Lima: CNV, 1958), 88, CDI-MVCS.

53. Eduardo Soler and John F. C. Turner, "Informe sobre la vivienda urbana en Paramonga: 1959–1960," 1960, 62, 61, JFCT-UW.

54. Turner, "Housing and Planning Problems," 54; Soler and Turner, "Informe sobre la vivienda," 65, 66.

55. Diego Robles Rivas, interview with the author, Oct. 28, 2008.

56. Soler and Turner, "Informe sobre la vivienda," 68.

57. "En la primera etapa del proyecto, 60 familias de Paramonga tendrán casa propia," *Paramonga: Organo Informativo de Paramonga*, 3, no. 13 (1961), JFCT-UW; Howard Wenzel, status report, Dec. 1, 1962, FF15, box 67, MS 94-09, Jean and Willard Garvey World Homes Collection, Wichita State University Libraries, Special Collections and University Archives, Wichita, KS (hereafter WHC-WSUL).

58. Howard Wenzel, status report, n.d., received Nov. 19, 1962, FF15, box 67, MS 94-09, WHC-WSUL.

59. T. Bachmann and W. H. Meier, "Confidential Report on Investigation of Defalcation," n.d. [ca. Sept. 1962], 4–5, JFCT-UW; Barbara Goldstein, "The Originators: John F. Charlewood Turner," *Architectural Design* 45, no. 9 (Sept. 1975): 525.

60. John F. C. Turner, "Consideraciones generales acerca del desarrollo de sistemas de diseño para casas económicas," and "Bases para un sistema de diseño (distribución) de casas economicas," Mar. 1963, JFCT-UW.

61. John F. C. Turner, "Criteria for the Development of Planning, Housing, and Construction Standards and for the Specifications of the Pilot Projects," Oct. 7, 1965, 2, JFCT-UW.

62. Patrick Crooke, "Village Artisan's Self-Built House," *Architectural Design* 33, no. 8 (Aug. 1963): 361.

63. Eduardo Neira Alva, "Un interesante ejemplo de arquitectura espontanea," *El Arquitecto Peruano* no. 246–248 (Jan.–Mar. 1958): n.p.; Neira, "Ahorro de Esfuerzo y Capital."

64. Turner, "Confidential Report," 7; Turner, "Housing and Planning Problems," 58.

65. John F. C. Turner, "Uncontrolled Urban Settlement: Problems and Policies," *International Social Development Review* 1 (1968): 112, 127, 128. In a 1964 article, Turner attributed the "working with/working for" distinction to Carola Ravell, the director of community development at the Venezuelan planning agency CORDIPLAN: John F. C. Turner, "La autoconstrucción," *Desarrollo Economico: Revista para el profesional del desarrollo* 1, no. 3 (1964): 34.

66. Turner, "Reeducation of a Professional," 144.

67. Turner, interview with the author, July 11, 2008.

68. John F. C. Turner, "Housing as a Verb," in Turner and Fichter, *Freedom to Build*, 158.

4. Mediating Informality, 1961–1963

1. Fondo Nacional de Salud y Bienestar Social (hereafter FNSBS), *La asistencia técnica a la vivienda y el problema de barriadas marginales* (Lima: FNSBS, 1958), 32, 46.

2. FNSBS, *La asistencia técnica*, 50; John F. C. Turner to César Solis, Dec. 5, 1958, John Francis Charlewood Turner Collection, University of Westminster, London (hereafter JFCT-UW).

3. "Con el aporte de varias familias y con la ayuda estatal se lleva adelante la proyectada Urbanización Cáceres," *La Prensa*, Dec. 31, 1959.

4. [FNSBS], "Contrato de Asistencia Técnica entre la Division de Asistencia Técnica a la Vivienda del Fondo Nacional de Salud y Bienestar Social y la Asociación Urbanizadora Andrés A. Cáceres," July 12, 1959, JFCT-UW.

5. [César Solis], memorandum, "La Ciudad de Chimbote," n.d. [ca. Jan. 1958], JFCT-UW.

6. "Construirán 1,412 casas en Chimbote," *La Prensa*, October 17, 1960; "Unas 300 casas por ayuda mutua fueron construídas en Chimbote," *La Prensa*, June 5, 1961; [FNSBS], "Contrato Provisional de adjucación de lotes en la Urbanización '21 de Abril' de Chimbote," n.d. [ca. October 1958], JFCT-UW.

7. FNSBS, *Anteproyecto de construcción de viviendas por ayuda mutua en la República* (Lima: FNSBS, Oct. 1960), 14, 15, 12, Centro de Documentación e Información, Ministerio de Vivienda, Construcción y Saneamiento, Lima (hereafter CDI-MVCS).

8. FNSBS, *Anteproyecto de construcción*, 11.

9. FNSBS, *La asistencia técnica*, 8, 10, 11.

10. El Comité de Defensa de las Urbanizaciones Populares, "El Proyecto de Ley sobre Barriadas" (advertisement), *La Prensa*, Jan. 17, 1961.

11. "Discurso pronunciado por el Presidente de la República, Dr. Manuel Prado," in Corporación Nacional de la Vivienda (hereafter CNV), *Ley de Remodelación, Saneamiento y Legalización de los barrios marginales* (Lima: CNV, 1961), 8, CDI-MVCS.

12. Manuel Valega, interview by Carlos Valladares and Eleodoro Ventocilla, "Para una concepción de la vivienda de interés social" (thesis, Universidad Nacional de Ingeniería, Lima, 1973), app. 6, 2:2.

13. "Reglamento de la Ley No. 13517," July 21, 1961, in *Lima: Historia y urbanismo en cifras, 1821–1970*, ed. Wiley Ludeña Urquizo (Lima: Ministerio de Vivienda, Construcción y Saneamiento, 2004), 436.

14. "Programa y metodo de trabajo de la Comisión en relación a vivienda," in Comisión para la Reforma Agraria y la Vivienda (hereafter CRAV), *Informe sobre la vivienda en el Perú* (Lima: CRAV, 1958), 307; FNSBS, *La asistencia técnica*, 51.

15. See CNV and Oliverio Portugal Alvarez, *Memoria del Departamento de Barrios Marginales, 1961–1962* (Lima: CNV, 1962).

16. Junta Nacional de la Vivienda (hereafter JNV), *Datos estadisticos de los Barrios Marginales de Lima: Distrito del Rímac*, vol. 1 (Lima: JNV, Dec. 1963), 114.

17. CNV and Mario Bernuy Ledesma, *Plan Río Rímac: Memoria Descriptiva* (Lima: CNV, Feb. 1962), 5, CDI-MVCS.

18. CNV and Bernuy Ledesma, *Plan Río Rímac*, 3.

19. CNV and Bernuy Ledesma, *Plan Río Rímac*, 12.

20. "Conclusiones aprobadas por el VI Congreso Panamericano de Arquitectos," *El Arquitecto Peruano* 11, no. 123 (Oct. 1947): n.p.

21. CNV and Alfredo Pérez Gonzáles, *Plan Río Rímac—Remodelación de la Zona 6* (Lima: CNV, Sept. 1962), CDI-MVCS.

22. "Esfuerzo propio o ayuda mutua para tener casa propia: San Juan, Ciudad que será edificada por sus habitantes," *La Prensa*, Jan. 3, 1962; "Se concretan los planes de vivienda," *La Prensa*, June 9, 1960.

23. "Corp. de la Vivienda hará enorme urbanización," *La Prensa*, Mar. 26, 1960.

24. Victor Smirnoff, interview by Valladares and Ventocilla, "Para una concepción," app. 4, 2:12–13.

25. Allan G. Austin and Sherman Lewis, *Urban Government for Metropolitan Lima* (New York: Praeger, 1970), 147.

26. "Dos mil casas de 'emergencia' hace la CNV de caña y estera," *La Prensa*, Feb. 24, 1962.

27. Ministerio de Vivienda y Construcción (hereafter MVC), "Evaluación técnica y social del programa 'Alojamiento H' en la Urbanización Valdiviezo," n.d. [ca. 1980–1981], n.p., CDI-MVCS.

28. MVC, "Plan 'U': Memoria Descriptiva," Mar. 1981, in MVC, "Evaluación técnica."

29. John F. C. Turner, "Minimal Government-Aided Settlements," *Architectural Design* 33, no. 8 (Aug. 1963): 379, 380.

30. Ministerio de Vivienda (hereafter MV), *Evaluación integral del proyecto de vivienda Caja de Agua-Chacarilla de Otero: Programa de núcleos básicos o viviendas semi-acabadas* (Lima: MV, 1970), 162.

31. See Helen Gyger, "Urbanización Caja de Agua, Lima," in *Woningbouw wereldwijd: betaalbare woningen voor groeiende steden* [*Global Housing: Affordable Dwellings for Growing Cities*], *DASH* (*Delft Architectural Studies on Housing*) 12–13, ed. Frederique van Andel (Rotterdam: NAi, 2015), 222–31.

32. John F. C. Turner, "Three Barriadas in Lima, Peru, and a Tentative Typology" (paper, Comparative Urban Settlements Seminar, Syracuse University, Oct. 1968), 16, 20, JFCT-UW.

33. CNV and Alfredo Pérez Gonzáles, *Plan Carabayllo—Anteproyecto de Urbanización Popular de la Pampa De Cueva: Memoria descriptiva* (Lima: CNV, Jan. 1962), 1, 2, CDI-MVCS.

34. "A Report on a Visit to the One-Month Old Squatter Settlement of Pampa del Ermitaño," attachment to USAID/Lima to AID/W, memorandum, "Housing and Urban Development Div. Semi-annual Summary Report—Jan. 1 to June 30, 1962," Aug. 17, 1962; Housing and Urban Development FY63; Central Subject Files, 1962–1968; USAID Mission to Peru, Executive Office, 11/4/1961–10/1/1979; Records of the Agency for International Development, 1948–2003, Record Group 286; National Archives at College Park, College Park, MD (hereafter RG 286; NACP).

35. "Report on a Visit," Aug. 17, 1962.

36. John F. C. Turner, "Lima Barriadas Today," *Architectural Design* 33, no. 8 (Aug. 1963): 376; John F. C. Turner, "Barriada Integration and Development," *Architectural Design* 33, no. 8 (Aug. 1963): 377.

37. CNV and Mario Bernuy Ledesma, *Plan Carabayllo—Proyecto de Urban-*

ización Popular de El Ermitaño: Memoria Descriptiva (Lima: CNV, Sept. 1962), 6, CDI-MVCS.

38. Horacio Caminos et al., *Urban Dwelling Environments: An Elementary Survey of Settlements for the Study of Design Determinants* (Cambridge, MA: MIT Press, 1969), 146.

39. Turner, "Minimal Government-Aided Settlements," 379; John F. C. Turner, "Popular Housing Policies and Projects in Peru" (lecture, Athens Centre of Ekistics, Athens, Greece, Nov. 1964), JFCT-UW.

40. Turner, "Minimal Government-Aided Settlements," 379.

41. JNV, "Plan trienal de inversiones en viviendas nuevas en Lima metropolitana," July 5, 1963, 7, 18, 14, JFCT-UW.

42. "JNV gestiona una expropiación para edificar 70 mil viviendas," *La Prensa*, June 7, 1963; Julio Calderón Cockburn, *La ciudad ilegal: Lima en el siglo XX* (Lima: Universidad Nacional Mayor de San Marcos, 2005), 66, 134.

43. JNV, "Plan trienal de inversiones," 21, 23. The administration fee was set at 15 percent "in accordance with the experience of INVI in 1962"—presumably a reference to the Perú-BID Plan Bienal 1962–1963 aided self-help program.

44. Turner, "Barriada Integration and Development," 377.

5. World Investments, Productive Homes, 1961–1967

1. Jose Figueres, former President of Costa Rica, qtd in introduction, Chase Manhattan Bank, *Housing in Latin America* (New York: Chase Manhattan Bank, 1962), n.p.; Chase Manhattan Bank, "Self-Help Housing," *Housing in Latin America*; Chase Manhattan Bank, introduction, *Housing in Latin America*.

2. Teodoro Moscoso, qtd in "Self-Help Housing," in Chase Manhattan Bank, *Housing in Latin America*; T. Graydon Upton, qtd in "The Role of US Business," in Chase Manhattan Bank, *Housing in Latin America*.

3. These included loans from Public Law 480 proceeds, the Development Loan Fund, and the Social Progress Trust Fund of the IDB, as well as a housing guaranty program managed by USAID. See Timothy Atkeson, "Aid for Latin American Housing," *George Washington Law Review* 31, no. 3 (Mar. 1963): 547–86.

4. Raymond P. Harold and Joseph T. Benedict, *Report on Savings and Loan Associations in Peru*, presented to David E. Bell of USAID, Mar. 29, 1963, p. 9, FF6, box 58, MS 94-09, Jean and Willard Garvey World Homes Collection, Wichita State University Libraries, Special Collections and University Archives, Wichita, KS (hereafter WHC-WSUL).

5. Father Daniel McLellan, "Puno Parish Credit Union," May 25, 1957, Maryknoll Mission Archives, Maryknoll, NY (hereafter MMA).

6. Father Daniel McLellan, "Memoria para la Asamblea Episcopal Peruana sobre el desarrollo de Cooperativas de Crédito Parroquiales en el año 1960," n.d. [ca. 1961], MMA; Lester Velie, "The Money Miracle of Father Dan," *Reader's Digest*, Apr. 1961; Joyce Donahue, "Father Dan's Big Adventure," *Saturday Evening Post*, July 8, 1961; "Father Dan the Money Man," *Time*, Apr. 22, 1966.

7. Barbara Goldstein, "The Originators: John F. Charlewood Turner," *Architectural Design* 45, no. 9 (Sept. 1975): 525; Donahue, "Father Dan's Big Adventure"; McLellan, "Puno Parish Credit Union."

8. Germán Tito Gutiérrez, "Verdad y mentira de las Mutuales de Vivienda (4)," *El Comercio*, Oct. 30, 1960, supplement; Sebastián Salazar Bondy, "El laberinto y

el hilo: la otra demogogia," *El Comercio*, Nov. 28, 1960, morning ed.; "La vivienda y la demagogia," *El Comercio*, Nov. 29, 1960, morning ed.

9. "Cooperativas y mutuales: Solución cristiana," *La Prensa*, Feb. 22, 1961; "El ahorro que a Usted le conviene," *Vivienda* 2, no. 23 (Nov. 1966): 9; "Casas de interés social con acabados de lujo se entregaron en Ingeniería," *Vivienda* 4, no. 45 (Sept. 1968): 7.

10. "Luz para el Pasaje Defensa," *Vivienda* 2, no. 22 (Oct. 1966): 7; Sean M. Elliott, *Financing Latin American Housing: Domestic Savings Mobilization and US Assistance Policy* (New York: F.A. Praeger, 1968), 86.

11. Willard Garvey, "This is a chronology of low-cost private housing as a Builders, Inc. concept," n.d. [ca. Mar. 1960], FF20, box 7, MS 94-09, WHC-WSUL.

12. Jerry Siebenmark, "Willard Garvey Has Built Legacy as Wichita Developer, Government Critic," *Wichita Business Journal*, Mar. 30, 2001, 4.

13. [Willard Garvey, Ronald Meredith, et al.], "Every Man a Capitalist," June 19, 1958, FF20, box 7, MS 94-09, WHC-WSUL.

14. Willard Garvey, "Talk presented by William Graham, Robert Martin, and Willard Garvey to the Committee on Foreign Economic Practices, Aug. 28, 1958," FF20, box 7, MS 94-09, WHC-WSUL; Willard W. Cochrane, "Public Law 480 and Related Programs," *Annals of the American Academy of Political and Social Science* 331 (Sept. 1960): 15.

15. "Garvey's Gravy," *Time*, June 8, 1959.

16. Willard Garvey to Pedro G. Beltrán, Mar. 19, 1959, FF14, box 58, MS 94-09, WHC-WSUL; Howard Wenzel (citing "Mr Stanley Baruch of the ICA, a good friend") to Pedro G. Beltrán, Nov. 18, 1959, FF13, box 58, MS 94-09, WHC-WSUL; Milton Eisenhower, *The Wine is Bitter: The United States and Latin America* (Garden City, NJ: Doubleday, 1963), 205–6.

17. Ralph Wulz, Treasurer of the University of Wichita, to Howard Wenzel, Jan. 6, 1960, FF29, box 58, MS 94-09, WHC-WSUL; Howard Wenzel to Floyd M. Baird, Feb. 9, 1960, FF29, box 58, MS 94-09, WHC-WSUL.

18. Howard Wenzel to the contest editor of *American Builder*, Oct. 5, 1962, FF15, box 65, MS 94-09, WHC-WSUL.

19. Howard Wenzel (reporting on a meeting with Export-Import Bank officials) to Floyd M. Baird, Oct. 23, 1960, FF30, box 58, MS 94-09, WHC-WSUL; Wenzel, memorandum, "Hogares Peruanos Sources of Additional Capital," Jan. 2, 1960, FF28, box 58, MS 94-09, WHC-WSUL; Hogares Peruanos, "Application for a Loan to the Inter-American Development Bank Washington DC, from Asociación Pro Vivienda Propia Villa Los Angeles," Aug. 10, 1961, FF21, box 65, MS 94-09, WHC-WSUL.

20. Howard Wenzel, "Preparation of Villa Los Angeles Project for Financing," Oct. 17, 1960, FF30, box 58, MS 94-09, WHC-WSUL.

21. Howard Wenzel to Robert Bell, Vice President, World Homes, July 20, 1960, FF29, box 58, MS 94-09, WHC-WSUL. Wenzel also recommended the report to Walter E. Arensberg, of the United States Operations Mission in Argentina: Wenzel to Arensberg, Aug. 24, 1960, FF29, box 58, MS 94-09, WHC-WSUL.

22. Hogares Peruanos, "Slide Show on Villa Los Angeles Project," Jan. 24, 1961, FF22, box 65, MS 94-09, WHC-WSUL. Howard Wenzel's manager back in Wichita approved of this approach, describing a similar deal projected for Sol de Oro as "in line with our idea of becoming consultants and financiers in this field."

He counseled: "Take a lesson from the Swiss, Howie. They contribute little or nothing except edelweiss, cheese, cuckoo clocks, and yodeling, but they are one of the richest countries in the world. They merely take a percentage of every dollar, franc, lire, sole, et cetera, ad infinitum passing through their country." Floyd M. Baird to Wenzel, June 14, 1960, FF3, box 67, MS 94-09, WHC-WSUL.

23. Hogares Peruanos, "Slide Show."

24. Willard Garvey to General Ricardo Pérez Godoy, memorandum, "Wheat for Homes," Aug. 22, 1962, FF20, box 67, MS 94-09, WHC-WSUL.

25. Howard Wenzel, status report, Mar. 5, 1962, FF19, box 65, MS 94-09, WHC-WSUL; Wenzel, status report, Sept. 8, 1962, FF1, box 64, MS 94-09, WHC-WSUL; Wenzel, status report, Sept. 15, 1962, FF19, box 65, MS 94-09, WHC-WSUL.

26. Howard Wenzel, status report, Sept. 8, 1962, FF1, box 64, MS 94-09, WHC-WSUL; Wenzel, status report, Sept. 22, 1962, FF19, box 65, MS 94-09, WHC-WSUL; Wenzel to Lee O. Thayer, memorandum, "Random Comments on My Experience in Peru," Mar. 12, 1963, FF2, box 1, MS 94-09, WHC-WSUL.

27. Howard Wenzel, memorandum, "Immediate Future for Hogares Peruanos SA," Aug. 1, 1962, FF23, box 58, MS 94-09, WHC-WSUL.

28. Jacob L. Crane to Ambassador Merwin L. Bohan, memorandum, "Technical Cooperation for Aided Self-Help Shelter Improvement in Latin America," Apr. 21, 1954; Latin America; Geographic Files, 1954–1956; Foreign Operations Administration (hereafter FOA) and International Cooperation Administration (hereafter ICA), Office of the Deputy Director for Technical Services, Office of Public Services, Housing Division; Records of US Foreign Assistance Agencies, 1942–1963, Record Group 469; National Archives at College Park, College Park, MD (hereafter RG 469; NACP).

29. George L. Reed, "Technical Cooperation for Aided Self-Help Housing in Latin America," Mar. 9, 1954; Subject Files Regarding Housing Assistance Programs, 1954–1956; Foreign Operations Administration and International Cooperation Administration, Office of the Deputy Director for Technical Services, Office of Public Services, Housing Division; RG 469; NACP.

30. Crane to Bohan, "Technical Cooperation."

31. B. Douglas Stone to George L. Reed, memorandum, "Aided Self-Help In Latin America," Nov. 10, 1954; Latin America—Programs; Geographic Files, 1954–1956; FOA and ICA, Office of the Deputy Director for Technical Services, Office of Public Services, Housing Division; RG 469; NACP.

32. FOA/W, memorandum, "FOA Housing Policy," Dec. 29, 1954; Subject Files Regarding Housing Assistance Programs, 1954–1956; FOA and ICA, Office of the Deputy Director for Technical Services, Office of Public Services, Housing Division; RG 469; NACP.

33. Stanley Baruch to George J. Greco, memorandum, "Technical Assistance Requirements," Sept. 27, 1960; Subject Files, 1955–1961; ICA, U.S. Operations Mission to Peru, Executive Office, 6/30/1955–11/3/1961; RG 469; NACP.

34. Osborne T. Boyd to Vance Rogers, Oct. 31, 1960; Subject Files, 1955–1961; ICA, U.S. Operations Mission to Peru, Executive Office, 6/30/1955–11/3/1961; RG 469; NACP.

35. Theodore C. Achilles to Pedro G. Beltrán, Nov. 1, 1960; Subject Files, 1955–1961; ICA, U.S. Operations Mission to Peru, Executive Office, 6/30/1955–11/3/1961; RG 469; NACP.

36. See Fondo Nacional de Salud y Bienestar Social (hereafter FNSBS), *Anteproyecto de construcción de viviendas por ayuda mutua en la República* (Lima: FNSBS, Oct. 1960), Centro de Documentación e Información, Ministerio de Vivienda, Construcción y Saneamiento, Lima (hereafter CDI-MVCS).

37. Memorandum to All American Diplomatic and Consular Posts, "US Housing Responsibility around the World," Aug. 2, 1960; Subject Files, 1934–1972; National Advisory Council on International Monetary and Financial Policies, ca. 1965–ca. 1989; Office of Assistant Secretary for International Affairs (hereafter OASIA); General Records of the Department of the Treasury, 1775–2005, Record Group 56; National Archives at College Park, College Park, MD (hereafter RG 56; NACP).

38. George A. Speer, "Draft of the Proposed Form E-1 for Housing," Jan. 9, 1961; Training; Subject Files, 1955–1961; ICA, U.S. Operations Mission to Peru, Executive Office, 6/30/1955–11/3/1961; RG 469; NACP.

39. "Project Agreement between the International Cooperation Administration (ICA), an Agency of the Government of the United States of America, and the Ministry of Finance and Commerce, an Agency of the Government of Peru, Project no. 527-83-046, Aided Self-Help Housing," June 28, 1961, and "Project no. 527-83-046, Aided Self-Help Housing, Revision," Sept. 6, 1961; Agreements—Housing; Central Subject Files, 1960–1962; USAID Mission to Peru, Executive Office, 11/4/1961–10/1/1979; Records of the Agency for International Development, 1948–2003, Record Group 286; National Archives at College Park, College Park, MD (hereafter RG 286; NACP).

40. AID/Washington, memorandum, "Instruction on Self-Help and Reform Measures," Dec. 1, 1961; Subject Files, 1934–1972; National Advisory Council on International Monetary and Financial Policies. ca. 1965–ca. 1989; OASIA; RG 56; NACP.

41. John F. C. Turner, interview with the author, June 2007.

42. Inter-American Development Bank (hereafter IDB), *Loan to the Republic of Peru for the Instituto de la Vivienda*, CO-FF/61/P-13 Rev., Oct. 11, 1961; Peru—1961 (1 of 2); National Advisory Council on International Monetary and Financial Policies, Reference Files Relating to Loans Issued by the Inter-American Development Bank, 1960–1966; OASIA; RG 56; NACP.

43. Banco Central de Reserva del Perú, *Plan nacional de desarrollo económico y social del Perú, 1962–1971* (Lima: Banco Central de Reserva del Perú, 1962), 241, 243.

44. Junta Nacional de la Vivienda (hereafter JNV), *Documento básico para el Plan Habitacional Urbano* (Lima: JNV, 1965), 167 graph, 133.

45. Instituto de la Vivienda (hereafter INVI), "Urbanización El Trapecio, Chimbote," brochure, ca. 1962, John Francis Charlewood Turner Collection, University of Westminster, London (hereafter JFCT-UW).

46. Humberto Ghersi and José Stretz, "Informe: Ciudad de Chimbote, investigaciones sociales," Mar. 16, 1963, 21–22, 17, JFCT-UW.

47. Elsa Samañez de Tovar, "Informe sobre el viaje a Chimbote," May 31, 1963, 18, 5, JFCT-UW.

48. USAID/Lima to AID/W, memorandum, "Senate Subcommittee on Housing, Study of International Programs," Mar. 7, 1963; Central Subject Files, 1962–1968; USAID Mission to Peru, Executive Office, 11/4/1961–10/1/1979; RG 286; NACP.

49. Teodoro Moscoso to Robert E. Culbertson, Feb. 13, 1963; Central Subject Files, 1962–1968; USAID Mission to Peru, Executive Office, 11/4/1961–10/1/1979; RG 286; NACP.

50. Howard Wenzel, status report, Dec. 27, 1962, FF19, box 67, MS 94-09, WHC-WSUL.

51. USAID/Lima to AID/W, memorandum, "Housing and Urban Development Div. Semi-annual Summary Report—Jan. 1 to June 30, 1962," Aug. 17, 1962; Housing and Urban Development FY63; Central Subject Files, 1962–1968; USAID Mission to Peru, Executive Office, 11/4/1961–10/1/1979; RG 286; NACP.

52. IDB, División de Administración de Préstamos, "Anexo H: Resumen del Informe de Evaluación del Préstamo 7/TF-PE," Oct. 1966, 2; in IDB, *Peru: Loan to the Banco de la Vivienda (PE0007)—Loan Proposal*, Apr. 21, 1968.

53. George W. Phillips to John K. Chattey, memorandum, "El Carmen Housing Project—Chimbote," Mar. 1, 1966; Central Subject Files, 1962–1968; USAID Mission to Peru, Executive Office, 11/4/1961–10/1/1979; RG 286; NACP.

54. IDB, División de Administración de Préstamos, "Anexo H: Resumen del Informe," 2.

55. George W. Phillips to William T. Dentzer, memorandum, "Housing Data and Activities," May 13, 1966; Housing and Urban Development, Housing—General; Subject Files, 1963–1973; USAID Mission to Peru, Housing Division, 11/4/1961–10/1/1979; RG 286; NACP.

56. Elsa Samañez de Tovar, "Informe sobre el viaje a Chimbote," May 31, 1963, 23, 10, JFCT-UW.

57. Henri Scioville-Samper, "Misión para analisis de recuperaciones en el campo de la vivienda: Colombia—Perú—Chile—Costa Rica" (Washington, DC: IDB, July–Aug. 1967), 40, JFCT-UW; "status" in English in original.

58. Scioville-Samper, "Misión para analisis," 35, 36, 38.

59. John F. C. Turner, "La autoconstrucción," *Desarrollo Economico: Revista para el profesional del desarrollo* 1, no. 3 (Sept.–Oct. 1964): 38, 37, 38.

60. International Bank for Reconstruction and Development, International Development Association, *An Appraisal of the 1966–1967 Public Investment Program of Peru*, vol. 7, *Housing* (Washington, DC: World Bank, 1965), 10, 11.

61. JNV, *Resumen del Programa BID-BVP-JNV*, July 1966, CDI-MVCS.

62. Centro de Investigaciones Sociales por Muestreo (hereafter CISM), *Barriadas de Lima: Actitudes de los habitantes respecto a servicios públicos y privados* (Lima: Ministerio de Trabajo y Comunidades, Servicio de Empleo y Recursos Humanos, CISM, June 1967), 58 app. 3, 17.

63. IDB, División de Análisis de Proyectos, "Anexo A: Informe técnico," Jan. 1967, DAP-42; in IDB, *Peru: Loan to the Banco de la Vivienda (PE0007)—Loan Proposal*.

64. "Fernando Belaúnde Terry ofreció charla," *El Comercio*, Mar. 18, 1961, morning ed.

65. "Decreto Supremo No. 066–68-FO," July 19, 1968, in *Normas Legales de Pueblos Jóvenes*, ed. Héctor E. Uchuya Reyes (Lima: Heur, 1971), 70.

6. Building a Better Barriada, 1968–1975

1. Fernando García-Huidobro et al., "Time Builds!," *Lotus International* 143 (Aug. 2010): 86–101; Justin McGuirk, "PREVI, The Metabolist Utopia," *Domus* 946 (Apr. 2011): 58–71; Sharif S. Kahatt, "PREVI-Lima's Time: Positioning Proyecto Experimental de Vivienda in Peru's Modern Project," *Architectural Design* 81, no. 3 (May–June 2011): 22–25.

2. Fernando García-Huidobro et al., *¡El tiempo construye! El Proyecto Experimental de Vivienda (PREVI) de Lima: Génesis y desenlace [Time Builds! The Experimental Housing Project (PREVI), Lima: Genesis and Outcome]* (Barcelona: Gustavo Gili, 2008); Kenneth Frampton, *Modern Architecture: A Critical History*, 4th ed. (London: Thames and Hudson, 2007), 377; Alejandro Aravena and Andrés Iacobelli, *Elemental: Manual de vivienda incremental y diseño participativo [Elemental: Incremental Housing and Participatory Design Manual]* (Ostfildern: Hatje Cantz, 2012), 41.

3. Peter Land, interview with the author, Apr. 2010; Supersudaca (Manuel de Rivero and Félix Madrazo), "¿Y PREVI? Proyecto de Investigación para la IV Bienal Iberoamericana de Arquitectura e Ingeniería Civil, Lima, Perú, 25 a 29 de Octubre de 2004," 18, exhibition material, collection of the author.

4. See Karin Kirsch, *The Weißenhofsiedlung: Experimental Housing Built for the Deutscher Werkbund, Stuttgart, 1927*, trans. Michael Knight (New York: Rizzoli, 1989).

5. Land, interview with the author, Apr. 2010.

6. A. C. Kayanan and Banco de la Vivienda del Perú, "Preliminary Report: Selection of Sites for an Experimental Housing Project, Lima, Peru," January 31, 1967, p. 3, TE 322/1 PERU (240-3), Jan. 1965–Dec. 1968, Archival Folder Series-0175-1686-11, United Nations Archives and Records Management Section, New York, NY (hereafter UN-ARMS).

7. Government of Peru and United Nations Development Program (hereafter UNDP), *Proyecto Experimental de Vivienda, Perú: Conclusiones y recomendaciones del proyecto*, DP/UN/PER-73-005/1 (New York: UN, 1976), 2, UN-ARMS; Government of Peru and United Nations (hereafter UN), "Concurso Internacional para el diseño de un proyecto piloto de vivienda de bajo costo en Lima," Sept. 1969, 2, Centro de Documentación e Información, Ministerio de Vivienda, Construcción y Saneamiento, Lima (hereafter CDI-MVCS).

8. A. C. Kayanan, "Final Report: Selection of Sites for an Experimental Housing Project, Lima, Peru," Mar. 31, 1967, 11, 37, TE 322/1 PERU (240-3), UN-ARMS.

9. The *empleado* was established as a legal category in Peru in the 1910s, granting additional social welfare benefits to office workers in recognition of their obligation to maintain a respectable standard of living. See David Parker, *The Idea of the Middle Class: White-Collar Workers and Peruvian Society, 1900–1950* (University Park: Pennsylvania State University Press, 1998).

10. Silvio Grichener, "PREVI/Perú: Un intento en el más alto nivel," *Summa: Revista de arquitectura, tecnología y diseño* 32 (Dec. 1970): 46; Government of Peru and UNDP, *Proyecto Experimental de Vivienda, Perú*, 6.

11. Instituto Nacional de Investigación y Normalización de la Vivienda (hereafter ININVI), *PREVI resultados y conclusiones: 20 años después* (Lima: ININVI, 1988), 41, collection of the author (thanks to Raquel Machicao); Land, phone conversation with the author, Apr. 2006. Land recalled that Giancarlo De Carlo and Balkrishna Doshi were also on the original shortlist, but he had not been able to meet with them on his research trip.

12. Government of Peru and UN, "Un concurso internacional para el diseño de un Proyecto Piloto de Vivienda de Bajo Costo en Lima, Perú," Sept. 2, 1968, 58, CDI-MVCS; Government of Peru and UN, "Concurso Internacional," Sept. 1969, 2.

13. Government of Peru and UN, "Un concurso internacional," Sept. 2, 1968, 15, 16, 19.

14. Peter Land, "The Experimental Housing Project (PREVI), Lima: Antecedents and Ideas," in García-Huidobro et al., *¡El tiempo construye!*, 22.

15. Government of Peru and UN, "Concurso Internacional," Sept. 1969, app. 4. The dissenting jurors were Carl Koch and Halldor Gunnlögsson; an additional juror, Alfredo Perez, endorsed their assessment of the CES project, but not their condemnation of Ohl's.

16. Government of Peru and UN, "Concurso Internacional," Sept. 1969, 4, 3.

17. Government of Peru and UNDP, *Proyecto Experimental de Vivienda, Perú*, 4.

18. Christopher Alexander et al., "Relational Complexes in Architecture," *Architectural Record* 140, no. 3 (Sept. 1966): 185–90; Christopher Alexander et al., *A Pattern Language Which Generates Multi-Service Centers* (Berkeley, CA: Center for Environmental Structure, 1968).

19. Christopher Alexander et al., *Houses Generated by Patterns* (Berkeley, CA: Center for Environmental Structure, 1969), 117; John F. C. Turner, "Lima Barriadas Today," *Architectural Design* 33, no. 8 (Aug. 1963): 375–76.

20. Alexander et al., *Houses Generated by Patterns*, 114, 129.

21. Sara Ishikawa, interview with the author, Jan. 2007; Sandy Hirshen, interview with the author, Jan. 2007.

22. Alexander et al., *Houses Generated by Patterns*, 39.

23. Alexander et al., *Houses Generated by Patterns*, 6; Government of Peru and UN, "Concurso Internacional," Sept. 1969, 9.

24. Ishikawa, interview with the author, Jan. 2007.

25. Herbert Ohl project statement, qtd. in "PREVI/Lima: Low Cost Housing Project," *Architectural Design* 40, no. 4 (Apr. 1970): 192.

26. Ohl, qtd. in "PREVI/Lima," 192.

27. Ohl, qtd. in "PREVI/Lima," 192; see also N. J. Habraken, *Supports: An Alternative to Mass Housing* (New York: Praeger, 1972).

28. Toivo Korhonen project statement, qtd. in "PREVI/Lima," 202.

29. Charles Correa project statement, qtd. in "PREVI/Lima," 198.

30. Atelier 5, "International Competition for an Experimental Housing Project in Lima, Peru," n.d. [ca. 1969], Plan No. 13, p. 25, collection of the author (thanks to Heinz Müller).

31. Atelier 5, "International Competition," Plan No. 2, p. 7.

32. James Stirling, qtd in *James Stirling, Buildings and Projects* (London: Architectural Press, 1984), 166.

33. James Stirling, qtd in *James Stirling: Exhibition, Royal Institute of British Architects*, exhibition catalogue, Heinz Gallery, Apr. 24–June 21, 1974 (London: Royal Institute of British Architects, 1974), 66.

34. Diana Ruiz and Juana Salcedo, "Barrio La Fragua," in *Casa + casa + casa = ¿ciudad? Germán Samper: Una investigación en vivienda,* ed. Marcela Ángel Samper and María Cecilia O'Byrne (Bogotá: Universidad de los Andes; Ediciones Uniandes, 2012), 121; Ángel Samper and O'Byrne, "Sidauto," in *Casa + casa + casa = ¿ciudad?*, 125.

35. Esguerra, Saenz, Urdaneta, Samper, "La ciudad como un organismo dinámico," in Ángel Samper and O'Byrne, *Casa + casa + casa = ¿ciudad?*, 140.

36. Oskar Hansen and Svein Hatløy project statement, qtd in "PREVI/Lima," 200.

37. Vincent Ligtelijn, ed. *Aldo van Eyck: Works* (Basel: Birkhäuser, 1999), 169.

38. Ligtelijn, *Aldo van Eyck*, 168; Aldo van Eyck project statement, qtd. in "PREVI/Lima," 205.

39. Ligtelijn, *Aldo van Eyck*, 168.

40. Aldo van Eyck, "Footnote: Who Are We Building for, and Why?" *Architectural Design* 40, no. 4 (Apr. 1970): 189. This image also appeared with a republication of the text: see Aldo van Eyck, "Footnote: Who Are We Building for, and Why?" in *Architecture in an Age of Scepticism: A Practitioners' Anthology*, ed. Denys Lasdun (London: Heinemann, 1984), 237.

41. Government of Peru and UNDP, *Proyecto Experimental de Vivienda, Perú*, 3.

42. Ministerio de Vivienda (hereafter MV), *PREVI Proyecto Piloto de Rehabilitación de Vivienda: Informe final de los estudios* (Lima: MV, July 1972), 66, collection of Lidia Gálvez, Lima.

43. MV and ININVI, *PREVI PP4: Auto-construcción post-sismo*, vol. 27 of *Publicación PREVI*, (Lima: MV; ININVI, 1979), 5, 65, caption, 66.

44. Government of Peru and UNDP, *Proyecto Experimental de Vivienda, Perú*, 6; MV and ININVI, *PREVI: Introducción*, vol. 1 of *Publicación PREVI* (Lima: MV; ININVI, 1979), 20.

45. Atelier 5, *Siedlungen und städtebauliche Projekte* (Braunschweig: Vieweg, 1994), 89.

46. McGuirk, "PREVI, The Metabolist Utopia," 70; Government of Peru and UNDP, *Proyecto Experimental de Vivienda, Perú*, 6.

47. Government of Peru and UNDP, *Proyecto Experimental de Vivienda, Perú*, 12.

48. See PCM Construction Control Consultants Limited and Julio Gianella Silva, *Affordable Housing for Low Income Families in Peru: A Study on Behalf of the Instituto Nacional de Investigación y Normalización de la Vivienda* (Lima: ININVI, 1985), app. C.

49. Instituto Nacional de Desarrollo Urbano (hereafter INADUR), *Estudio de evaluación integral de los programas de vivienda ejecutados y/o promovidos por el Estado*, vol. 1, *Informe período 1969–1979* (Lima: INADUR, 1991), 42, 74, CDI-MVCS; Alfredo Montagne, "Maisons expérimentales Previ, Lima, Perou," *Archithese* 14, no. 5 (1984): 6; INADUR, *Estudio de evaluación integral*, 1:74.

50. García-Huidobro et al., *¡El tiempo construye!*, 87.

51. Josefina Mena, "News from PREVI," *Architectural Design* 44, no. 1 (Jan. 1974): 53.

52. Forum Nacional de Vivienda, Comisión de Trabajo, "Hacia una política de vivienda por autoconstrucción," November 1970, i, 13, CDI-MVCS.

53. MV and ININVI, *PREVI PP3: Proyecto de lotes y servicios*, vol. 26 of *Publicación PREVI*, (Lima: MV; ININVI, 1979), 37, 55. Federico Mevius was the lead author on this publication.

54. MV and ININVI, *PREVI PP3*, 46, 72.

55. MV and ININVI, *PREVI PP3*, 71, 64, 67.

56. MV and ININVI, *PREVI PP3*, 70, 71.

57. MV and ININVI, *PREVI PP3*, 73, 75.

7. Revolutions in Self-Help, 1968–1980

1. Barbara Ward, "The Home of Man: What Nations and the International Must Do," *Habitat International* 1, no. 2 (1976): 125, 130; Barbara Ward, *The Home of Man* (New York: Norton, 1976), 268, 289.

2. For further discussion see John P. Renninger, "After the Seventh Special General Assembly Session: Africa and the New Emerging World Order," *African Studies Review* 19, no. 2 (Sept. 1976): 35–48.

3. Juan Velasco Alvarado, qtd in Carlos Delgado, *SINAMOS: La participación popular an el Revolución Peruana* (Lima: SINAMOS, 1972), 1.

4. "Manifiesto del Gobierno Revolucionario de la Fuerza Armada," Oct. 2, 1968, http://www.congreso.gob.pe/participacion/museo/congreso/mensajes/mani fiesto_nacion_3_octubre_1968.

5. "Manifiesto," Oct. 2, 1968.

6. Oficina Nacional de Estadística y Censos (hereafter ONEC), *La Población del Perú* (Lima: ONEC, 1974), 38 gráfico 5; Abraham F. Lowenthal, "The Peruvian Experiment Reconsidered," in *The Peruvian Experiment Reconsidered*, ed. Cynthia McClintock and Lowenthal (Princeton, NJ: Princeton University Press, 1983), 421.

7. See José María Caballero, *From Belaunde to Belaunde: Peru's Military Experiment in Third-Roadism* (Cambridge: Centre of Latin American Studies, University of Cambridge, 1981).

8. Carlos Delgado, "Desarrollo social: Reconsideracions y planteamientos," in Delgado, *Problemas sociales en el Perú contemporáneo* (Lima: Instituto de Estudios Peruanos, 1971), 31, 34, 35, 37.

9. Sistema Nacional de Apoyo a la Movilización Social (hereafter SINAMOS), *8 preguntas a la revolución peruana* (Lima: SINAMOS, 1973), 10.

10. Oficina Nacional de Desarrollo de Pueblos Jóvenes (hereafter ONDEPJOV), *Boletín 1, La organización para el desarrollo de los pueblos jóvenes* (Lima: ONDEPJOV, 1969), 5.

11. Diego Robles Rivas, interview with the author, Nov. 13, 2008.

12. Abelardo Sánchez-León and Julio Calderón Cockburn, *El laberinto de la ciudad: Políticas urbanas del Estado 1950–1979* (Lima: Centro de Estudios y Promoción del Desarrollo [hereafter DESCO], 1980), 64.

13. Carlos Delgado, "Introducción," *La Unidad Vecinal No. 3 y Matute: Estudio social comparativo referido a problemas de planeamiento físico* (Lima: Oficina de Planificación Sectorial de Vivienda y Equipamiento Urbano, 1966), n.p.

14. Carlos Delgado, *Tres planteamientos en torno a problemas de urbanización acelerada en áreas metropolitanas: El caso de Lima* (Lima: Oficina Nacional de Planeamiento y Urbanismo, Plan de Desarrollo Metropolitano Lima-Callao [hereafter PLANDEMET], Oct. 1968), 11, 10, 12, 45.

15. Delgado, *Tres planteamientos*, 47.

16. Alfred Stepan, *The State and Society: Peru in Comparative Perspective* (Princeton, NJ: Princeton University Press, 1978), 164, 165n14.

17. Sara Michl, "Urban Squatter Organization as a National Government Tool: The Case of Lima, Peru," in *National-Local Linkages: The Interrelationship of Urban and National Polities in Latin America*, ed. Francine F. Rabinovitz and Felicity M. Trueblood (Beverly Hills, CA: Sage, 1973), 166.

18. ONDEPJOV, *Plan de acción inmediata: A ejecutarse en los Pueblos Jóvenes de los Distritos de San Martín de Porres, Independencia, Comas, Surco y Chorrillos* (Lima: ONDEPJOV, 1969), 58.

19. Diego Robles Rivas, "El proceso de urbanización y los sectores populares en Lima," *Cuadernos DESCO*, serie A, no. 1 (Feb. 1969): 63, 52–53; Diego Robles Rivas, "Development Alternatives for the Peruvian Barriada," in *Regional and*

Urban Development Policies: A Latin American Perspective, ed. Guillermo Geisse and Jorge Enqrique Hardoy (Beverly Hills, CA: Sage, 1972), 229, 234–35.

20. ONDEPJOV, *Boletin* 5, *Ponencia presentada por la Oficina Nacional de Desarrollo de Pueblos Jóvenes al Seminario de Asentamientos Populares organizado por la Agencia Internacional para el Desarrollo, Washington DC, noviembre de 1969* (Lima: ONDEPJOV, 1969), 25, 29.

21. "Decreto Ley No. 18896: Se crea el Sistema Nacional de Apoyo a la Movilización Social," June 22, 1971, http://peru.justia.com/federales/decretos-leyes/18896-jun-22-1971/gdoc/.

22. Interview with Carlos Arriola, qtd in Dirk Kruijt, *Revolution by Decree: Peru, 1968–1975* (Amsterdam: Thela, 1994), 120.

23. SINAMOS, *¿Qué son los títulos de propiedad?* (Arequipa: Oficina Regional de Apoyo a la Movilización Social [hereafter ORAMS] IX, n.d. [ca. 1971]), Centro de Documentación e Información, Ministerio de Vivienda (hereafter CDI-MVCS).

24. Juan Velasco Alvarado, "The Master Will No Longer Feed Off Your Poverty," in *The Peru Reader: History, Culture, Politics*, ed. Orin Starn et al. (Durham, NC: Duke University Press, 1995), 267.

25. Stepan, *State and Society*, 169, 168; Interview with the "official in charge of organizing Lima and Callao into neighborhood committees," Nov. 1972, qtd in Stepan, *State and Society*, 165.

26. SINAMOS, ORAMS X, and Comisión Especial sobre Villa El Salvador, *Informe sobre Villa El Salvador* (Lima: SINAMOS; ORAMS X, 1974), 12, CDI-MVCS.

27. Gustavo Riofrío Benavides, *Habilitación urbana con participación popular: Tres casos en Lima, Perú* (Eschborn: Deutsche Gesellschaft für Technische Zusammenarbeit, 1986), 91, 70.

28. SINAMOS et al., *Informe*, 14; "Los 'invasores' se fueron masivamente," *Expreso*, May 17, 1971.

29. Reinhard Skinner, "Self-Help, Community Organization, and Politics: Villa El Salvador, Lima," in *Self-Help Housing: A Critique*, ed. Peter M. Ward (London: Mansell, 1982), 218.

30. SINAMOS et al., *Informe*, 26, 27.

31. SINAMOS et al., *Informe*, 32.

32. SINAMOS et al., *Informe*, 48, 45, 46.

33. SINAMOS et al., *Informe*, 60.

34. SINAMOS et al., *Informe*, 56, 57.

35. Gustavo Riofrío Benavides and Jean-Claude Driant, *¿Qué vivienda han construido? Nuevos problemas en viejas barriadas* (Lima: CIDAP, Centro de Investigación, Desarrollo y Asesoría Poblacional; IFEA, Instituto Francés de Estudios Andinos; TAREA, Asociación de Publicaciones Educativas, 1987), 97.

36. Instituto Nacional de Estadística e Informática (hereafter INEI), *Una mirada a Lima Metropolitana* (Lima: INEI, 2014), 11.

37. Ministerio de Vivienda (hereafter MV), Oficina Sectorial de Planificación, *Desarrollo integral del área Canto Grande* (Lima: MV, 1976), 1, CDI-MVCS.

38. Robles, interview with the author, Oct. 28, 2008.

39. John F. C. Turner, "Uncontrolled Urban Settlement: Problems and Policies," *International Social Development Review* 1 (1968): 128.

40. John F. C. Turner, "A New View of the Housing Deficit," *Architects' Yearbook* 13 (1971): 115.

41. John F. C. Turner, "Housing Issues and the Standards Problem," *Ekistics* 196, no. 33 (1972): 154, 157, 158.

42. World Bank, *Urbanization Sector*, Working Paper 11072 (Washington, DC: World Bank, June 1972), 7.

43. John F. C. Turner, "Levels of Housing Action," Nov. 1971, attachment to Turner to Robert Sadove, memorandum, "Sites and Services Programs," Nov. 30, 1971, John Francis Charlewood Turner Collection, University of Westminster, London (hereafter JFCT-UW). Turner's "Levels of Housing Action" drew upon a report cowritten with colleagues from MIT: John F. C. Turner, with Clinton Bourdon, Robert Ledogar, and Tomasz Sudra, "Notes for a Housing Policy with Special Reference to Low-Income Housing Systems in Metropolitan Mexico," July-November 1971, JFCT-UW.

44. Turner, "Levels of Housing Action"; Turner to Robert Sadove, memorandum, "Sites and Services Programs," Nov. 30, 1971, JFCT-UW; Turner to Sadove, Nov. 30, 1971, JFCT-UW.

45. John F. C. Turner, *Housing by People: Towards Autonomy in Building Environments*, 1st American ed. (New York: Pantheon, 1977), xiv; John F. C. Turner, "The Housing and Planning Problems of Arequipa, Peru: A Case Study with Particular Reference to the Application of Self-Help Methods in Relation to the Squatter Settlements," n.d. [ca. 1959–1960], 58, JFCT-UW.

46. Rod Burgess, "Petty Commodity Housing or Dweller Control? A Critique of John Turner's Views on Housing Policy," *World Development* 6, no. 9/10 (1978): 1119; John F. C. Turner, "Housing in Three Dimensions: Terms of Reference for the Housing Question Redefined," *World Development* 6, no. 9/10 (1978): 1136; Patrick Geddes, *What To Do?* (1912), qtd in Turner, "Housing in Three Dimensions," 1142.

47. Turner, *Housing by People*, 1st American ed., xvi.

48. John F. C. Turner, "The Squatter Settlement: An Architecture that Works," *Architectural Design* 38, no. 8 (Aug. 1968): 357.

49. William Mangin and John F. C. Turner, "The Barriada Movement," *Progressive Architecture* 49 (May 1968): 162.

50. UN-Habitat, *Dubrovnik: An Analysis of the Crisis in Human Settlements* (N.p.: United Nations Human Settlements Programme, n.d. [ca. 1975]), 1, 4, 8, 6.

51. John F. C. Turner, "Issues for Discussion on Self-Help and Low-Cost Housing," keynote lecture, Self-Help and Low-Cost Housing Symposium, Habitat Forum, Vancouver, June 1, 1976, JFCT-UW.

52. United Nations Conference on Human Settlements, *Report of Habitat: United Nations Conference on Human Settlements, Vancouver, 31 May–11 June 1976*, A/CONF.70/15 (New York: United Nations, 1976), 7, 58, 48.

53. Aprodicio A. Laquian, "Whither Sites and Services?" *Science* 192, no. 4243 (1976): 951, 954.

54. Diego Robles Rivas, "Limitations of Self-Help," *Architectural Design* 46, no. 4 (Apr. 1976): 231; Diego Robles Rivas, "La marginalidad urbana," in *América Latina en su arquitectura*, ed. Roberto Segre (Mexico City: Siglo XXI, 1975), 103, 104.

55. Emilio Pradilla, "La ideología burgesa y el problema de la vivienda: Crítica de dos teorías," *Ideología y Sociedad* 19 (Oct.–Dec. 1976): 44, 47.

8. Other Paths, 1980–1986

1. Steve J. Stern, "Beyond Enigma: An Intepreting Shining Path and Peru, 1980–1995," in *Shining and Other Paths: War and Society in Peru, 1980–1995*, ed. Stern (Durham, NC: Duke University Press, 1998), 5.

2. Empresa Nacional de Edificaciones (hereafter ENACE), *Revolución habitacional en democracia: Plan de vivienda del gobierno peruano, 1980–1985* (Lima: ENACE, 1985), front cover.

3. Jean-Claude Driant, *Las barriadas de Lima: Historia e interpretación* (Lima: IFEA, Instituto Francés de Estudios Andinos; Centro de Estudios y Promoción del Desarrollo [hereafter DESCO], 1991), 198.

4. Manuel Castells, *The City and the Grassroots: A Cross-Cultural Theory of Urban Social Movements* (Berkeley: University of California Press, 1983), 179, 212.

5. Gustavo Riofrío Benavides, *Habilitación urbana con participación popular: Tres casos en Lima, Perú* (Eschborn: Deutsche Gesellschaft für Technische Zusammenarbeit, 1986), 188.

6. Riofrío, *Habilitación urbana*, 154.

7. Municipalidad de Lima Metropolitana (hereafter MLM), *Programa Especial Huaycán* (Lima: MLM, n.d. [ca. 1985]), n.p.

8. MLM, *Programa Especial Huaycán*, n.p.

9. Eduardo Figari Gold, "Huaycán: Una experiencia de urbanismo popular," *Historia, urbanismo, arquitectura, construcción arte (HUACA)* 1 (July 1987): 29.

10. MLM, *Programa Especial Huaycán*, n.p.

11. Figari, "Huaycán," 30.

12. Figari, "Huaycán," 26.

13. MLM, *Programa Especial Huaycán*, n.p.

14. Reynaldo Ledgard, "Imaginando otro espacio urbano: La experiencia de Huaycán," *Márgenes* 1, no. 1 (Mar. 1987): 37.

15. Figari, "Huaycán," 29.

16. Figari, "Huaycán," 29, 30.

17. Figari, "Huaycán," 30.

18. Figari, "Huaycán," 30.

19. Ledgard, "Imaginando otro espacio urbano," 37, 40, 42.

20. Ledgard, "Imaginando otro espacio urbano," 41.

21. Ledgard, "Imaginando otro espacio urbano," 44.

22. Julio Calderón Cockburn and Luis Olivera Cárdenas, *Municipio y pobladores en la habilitación urbana: Huaycán y Laderas del Chillón* (Lima: DESCO, 1989), 99.

23. Carlos Roel, "Huaycán: Dos años de lucha por la forja de una ciudad modelo," in *Estrategias de vida en el sector urbano popular*, ed. Roelfien Haak and Javier Diaz-Albertini (Lima: FOVIDA (Asociación Fomento de la Vida); DESCO, 1987), 314.

24. Calderón Cockburn and Olivera Cárdenas, *Municipio y pobladores*, 59.

25. Javier Díaz-Albertini, qtd in Calderón Cockburn and Olivera Cárdenas, *Municipio y pobladores*, 104.

26. Driant, *Las barriadas de Lima*, 211.

27. Pedro Arévalo T., "Huaycán Self-Managing Urban Community: May Hope be Realized," *Environment and Urbanization* 9, no. 1 (1997): 66, 68.

28. Michael L. Smith, "Shining Path's Urban Strategy: Ate Vitarte," in *The Shining Path of Peru*, ed. David Scott Palmer (New York: St. Martin's, 1992), 137, 138; Deborah Poole and Gerardo Rénique, *Peru: Time of Fear* (London: Latin American Bureau, 1992), 91.

29. Abimael Guzmán, qtd in Jo-Marie Burt, "Shining Path and the 'Decisive Battle' in Lima's Barriadas: The Case of Villa El Salvador," in *Shining and Other Paths*, ed. Stern, 269.

30. *El Diario* 551, June 7, 1989, qtd in Burt, "Shining Path," 305n48.

31. Burt, "Shining Path," 304n41.

32. Hernando de Soto with Instituto Libertad y Democracia, *The Other Path: The Invisible Revolution in the Third World*, trans. June Abbott (New York: Harper & Row, 1989), 261; Mario Vargas Llosa, "In Defense of the Black Market," *New York Times Magazine*, Feb. 22, 1987. This article was adapted from Vargas Llosa's preface to *El otro sendero*.

33. This is my translation of the phrase "incipiente economía de mercado que están generado las clases populares del Perú." De Soto et al., *El otro sendero: La revolución informal* (Lima: Instituto Libertad y Democracia, 1986), 60. June Abbott's translation of this phrase sidesteps the issue of class: "incipient market economy generated by Peru's people." De Soto, *Other Path*, 56.

34. de Soto, *Other Path*, 50, 55, 50, 56.

35. de Soto, *Other Path*, 18.

36. de Soto, *Other Path*, 56.

37. Mike Davis, *Planet of Slums* (New York: Verso, 2006), 79; John F. C. Turner, interview with the author, June 2007, transcript, Oral History Research Office, Columbia University, New York.

38. Peter M. Ward, "Self Help Housing in Mexico City: Social and Economic Determinants of Success," *Town Planning Review* 49, no. 1 (Jan. 1978): 46.

39. John F. C. Turner, *Housing by People: Towards Autonomy in Building Environments*, 1st American ed. (New York: Pantheon, 1977), xiv; see Samuel Smiles, *Self-Help: With Illustrations of Character and Perseverance* (1859).

40. See John F. C. Turner, "The Squatter Settlement: An Architecture that Works," *Architectural Design* 38, no. 8 (Aug. 1968): 355–60.

41. Gustavo Riofrío Benavides, *Producir la ciudad (popular) de los '90: Entre el mercado y el Estado* (Lima: DESCO, 1991), 114, 115.

42. Riofrío, *Producir la ciudad*, 133.

43. Riofrío, *Producir la ciudad*, 149, 150, 151.

44. Riofrío, *Producir la ciudad*, 122, 123.

45. Ray Bromley, "Power, Property, and Poverty: Why De Soto's 'Mystery of Capital' Cannot Be Solved," in *Urban Informality: Transnational Perspectives from the Middle East, Latin America, and South Asia*, ed. Ananya Roy and Nezar AlSayyad (Lanham, MD: Lexington, 2004), 284.

46. United Nations Centre for Human Settlements, *Executive Summary of the Global Report on Human Settlements* (Nairobi: United Nations Centre for Human Settlements, 1988), 10, 40, 44.

47. World Bank, *Housing: Enabling the Market to Work* (Washington, DC: World Bank, 1993), 58, 64, 116 citing de Soto, *Other Path*.

48. David F. Varela and Jorge L. Archimbaud, "Property Rights and Land Tenancy," in *An Opportunity for a Different Peru: Prosperous, Equitable, and Gov-*

ernable ed. Marcelo Giugale, Vicente Fretes-Cibils, and John L. Newman (Washington, DC: World Bank, 2007), 570, 572.

49. William Britt Gwinner, "Housing," in Giugale, Fretes-Cibils, and Newman, *Opportunity for a Different Peru,* 353, 355.

50. Gustavo Riofrío Benavides and Daniel Ramírez Corzo N., *Formalización de la propiedad y mejoramiento de barrios: Bien legal, bien marginal* (Lima: DESCO, 2006), 33, emphasis in original.

51. Gustavo Riofrío Benavides and Jean-Claude Driant, *¿Qué vivienda han construido? Nuevos problemas en viejas barriadas* (Lima: CIDAP, Centro de Investigación, Desarrollo y Asesoría Poblacional; IFEA, Instituto Francés de Estudios Andinos; TAREA, Asociación de Publicaciones Educativas, 1987), 135.

52. Riofrío and Driant, *¿Qué vivienda han construido?,* 136, 138; Danielle M. Rojas et al, "Rehab, 'Los Aires' and Densification of Consolidated Settlements in Lima, Peru," in *Housing Policy in Latin American Cities: A New Generation of Strategies and Approaches for 2016 UN-Habitat III,* ed. Peter M. Ward et al. (London: Routledge, 2015), 177, 180.

53. Riofrío and Driant, *¿Qué vivienda han construido?,* 79, 156.

54. Riofrío and Driant, *¿Qué vivienda han construido?,* 140.

Epilogue

Epigraph: *Relaciones de los virreyes y audiencias que han gobernado el Perú,* 3 vols. (Lima and Madrid: 1867–1872), 3: 90; qtd. in Richard M. Morse, "Recent Research on Latin American Urbanization: A Selective Survey with Commentary," *Latin American Research Review* 1, no. 1 (Autumn 1965): 71n77.

BIBLIOGRAPHY

Archives

Centro de Documentación e Información, Ministerio de Vivienda,
Construcción y Saneamiento (CDI-MVCS), Lima

Jean and Willard Garvey World Homes Collection, Wichita State University
Libraries, Special Collections and University Archives (WHC-WSUL),
Wichita, KS

John Francis Charlewood Turner Collection, University of Westminster
(JFCT-UW), London

Maryknoll Mission Archives (MMA), Maryknoll, NY

National Archives at College Park, College Park, MD
General Records of the Department of the Treasury, 1775–2005, Record
Group 56 (RG 56; NACP)
Records of the Agency for International Development, 1948–2003, Record
Group 286 (RG 286; NACP)
Records of US Foreign Assistance Agencies, 1942–1963, Record Group 469
(RG 469; NACP)

United Nations Archives and Records Management Section (UN-ARMS),
New York, NY

Published Sources

Abrams, Charles. "Urban Land Problems and Policies." In *Urban Land Problems
and Policies*, bulletin 7 of *Housing and Town and Country Planning*, 2–58.
New York: United Nations, Department of Social Affairs, 1953.

Abrams, Charles. *Man's Struggle for Shelter in an Urbanizing World*. Cambridge,
MA: MIT Press, 1964.

Abrams, Charles. *Squatter Settlements: The Problem and the Opportunity*. Ideas
and Methods Exchange, 63. Washington, DC: Agency for International
Development, Department of Housing and Urban Development, 1966.

Agrupación Espacio. "Expresión de principios de la Agrupación Espacio." *El
Arquitecto Peruano* 11, no. 119 (June 1947): n.p.

Alexander, Christopher, Sanford Hirshen, Sara Ishikawa, Christie Coffin, and
Shlomo Angel. "Houses Generated by Patterns." *Architects' Yearbook* 13
(1971): 84–114.

Alexander, Christopher, Sanford Hirshen, Sara Ishikawa, Christie Coffin, and Shlomo Angel. *Houses Generated by Patterns.* Berkeley, CA: Center for Environmental Structure, 1969.

Alexander, Christopher, Sara Ishikawa, and Murray Silverstein. *A Pattern Language Which Generates Multi-Service Centers.* Berkeley, CA: Center for Environmental Structure, 1968.

Alexander, Christopher, Van Maren King, Sara Ishikawa, Michael Baker, and Patrick Hyslop. "Relational Complexes in Architecture." *Architectural Record* 140, no. 3 (Sept. 1966): 185–90.

Andrews, Frank M., and George W. Phillips. "The Squatters of Lima: Who They Are and What They Want." *Journal of Developing Areas* 4, no. 2 (Jan. 1970): 211–24.

Ángel Samper, Marcela, and María Cecilia O'Byrne. *Casa + casa + casa = ¿ciudad? Germán Samper: Una investigación en vivienda.* Bogotá: Universidad de los Andes, Facultad de Arquitectura y Diseño, Departamento de Arquitectura; Ediciones Uniandes, 2012.

Aravena, Alejandro, and Andrés Iacobelli. *Elemental: Manual de vivienda incremental y diseño participativo* [*Elemental: Incremental Housing and Participatory Design Manual*]. Ostfildern: Hatje Cantz, 2012.

Arévalo T., Pedro. "Huaycán Self-Managing Urban Community: May Hope Be Realized." *Environment and Urbanization* 9, no. 1 (Apr. 1997): 59–79.

Arndt, H. W. *Economic Development: The History of an Idea.* Chicago: University of Chicago Press, 1987.

Atelier 5. *Siedlungen und städtebauliche Projekte.* Braunschweig: Vieweg, 1994.

Atkeson, Timothy. "Aid for Latin American Housing." *George Washington Law Review* 31, no. 3 (Mar. 1963): 547–86.

Atwood, Rollin S. "The United States Point Four Program—A Bilateral Approach." *Annals of the American Academy of Political and Social Science* 323, no. 1 (May 1959): 33–39.

Austin, Allan G., and Sherman Lewis. *Urban Government for Metropolitan Lima.* Praeger Special Studies in International Politics and Public Affairs. New York: Praeger, 1970.

Ballent, Anahí. "Learning from Lima." *Block* 6 (Mar. 2004): 86–95.

Banco Central de Reserva del Perú. *Plan nacional de desarrollo económico y social del Perú, 1962–1971.* Lima: Banco Central de Reserva del Perú, 1962.

Belaúnde Terry, Fernando. "Construyamos hoy para no tener que expropriar y demoler mañana." *El Arquitecto Peruano* 18, no. 204–5 (July–Aug. 1954): n.p.

Belaúnde Terry, Fernando. "El barrio unidad: Intento de decentralización urbana." *El Arquitecto Peruano* 8, no. 83 (June 1944): n.p.

Belaúnde Terry, Fernando. "El planeamiento en el antiguo y moderno Perú." *El Arquitecto Peruano* 18, no. 202 (May–June 1954): n.p.

Belaúnde Terry, Fernando. "La ciudad risueña: Significado y misión de la Unidad Vecinal No. 3." *El Arquitecto Peruano* 13, no. 146 (Sept. 1949): n.p.

Belaúnde Terry, Fernando. *La conquista del Perú por los Peruanos.* Lima: Ediciones Tawantinsuyo, 1959.

Belaúnde Terry, Fernando. "La incultura de las ciudades." *El Arquitecto Peruano* 17, no. 192–93 (Aug. 1953): n.p.

Belaúnde Terry, Fernando. *Peru's Own Conquest.* Lima: American Studies, 1965.

Benmergui, Leandro. "The Alliance for Progress and Housing Policy in Rio de Janeiro and Buenos Aires in the 1960s." *Urban History* 36, no. 2 (2009): 303–26.

Billone, Jorge, Daniel Martínez, and Jorge Carbonel. "La política gubernamental en los pueblos jóvenes y la experiencia de Villa El Salvador." In *El Perú de Velasco*, vol. 3, edited by Carlos Franco, 881–909. Lima: CEDEP, Centro de Estudios para el Desarrollo y la Participación, 1983.

Blau, Eve. *The Architecture of Red Vienna, 1919–1934*. Cambridge, MA: MIT Press, 1999.

Boudon, Philippe. *Lived-in Architecture: Le Corbusier's Pessac Revisited*. Cambridge, MA: MIT Press, 1972.

Britt Gwinner, William. "Housing." In *An Opportunity for a Different Peru: Prosperous, Equitable, and Governable*, edited by Marcelo Giugale, Vicente Fretes-Cibils, and John L. Newman, 349–59. Washington, DC: World Bank, 2007.

Bromley, Ray. "Informality, de Soto Style: From Concept to Policy." In *Contrapunto: The Informal Sector Debate in Latin America*, edited by Cathy A. Rakowski, 131–51. Albany: State University of New York Press, 1994.

Bromley, Ray. "A New Path to Development? The Significance and Impact of Hernando de Soto's Ideas on Underdevelopment, Production, and Reproduction." *Economic Geography* 66, no. 4 (Oct. 1990): 328–48.

Bromley, Ray. "Peru 1957–1977: How Time and Place Influenced John Turner's Ideas on Housing Policy." *Habitat International* 27, no. 2 (2003): 271–92.

Bromley, Ray. "Power, Property, and Poverty: Why De Soto's 'Mystery of Capital' Cannot Be Solved." In *Urban Informality: Transnational Perspectives from the Middle East, Latin America, and South Asia*, edited by Ananya Roy and Nezar AlSayyad, 271–88. Lanham, MD: Lexington, 2004.

Browning, Harley L. "Recent Trends in Latin American Urbanization." *The Annals of the American Academy of Political and Social Science*, vol. 316, *A Crowding Hemisphere: Population Change in the Americas* (Mar. 1958): 111–20.

Bullrich, Francisco. *New Directions in Latin American Architecture*. New York: George Braziller, 1969.

Burgess, Rod. "Petty Commodity Housing or Dweller Control? A Critique of John Turner's Views on Housing Policy." *World Development* 6, no. 9/10 (1978): 1105–33.

Burt, Jo-Marie. "Shining Path and the 'Decisive Battle' in Lima's Barriadas: The Case of Villa El Salvador." In *Shining and Other Paths: War and Society in Peru, 1980–1995*, edited by Steve J. Stern, 267–306. Durham, NC: Duke University Press, 1998.

Burt, Jo-Marie, and César Espejo. "The Struggles of a Self-Built Community." *NACLA Report on the Americas* 28, no. 4 (Jan.–Feb. 1995): 19–25.

Caballero, José María. *From Belaunde to Belaunde: Peru's Military Experiment in Third-Roadism*. Cambridge: Centre of Latin American Studies, University of Cambridge, 1981.

Calderón Cockburn, Julio. *La ciudad ilegal: Lima en el siglo XX*. Lima: Universidad Nacional Mayor de San Marcos, 2005.

Calderón Cockburn, Julio. "Villa El Salvador: Twenty Years of Self-Management and Self-Government in Lima, Peru." In *Beyond Self-Help Housing*, edited by Kosta Mathéy, 311–21. London: Mansell, 1992.

Calderón Cockburn, Julio, and Luis Olivera Cardenas. *Municipio y pobladores en la habilitación urbana: Huaycán y Laderas del Chillón*. Lima: DESCO (Centro de Estudios y Promoción del Desarrollo), 1989.

Calderón Cockburn, Julio, and Paul Maquet Makedonski. *Las ideas urbanas en el Peru (1958–1989)*. Lima: CENCA (Instituto de Desarrollo Urbano), 1990.

Caminos, Horacio, John F. C. Turner, and John A. Steffian. *Urban Dwelling Environments: An Elementary Survey of Settlements for the Study of Design Determinants*. Cambridge, MA: MIT Press, 1969.

Caravedo, Baltazar, Humberto Rotondo, and Javier Mariátegui. *Estudios de psiquiatría social en el Perú*. Lima: Ediciones del Sol, 1963.

Carey, James C. *Peru and the United States, 1900–1962*. Notre Dame, IN: University of Notre Dame Press, 1964.

Castañeda, Luis. "Pre-Columbian Skins, Developmentalist Souls: The Architect as Politician." In *Latin American Modern Architectures: Ambiguous Territories*, edited by Patricio del Real and Helen Gyger, 93–114. London: Routledge, 2013.

Castells, Manuel. "La urbanización dependiente en América Latina." In *Imperialismo y Urbanización en América Latina*, edited by Manuel Castells, 7–26. Barcelona: Gustavo Gili, 1973.

Castells, Manuel. *The City and the Grassroots: A Cross-Cultural Theory of Urban Social Movements*. Berkeley: University of California Press, 1983.

Centro Interamericano de Vivienda. *Unidad Vecinal No. 3, Lima-Callao, de la Corporación Nacional de Vivienda del Perú: Informe*. Bogotá: Centro Interamericano de Vivienda, 1958.

Centro de Investigación, Documentación y Asesoría Poblacional. *Gobiernos y Barriadas 1950–1985*. Lima: CIDAP (Centro de Investigación, Documentación y Asesoría Poblacional), June 1988.

Centro de Investigaciones Sociales por Muestreo. *Barriadas de Lima: Actitudes de los habitantes respecto a servicios públicos y privados*. Lima: Ministerio de Trabajo y Comunidades, Servicio de Empleo y Recursos Humanos, Centro de Investigaciones Sociales por Muestreo, June 1967.

Chase Manhattan Bank. *Housing in Latin America*. New York: Chase Manhattan Bank, 1962.

Clayton, Lawrence A. *Peru and the United States: The Condor and the Eagle*. Athens: University of Georgia Press, 1999.

Cochrane, Willard W. "Public Law 480 and Related Programs." *Annals of the American Academy of Political and Social Science* 331 (Sept. 1960): 14–19.

Collier, David. "Squatter Settlements and Policy Innovation in Peru." In *The Peruvian Experiment: Continuity and Change under Military Rule*, edited by Abraham F. Lowenthal, 128–78. Princeton, NJ: Princeton University Press, 1975.

Collier, David. *Squatters and Oligarchs: Authoritarian Rule and Policy Change in Peru*. Baltimore, MD: Johns Hopkins University Press, 1976.

Comisión para la Reforma Agraria y la Vivienda. *Informe sobre la vivienda en el Perú*. Lima: Comisión para la Reforma Agraria y la Vivienda, 1958.

Comisión para la Reforma Agraria y la Vivienda. *Report on Housing in Peru*. 1st English ed. Mexico City: Regional Technical Aids Center, International Cooperation Administration, 1959.

"Conclusiones aprobadas por el VI Congreso Panamericano de Arquitectos." *El Arquitecto Peruano* 11, no. 123 (Oct. 1947): n.p.

Córdova Valdivia, Adolfo. *La vivienda en el Perú: Estado actual y evaluación de las necesidades.* Lima: Comisión para la Reforma Agraria y la Vivienda, 1958.

Corporación Nacional de la Vivienda. *Información básica sobre barrios marginales en la República del Perú.* Lima: Corporación Nacional de la Vivienda, 1962.

Corporación Nacional de la Vivienda. *Planteamientos generales sobre el problema de la vivienda social.* Lima: Corporación Nacional de la Vivienda, 1956.

Corporación Nacional de la Vivienda and Oliverio Portugal Alvarez. *Memoria del Departamento de Barrios Marginales, 1961–1962.* Lima: Corporación Nacional de la Vivienda, 1962.

Correa, Charles. *Charles Correa: Housing and Urbanisation.* New York: Thames & Hudson, 2000.

Cotler, Julio. "Peru since 1960." In *The Cambridge History of Latin America.* Vol. 7, *Latin America since 1930: Spanish South America*, edited by Leslie Bethell, 451–507. Cambridge: Cambridge University Press, 1991.

Crane, Jacob L. "Huts and Houses in the Tropics." *Unasylva* 3, no. 3 (May–June 1949): 100–105.

Crane, Jacob L. "Workers' Housing in Puerto Rico." *International Labour Review* 49, no. 6 (June 1944): 608–29.

Crane, Jacob L., and Robert E. McCabe. "Programmes in Aid of Family House-building: 'Aided Self-Help Housing.'" *International Labour Review* 61, no. 4 (Apr. 1950): 367–84.

Crooke, Patrick. "Village Artisan's Self-Built House." *Architectural Design* 33, no. 8 (Aug. 1963): 361–62.

Crooke, Patrick, and Carlo Doglio. "Scuole e comunità." *Comunità: Rivista mensile di cultura e informazione fondata da Adriano Olivetti* 14, no. 84 (1960): 28–57.

Cupers, Kenny. *The Social Project: Housing Postwar France.* Minneapolis: University of Minnesota Press, 2014.

Davis, Mike. *Planet of Slums.* New York: Verso, 2006.

d'Auria, Viviana. "In the Laboratory and in the Field: Hybrid Housing Design for the African City in Late-Colonial and Decolonising Ghana, 1945–1957." *Journal of Architecture* 19, no. 3 (2014): 329–56.

d'Auria, Viviana, and Hannah le Roux. "Quand la vie prend le dessus: Les interactions entre l'utopie bâtie et l'habiter." In "Modernisme(s) Approprié(s)?" Special issue, *CLARA Architecture/Recherche* 4 (2017): 9–28.

de la Cadena, Marisol. "Silent Racism and Intellectual Superiority in Peru." *Bulletin of Latin American Research* 17, no. 2 (1998): 143–64.

de Soto, Hernando, with Enrique Ghersi and Mario Ghibellini. *El otro sendero: La revolución informal.* Lima: Instituto Libertad y Democracia, 1986.

de Soto, Hernando, with Instituto Libertad y Democracia. *The Other Path: The Invisible Revolution in the Third World.* Translated by June Abbott. New York: Harper & Row, 1989.

Degregori, Carlos Iván, and Pablo Sandoval. "Peru: From Otherness to a Shared Diversity." In *A Companion to Latin American Anthropology*, edited by Deborah Poole, 150–73. Malden, MA: Blackwell, 2008.

Delgado, Carlos. "Desarrollo social: Reconsideracions y planteamientos." In

Problemas sociales en el Perú contemporáneo, by Carlos Delgado, 15–38. Colección Perú Problema 6. Lima: Instituto de Estudios Peruanos, Campodónico, 1971.

Delgado, Carlos. *La Unidad Vecinal No. 3 y Matute: Estudio social comparativo referido a problemas de planeamiento físico*. Lima: Oficina de Planificación Sectorial de Vivienda y Equipamiento Urbano, 1966.

Delgado, Carlos. *SINAMOS: La participación popular en la revolución peruana*. Lima: SINAMOS, 1972.

Delgado, Carlos. "Three Proposals Regarding Accelerated Urbanization Problems in Metropolitan Areas: The Lima Case." In *Latin American Urban Policies and the Social Sciences*, edited by John Miller and Ralph Albert Gakenheimer, 271–99. Beverly Hills, CA: Sage, 1971.

Delgado, Carlos. *Tres planteamientos en torno a problemas de urbanización acelerada en áreas metropolitanas: El caso de Lima*. Cuadernos PLANDEMET, Serie Anaranjada: Asuntos Sociales No. 1. Lima: Oficina Nacional de Planeamiento y Urbanismo, Plan de Desarrollo Metropolitano Lima-Callao, 1968.

Dietz, Henry A. "Bureaucratic Demand-Making and Clientelistic Participation in Peru." In *Authoritarianism and Corporatism in Latin America*, edited by James M. Malloy, 413–58. Pittsburgh, PA: University of Pittsburgh Press, 1977.

Dietz, Henry A. *Poverty and Problem-Solving under Military Rule: The Urban Poor in Lima, Peru*. Austin: University of Texas Press, 1980.

Dorich, Luis. "Urbanization and Physical Planning in Peru." In *Urbanization in Latin America*, edited by Philip M. Hauser, 280–93. New York: United Nations Educational, Scientific and Cultural Organization (UNESCO), 1961.

Driant, Jean-Claude. *Las barriadas de Lima: Historia e interpretación*. Lima: IFEA (Instituto Francés de Estudios Andinos), DESCO (Centro de Estudios y Promoción del Desarrollo), 1991.

Elliott, Sean M. *Financing Latin American Housing: Domestic Savings Mobilization and US Assistance Policy*. Praeger Special Studies in International Economics and Development. New York: F. A. Praeger, 1968.

Empresa Nacional de Edificaciones. *Revolución habitacional en democracia: Plan de vivienda del gobierno peruano, 1980–1985*. Lima: Empresa Nacional de Construcción y Edificaciones, 1985.

Erb, Claude C. "Prelude to Point Four: The Institute of Inter-American Affairs." *Diplomatic History* 9 (Summer 1985): 249–69.

Escobar, Arturo. *Encountering Development: The Making and Unmaking of the Third World*. Princeton, NJ: Princeton University Press, 1995.

Ferguson, James. "Anthropology and Its Evil Twin: 'Development' in the Constitution of a Discipline." In *International Development and the Social Sciences: Essays on the History and Politics of Knowledge*, edited by Frederick Cooper and Randall M. Packard, 150–75. Berkeley: University of California Press, 1997.

Ferguson, James. "Decomposing Modernity: History and Hierarchy after Development." In *Postcolonial Studies and Beyond*, edited by Ania Loomba, 166–81. Durham, NC: Duke University Press, 2005.

Figari Gold, Eduardo. "Huaycán: Una experiencia de urbanismo popular." *Historia, urbanismo, arquitectura, construcción, arte (HUACA)* 1 (July 1987): 26–30.

Fischer, Brodwyn. *A Poverty of Rights: Citizenship and Inequality in Twentieth-Century Rio de Janeiro.* Stanford, CA: Stanford University Press, 2008.

Fondo Nacional de Salud y Bienestar Social. *Barriadas de Lima Metropolitana.* Lima: Fondo Nacional de Salud y Bienestar Social, 1960.

Fondo Nacional de Salud y Bienestar Social. *La asistencia técnica a la vivienda y el problema de barriadas marginales.* Lima: Fondo Nacional de Salud y Bienestar Social, Division de Asistencia Técnica a la Vivienda, 1958.

Frampton, Kenneth. *Modern Architecture: A Critical History.* 4th ed. London: Thames and Hudson, 2007.

Fromm, Dorit. "Alternatives in Housing: 1—Peru: PREVI." *Architectural Review* 178, no. 1062 (1985): 48–54.

Gálvez Velarde, Augusto. *Política de vivienda y construcción en el Perú, 1975–1976.* Lima: Ministerio de Vivienda y Construcción, 1975.

García-Huidobro, Fernando, Diego Torres Torriti, and Nicolás Tugas. *¡El tiempo construye! El Proyecto Experimental de Vivienda (PREVI) de Lima: Génesis y desenlace [TimeBuilds! The Experimental Housing Project (PREVI), Lima: Genesis and Outcome].* Barcelona: Gustavo Gili, 2008.

García-Huidobro, Fernando, Diego Torres Torriti, and Nicolás Tugas. "Time Builds!" *Lotus International* 143 (Aug. 2010): 86–101.

Geddes, Patrick. *Patrick Geddes in India.* Edited by Jaqueline Tyrwhitt. London: L. Humphries, 1947.

Geddes, Patrick. *Town Planning towards City Development: A Report to the Durbar of Indore.* 2 vols. Indore, India: Holkar State Printing Press, 1918.

Gibbons, Ronald, Javier Diaz-Albertini, Adolfo Cabrera, and Flor de María Vásquez. "Proyecto piloto habitacional Laderas del Chillón: Hacia un modelo de gestión popular." In *Estrategias de vida en el sector urbano popular*, edited by Roelfien Haak and Javier Diaz-Albertini, 283–300. Lima: FOVIDA (Asociación Fomento de la Vida); DESCO (Centro de Estudios y Promoción del Desarrollo), 1987.

Gilbert, Alan. "On the Mystery of Capital and the Myths of Hernando de Soto: What Difference Does Legal Title Make?" *International Development Planning Review* 24, no. 1 (2002): 1–19.

Gilbert, Alan. "The Return of the Slum: Does Language Matter?" *International Journal of Urban and Regional Research* 31, no. 4 (Dec. 2007): 697–713.

Goldstein, Barbara. "The Originators: John F. Charlewood Turner." *Architectural Design*, 45, no. 9 (Sept. 1975): 524–25.

González Malpartida, Eduardo. "Barrio El Acero de Chimbote, Perú: Un programa de erradicación y de rehabilitación de vivienda." In *Barrio El Acero de Chimbote, Perú*, 1–32. Lima: Colegio de Arquitectos del Perú, 1969.

Grichener, Silvio. "PREVI/Perú: Un intento en el más alto nivel." *Summa: Revista de arquitectura, tecnología y diseño* 32 (Dec. 1970): 42–57.

Grillo, María Teresa, and Tucker Sharon. "Peru's Amazonian Imaginary: Marginality, Territory and National Integration." In *Environment and Citizenship in Latin America: Natures, Subjects and Struggles*, edited by Alex Latta and Hannah Wittman, 112–28. New York: Berghahn, 2012.

Guerra García, Francisco. "SINAMOS y la promoción de la participación." In *El Perú de Velasco*, vol. 3, edited by Carlos Franco, 681–99. Lima: Centro de Estudios para el Desarrollo y la Participación, 1983.

Gutierrez, Germán Tito. *Análisis censal para una evaluación de vivienda*. Lima: Oficina de Planificación Sectorial de Vivienda y Equipamiento Urbano, 1966.

Gyger, Helen. "Urbanización Caja de Agua, Lima." In *Woningbouw wereldwijd: Betaalbare woningen voor groeiende steden* [*Global Housing: Affordable Dwellings for Growing Cities*], edited by Frederique van Andel, 36–51. No. 12–13 of *DASH* (*Delft Architectural Studies on Housing*). Rotterdam: NAi, 2015.

Habraken, N. J. *Supports: An Alternative to Mass Housing*. New York: Praeger, 1972.

Harris, Richard. "'A Burp in Church': Jacob L. Crane's Vision of Aided Self-Help Housing." *Planning History Studies* 11, no. 1 (1997): 3–16.

Harris, Richard. "A Double Irony: The Originality and Influence of John F. C. Turner." *Habitat International* 27, no. 2 (2003): 245–69.

Harris, Richard. "Slipping through the Cracks: The Origins of Aided Self-Help Housing, 1918–1953." *Housing Studies* 14, no. 3 (1999): 281–309.

Harris, Richard. "The Silence of the Experts: Aided Self-Help Housing, 1939–1954." *Habitat International* 22, no. 2 (1998): 165–89.

Harris, Richard, and Godwin Arku. "Housing as a Tool of Economic Development since 1929." *International Journal of Urban and Regional Research* 29, no. 4 (Dec. 2005): 895–915.

Harris, Walter D., and Hans A. Hossé. *La vivienda en el Perú: estudio realizado en el Departamento de Asuntos Sociales, Unión Panamericana* [*Housing in Peru: A research study conducted in the Department of Social Affairs, Pan American Union*]. Washington, DC: Pan American Union, 1963.

Hauser, Philip M., ed. *Urbanization in Latin America*. New York: United Nations Educational, Scientific and Cultural Organization (UNESCO), 1961.

Henderson, Susan R. "Self-Help Housing in the Weimar Republic: The Work of Ernst May." *Housing Studies* 14, no. 3 (1999): 311–28.

Hobsbawm, Eric. "Peasant Land Occupations." *Past and Present* 62 (Feb. 1974): 120–52.

Hochhäusl, Sophie. "From Vienna to Frankfurt Inside Core-House Type 7: A History of Scarcity through the Modern Kitchen." *Architectural Histories* 1, no. 1 (2013): 1–19.

Holston, James. "Autoconstruction in Working-Class Brazil." *Cultural Anthropology* 6, no. 4 (Nov. 1991): 447–65.

Holston, James. "Housing Crises, Right to the City, and Citizenship." In *The Housing Question: Tensions, Continuities, and Contingencies in the Modern City*, edited by Edward Murphy and Najib B. Hourani, 188–98. London: Routledge, 2013.

Holston, James. *Insurgent Citizenship: Disjunctions of Democracy and Modernity in Brazil*. Princeton, NJ: Princeton University Press, 2008.

Hordijk, Michaela. "Debe Ser Esfuerzo Propio: Aspirations and Belongings of the Young Generation in the Old Barriadas of Southern Lima, Peru." In *Housing and Belonging in Latin America*, edited by Christien Klaufus and Arij Ouweneel, 81–103. New York: Berghahn, 2015.

"Housing in the Tropics." In *Housing in the Tropics*, bulletin 6 of *Housing and Town and Country Planning*, 2–6. New York: United Nations, Department of Social Affairs, 1952.

Instituto Nacional de Desarrollo Urbano. *Estudio de evaluación integral de los programas de vivienda ejecutados y/o promovidos por el Estado*, 7 vols. Lima: Instituto Nacional de Desarrollo Urbano, 1991.

International Bank for Reconstruction and Development, International Development Association. *An Appraisal of the 1966–1967 Public Investment Program of Peru*. Vol. 7, *Housing*. Washington, DC: World Bank, 1965.

Junta Nacional de la Vivienda. *Datos estadisticos de los Barrios Marginales de Lima: Distrito del Rímac*. Vol. 1. Lima: Junta Nacional de la Vivienda, Departamento de Catastro, 1963.

Junta Nacional de la Vivienda. *Datos estadisticos de los Barrios Marginales de Lima: Distritos de Breña—Pueblo Libre—Magdalena*. Lima: Junta Nacional de la Vivienda, Departamento de Catastro, 1963.

Junta Nacional de la Vivienda. *Documento básico para el Plan Habitacional Urbano: Documento general del estudio de 42 ciudades del país y fundamentos para la política habitacional urbana*. Lima: Junta Nacional de la Vivienda, Mar. 1965.

Junta Nacional de la Vivienda. *Informe de situación sobre vivienda, construcción y desarrollo urbano, 1963*. 2 vols. Lima: Junta Nacional de la Vivienda, Asesoría de la Planificación, June 1963.

Junta Nacional de la Vivienda. *Obra de la Junta Nacional de la Vivienda de julio de 1963 a octubre de 1967*. Lima: Junta Nacional de la Vivienda, 1967.

Kahatt, Sharif S. "PREVI-Lima's Time: Positioning Proyecto Experimental de Vivienda in Peru's Modern Project." *Architectural Design* 81, no. 3 (May–June 2011): 22–25.

Kahatt, Sharif S. *Utopías construidas: Las Unidades Vecinales de Lima*. Lima: Fondo Editorial Pontificia Universidad Católica del Perú, 2015.

Kedziorek, Aleksandra, and Łukasz Ronduda, eds. *Oskar Hansen: Opening Modernism—On Open Form Architecture, Art and Didactics*. Warsaw: Museum of Modern Art in Warsaw, 2014.

Kirsch, Karin. *The Weißenhofsiedlung: Experimental Housing Built for the Deutscher Werkbund, Stuttgart, 1927*. Translated by Michael Knight. New York: Rizzoli, 1989.

Kropotkin, Peter. *Mutual Aid, A Factor of Evolution*. New York: McClure Phillips, 1903.

Kruijt, Dirk. *Revolution by Decree: Peru, 1968–1975*. Amsterdam: Thela, 1994.

Kuczynski Godard, Pedro-Pablo. *Peruvian Democracy under Economic Stress: An Account of the Belaúnde Administration, 1963–1968*. Princeton, NJ: Princeton University Press, 1977.

Lagae, Johan, and Kim De Raedt. Editorial. In "Global Experts 'Off Radar.'" Special issue, *ABE Journal* 4 (2013): 1–17. http://abe.revues.org/3384.

Land, Peter. "Peru, Self-Help Building: Two Demonstration Pilot Projects." *AC: International Asbestos-Cement Review* 24, no. 93 (1979): 59–62.

Laquian, Aprodicio A. "Whither Sites and Services?" *Science* 192, no. 4243 (1976): 950–55.

Ledgard, Reynaldo. "Imaginando otro espacio urbano: La experiencia de Huaycán." *Márgenes* 1, no. 1 (Mar. 1987): 34–47.

Liernur, Jorge Francisco. "Vanguardistas versus expertos." *Block* 6 (Mar. 2004): 18–39.

Ligtelijn, Vincent, ed. *Aldo van Eyck: Works*. Basel: Birkhäuser, 1999.

Lloyd, Peter. *The "Young Towns" of Lima: Aspects of Urbanization in Peru*. Cambridge: Cambridge University Press, 1980.

Lowenthal, Abraham F. "Peru's Ambiguous Revolution." In *The Peruvian Experiment: Continuity and Change under Military Rule*, edited by Abraham F. Lowenthal, 3–43. Princeton, NJ: Princeton University Press, 1975.

Lowenthal, Abraham F. "The Peruvian Experiment Reconsidered." In *The Peruvian Experiment Reconsidered*, edited by Cynthia McClintock and Abraham F. Lowenthal, 415–30. Princeton, NJ: Princeton University Press, 1983.

Ludeña Urquizo, Wiley. *Lima: Historia y urbanismo en cifras, 1821–1970*. Lima: Ministerio de Vivienda, Construcción y Saneamiento, 2004.

Ludeña Urquizo, Wiley. *Tres buenos tigres: Vanguardia y urbanismo en el Perú del siglo XX*. Huancayo: Colegio de Arquitectos del Perú, Regional Junín; Ur[b]es, 2004.

Manaster, Kenneth. "The Problem of Urban Squatters in Developing Countries: Peru." *Wisconsin Law Review* 23, no. 1 (1968): 23–61.

Maneville, Roger. "L'expérience 'Castor' aux Carrières Centrales de Casablanca." *Notes marocaines*, no. 7 (July 1956): 2–8.

Mangin, William. "Latin American Squatter Settlements: A Problem and a Solution." *Latin American Research Review* 2, no. 3 (1967): 65–98.

Mangin, William. "Thoughts on 24 Years of Work in Peru: The Vicos Project and Me." In *Long-Term Field Research in Social Anthropology*, edited by George Foster et al., 65–84. New York: Academic Press, 1979.

Mangin, William. "Urbanisation Case History in Peru." *Architectural Design* 33, no. 8 (Aug. 1963): 366–70.

Mangin, William, and John F. C. Turner. "The Barriada Movement." *Progressive Architecture* 49 (May 1968): 154–62.

Martuccelli, Elio. *Arquitectura para una ciudad fragmentada: Ideas, proyectos y edificios en la Lima del siglo XX*. Lima: Universidad Ricardo Palma, 2000.

Mathéy, Kosta, ed. *Beyond Self-Help Housing*. London: Mansell, 1992.

Matos Mar, José. *Estudio de las barriadas limeñas: Informe presentado a Naciones Unidas en diciembre de 1955*. Lima: Instituto de Estudios Peruanos, 1966.

Matos Mar, José. *Las barriadas de Lima, 1957*. Lima: Instituto de Estudios Peruanos, 1977.

Matos Mar, José. "Migration and Urbanization: The Barriadas of Lima, an Example of Integration into Urban Life." In *Urbanization in Latin America*, edited by Philip M. Hauser, 170–90. New York: United Nations Educational, Scientific and Cultural Organization (UNESCO), 1961.

Matos Mar, José. "Una experiencia de mejoramiento de comunidades indígenas en el Perú: El Proyecto Huarochirí." *Boletín Trimestral: Centro Regional de Educación Fundamental para la América Latina* 6, no. 3 (July 1954): 2–12.

Matos Mar, José, Teresa Guillén de Boluarte, Julio Cotler, Eduardo Soler, and Francisco Boluarte. *Las actuales comunidades indígenas: Huarochirí en 1955*. Lima: Universidad Nacional Mayor de San Marcos, Instituto de Etnología y Arqueología, 1958.

McCurry, Dan C. "US Church-Financed Missions in Peru." In *US Foreign Policy and Peru*, edited by Daniel A. Sharp, 379–415. Austin: University of Texas Press, 1972.

McGuirk, Justin. "PREVI: The Metabolist Utopia." *Domus* no. 946 (Apr. 2011): 58–71.

Mena, Josefina. "News from PREVI." *Architectural Design* 44, no. 1 (Jan. 1974): 53–54.

Mendez G., Cecilia. "Incas Sí, Indios No: Notes on Peruvian Creole Nationalism and Its Contemporary Crisis." *Journal of Latin American Studies* 28, no. 1 (Feb.1996): 197–225.

Mevius Andersen, Federico. *Problema de vivienda en Lima Metropolitana: Forum Lima Año 2000, Lima, 16 al 19 de noviembre '77*. Lima: Forum Año 2000, 1977.

Michl, Sara. "Urban Squatter Organization as a National Government Tool: The Case of Lima, Peru." In *National-Local Linkages: The Interrelationship of Urban and National Polities in Latin America*, edited by Francine F. Rabinovitz and Felicity M. Trueblood, 155–78. Vol. 3 of *Latin American Urban Research*. Beverly Hills, CA: Sage, 1973.

Miner, Craig. "R. H. Garvey: 'Operations are Interesting.'" In *John Brown to Bob Dole: Movers and Shakers in Kansas History*, edited by Virgil W. Dean, 253–64. Lawrence: University Press of Kansas, 2006.

Ministerio de Vivienda. *Evaluación integral del proyecto de vivienda Caja de Agua-Chacarilla de Otero: Programa de núcleos básicos o viviendas semi-acabadas*. Lima: Ministerio de Vivienda, Dirección General de Edificaciones, 1970.

Ministerio de Vivienda and Instituto Nacional de Investigación y Normalización de la Vivienda. *PREVI: Introducción*. Vol. 1 of *Publicación PREVI*. Lima: Ministerio de Vivienda; Instituto Nacional de Investigación y Normalización de la Vivienda, 1979.

Ministerio de Vivienda and Instituto Nacional de Investigación y Normalización de la Vivienda. *PREVI PP3: Proyecto de lotes y servicios*. Vol. 26 of *Publicación PREVI*. Lima: Ministerio de Vivienda; Instituto Nacional de Investigación y Normalización de la Vivienda, 1979.

Ministerio de Vivienda and Instituto Nacional de Investigación y Normalización de la Vivienda. *PREVI PP4: Auto-construcción post-sismo*. Vol. 27 of *Publicación PREVI*. Lima: Ministerio de Vivienda; Instituto Nacional de Investigación y Normalización de la Vivienda, 1979.

Montagne, Alfredo. "Maisons expérimentales Previ, Lima, Perou." *Archithese* 14, no. 5 (1984): 6–7.

Montero López, Víctor. *Huaycán: Un pueblo que construye, lucha y celebra*. Lima: EDAPROSPO (Equipo de Asesoramiento a Actividades Productivas en Sectores Populares), 1992.

Morse, Richard M. "Recent Research on Latin American Urbanization: A Selective Survey with Commentary." *Latin American Research Review* 1, no. 1 (1965): 35–74.

Mumford, Lewis. *The Culture of Cities*. New York: Harcourt, Brace and Company, 1938.

Municipalidad de Lima Metropolitana, Unidad de Promoción Social. *Programa Especial Huaycán*. Lima: Municipalidad de Lima Metropolitana, n.d. [ca. 1985].

Muñoz, Hortensia. "Believers and Neighbors: 'Huaycán Is One and No One Shall Divide It.'" *Journal of Interamerican Studies and World Affairs* 41, no. 4 (1999): 73–92.

Muñoz, José, and Diego Robles Rivas. *Estudio de tugurios en los distritos de Jésus María y La Victoria*. Cuadernos PLANDEMET, Serie Violeta: Asuntos Físicos No. 2. Lima: Oficina Nacional de Planeamiento y Urbanismo, 1968.

Murphy, Edward. *For a Proper Home: Housing Rights in the Margins of Urban Chile, 1960–2010.* Pittsburgh, PA: University of Pittsburgh Press, 2015.

Murra, John V. "Andean Societies." *Annual Review of Anthropology* 13 (1984): 119–41.

Muzaffar, M. Ijlal. "The Periphery Within: Modern Architecture and the Making of the Third World." PhD diss., Massachusetts Institute of Technology, 2007.

Neira Alva, Eduardo. "El desarrollo regional y su vinculación con la arquitectura." *El Arquitecto Peruano* no. 297–99 (Apr.–June 1962): n.p.

Neira Alva, Eduardo. "El problema de la vivienda en el Perú." *El Arquitecto Peruano* 20, no. 224–25 (Mar.–Apr. 1956): n.p.

Neira Alva, Eduardo. "Un arquitecto viaja por Europa." *El Arquitecto Peruano* 17, no. 188–89 (Mar.–Apr. 1953): n.p.

Neira Alva, Eduardo. "Un interesante ejemplo de arquitectura espontanea." *El Arquitecto Peruano* no. 246–48 (Jan.–Mar. 1958): n.p.

Oficina Nacional de Desarrollo de Pueblos Jóvenes. *Boletín* 1, *La organización para el desarrollo de los pueblos jóvenes*. Lima: Oficina Nacional de Desarrollo de Pueblos Jóvenes, 1969.

Oficina Nacional de Desarrollo de Pueblos Jóvenes. *Boletín* 3, *Normas generales para el establecimiento de oficinas locales*. Lima: Oficina Nacional de Desarrollo de Pueblos Jóvenes, 1969.

Oficina Nacional de Desarrollo de Pueblos Jóvenes. *Boletín* 4, *Organización y funcionamiento de las Oficinas Locales de Desarrollo de Pueblos Jóvenes*. Lima: Oficina Nacional de Desarrollo de Pueblos Jóvenes, 1969.

Oficina Nacional de Desarrollo de Pueblos Jóvenes. *Boletín* 5, *Ponencia presentada por la Oficina Nacional de Desarrollo de Pueblos Jóvenes al Seminario de Asentamientos Populares organizado por la Agencia Internacional para el Desarrollo, Washington DC, noviembre de 1969*. Lima: Oficina Nacional de Desarrollo de Pueblos Jóvenes, 1969.

Oficina Nacional de Desarrollo de Pueblos Jóvenes. *Folleto de Divulgación* 1, *Guia para la organización de los Pueblos Jóvenes*. Lima: Oficina Nacional de Desarrollo de Pueblos Jóvenes, n.d. [ca. 1970].

Oficina Nacional de Desarrollo de Pueblos Jóvenes. *Oficina Nacional de Desarrollo de Pueblos Jóvenes*. Lima: Oficina Nacional de Desarrollo de Pueblos Jóvenes, Apr. 1969.

Oficina Nacional de Desarrollo de Pueblos Jóvenes. *Plan de acción inmediata: A ejecutarse en los Pueblos Jóvenes de los Distritos de San Martín de Porres, Independencia, Comas, Surco y Chorrillos*. Lima: Oficina Nacional de Desarrollo de Pueblos Jóvenes, June 1969.

Oficina Nacional de Planeamiento y Urbanismo. *Construcciones efectuadas por particulares y por entidades estatales en Lima Metropolitana, durante el período 1949–1960*. Lima: Oficina Nacional de Planeamiento y Urbanismo, June 1961.

Oficina Nacional de Planeamiento y Urbanismo. *Lima Metropolitana: Algunos aspectos de su expediente urbano y soluciones parciales varias*. Lima: Oficina Nacional de Planeamiento y Urbanismo, December 1954.

Oficina Nacional de Planeamiento y Urbanismo. *Plan de Desarrollo Metro-politano Lima-Callao a 1980*. Vol. 1, *Aspectos Globales: Esquema Director, 1967–1980*. Lima: Oficina Nacional de Planeamiento y Urbanismo; Ministe-rio de Vivienda; Concejo Provincial de Lima; Dirección General de Desarrol-lo Urbano, 1967–1972.

Oficina Nacional de Planeamiento y Urbanismo. *Plan Regulador de Arequipa*. Lima: Oficina Nacional de Planeamiento y Urbanismo, 1957.

Oficina Regional de Apoyo a la Movilización Social IV. *Bases ideologicas de la revolución peruana*. N.p.: Oficina Regional de Apoyo a la Movilización Social IV, n.d. [ca. 1972].

Osterling, Jorge P., and Héctor Martínez. "Notes for a History of Peruvian Social Anthropology, 1940–1980." *Current Anthropology* 24, no. 3 (June 1983): 343–60.

Parker, David S. "Civilizing the City of Kings: Hygiene and Housing in Lima, Peru." In *Cities of Hope: People, Protests, and Progress in Urbanizing Latin America, 1870–1930*, edited by Ronn Pineo and James A. Baer, 153–78. Boulder, CO: Westview Press, 1998.

Parker, David S. *The Idea of the Middle Class: White-Collar Workers and Peru-vian Society, 1900–1950*. University Park: Pennsylvania State University Press, 1998.

Pastor, Manuel, Jr., and Carol Wise. "Peruvian Economic Policy in the 1980s: From Orthodoxy to Heterodoxy and Back." *Latin American Research Review* 27, no. 2 (1992): 83–117.

Paz-Soldán, Carlos Enrique, ed. *Lima y sus suburbios*. Lima: Universidad Nacio-nal de San Marcos, Instituto de Medicina Social, 1957.

PCM Construction Control Consultants Limited and Julio Gianella Silva. *Affordable Housing for Low Income Families in Peru: A Study on Behalf of the Instituto Nacional de Investigación y Normalización de la Vivienda*. Lima: Instituto Nacional de Investigación y Normalización de la Vivienda, 1985.

Peattie, Lisa. "Participation: A Case Study of How Invaders Organize, Negotiate, and Interact with Government in Lima, Peru." *Environment and Urbaniza-tion* 2, no. 1 (Apr. 1990): 19–30.

Peattie, Lisa. "Some Second Thoughts on Sites-and-Services." *Habitat Interna-tional* 6, no. 1/2 (1982): 131–39.

Perlman, Janice. *Favela: Four Decades of Living on the Edge in Rio de Janeiro*. New York: Oxford University Press, 2010.

Perlman, Janice. *The Myth of Marginality: Urban Poverty and Politics in Rio de Janeiro*. Berkeley: University of California Press, 1976.

Philip, George. "The Soldier as Radical: The Peruvian Military Government, 1968–1975." *Journal of Latin American Studies* 8, no. 1 (1976): 29–51.

Plöger, Jörg. "Gated Barriadas: Responses to Urban Insecurity in Marginal Settlements in Lima, Peru." *Singapore Journal of Tropical Geography* 33, no. 2 (July 2012): 212–25.

Poole, Deborah, and Gerardo Rénique. *Peru: Time of Fear*. London: Latin Ameri-can Bureau, 1992.

Portes, Alejandro. "Rationality in the Slum: An Essay on Interpretive Sociology." *Comparative Studies in Society and History* 14, no. 3 (June 1972): 268–86.

Pradilla, Emilio. "La ideología burguesa y el problema de la vivienda: Crítica de dos teorías." *Ideología y Sociedad* 19 (Oct.–Dec. 1976): 5–48.

"PREVI/Lima: Low Cost Housing Project." *Architectural Design* 40, no. 4 (Apr. 1970): 187–205.

"¿Qué es una unidad vecinal?" *El Arquitecto Peruano* 9, no. 98 (Sept. 1945): n.p.

Quijano, Aníbal. "Dependencia, cambio social y urbanización en Latinoamérica." *Revista Mexicana de Sociología* 30, no. 3 (1968): 525–70.

Rama, Ángel. *The Lettered City*. Translated by John Charles Chasteen. Durham, NC: Duke University Press, 1996.

Read, Herbert. "The Paradox of Anarchism" (1941). In *A Coat of Many Colours: Essays*, by Herbert Read, 59–67. London: Routledge & Paul, 1956.

Regional and Urban Planning Implementation. *Urban Redevelopment in Peru*. Washington, DC: Regional and Urban Planning Implementation, 1966.

Renninger, John P. "After the Seventh Special General Assembly Session: Africa and the New Emerging World Order." *African Studies Review* 19, no. 2 (Sept. 1976): 35–48.

Riofrío Benavides, Gustavo. *Habilitación urbana con participación popular: Tres casos en Lima, Perú*. Eschborn: Deutsche Gesellschaft für Technische Zusammenarbeit, 1986.

Riofrío Benavides, Gustavo. *Producir la ciudad (popular) de los '90: Entre el mercado y el Estado*. Lima: DESCO (Centro de Estudios y Promoción del Desarrollo), 1991.

Riofrío Benavides, Gustavo, and Daniel Ramírez Corzo N. *Formalización de la propiedad y mejoramiento de barrios: Bien legal, bien marginal*. Lima: DESCO (Centro de Estudios y Promoción del Desarrollo), 2006. http://urbano.org.pe/descargas/investigaciones/Estudios_urbanos/EU_1.pdf.

Riofrío Benavides, Gustavo, and Jean-Claude Driant. *¿Qué vivienda han construido? Nuevos problemas en viejas barriadas*. Lima: CIDAP (Centro de Investigación, Desarrollo y Asesoría Poblacional), IFEA (Instituto Francés de Estudios Andinos), TAREA (Asociación de Publicaciones Educativas), 1987.

Rivera Santos, Luis. "A New Approach to Low Cost Rural Housing in Puerto Rico." *Monthly Bulletin—Caribbean Commission* 3, no. 12 (July 1950): 422–23.

Rivera Santos, Luis. "Experiencia de Puerto Rico en ayuda propia y ayuda mutua." *El Arquitecto Peruano* 19, no. 216–18 (July–Sept. 1955): n.p.

Rivera Santos, Luis, Enrique Bird Piñero, Lorenzo Muñoz Morales, and Emilio A. Dávila. *Manual para la organización de proyectos piloto de ayuda propia y ayuda mutua en vivienda*. Bogotá: Centro Interamericano de Vivienda, Servicio de Intercambio Científico, 1953.

Robles Rivas, Diego. "Development Alternatives for the Peruvian Barriada." In *Regional and Urban Development Policies: A Latin American Perspective*, edited by Guillermo Geisse and Jorge E. Hardoy, 229–37. Vol. 2 of *Latin American Urban Research*, edited by Francine F. Rabinovitz and Felicity M. Trueblood. Beverly Hills, CA: Sage, 1972.

Robles Rivas, Diego. "El proceso de urbanización y los sectores populares en Lima." *Cuadernos DESCO*, serie A, no. 1 (Feb. 1969): 49–63.

Robles Rivas, Diego. "La marginalidad urbana." In *América Latina en su arquitectura*, edited by Roberto Segre, 87–104. Mexico City: Siglo XXI, 1975.

Robles Rivas, Diego. "Limitations of Self-Help." *Architectural Design* 46, no. 4 (Apr. 1976): 231.

Robles Rivas, Diego, and Juan Sierra. "Síntesis del desarrollo del Barrio La

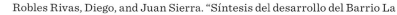

Libertad, Chimbote, Ancash, Perú." In *Barrio El Acero de Chimbote, Perú*, 33–47. Lima: Colegio de Arquitectos del Perú, 1969.

Roel, Carlos. "Huaycán: Dos años de lucha por la forja de una ciudad modelo." In *Estrategias de vida en el sector urbano popular*, edited by Roelfien Haak and Javier Diaz-Albertini, 301–18. Lima: FOVIDA (Asociación Fomento de la Vida); DESCO (Centro de Estudios y Promoción del Desarrollo), 1987.

Roesler, Sascha, ed. *Habitat Marocain Documents: Dynamics between Formal and Informal Housing.* Zurich: Park, 2015.

Rojas, Danielle M., and Peter M. Ward, with Olga Peek and Martha Lazarte Salinas. "Rehab, 'Los Aires' and Densification of Consolidated Settlements in Lima, Peru." In *Housing Policy in Latin American Cities: A New Generation of Strategies and Approaches for 2016 UN-Habitat III*, edited by Peter M. Ward, Edith R Jiménez Huerta, and María Mercedes Di Virgilio, 160–91. London: Routledge, 2015.

Roy, Ananya. "The 21st-Century Metropolis: New Geographies of Theory." *Regional Studies* 43, no. 6 (2009): 819–30.

Roy, Ananya, and Nezar AlSayyad, eds. *Urban Informality: Transnational Perspectives from the Middle East, Latin America, and South Asia.* Lanham, MD: Lexington, 2004.

Salazar Larraín, Arturo, ed. *Pedro G. Beltrán: Pensamiento y acción.* Lima: Instituto de Economía de Libre Mercado, 1994.

Salinas, Fernando. "La arquitectura revolucionaria del Tercer Mundo." *Tricontinental* no. 1 (July–Aug. 1967): 93–102.

Samper, Germán. *Germán Samper: La evolución de la vivienda.* Bogotá: Escala, 2003.

Samper, Germán. "Responsibilidad social del arquitecto." In *América Latina en su arquitectura*, edited by Roberto Segre, 204-215. Mexico City: Siglo XXI, 1975.

Sánchez-León, Abelardo, and Julio Calderón Cockburn. *El laberinto de la ciudad: Políticas urbanas del Estado 1950–1979.* Lima: DESCO (Centro de Estudios y Promoción del Desarrollo), 1980.

Segre, Roberto. "Comunicación y participación social." In *América Latina en su arquitectura*, edited by Roberto Segre, 269-299. Mexico City: Siglo XXI, 1975.

Sistema Nacional de Apoyo a la Movilización Social. *8 preguntas a la revolución peruana.* Lima: Sistema Nacional de Apoyo a la Movilización Social, 1973.

Sistema Nacional de Apoyo a la Movilización Social, Oficina Regional de Apoyo a la Movilización Social X, and Comisión Especial sobre Villa El Salvador. *Informe sobre Villa El Salvador.* Lima: Sistema Nacional de Apoyo a la Movilización Social; Oficina Regional de Apoyo a la Movilización Social X, 1974.

Skinner, Reinhard. "Self-Help, Community Organization, and Politics: Villa El Salvador, Lima." In *Self-Help Housing: A Critique*, edited by Peter M. Ward, 209–29. London: Mansell, 1982.

Smirnoff, Victor. "25 años de vivienda en el Perú." *El Arquitecto Peruano*, no. 306–8 (Jan.–Mar. 1963): 44–80.

Smith, Michael L. "Shining Path's Urban Strategy: Ate Vitarte." In *The Shining Path of Peru*, edited by David Scott Palmer, 127–47. New York: St. Martin's, 1992.

Starn, Orin, Carlos Iván Degregori, and Robin Kirk, eds. *The Peru Reader: History, Culture, Politics*. Durham, NC: Duke University Press, 1995.

Stepan, Alfred. *The State and Society: Peru in Comparative Perspective*. Princeton, NJ: Princeton University Press, 1978.

Stern, Steve J., ed. *Shining and Other Paths: War and Society in Peru, 1980–1995*. Durham, NC: Duke University Press, 1998.

Stirling, James. *James Stirling, Buildings and Projects: James Stirling, Michael Wilford and Associates*. London: Architectural Press, 1984.

Stirling, James. *James Stirling: Exhibition, Royal Institute of British Architects*. Exhibition catalogue, Heinz Gallery, Apr. 24–June 21, 1974. London: Royal Institute of British Architects, 1974.

Supersudaca (Manuel de Rivero and Félix Madrazo). "¿Y PREVI? Proyecto de Investigación para la IV Bienal Iberoamericana de Arquitectura e Ingeniería Civil, Lima, Perú, 25 a 29 de Octubre de 2004." Lima: 2004.

Turner, John F. C. "Barriers and Channels for Housing Development in Modernizing Countries." *Journal of the American Institute of Planners* 33, no. 3 (May 1967): 167–81.

Turner, John F. C. "Housing as a Verb." In *Freedom to Build: Dweller Control of the Housing Process*, edited by John F. C. Turner and Robert Fichter, 148–75. New York: Macmillan, 1972.

Turner, John F. C. *Housing by People: Towards Autonomy in Building Environments*. London: Marion Boyars, 1976.

Turner, John F. C. *Housing by People: Towards Autonomy in Building Environments*. 1st American ed. New York: Pantheon, 1977.

Turner, John F. C. "Housing in Three Dimensions: Terms of Reference for the Housing Question Redefined." *World Development* 6, no. 9/10 (1978): 1135–45.

Turner, John F. C. "Housing Issues and the Standards Problem." *Ekistics* 196, no. 33 (1972): 152–58.

Turner, John F. C. "Housing Priorities, Settlement Patterns, and Urban Development in Modernizing Countries." *Journal of the American Institute of Planners* 34, no. 6 (Nov. 1968): 354–63.

Turner, John F. C. "La autoconstrucción." *Desarrollo Economico: Revista para el profesional del desarrollo* 1, no. 3 (Sept.–Oct. 1964): 32–39.

Turner, John F. C. "Lima Barriadas Today." *Architectural Design* 33, no. 8 (Aug. 1963): 375–76.

Turner, John F. C. "Lima's Barriadas and Corralones: Suburbs versus Slums." *Ekistics* 19, no. 112 (Mar. 1965): 152–55.

Turner, John F. C. "A New View of the Housing Deficit." *Architects' Yearbook* 13 (1971): 115–24.

Turner, John F. C. "The Reeducation of a Professional." In *Freedom to Build: Dweller Control of the Housing Process*, edited by John F. C. Turner and Robert Fichter, 122–47. New York: Macmillan, 1972.

Turner, John F. C. "The Scope of the Problem." *Architectural Design* 33, no. 8 (Aug. 1963): 363–65.

Turner, John F. C. "The Squatter Settlement: An Architecture that Works." *Architectural Design* 38, no. 8 (Aug. 1968): 355–60.

Turner, John F. C. "Uncontrolled Urban Settlement: Problems and Policies." *International Social Development Review* 1 (1968): 107–30.

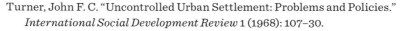

Turner, John F. C. "Who Is Teaching Whom to Do What?" *Bulletin of Environmental Education* 59 (Mar. 1976): 17–20.

Turner, John F. C., and Robert Fichter, eds. *Freedom to Build: Dweller Control of the Housing Process.* New York: Macmillan, 1972.

Turner, John F. C., and W. P. Keatinge-Clay. "The Geddes Diagrams: The Contribution of the Diagrams towards a Synthetic Form of Thought." In *Cities in Evolution*, by Patrick Geddes, 2nd ed., edited by Jaqueline Tyrwhitt, app. 1, pt. 2, 201–5. London: Williams & Norgate, 1949.

Turner, John F. C., ed. "Dwelling Resources in South America." Special issue, *Architectural Design* 33, no. 8 (Aug. 1963).

Uchuya Reyes, Héctor E., ed. *Normas Legales de Pueblos Jóvenes.* Lima: Heur, 1971.

UN-Habitat. *Dubrovnik: An Analysis of the Crisis in Human Settlements.* N.p.: United Nations Human Settlements Programme, n.d. [ca. 1975].

United Nations Centre for Housing, Building, and Planning. *Global Review of Human Settlements: A Support Paper for Habitat: United Nations Conference on Human Settlements.* A/CONF.70/A/1. Oxford: Pergamon, 1976.

United Nations Centre for Human Settlements. *Executive Summary of the Global Report on Human Settlements.* Nairobi: United Nations Centre for Human Settlements, 1988.

United Nations Conference on Human Settlements. *Report of Habitat: United Nations Conference on Human Settlements, Vancouver, 31 May–11 June 1976.* A/CONF.70/15. New York: United Nations, 1976.

United Nations Tropical Housing Mission. *Low Cost Housing in South and South-East Asia.* New York: UN, Department of Social Affairs, 1951.

United Nations. "Housing and Town and Country Planning." *Annals of Public and Cooperative Economics* 20, no. 3 (Sept. 1949): 302–61.

United Nations. *Manual on Self-Help Housing.* New York: UN, Deptartment of Economic and Social Affairs, 1964.

United Nations. *Survey of Problems of Low Cost Rural Housing in Tropical Areas: A Preliminary Report with Special Reference to the Caribbean Area.* New York: UN, Department of Social Affairs, 1950.

United States Agency for International Development, Bureau for Latin America. *Mesa redonda sobre el problema de la vivienda en las urbanizaciones marginales.* Panama City: Agency for International Development, 1970.

Valladares Osso, Carlos, and Eleodoro Ventocilla Cuadros. "Para una concepción de la vivienda de interés social." 2 vols. Thesis, Universidad Nacional de Ingeniería, Lima, 1973.

van Eyck, Aldo. "Footnote: Who Are We Building for, and Why?" *Architectural Design* 40, no. 4 (Apr. 1970): 189.

Varela, David F., and Jorge L. Archimbaud. "Property Rights and Land Tenancy." In *An Opportunity for a Different Peru: Prosperous, Equitable, and Governable*, edited by Marcelo Giugale, Vicente Fretes-Cibils, and John L. Newman, 553–87. Washington, DC: World Bank, 2007.

Vega Christie, David. "Impresiones del Ingeniero Vega Christie a su retorno de los Estados Unidos." *El Arquitecto Peruano* 11, no. 119 (June 1947): n.p.

Velasco, Alejandro. *Barrio Rising: Urban Popular Politics and the Making of Modern Venezuela.* Oakland: University of California Press, 2015.

Violich, Francis. "Urban Land Policies: Latin America." In *Urban Land Problems and Policies*, bulletin 7 of *Housing and Town and Country Planning*, 90–97. New York: United Nations, Department of Social Affairs, 1953.

Wagner, Martin. *Das wachsende Haus: Ein Beitrag zur Lösung der städtischen Wohnungsfrage*. Berlin: Bong, 1932.

Wakeman, Rosemary. "Reconstruction and the Self-Help Housing Movement: The French Experience." *Housing Studies* 14, no. 3 (May 1999): 355–66.

Walter, Richard J. *Peru and the United States, 1960–1975: How Their Ambassadors Managed Foreign Relations in a Turbulent Era*. University Park: Pennsylvania State University Press, 2010.

Ward, Barbara. *The Home of Man*. New York: Norton, 1976.

Ward, Barbara. "The Home of Man: What Nations and the International Must Do." *Habitat International* 1, no. 2 (Sept. 1976): 125–32.

Ward, Peter M. "The Lack of 'Cursive Thinking' with Social Theory and Public Policy: Four Decades of Marginality and Rationality in the So-Called Slum." In *Rethinking Development in Latin America*, edited by Charles H. Wood and Bryan R. Roberts, 271–96. University Park: Pennsylvania State University Press, 2005.

Ward, Peter M., ed. *Self-Help Housing: A Critique*. London: Mansell, 1982.

Ward, Peter M. "Self Help Housing in Mexico City: Social and Economic Determinants of Success." *Town Planning Review* 49, no. 1 (Jan. 1978): 38–50.

Ward, Peter M., Edith R. Jiménez Huerta, and Mercedes Di Virgilio, eds. *Housing Policy in Latin American Cities: A New Generation of Strategies and Approaches for 2016 UN-Habitat III*. New York; London: Routledge, 2015.

Weissmann, Ernest. "Human Settlements—Struggle for Identity." *Habitat International* 3, no. 3–4 (1978): 227–41.

Weissmann, Ernest. "Mutual Aid in Low-Cost Housing." *Annals of the American Academy of Political and Social Science* 329 (1960): 107–14.

Welter, Volker M. *Biopolis: Patrick Geddes and the City of Life*. Cambridge, MA: MIT Press, 2002.

White, Stephen. "PREVI Twenty Years After." *Architecture and Design: A Journal for the Indian Architect* 11, no. 2 (Mar.–Apr. 1994): 53–59.

Wiener, Paul Lester, and José Luis Sert. "Five Civic Centers in South America." *Architectural Record* 114 (Aug. 1953): 121–36.

World Bank. *Housing: Enabling the Market to Work*. Washington, DC: World Bank, 1993.

World Bank. *Housing*. Sector Policy Paper 11023. Washington, DC: World Bank, 1975.

World Bank. *Urbanization Sector*. Working Paper 11072. Washington, DC: World Bank, 1972.

Woy, Sandra L. "Infrastructure of Participation in Peru: SINAMOS." In *Political Participation in Latin America*, vol. 1, *Citizen and State*, edited by John A. Booth and Mitchell A. Seligson, 189–208. New York: Holmes and Meier, 1978.

Zimmermann Zavala, Augusto. *El Plan Inca: Objetivo: Revolución peruana*. Lima: Diario Oficial El Peruano, 1974.

Zoumanas, Thomas. "Containing Castro: Promoting Homeownership in Peru, 1956–1961." *Diplomatic History* 10, no. 2 (1986): 161–81.

INDEX

Note: Page numbers in *italics* refer to figures.